D1529053

SCIENCE FICTION IN AMERICA, 1870s-1930s

SCIENCE FICTION IN AMERICA, 1870s-1930s

AN ANNOTATED
BIBLIOGRAPHY OF
PRIMARY SOURCES

COMPILED BY
THOMAS D. CLARESON

Bibliographies and Indexes in American Literature, Number 1

Greenwood Press
Westport, Connecticut • London, England

Library of Congress Cataloging in Publication Data

Main entry under title:

Science fiction in America, 1870s-1930s.

(Bibliographies and indexes in American literature, ISSN 0742-6860 ; no. 1)
Includes indexes.
1. Science fiction, American—Bibliography. 2. Science fiction—Bibliography. I. Clareson, Thomas D. II. Series.
Z1231.F4S38   1984   016.813'0876   84-8934
[PS374.S35]
ISBN 0-313-23169-9 (lib. bdg.)

Library of Congress Catalog Card Number: 84-8934
ISBN: 0-313-23169-9
ISSN: 0742-6860

First published in 1984

Greenwood Press
A division of Congressional Information Service, Inc.
88 Post Road West, Westport, Connecticut 06881

Printed in the United States of America

10 9 8 7 6 5 4 3 2 1

For
Ossie Train
and
"Doc" Barrett,
who provided
so many books

CONTENTS

INTRODUCTION

The present *Annotated Bibliography* has grown out of work that I did under the direction of Professor Robert E. Spiller at the University of Pennsylvania. Its first appearance as a bibliography occurred in the initial number of *Extrapolation* (December 1959) when that journal served as the *Newsletter* of the Conference on Science Fiction held annually at the December meeting of the Modern Language Association. At that time it was less than one-quarter its present length, the notations were much briefer, and titles as early as Captain Adam Seaborn's *Symzonia: A Voyage of Discovery* were included in order to indicate the literary tradition from which American science fiction had developed.

In its present form I have tried to be comprehensive but not definitive. The concentration upon the period from the 1870s to the 1930s is deliberate, for those years remain crucial to the emergence of modern science fiction. Moreover, they have not previously been treated as a single unit; too often they are glossed over. (My own annotated bibliographies for the two editions of *Anatomy of Wonder* were keyed to more restrictive dates and were, obviously, much more limited in the number of titles that they could consider.) As for the works of other individuals, even I. F. Clarke's fine, pioneering *The Tale of the Future* (1961, 1972) used annotations seldom running to more than a single sentence primarily because it sought to cover the books issued during two centuries. Lyman Tower Sargent's *British and American Utopian Literature, 1516-1975* (1979) becomes even more succinct, often relying on no more than a phrase. *"333": A Bibliography of the Science-Fantasy Novel* (1953, 1975), edited by Joseph H. Crawford, James H. Donahue, and Donald M. Grant, has lengthier notations but ranges from "The

Gothic Romance" and "The Oriental Novel" to "Associational" items published between 1798 and 1950.

R. Reginald's *Science Fiction and Fantasy Literature* (1979) comes as near to a definitive listing of titles as one can hope for. Yet it contains no annotations whatsoever and in the interest of being complete brings together both fiction and nonfiction titles. Nor does it always indicate whether or not there were both American and British editions of a single work. Finally, like E. F. Bleiler's *The Checklist of Fantastic Literature* (1948) and *The Checklist of Science-Fiction & Supernatural Fiction* (1978), it makes no distinction between fantasy and science fiction. That fact, as may be seen in certain entries in this volume, can provide the researcher with a variety of problems. Quite simply, titles can be deceptive. And in Bleiler's recent, fully annotated *The Guide to Supernatural Fiction* (1983) science fiction becomes incidental. Such an appraisal of the work of Reginald and Bleiler should not be interpreted as criticism of their invaluable books; it simply points out the limitations within which they chose to work.

As I mentioned, the period beginning with the 1870s remains central to the development of modern science fiction. By then most of Jules Verne's early novels had been translated into English. In addition, drawing on themes voiced by Mary Shelley, Edgar Allan Poe, Mary Griffith, and FitzJames O'Brien, to name only those earlier writers who come readily to mind, both American and British writers had begun to make greater use of *contemporary* scientific fact and theory. In 1971 I suggested that science fiction should be regarded as the other side of realism. Perhaps I should have used the term literary naturalism, though such scholars as J. O. Bailey and Dale Mullen were satisfied with the aptness of the former phrasing. Whatever the wording, the intent of the idea was to stress concurrent literary reactions. There is no need to rehearse here the despair that the concept of naturalism (including determinism) evoked in such writers as Mark Twain, William Dean Howells, Matthew Arnold, and Henry Adams. What is still too often overlooked (ignored?) is that simultaneously, perhaps, a second, smaller group of writers enthusiastically embraced the new science, especially its technology. To call this latter group estranged and alienated seems a grievous error unless the critic-historian himself has either a political ax to grind or is disenchanted by the assumption that mankind can be accounted for solely in terms of psychological, sociological, and environmental data. (I personally believe that dread of this assumption has deeply colored modern scholarship, not only literary criticism. It raises a telling question: can mankind build a humane philosophy in a completely secular universe?)

Certainly most of the writers dealt with in this volume—from the 1870s on—tried to do so. How often has it been emphasized that the period between the American Civil War and World War I produced the greatest number of fictional utopias of any single historical era? Yet as I pointed out in *A Spectrum of Worlds* (1972), to confine one's attention only to utopian societies misses the rich diversity of the literary expression of those enthusiasts of science. I suggested then that among the motifs to which any historian of science fiction must give attention were those involving future wars, lost races, interplanetary voyages, prehistory, wonderful inventions and discoveries, and natural and man-made catastrophes as well as utopian societies.

In short, what I have attempted to do in the present *Annotated Bibliography* is to show in some detail the variety of responses to science between the 1870s and 1930s made by writers who used some aspect of the new sciences as a basis for their fantasy or extrapolations.

If science fiction is a separate genre—and that premise can certainly be argued—then it emerged as an independent form during the seven decades this volume covers. I have not imposed any strict, recently developed definition upon the field because to do so might exclude works that illuminate the evolution of the field. For example, a number of entries concern novels dealing with the occult; to ignore them entirely would be to overlook deliberately one of the chief intellectual debates of the late nineteenth and early twentieth centuries: namely, the attempts of writers (and their readers) to reconcile—perhaps a better term would be to restate—traditional philosophical and religious beliefs in terms that would subsume the new scientific theories and findings. Similarly, to omit the so-called lost race motif would be to ignore the impact that the fields of geology, archaeology, and anthropology—as well as exploration (geography) had upon the literary and literate imaginations of the period. Dismissing the motif out of hand as mere fantasy because a number of particulars voiced during the period have been disproved smacks of a narrow elitism, at best. One might as well dismiss from any historical consideration of the growth of science fiction the many interplanetary voyages that built upon the concept of parallel evolution—indeed, dismiss all of those stories that found any form of life on the planets of this solar system. Such exclusions forget that one of the values of science fiction lies in its ability to provide an index to the popular response to science during any given period. And certainly they turn their backs upon a basic lesson that H. G. Wells and so many others have reiterated over and over again: change is inevitable.

Thus in this volume I have tried to be as inclusive (comprehensive) as possible in order to show the breadth of the literary response that has created modern science fiction. Consequently, I have not been so pedantic as to enumerate titles that should *not* be considered science fiction; instead I have included a few entries that show how misleading titles can be. I have done this in part, at least, because despite the fine work of J. O. Bailey, Marjorie Nicolson, and I. F. Clarke, there has not yet been a scholarly literary/intellectual history of the field as a whole. (I do not forget or dismiss the sound work of popular writers such as Brian Aldiss when I say this; after all, the first chapter of *Billion Year Spree* was initially published in *Extrapolation*.) I hope that to some small extent my own *Some Kind of Paradise* will remedy this lack. That monograph (to be published by Greenwood Press) should be regarded as a companion volume to this *Bibliography*, for only in such a study can one trace the patterns and implications that surface in the annotations to the books cited here.

I have abandoned my original impulse to restrict the *Bibliography* to titles by American authors only, although I have tried to emphasize American editions. Of the 838 entries in this volume, I note that the vast majority are the sole efforts in the field by their authors. I do not try to interpret the significance of that fact here. I have deliberately not annotated every work by such familiar writers as Sir Arthur Conan Doyle, Sir H. Rider Haggard, Jules Verne, and

H. G. Wells. I have chosen what I regard as their most representative and significant contributions to the field, but I recognize that any selection involving such writers will bring disagreement from someone. To those who suggest that I have not given adequate attention to Continental writers, I can only reply that to be of influence in Britain and, especially, America, their work had to be translated. I believe I have included significant translations made during the period under consideration. In addition, by and large, I have omitted those works that were published only in magazines during the period. That exclusion looms most noticeably in terms of the short stories and serials issued in the Munsey magazines. As I suggested in regard to another matter in *SF Criticism: An Annotated Checklist* (1972), such an effort merits the labor. But it involves a separate (and needed) volume. My emphasis here has been on book publication, for I believe that the success of the early books created the magazine market.

In short, to repeat, I have tried to give a detailed and comprehensive overview of the field during the period from the 1870s to the 1930s. I have thought this could best be done by showing the extent to which the field found publication in book form.

Such a work as this could not be completed without the aid of innumerable friends. I must extend special thanks to Ossie Train of Philadelphia and to "Doc" C. L. Barrett of Bellefontaine, Ohio; oftentimes both men allowed me to borrow rare items from their personal collections. Stu Teitler, whose knowledge of the lost race motif is unexcelled, gave me many suggestions and helped me obtain access to rare volumes. (I recall a number of times when we "read shelves" in various parts of California.) Sam Moskowitz helped me, always keeping me posted regarding his latest discoveries among the writers of the nineteenth century. I must also single out I. F. Clarke, especially for his advice regarding the future war motif. As I have said elsewhere, his *Voices Prophesying War* provides a model of scholarship that we all might emulate.

I am also greatly indebted to the staffs of the British Museum, the Huntington Library, and U.C.L.A.; and to George Slusser of the University of California—Riverside, John Newman of Colorado

State University, Robert A. Tibbetts of Ohio State University, and to Michael Freeman of The College of Wooster.

Nor could I have completed the travel and research necessary without a grant from N.E.H. in 1976 and the truly fine support of The College of Wooster Research Leave Program.

I am, of course, as indebted as ever to my wife, Alice, who has by now assimilated more information about science fiction through reading copy and proofs than anyone I know. This time out, I could not have completed the manuscript of the *Bibliography* without Marlene Zimmerman—my word processing woman, as I call her—who brought something of the awe and wonder of high tech to the preparation of the volume.

To come full circle, I must extend thanks to Professor Spiller, who saw, in the suggestion of the topic, a source that might add new insight into modern American civilization. Nor, perhaps, would it be amiss to recall those hundreds of writers who created the field of science fiction in the late nineteenth and early twentieth centuries.

SCIENCE FICTION IN AMERICA, 1870s-1930s

ANNOTATED BIBLIOGRAPHY

001. Abbot, Edwin A. [as A. Square]. Flatland; A Romance of Many Dimensions. London: Seeley, 1884.

The narrator presents his two-dimensional world as though describing a utopia, giving attention to its daily life while satirizing education and women. His real aim, however, is to explore the concept of dimensions. He imagines a one-dimensional world (Lineland), in which motion is impossible, and meets a three-dimensional man (Sphere), who informs him of Spaceland. They speculate about a fourth dimension. His grandson and others cannot comprehend the idea of a third dimension, and he is imprisoned for his teaching. A classic of the period often reprinted.

002. About, Edmond. The Man with the Broken Ear. [Trans. from the French by Henry Holt]. New York: Holt & Williams, 1872.

A slight, humorous tale of suspended animation: Professor Meiser of Dantzic believed that humans are watches, water acting as oil. In 1813 he subjected Colonel Fougas, a Frenchman condemned as a spy, to various experiments resulting in his desiccation. Returning from Russia, Leon Renault brings the mummy to his father, a scientist. Fougas is revived in 1859 amid the scientific jargon of the period. He obtains the fortune left him by Meiser and seeks the hand of lovely Clementine until he learns that she is the granddaughter of a woman he loved. Clementine and Leon marry; Colonel Fougas dies a month after his revival.

003. Adams, Frederick Upham. President John Smith; The Story of a Peaceful Revolution. New York: Kerr, 1897.

A socialist utopia in which capitalists and their misuse of technology are criticized, this novel has its chief importance as one of the first stories to create an imaginary president as its protagonist--in this instance, a Boston judge. He overcomes the threat of anarchists and supports a new constitution calling for the "right to work" and abolishing the Senate.

004. Adams, Jack [pseud. of Alcanoan O. Grigsby]. Nequa; or, The Problem of the Ages. Topeka, Ks.: Equity, 1900.

Within the framework of a love story--in which the heroine disguises herself as a man in order to be near the man she loves and to gain a berth on a ship seeking the North Pole--the voyagers discover an interior world which has attained the utopian level because women have "carried their humanitarian work to such perfection" that society's ills have been overcome. The society is deeply religious, but "Mother-love completed the work of human redemption." Direct reference is made to Symmes' theory, and the country is several times called Altruria.

005. Adams, Samuel Hopkins. The Flying Death. New York: McClure, 1908.

Mysterious deaths occur on the beach at Montauk Point. The wonderful Whalley, a mad knife juggler, confesses to several, but the other killer is a pteranodon, a flying reptile. The investigations of the scientist, Professor Ravenden, are emphasized, as is the rationale explaining how prehistoric creatures, both of the sea and the air, can survive. Originally published in McClure's Magazine in 1903, the narrative was expanded to novel length by adding to the love story.

006. Adams, Samuel Hopkins. The World Goes Smash. Boston: Houghton Mifflin, 1938.

Adams projects a civil war in 1940 when gangsters and corrupt politicians attempt to gain control of Congress and the presidency. Against this background the main storyline centers on the love of Hugh Farragut, New York District Attorney, and Dorrie, daughter of Happy James, the secret leader of the conspiracy. The war ends after the development of the Azrael bomb, which causes blindness. At the end the couple stands near the crater that was Columbus Circle. Obviously society must be rebuilt. Incidentally, Europe was destroyed by Fascism and Communism.

007. Aikin, Charles. Forty Years with the Damned; or, Life Inside the Earth. Chicago: Regan, 1895.

A strange mixture of mysticism and utopianism: the envelope for the narrative is a hunter's discovery of a cave in Virginia and his awakening from a dream. A runaway slave and his wife penetrate into an interior world inhabited by people from various eras and planets. The latter part describes the civilization of Mars. Much is made of redemption.

008. Aldrich, Thomas Bailey. The Queen of Sheba and My Cousin the Colonel. Boston: Osgood, 1877.

The Queen of Sheba exemplifies the early psychological case study. Following an attack of typhoid fever, the heroine suffers a mental disorder involving amnesia and the delusion that she is the Queen of Sheba. The trouble is temporary, however, not some "hereditary doom" which would prevent her marriage to the protagonist who has sought an explanation of her condition.

009. Alexander, James B. The Lunarian Professor, and His Remarkable Revelations Concerning the Earth, the Moon and Mars, Together with an Account of the Cruise of the Sally Ann. Minneapolis, Mn.: no publisher, 1909.

The narrator encounters the Lunarian Professor--shaped like an insect--in the Minnesota woods in 1892. He listens to a history of the Earth throughout the twentieth century because his visitor is from the twenty-first century. In addition to such topical matters as the single tax, the growing socialism in cities, the changes in agriculture, and the improvements in transportation, he learns that Russia dominated most of Asia, that Britian declined after losing India in a war with Russia and France, and that the United States formed the Great Union, which involved Central and North America, the British colonies, and many islands in the Pacific, including Japan. After society learns how to determine the sex of a fetus, women become the ruling sex, gaining complete equality. But society balks at polyandry. All of the developments of the twentieth century fail because of the problem of overpopulation. Just twenty years earlier the Lunarians solved that difficulty by introducing the third (neuter) sex which will make up the majority of humanity. The Professor declares that environment determines the nature of the race and the individual. He departs for Mars, where the dominant species resembles the starfish. The ending implies that the narrator has dreamed the entire encounter.

010. Allen, [Charles] Grant. The British Barbarians; A Hilltop Novel. New York: Putnam, 1895.

Also published in London by John Lane (1895): in Surrey Philip Christy encounters a man from the twenty-fifth century and takes him into his family group. Since the visitor, Bertram Ingledew, wishes to study Victorian "taboos," this device serves as a means of satirizing British social customs, especially the obsession with respectability. Bertram explains that European man is descended from Andropithecus of Upper Uganda, an irrational species. When he would marry Frida spiritually, her jealous husband, Robert Monteith, accuses him of adultery and shoots him.   Bertram fades back into the twenty-fifth century.

011.   Allen, Lumen.   <u>Pharaoh's</u> <u>Treasure</u>; <u>An</u> <u>Egyptian</u> <u>Romance</u>. Chicago: Donohue & Henneberry, 1891.

An ancient manuscript, recently discovered, gives an account of the adventures of Athene in Egypt circa 1345 B.C.   At the end a Hebrew seer laments the bondage of the Israelites.   Such a novel underscores the continuing interest in Egyptology and Biblical materials at the turn of the century; it should be regarded as a pseudo-historical novel instead of fantasy or science fiction.

012.   Allen, Willis Boyd.   <u>The</u> <u>Lion</u> <u>City</u> <u>of</u> <u>Africa</u>; <u>A</u> <u>Story</u> <u>of</u> <u>Adventure</u>.   Boston: Lothrop, 1890.

Boyd asserts that he is the editor of a manuscript given him by a David Livingstone Scott.   Many references to con-temporary explorers as well as to legends of lost cities from Moses to Herodotus.   Specific reference is made to H. Rider Haggard.   The narrative becomes something of a travelogue as Scott penetrates the interior near Lakes Tanganyika and Victoria.   The ruins--"long mounds and hollows"--of the City of Lions, Simbamwenni, are found.   In a prefatory note Boyd insists that "the real Africa is sufficiently marvellous" without the invention of "new wonders"; the book thus illustrates the continuing impact of Africa on the popular imagination.   It is neither fantasy nor science fiction.

013.   Ames, Joseph Bushnell.   <u>The</u> <u>Bladed</u> <u>Barrier</u>.   New York: Century, 1929.

This lost race novel takes its protagonists, Stillman and Cavanaugh, into Lower California, where they find a race of Chinese in a hidden valley.   An American girl, Phyllis Brooks, believed to have been lost at sea, acts as a kind of goddess/priestess to the Chinese.   She helps the two to escape with a treasure of jewels.   At the end Stillman reveals his love for her.

014.   Anderson, Olof W.   <u>The</u> <u>Treasure</u> <u>Vault</u> <u>of</u> <u>Atlantis</u>. Minneapolis, Mn.: Midland, 1925.

This novel illustrates the persistence both of a concern for the occult and of a belief in Atlantis as the mother continent of civilization.   As a youth its narrator had dreams of a former existence.   He is one of the explorers who venture into the Amazon valley and find a vault con-taining Atlantean leaders in a state of suspended ani-mation; they sought to escape the destruction of the continent in order to give their vast knowledge to future peoples.   One of them, the protagonist believes, is the matured girl of whom he dreamed; he names her Dogma, Goddess of the Dawn. Revived, the Atlanteans share their technical knowledge and travel the world with the explorers. They offer to provide a means of ending war. Yet thematically the novel from its beginning emphasizes the problem of life after death and communication with the dead. The final achievement is the development of a machine enabling the protagonist to talk with his deceased mother.

015. Anet, Claude [pseud. of Jean Schopfer]. The End of a World. New York: Knopf, 1927.

Focusing upon a brother and sister, the novel portrays the disappearance of a prehistoric race, the "People of the River," who worship the mammoth and cave bear at the end of the last ice age. Merchants of an advanced culture visit them, and a group called Round Heads, who build a village and disrupt the old hunting culture, absorb them. The tribe is identified with the artists of the grottoes near Dordogne on the banks of the Vézère.

016. Angelo [pseud.]. The Adventures of an Atom, Its Autobiography by Itself. New York: Hurst, 1880.

Although the novel contains satire of such matters as drama and women, it becomes a celebration of God and his universe.

017. Anonymous. What May Happen in the Next 90 Days; The Disruption of the United States, or the Origin of the Second Civil War. New York: no publisher, 1877.

In a retrospective letter to a nephew, the writer asserts that just prior to the 1876 election the reputation of Senator Blaine was besmirched; he calls for resistance to the inauguration of Tilden, should he win. When he does, the returns in Florida, Louisiana, and South Carolina, especially, are questioned. Congress does not carry out any of its business, banks refuse to pay out more than $100. at a time, and soldiers guard Congress. Grant proclaims himself "Protector of the Republic," while Hayes calls out the Ohio militia. Fighting breaks out in Ohio and New York, continuing for years and devastating the country. This volume remains unique among portrayals of imaginary conflicts because of its topicality.

018. Appleton, Victor [house name]. Tom Swift. . . .

Beginning in 1910, using the pseudonym Victor Appleton, the Edward Stratemeyer syndicate made the name Tom Swift synonymous with the idea of a youthful American genius turning out innumerable inventions which were always used for humane, moral purposes. The plots involved little more

than capture and escape, as well as the threats of villain-
nous middle-Europeans (usually) to steal Tom's inventions.
Between 1910 and 1912 fifteen titles were issued; by 1935
thirty-eight titles had been published. Significantly, as
in the case of Jules Verne, whose basic influence is
apparent, most of Tom's inventions were not far in advance
of his contemporaries but simply reflect work already
undertaken in contemporary laboratories. At present
perhaps the best detailed discussion of his works occurs in
three chapters of John T. Dizer's Tom Swift & Company
(1982).

019. Armour, J[ohn] P.   Edenindia; A Tale of Adventure.   New
York: Dillingham, 1905.

A storm blows Horace Mayfield and his new airship into the
Arctic, where he finds an unknown kingdom whose governing
family is descended from Henry Hudson. A utopian element
stresses good physical health, while electric power assures
that everyone has an "abundance of the necessaries of
life." The plot turns upon an unsuccessful flight to Mars
(ending up in Siberia) and the discovery that one of the
young women is Mayfield's niece, supposedly lost in the
Arctic years ago.

020. Arnold, Edwin Lester.   Lepidus the Centurion.   New York:
Crowell, 1901.

On the grounds of his estate, Louis Allanby, "Squire and
J.P.," as well as a devoted student of the classics,
accidentally excavates a vault containing the body of a
Roman, whose epitaph reads, "Marcus Lepidus, the Centurion
. . . is Asleep."   Almost by an act of will, Allanby
revives him. Spiritually akin, they love the same woman,
Priscilla Smith, whom Lepidus believes to be the incarnation of Prisca Quintilia.   Rivals for her hand, they
finally decide to confront her after preparing a potion for
the loser. Priscilla chooses Allanby from a sense of duty
because she is already betrothed to him. Lepidus takes the
potion.   A gentle satire of the British landed gentry
pervades the narrative.

021. Arnold, Edwin Lester.   Lieut. Gullivar Jones; His Vaca-
tion. London: Brown, Langham, 1905.

Alone in New York on an extended shore leave and refused a
promotion, the frustrated American, Jones, finds a magic
carpet which takes him to Mars when he wishes he were
there. Although a first-person narrator, Jones does not
give a graphic description of the gentle, primitive Hither
people. Almost all of the action involves his rescues of
the beautiful princess Heru. He first saves her from
drowning; then when the barbarous Ar-hap claims her as part
of his annual tribute, Jones sets out across Mars to find

her. He fulfills several tasks set for him by Ar-hap, but
the appearance of a giant meteor delays her release. After
they return to the Hither kingdom, Ar-Kap and his men
attack; hard pressed, Jones wishes he were on Earth. The
carpet returns him to New York, where a letter tells him of
his promotion, and a faithful, unquestioning Polly agrees
to marry him. While Bleiler dismisses the novel as "a
minor oddity only," others, like Richard Lupoff, see it as
a major source for Burroughs' John Carter tales. An
equally strong argument could be made for the two novels by
Gustavus W. Pope.

022. Arnold, Edwin Lester. The Wonderful Adventures of Phra
the Phoenician. New York: Harper, 1890.

The novel has importance because it portrays a series of
reincarnations, though Arnold refers to his protagonist's
sleeping for long periods. Originally, Phra, a merchant,
buys the freedom of a British princess and takes her to
England. When Romans invade the island, the Britons
sacrifice Phra as a traitor. He awakens as a member of a
Roman legion recalled from Britain at the time of the fall
of Rome; he fights at the battle of Crécy; and his final
"life" occurs during the reign of Elizabeth.

023. Ash, Fenton [pseud. of Frank Atkins]. By Airship to
Ophir. London: Shaw, 1911.

A voyage filled with Verne-like espisodes takes its juvenile protagonists to a city inhabited by descendants of the
Queen of Sheba.

024. Ash, Fenton [pseud. of Frank Atkins]. The Radium Seekers;
or, The Wonderful Black Nugget. London: Pitman & Sons, 1905.

Wilfrid Moray develops an airship powered by the black
nugget, which was brought back from South America. He and
his companions undertake an expedition, especially when
they hear of the existence of an ancient city. Many
adventures befall them, including encounters with bird men,
before they reach the city, Raneema. They become involved
in a struggle for power between the birdmen and the natives. They place the rightful heir on the throne, but the
island containing the "Moradium"--as they call the metal--
sinks beneath the great lake. Wilfrid remains in the city,
but his companions return to Britain.

025. Ash, Fenton [pseud. of Frank Atkins]. A Trip to Mars.
Philadelphia: Lippincott, 1909.

Also published in London by Chambers (1909): in a prefatory
note Atkins asserts that his portrayal of Mars is based
upon some "quasi-scientific foundation," although he had
difficulty regarding verisimilitude and his choice of what

theories to adopt. What appears to be a meteor proves to be an "aerostat," the _Ivenia_, which lands near the home of Gerald Wilton and Jack Lawford, wards of the scientist Armeath. The ship was sent to Earth to obtain diamonds, which are highly prized by the Martians. (Armeath reveals that he has tried to produce the gems synthetically, but nothing is made of this.) Taken to Mars--the journey requires several months--the boys and their guardian undergo various conventional adventures, and they become involved in a rebellion between Agronia and King Ivanta. When Ivanta wins, he returns them to Earth-- sending with them all of the diamonds which have been acquired.

026. Astor, John Jacob. _A Journey in Other Worlds_. New York: D. Appleton, 1894.

Although Astor employs apergy to propel his ship, as did Percy Greg earlier, this novel differs from _Across the Zodiac_. Through the character of Professor Cortlandt, it promotes the concept of progressive or parallel evolution throughout the universe. The first part provides a utopian description of Earth in the year 2000; the second takes the voyagers to a prehistoric Jupiter, where they indulge in a fantastic hunting foray; finally, on Saturn they meet a variety of disembodied spirits, among them an Anglican bishop. He describes the wonders of many worlds beyond the solar system and reaffirms the theme of the basic perfectability of man.

027. Aubrey, Frank [pseud. of Frank Atkins]. _The Devil Tree of El Dorado_. New York: New Amsterdam, 1897.

Monella, who will figure in _A Queen of Atlantis_, leads an expedition to the South American mountain, Roraima, which Conan Doyle will use in his _The Lost World_. There the explorers find the beautiful city of Manoa, the golden El Dorado, and become involved in the struggle between the priests who make human sacrifices to the carnivorous tree and the hereditary rulers. They save Princess Uluma. Monella is revealed as the king of Manoa, the tree is destroyed, and Leonard Elwood marries Uluma and remains in Manoa although his British companions return to the outside world.

028. Aubrey, Frank [pseud. of Frank Atkins]. _King of the Dead; A Weird Romance_. London: Macqueen, 1903.

The novel is based upon the premise that thousands of years ago a great white race ruled the entirety of both North and South America, achieving a height of civilization not equalled even by ancient Egypt. When Arnold Neville refuses to accompany Don Lorenzo to the Roraima area of South America, Lorenzo kidnaps Neville's fiancee, Beryl Atherton. Neville and a companion follow them and meet

Manzoni, a white man, and Rhelma, his daughter, in the jungle. They go to Myrvonia, the last city of the old race. Lorenzo proves to be Lyostrah, the high priest of the city; Manzoni is its king, though in voluntary exile. Manzoni has a red ray--which he compares to a galvanic battery--capable of restoring mummies to a kind of life. Lorenzo/Lyostrah sees this as a means of providing armies of the dead with which to conquer the world and restore the ancient kingdom. He loves Alloyah, who worships the Spirit of Evil. When Alloyah would sacrifice Beryl to the Spirit, Lorenzo and Manzoni stop her. Lorenzo gives his life to destroy the Spirit.

029. Aubrey, Frank [pseud. of Frank Atkins]. A Queen of Atlantis; A Romance of the Caribbean. Philadelphia: Lippincott, 1900.

The stepfather of George and Vanina Dareville conspires to have them and their friend, Owen Wydale, abandoned in the Sargasso Sea. They find an island which George calls Atlantis. Cuttlefish attack them, and they find an empty city. The natives of the island hail Vanina as their queen, and the young protagonists become involved in the warfare between the Atlanteans and the natives of a second island, Dilantis. Vanina is bewitched and supposedly will marry King Kara of Dilantis, but George goes to yet another island and obtains an antidote from the "Flower Dwellers." The shadowy figure of Monella helps in the final defeat of Dilantis. Vanina marries Owen, and George studies chemistry. Serialized in Lippincott's Magazine in 1899.

030. Austin, F[rederick] Britten. Thirteen. Garden City, N.Y.: Doubleday, Page, 1925.

The lead story, "Under the Lens," has been compared to Oliver Wendell Holmes' Elsie Venner because of its emphasis upon the degree to which human behavior is controlled by inherited characteristics. "The Infernal Machine" recalls the stories of Ambrose Bierce because the protagonist literally frightens himself to death.

031. Austin, F[rederick] Britten. The War God Walks Again. Garden City, N.Y.: Doubleday, Page, 1926.

"When the War God Walks Again" emphasizes the use of tanks in a future battle, suggesting that they will replace infantry. "In the China Sea" reports the destruction of British ships by the Japanese and warns that the Japanese will attack Guam. "A Battlepiece: New Style" suggests victory attained by an enormous raid on the city by planes using gas bombs. Both "Goliath" and "They Who Laughed" also concentrate upon attacks by airplanes and gas. The former refers to aircraft carriers. The stories remain interesting because of their predictions in light of the events of World War Two.

032. Austin, F[rederick] Britten. <u>When</u> <u>Mankind</u> <u>Was</u> <u>Young</u>. Garden City, N.Y.: Doubleday, Page, 1927.

Most of the stories deal with prehistory, ranging from "The Taming of the Brute," which deals with the acceptance of exogamy, to "The Covered Wagon--2000 B.C.," which deals with the migration of a tribe settling in Greece. Other titles include "In the Land of Osiris," "Midsummer at Stonehenge," and "Rome Begins."

033. Bachelder, John. <u>A.D. 2050; Electrical Development at Atlantis</u>. San Francisco: Bancroft, 1890.

The narrator asserts that Bellamy's West and Leete had taken "a hasty and superficial view" of the year 2000, especially in regard to "scientific and material development." He dreams of a future in which Captain Jones, a wealthy shipowner, has christened a Capitalist utopia Atlantis. Electricity, a cheap building material, and aluminum have contributed to the health and comfort of the people. There are nurseries for infants, and marriage must be approved by both parents and a Board of Health. In 2034 there was a brief war with China, which was won with "Eurekite" shells and torpedo boats. Meanwhile, anarchists and communists from Europe flood the United States and "inflamed the passions of the ignorant masses."

034. Bacheller, Irving. <u>The Master of Silence</u>. New York: Webster, 1892.

Kendric Lane visits his American uncle who investigates the psychic and occult. He has raised his motherless son, Rayel, the personification of innocence, who is able to read minds and perceive dreams. At his uncle's request Lane teaches Rayel to speak. When the uncle dies, the two young men go out into the world. Rayel gains a reputation as an artist and an eccentric. Lane meets his former sweetheart, but the main storyline involves a scheme by Lane's remarried stepmother to obtain his money. Rayel foils the plot but dies. Lane and his sweetheart are married. Bacheller makes a savage attack on parents who do not realize that caring for the mind and body of a child is their highest "mission."

035. Badger, Joseph Edward, Jr. <u>The Lost City</u>. Boston: Estes, 1898.

A tornado carries the juvenile protagonists and Professor Featherwit aboard an airship to the Olympic Mountains of Washington. They discover a city of Aztecs and rescue a mother and daughter who have long been held as prisoners.

036. Balch, Frank. A Submarine Tour. New York: Broadway,
1905.

> An obvious imitation of Twenty Thousand Leagues under the
> Sea: the narrator, Professor Baker, is swept from the deck
> of a ship headed for the North Pole and is picked up by the
> submarine Victor.   Its commander, Captain Hake, takes Baker
> on a world tour, including Naples, Port Said, Atlantis, and
> Manila, where they witness Dewey's victory.   Off South
> America they discover the ruins of a city several thousand
> years old; passing through a tunnel, they emerge in a
> cavern so large that it contains an island on which a city
> of Incas is at war with a city of Aztecs.   They destroy the
> Aztecs with nitro-glycerine.   Baker falls in love with the
> beautiful Actlea, but cannot marry her because the law will
> not allow her to wed a stranger.   Baker is swept off the
> submarine near Cape Hatteras and returns to the United
> States.

037. Balfour, David.   The Golden Kingdom; Being an Account of
the Quest for the Same as Described in the Remarkable Narrative
of Doctor Henry Mortimer, Contained in the Manuscript Found
within the Boards of a Boer Bible During the Late War, and
Edited with a Prefatory Note. Boston: Page, 1903.

> The prefatory note dates the manuscript from the late
> seventeenth-early eighteenth centuries.   On its last page
> the first-person narrator calls it "a false quest," al-
> though he and his companions find a ruined city which seems
> golden seen from afar.   Christopher Melinda, a Portugese,
> has founded a private kingdom among the natives of the
> interior.   But the value of the novel lies in its realistic
> detail as Mortimer journeys from England to the Transvaal.
> He speaks of the "great apes," identifying them as goril-
> las.   A companion of his, Corkran, who has a map that leads
> them into the heart of Africa, becomes the new king.
> Mortimer finds the beautiful, English-speaking girl, Cira,
> whose parents are dead.   They return to Capetown and are
> married.   So realistic is most of its detail that it could
> be mistaken for an historical novel.

038. Ball, Frank P.   My Wondrous Dream New York: Ball, 1923.

> In a prefatory note Ball explains that in 1922 he obtained
> a copy of Donnelly's Atlantis; The Antediluvian World.   He
> dreams of a miniaturized world which is essentially uto-
> pian.   The novel is unique in the degree to which it empha-
> sizes the issue of race.   Repeadtedly he refers to statues
> of black and white marble as symbolic of "National Purity."
> Shiny "ebony blacks" are obviously the workers and are
> supervised by "ivory-like whites."   No other book of the
> period takes so explicit and narrow a view concerning
> racial matters.

039. Ballou, William Hosea. The Bachelor Girl; A Novel of the
1400. New York: Lovell, 1890.

A slight romance that deserves attention because of its emphasis upon ballooning: a wealthy young society woman, Lily
Carolyn Douvre, disappears during a violent storm in New
York City. Her horse is killed. Some think she may have
been struck by a meteor; her father thinks it is a prank.
She is caught up in the guy ropes of a balloon built and
flown by a wealthy young English scientist. His Americus
can achieve thirty mph.   Much information about the
history of the balloon is included. They fall in love and
sink the balloon so that all evidence of the aerial trip
will be their secret. It also contains high praise of the
"New York fashionable girl."

040. Balmer, Edwin and William MacHarg.   The Achievements of
Luther Trant. Boston: Small, Maynard, 1910.

Once an assistant in a psychology laboratory, Trant has
turned detective. Although some of the stories are merely
problems in deduction in the manner of Sherlock Holmes,
Trant does employ current theory and experiment to trap
criminals, using such means as the cardiograph and the word
association test. In its preface the authors stress the
factual basis of the stories. Howard Haycraft states in
Murder for Pleasure that one story, "The Man Higher Up,"
includes the first use of the lie detector in fiction.

041. Balmer, Edwin and Philip Wylie. After Worlds Collide.
New York: Stokes, 1934.

The sequel to When Worlds Collide: after landing on Bronson
Beta, which is conveniently much like the Earth, the
American survivors find an ancient city in which they take
up residence. A British group of survivors joins them, and
together they fight off a third group, Asiatic communists.
This does not achieve the quality of the earlier work.

042. Balmer, Edwin and Philip Wylie. When Worlds Collide. New
York: Stokes, 1933.

Earth cannot escape collision with a planet which intrudes
into the solar system. Cole Hendron organizes a group to
build a spaceshihp so that humanity can survive the catastrophe. The group must also fight off hysterical mobs
which try to storm the construction site. After take-off
the crew watches the destruction of Earth and lands on
Bronson Beta, which now orbits the sun.

043. Barker, Arthur W. <u>The Light from Sealonia</u>. Boston: Four Seasons, 1927.

The captain of a ship in the North Sea discovers an object containing the manuscript of Lee Raymond, one of two Americans who started by balloon for the North Pole some years ago. For a time the two are unconscious, thereby not knowing where they are. As they sight land and people, Raymond's companion falls to his death. Raymond lands in Sealonia; he finds two technically advanced societies which have fought each other frequently. Old books containing information antedating Chinese records lead him to equate Cain's banishment to the land of Nod with the ancient appearance of Kana in the other nation, Nodalia. Kana bore a mark on his forehead, as does the present queen of Nodalia. The Sealonians believe that he fulfills an old prophecy of a sky king who will establish a kingdom of love on Earth. Nodalia prepares aircraft for war; he wishes to marry the queen of Sealonia; and he sets his manuscript adrift. An anachronism at so late a date.

044. Barnes, James. <u>The Unpardonable War</u>. New York and London: Macmillan, 1904.

To keep the "People's Party" from losing the next election, a journalist and a cabinet member distract America from its domestic problems by inciting a war with Great Britain. They justify their actions in terms of the annexation of Canada and the freedom of Ireland. Although a device like radar is described, the war does not end until Westland, "the Wizard of Staten Island," introduces an electrical force which explodes all kinds of gunpowder. This success leads him to suggest that the President head a league to suppress war. Theodore Roosevelt re-enters politics, and America and Britain sign an alliance.

045. Barney, John Stewart. <u>L.P.M.; The End of the Great War</u>. New York: Putnam, 1915.

The American scientist, Edestone, develops an anti-gravity force permitting him to build a fortress-like flying machine. He persuades the King of England and the Kaiser to support his demand that all war end, and he calls for an authoritarian world government to be led by "the Aristocracy of Intelligence." He insists that governments should be organized like "the great corporations of America." Not only does he deny equality and majority rule, but he also demands that the races be segregated geographically.

046. Barr, Robert. The Face and the Mask. New York: Stokes, 1895.

The narrator of "The Doom of London" explains that a combination of coal smoke and fog suffocated almost everyone by consuming the oxygen in the air. He escaped by train after using an oxygen-producing machine invented in America. In "The New Explosive" the French Minister of War blows up the inventor of an explosive detonated by exposure to the sunlight.

047. Barry, Richard. Fruit of the Desert. Garden City, N.Y.: Doubleday, Page, 1920.

In an attempt to regain his health which he lost because he studied too hard--he is called "a victim of the colleges"-- Ranor Gaul goes into the California desert. Abandoned there by an outlaw who steals all of his possessions, he is rescued by the Indian, Tuwah, who takes him deeper into the desert beyond the Grand Canyon to the lost city of the Nahneet tribe, survivors from the period of the Aztecs and Toltecs. He falls in love with Izara, their high priestess, whom he saves from a puma. When Gaul shows the Indians how to irrigate their crops--threatened by a drought--Izara is tried by the patriarchs for failing as a priestess and is banished into the desert. Gaul finds her, and they return to civilization. Yet as they go by train toward Philadelphia, Barry questions whether or not the better life was the primitive existence in the desert, where Gaul did recover his health and find his beloved.

048. Barton, Samuel. The Battle of the Swash, and the Capture of Canada. New York: Dillingham, 1888.

Apparently the first American novel to treat the future war motif, this narrative emphasizes the enthusiasm with which Canada accepts union with the United States. As was typical of so many early treatments of the motif, Barton warned that the failure "to adopt ordinary defensive precautions," including not rebuilding the merchant marine, led to the conflict. Although the British navy sacks such cities as New York, the United States finally annihilates the British fleet when American science develops self-destroying torpedo boats. Both Canada and the West Indies are ceded to the United States, while Great Britain is so badly mauled that she must remain an observer in an ensuing European war. The novel reflects an early view which was to be replaced by the concept of some kind of Anglo-American alliance or of Anglo-Saxon supremacy.

049. Baum, L[yman] Frank. <u>The</u> <u>Master</u> <u>Key</u>; <u>An</u> <u>Electrical</u> <u>Fairy</u>
<u>Tale</u>. Indianapolis, In.: Bowen-Merrill, 1901.

> Baum models the youthful protagonist on his son who was
> interested in electricity. The boy Rob accidentally calls
> forth The Demon of Electricity, who gives him three gifts--
> a food tablet, a tube (weapon) causing unconsciousness, and
> an arm band permitting aerial flight.   Rob's adventures
> parallel those of other juveniles. Given still more gifts,
> he finally returns them all, saying that humanity is not
> yet intelligent enough to use them.   In the initial dia-
> logue the Demon belittles Edison and Tesla and asserts that
> neither Mars nor any other planet of the solar system is
> inhabited.

050. Beale, Charles Willing.   <u>The</u> <u>Secret</u> <u>of</u> <u>the</u> <u>Earth</u>.   New
York and London: Neely, 1899.

> From the ocean near the Celebes Beale obtains the manu-
> script of Gurthrie and Torrence Attlebridge, Americans who
> went to England to build an airship to fly to the North
> Pole. Almost half the narrative deals with their diffi-
> culties in finishing the ship. Eventually they pass into
> an inner world through a polar opening having a thousand-
> mile diameter. They obtain a treasure, and natives regard
> them as gods, but theirs is a scenic cruise; they do not
> pause at great cities because of their "utter inability to
> communicate with the inhabitants."   Emerging from the
> Antarctic opening, they fly across the Pacific until
> mechanical failure maroons them on the island from which
> they send their manuscript.

051. Beatty, John. <u>The</u> <u>Alcohuans</u>; <u>A</u> <u>Narrative</u> <u>of</u> <u>Sojourn</u> <u>and</u>
<u>Adventure</u> among the <u>Mound</u> <u>Builders</u> <u>of</u> <u>the</u> <u>Ohio</u> <u>Valley</u> . . .
Columbus, Oh: McClelland, 1902.

> The "memoirs of Ivarr Bartholdsson," this pseudo-historical
> novel permits a tenth-century Viking to save the Mound
> Builders from northern barbarians before he visits the
> Toltec empire, described as though it were a profligate
> Rome. He returns to Normandy, where his mother is a queen.

052. Bechdolt, Jack [John Ernest].   <u>The</u> <u>Lost</u> <u>Vikings</u>.   New
York: Cosmopolitan, 1931.

> The juvenile protagonists find a colony of Vikings some-
> where north of Point Barrow. They apparently made their
> way to the area of Alaska from the Norse colony in Green-
> land.

053. Beeding, Francis [pseud. of John Palmer and Hilary Saunders]. The Hidden Kingdom. Boston: Little, Brown, 1927.

A sequel to The Seven Sleepers: the protagonist and two friends who belong to the French secret service follow Professor Kreutzemark, a chemist, from western Europe to Outer Mongolia, where with the aid of Baron Konrad Von Hefflebech, he hopes to set himself up as the so-called Deliverer and lead the Mongol Hordes to world conquest. Speaking of a moral bankruptcy of Europe and the "democractic malady" of the West, he hopes to establish an authoritarian state having the virtues of old Germany. He can be interpreted as a kind of anti-Christ. The protagonist must also rescue Suzanne, whom Kreutzemark has carried off.

054. Beeding, Francis [pseud. of John Palmer and Hilary Saunders]. The Seven Sleepers. Boston: Little, Brown, 1925.

The British protagonist prevents the diabolical Professor Kreutzemark from masterminding a plot involving German Capitalists and generals to start a new war and conquer the world.

055. Bell, George W. Mr. Oseba's Last Discovery. Wellington, New Zealand: New Zealand Times, 1904.

Amoora Oseba inhabits a Symmesian world rich in "electrical science" in a novel aimed primarily at promoting New Zealand. It contains many photographs of New Zealand's outstanding citizens and its scenery. It also expounds the idea of Anglo-Saxon supremacy.

056. Bellamy Edward. The Blindman's World. Boston: Houghton Mifflin, 1898.

The most important story in this volume, "To Whom This May Come," looks back past Bellamy's social criticism to his early interest in the occult. Shipwrecked on an unknown island in the Pacific, the narrator describes a utopia achieved because the people--originally from Persia some time ago--have developed the power of telepathy through evolution. Bellamy suggests that telepathy will eventually appear throughout humanity and, making secrecy and deceit impossible, will bring about utopia.

057. Bellamy Edward. Dr. Heidenhoff's Process. New York: D. Appleton, 1880.

In this first novel Bellamy uses the scientific theory of the period to express an essentially mystical theme. Using the galvanic battery to destroy "morbid tissues," Dr. Heidenhoff invents a device which erases from the mind the memory of any evil deed which a patient may have committed.

Bellamy emphasizes that the process merely completes what has already begun through Christian repentence.

058. Bellamy Edward. Equality. New York: D. Appleton, 1897.

More of an essay than a novel, this sequel to Looking Backward elaborates upon his previous thesis. He gives more attention to women and education, as well as emphasizing the lack of sectarianism in religion. He does criticize technology somewhat in that inventions often increased production and left the profit in the hands of the capitalists. The society is vegetarian, and there is an emphasis upon exercise. Equality reflects his political activity and considers the various reforms proposed by the Populists.

059. Bellamy Edward. Looking Backward; A.D. 2000-1887. Boston: Ticknor, 1888.

This became the most influential of the American utopias not so much for its merit as a novel as for the sharp disagreement over Bellamy's basic theses: namely, that economic equality was the necessary cornerstone of a democracy and that the government assume responsibility for all service organizations and all production. The basic argument became the issue of socialism. Bellamy gave little explicit attention to specific developments in science and technology. This contains the parable of the stagecoach, perhaps the single best image attacking the capitalistic system.

060. Bellamy Edward. Miss Ludington's Sister; A Romance of Immortality. Boston: Osgood, 1884.

The slightest of Bellamy's fictions, although it established his popularity both in America and Britain, this story illustrates the period's interest in psychical research and "mediumship."

061. Bennet, Robert Ames. The Bowl of Baal. West Kingston, R.I.: Donald M. Grant, 1975.

Originally serialized in All Around Magazine (November 1916-February 1917): the war prevents Professor Searing from leading an archaeological expedition into the interior of Arabia. His devoted student, Larry O'Brien, flies into the unknown area north of Aden to photograph artifacts for Searing. He finds the "Lost Garden of Irem," where he becomes involved with two priestesses: the brunette Tigra and the golden Istara. Tigra performs a ritual dance which makes her his wife, at least in name, but he refuses her advances, declaring his love for Istara. Bennet retains a tribe of savage cavemen (the Noadites) and a blind saurian monster which they worship (the "Dweller"; the "Devourer").

O'Brien kills the monster. During a final battle with the Noadites, he realizes that he loves Tigra and fights by her side. When she is wounded, they flee by airplane only to go down in the desert where she dies in his arms. O'Brien regains consciousness in a British camp and learns that he has had amnesia. The British dismiss his story, official- ly, as hallucinations during his amnesia. But he knows that Searing will believe, and he cannot return to civili- zation. No single story better illustrates the way in which the lost race novel evolved in America. Perhaps most important is the eroticism introduced by Tigra.

062. Bennet, Robert Ames. _Thyra; A Romance of the Polar Pit_. New York: Holt, 1901.

After the horrors of an Arctic winter, the first-person narrator and his companions find a balloon enabling them to continue northward. On the ice they save a "Polar Val- kyrie"--Thyra--as she struggles with a cave bear. She leads them to a vast, temperate chasm inhabited by various prehistoric creatures, including a race of beast-men (the Dwerger) who worship a great serpent. There in Biornstad live a lost race of Vikings, descendants of a tenth-century expedition. Despite praise of the Vikings' "full fledged democracy," the novel emphasizes the warfare with the beast-men and the killing of the serpent-god.

063. Benoit [Ferdinand Marie] Pierre. _The Queen of Atlantis_. London: Hutchinson, 1920.

Published in the U.S. in 1920 as _Atlantida (L'Atlantide)_ by Duffield, this novel combines the interest in such Arab tribes as the Tauregs and the legend of Atlantis. In France, especially, it was compared to Rider Haggard's _She_. Officers of the French foreign legion enter an unknown area of the Sahara ruled by Antinea, "the grand-daughter of Neptune, the last descendant of the Atlantes." Another ancestor, however, is the daughter of Cleopatra and Mark Antony. It is basically a love story.

064. Benson, Robert Hugh. _The Dawn of All_. London: Hutchin- son, 1911.

Benson names this as a sequel to _Lord of the World_, in which he explores the alternative ("the opposite process") to the earlier novel. Within the narrative frame of a dying man's dream vision, Benson argues for a world ruled by the Pope because he is the Emissary of God. The story- line, such as it is, centers on the vote of Parliament to recognize the Pope. Benson casts the action into the future, 1973. He argues at length against the superfi- ciality of science (materialism), realism in the arts, and especially socialism. Catholicism is triumphant throughout the world.

065.   Benson, Robert Hugh.   Lord of the World.   New York: Dodd, Mead, 1908.

>   First published in London (1907) by Sir Isaac Pitman: Benson attacks the Bellamy-Wellsian projection of humanistic Utopias.   He places the action a century in the future.   The religion of Humanitarianism is led by its prophet, Felsenburgh, perhaps a kind of anti-Christ, who becomes President of the World.   Rome is destroyed; the Pope and his few followers are forced to Palestine.   The novel ends in an enigmatic vision which may signify the Second Coming and the end of the world.   A "Prologue" denounces the spread of socialism.

066.   Beresford, J[ohn] D[avys].   The Camberwell Miracle. London: Heinemann, 1933.

>   This novel becomes an attack upon modern medicine in so far as it views the human being as no more than "a complicated machine."   At the age of two, Rosemary Henderson is stricken by a disease, apparently infantile paralysis.   The storyline centers upon the career of Martin Davies, who does not regard himself as a "faith-healer," as he tries to help her and others.   Part of the narrative deals with his trial.   Through "the power of love" Rosemary overcomes her own weaknesses and may be able to help others, though she remains lame.   Beresford rejects any purely "mechanistic theory of the universe."

067.   Beresford, J[ohn] D[avys].   Revolution; A Story of the Near Future in England.   New York: Putnam, 1921.

>   Also published in London by W. Collins (1921): the introduction to the American edition suggests that European civilization has reached its height and can only decline. Paul Leaming, the narrator and son of a conservative, describes the attempts of the Labor Party to come to power. There is a General Strike.   Isaac Perry, the Labor leader who issues an idealistic manifesto calling for change and has the charisma to effect change, is assassinated by a sniper.   Beresford remains somewhat ambivalent in his attitude.   One character asserts the working men had hoped for a kind of Utopia; another sees civilization dying, "full of sin and splendor, of fierce incompleted ideas and glorious accomplishments."

068.   Beresford, J[ohn] D[avys].   The Wonder.   New York: Doran, 1917.

>   First published in England by Sidgwick & Jackson (1911): this remains one of the early classic treatments of the "superman" theme.   It concentrates upon a young boy whose mind is thousands of years in advance of contemporary man's.   Yet society regards him as little more than an

idiot because he does not speak. The local vicar is his main enemy. When the boy drowns, the question remains whether or not he was murdered. Perhaps its most notable feature is the wonder and awe the narrator has for a superior, rational mind.

069. Beresford, J[ohn] D[avys]. A World of Women. New York: Macaulay, 1913.

Published in London as Goslings by Heinemann (1913): a plague spreads westward from Asia (Tibet), killing only men. Despite a strict quarantine it invades England. An exodus from London begins; famine haunts the Home Counties and areas near cities. Jasper Thrale, the protagonist, accompanies the Gosling family, which breaks up. At Marlow he becomes chief mechanic. Despite the efforts of the Jenkynites, religious zealots, he survives and falls in love with the girl Eileen. Together they go downstream to open all the weirs so there will be no flooding. An ocean liner from America arrives with some 1200 men; in America both men and women caught the plague, but paralysis did not last beyond six months. The novel serves as a vehicle for commentary on the status of women. Thrale observes that most of the women were unable to "think out a new morality for themselves," while Eileen is pleased that the new situation, though perilous before the arrival of the Americans, has done away with all the "silly" manners and reserve which made love "abominable." One cannot be certain of the time lapse covered by the narrative: a number of years at least.

070. Beresford, Leslie. The Venus Girl. London: Long, 1925.

A light-hearted spoof on interplanetary love affairs, the novel nevertheless remarks upon the status of women. With his fiancée, Barbara Wainwright in mind, Milton Hastings writes The Venus Girl, the "first English opera of note" in a number of years. Alone, Hastings puts on an armlet supposedly from Peru. As soon as he does there appears a beautiful young woman who declares that she is from Venus and must find an Earthman to be her lover and return to Venus with her. She is Una, and he wore the Bracelet of Bhor, Queen of Venus. When he does not respond, Una influences others to become infatuated with him. Her efforts provide the basis for the comedy and the satire of English manners. Una explains that on Venus each girl seeks out her own man, but there is no marriage in her society. At the end he awakens to find that he has been ill with brain fever for a week. Una is gone; he removed the armlet in the woods before he became ill. He and Barbara marry.

071. Besant, Walter. The Revolt of Man. London: Chatto & Windus, 1897.

Originally published anonymously by Blackwood (1882): in an essentially unchanged England women hold all positions of authority. Most importantly, they control the social scene, including marriage. The revolt occurs because wealthy old women choose to marry young husbands, thereby depriving the men of the right to woo and wed young women. The storyline centers on the Duchess of Dunstanburgh, who offers her hand to Edward, Lord Chester. He loves the beautiful young Constance, Countess of Calyon. The idea that the novel calls for the submissiveness of women must be tempered by the satire of the disparity of ages in marriage.

072. Bierbower, Austin. From Monkey to Man; or, Life in the Tertiary Age. Chicago: Dibble, 1894.

In his earlier books Bierbower had written about Christian ethics, suggesting in one that Christ was a Socialist. Racial memory plays an important role in this attempt to reconcile new theories with traditional beliefs. An on-coming glacier forced the "Missing Link" from his Edenic home in the North, while snakes were the obvious enemies of the apemen and so became symbolic of evil. Equally impor-tant, Bierbower showed the first steps the apemen took in their evolution toward true mankind. In doing so, he helped to establish the main storyline for most of the novels dealing with prehistoric man.

073. Bierce, Ambrose. In the Midst of Life (1891); Can Such Things Be? (1893). Works. Washington, D.C.: Neale, 1909-1912, vols 2, 3.

Stories in these two early volumes establish Bierce as a significant figure in the transformation of the traditional ghost story into the modern case history. He dramatized fear, as in "The Man and The Snake." He spoke of racial memory, as in "A Watcher by the Dead" and "A Tough Tussle." The former of these exemplifies a plot he developed which became widely popular and often imitated: a man literally frightens himself to death given "The Suitable Surround-ings." His most successful venture into science fiction remains "The Damned Thing," in which he explained the phenomenon in terms of light rays beyond the range of man's vision.

074. Bigly, Cantell A. [pseud. of George Washington Peck]. Aurifodina; or, Adventures in the Gold Region. New York: Baker and Scribner, 1849.

Apparently the earliest lost race novel whose setting is the United States. Its protagonist searches for a pass

though the Sierra Mountains. He finds a pastoral utopia
whose people have "golden hair, like our Saxon ancestors."
They are not otherwise identified. Gold is so plentiful as
to be valueless. He marries the princess Mideere. Ascend-
ing in a balloon, he is blown to Kentucky. In New York he
longs to return to his princess and his kingdom, but he
fears that he cannot survive another journey into the
Sierras and that he cannot find the idyllic mountain
valley.

075. Birch, A[lbert] G.   The Moon Terror and Other Stories.
Indianapolis, In.: Popular Fiction, 1927.

A variation of the "Yellow Peril": an ancient sect of
Chinese sorcerers/scientists (the Seuen H'sin led by Kwo-
Sung-tao) threatens to destroy the world by catastrophic
earthquakes. They have developed an electrical force which
matches the Earth's vibrations and can tear it apart.
Although they are foiled by an American scientist, Gresham,
and his narrator friend, their effort changes the face of
the Earth.   The volume also includes Anthony M. Rud's
"Ooze," dealing with the giant amoeba, as well as Vincent
Starrett's "Penelope" and Farnsworth Wright's "An Adventure
in the Fourth Dimension." All were reprinted from early
issues of Weird Tales.

076. Birkmaier, Elizabeth G.   Poseidon's Paradise; The Romance
of Atlantis. San Francisco: Clemens, 1892.

This is the earliest pseudo-historical novel by an American
to use Atlantis as a setting.   It deals with the war
between Atlantis and the kingdom of Pelasgia, ruled by King
Deucalion. His children are taken as hostages to Atlantis,
but he rescues them before the continent sinks.   The
knowledge they have gained lays the foundation for the
Hellenic civilization.

077. Bisbee, Eugene Shade.   The Treasure of the Ice.   London
and New York: Neely, 1898.

Near a volcano close to the South Pole a party of Americans
discovers a lost colony of Greeks.   A year after the
assassination of Caesar, their ancestors sought a new home
in the southern temperate zone. The plot centers upon the
love of the narrator, Robert Bardwell, and the beautiful
Cleo Andromeda, sister of Queen Eurydice. The explorers
are rescued by an American ship. There are three weddings,
but ". . . the peerless Cleo [is] the Treasure of the Ice."

078. Black, William.   A Princess of Thule.   Philadelphia:
Coates, n.d.

The title is deceptive; this is neither sf nor fantasy. It
is a romance of the northern Scottish islands.

079. Blanchard H[enry] Percy. After the Cataclysm; A Romance of the Age to Come. New York: Cochrane, 1909.

A native of Rochester, New York, goes into suspended animation during a great fire and awakens in 1934 to find a pastoral, Christian society in which there is no marriage. He learns that early in the century there was much strife between a monopolistic syndicate and labor. Germany, Great Britain, and the new state of Israel are at war with Russia in 1914. Then a vast comet passes close to the Earth, with resulting tidal waves sinking much of eastern America, Europe, and Japan. Mankind is thus given a second chance. The change in the Earth's orbit caused by the passage of the meteor brings about a universally temperate climate.

080. Blayre, Christopher [pseud. of Edward Heron-Allen]. The Purple Sapphire, and Other Posthumous Papers. London: Allan, 1921.

Blayre, the Registrar of the University of Cosmopoli, poses as editor of various manuscripts left in his hands. "The Purple Sapphire" involves a jewel which brings its possessor bad luck. "Aalita" chronicles the love of an astronomer for a Venusian girl who appears because of a "photo-telephone" device. "The Thing That Smelt" deals with Austin Black, a spiritualist, who is killed by something he called forth at a séance. "The Demon" takes possession of a woman who has died of cancer. "The Cosmic Dust" suggests that life originates from radium. "The Publishers regret that they are unable to print" a story entitled "The Cheetah Girl."

081. Bleunard, A[lbert]. [Trans. from the French by Frank Linston White]. Babylon Electrified; The History of an Expedition Undertaken to Restore Ancient Babylon by the Power of Electricity, and How it Resulted. Philadelphia: Gebble, 1889.

Sir James Badger, interested in science, backs an expedition which seeks to restore the glory of ancient Mesopotamia; his efforts come to naught when the Kurds oppose him and destroy what he has built.

082. Blodgett, Mabel Fuller. At the Queen's Mercy. Boston: Lamson, Wolffe, 1897.

An imitation of Rider Haggard: the first-person narrator and his companion, Gaston Lastrade, find a mysterious walled city, apparently Phoenician in origin. Lastrade flees with the queen's handmaiden, but the narrator remains with the beautiful, capricious Lah. She returns his love and would give up her kingdom for him, but she is killed by the high priest. The narrator escapes and tells the story in his old age.

083. Blot, Thomas [pseud. of William Simpson]. The Man from
Mars, His Morals, Politics and Religion. San Francisco: Bacon,
1891.

> By metempsychosis (teleportation) a Martian appears on
> Earth. He describes at length a utopian civilization on
> Mars during a conversation with a hermit.

084. Bogaras, Waldemar. [Trans. from the Russian by Stephen
Graham]. Sons of the Mammoth. New York: Cosmopolitan, 1929.

> This account of cavemen living near the Dadana River
> vividly portrays such rituals as the annual love festival
> (marriage). Not yet initiated as an adult, Yarry breaks
> taboos and proves such a skilled hunter that his angered
> elders drive him from the tribe. From the women's camp he
> takes Ronta with him into exile. Their meeting with the
> Grrams suggests an encounter with the Neanderthal because
> the Grrams are fascinated with Ronta's white skin. Unable
> to get along with Yarry, Ronta returns to the tribe.
> Plague strikes the cavemen, and a dragonlike creature, Moon
> Rek, makes its appearance. Ronta is to be sacrificed to
> him. As the tribe howls its disapproval, Yarry intervenes.
> The novel is unique in that there is no resolution, only
> the final confrontation between Yarry and a creature which
> he realizes is no god but only an animal.

085. Boisgilbert, Edmund [see Ignatius Donnelly].

086. Bolton, Charles E. The Harris-Ingram Experiment. Cleveland, Oh.: Burrows, 1905.

> Posthumously published, Bolton's narrative blends together
> a novel of manners portraying wealthy American society, a
> confrontation between capital and labor, and gold-hunting
> in the Rockies as background for the love story of George
> Ingram, a young genius schooled as an engineer, and Ger-
> trude Harris, daughter of the wealthy steel manufacturer
> who becomes George's sponsor-partner. After outside
> agitators cause a strike at the plant in Harrisville, flee
> the city after police and militia intervene, and blow up
> the old mill, the protagonists build the finest steel mill
> in the world, completely powered by electricity. Equally
> important, they establish a utopian community which man-
> agement and labor share. Harris' only son, who wished to
> be an artist, finds the Mariposa Gold Mine and rescues
> George and the new mill at a financially crucial time. The
> novel has significance both because of the reconciliation
> between labor and management and because of its topical
> detail regarding American society.

087. Boussenard, Louis.   [Trans. from the French by Louis Paret]. 10,000 Years in a Block of Ice. New York: Neely, 1898.

As a result of exposure a scientist exploring the Arctic is frozen into suspended animation.   He awakens to find a world much transformed by a new ice age.   The center of civilization is a utopian state in Africa, where a race descended from the Chinese and Africans is dominant.   The psychic power of these people, the Cerebrals, is emphasized as much as the technology.   There is the suggestion that they will try to colonize other areas, but their culture seems to be dying.

088. Bouve, Edward T[racy]. Centuries Apart. Boston: Little, Brown, 1894.

Supposedly the narrative reproduces the diary of Captain Arthur Percy, which was destroyed in the great Boston fire of 1872.   During the Civil War a Union force sent to Califronia via Cape Horn is driven into the Antarctic past the ice fields to an open polar sea.   There they discover "South England" and "La Nouvelle France," settled by refugees from the War of the Roses.   The narrative reads like Sir Walter Scott.   It even contains Ruval Ben-Ardlac, described as a Robin Hood, who lives in the White Forest of Humber.   The main action dwells upon Captain Percy's journey to Fair Northumbria, where he falls in love with Kate Percy.   When the American ship is repaired, however, Percy returns to the U.S.   Just before Appomattox he is killed by a sniper, but as he dies he has a vision of Kate. His ghost appears to the narrator, who identifies himself as Percy's brother-in-law and believes the story to be true.

089. Bower, B.M. [pseud. of Bertha Muzzy Bower Sinclair]. The Adam Chasers. Boston: Little, Brown, 1927.

After referring to the discovery of the skull of an ape-man in Rhodesia, the archaeologist, Lewis Abington, wishes that he could find the remains of prehistoric man in the mountains of Nevada.   He and a companion do find numerous glyphs and some artifacts in a maze of caves.   They encounter two women, one of whom, Jean Pattison, is psychic. In her sleep she speaks as "Many Feathers," who once lived nearby.   She leads Abington to a cavern chamber which does contain fossils of a giant manlike being.

090. Bradford, Columbus. Terrania; or, The Feminization of the World. Boston: Christopher, 1930.

The story is presented as though written by a future historian.   This is a platonic, cerebralized Lysistrata. Amy Mortimer, whose brother was killed in World War I, becomes the stenographer for Major John Goff of the War

Department.   He falls in love with her, but she will not
marry him unless he helps her to outlaw war.   She proposes
a universal strike against matrimony until disarmament
takes place. Women who have lost lovers in the War come to
her support.   The National Women's Party is organized to
promote Equal Rights.   She commands him to scrap all
weapons and promises to marry if there is progress.   Women
are elected to Congress, and there is a woman as President.
Eventually the United States of Terrania becomes the world-
wide state.

091.   Bradshaw, William R[ichard].   The Goddess of Atvatabar,
Being the History of the Discovery of the Interior World and the
Conquest of Atvatabar.   New York: Douthitt, 1892.

The narrator, White, describes his entry into a Symmesian
world where magic and technical advancements exist side by
side, although he gives no details of the machines.   The
storyline concentrates upon his love for the goddess Lyone.
When she explains that the essence of their belief ("Life
and love are synonymous.") is a romantic, platonic passion
which keeps lovers apart, he soundly kisses her.   The
goddess vows her love for him and desires to abdicate her
position.   This apostasy leads to civil war, which the
lovers win with the aid of American and British warships
sent in search of White after news of his discovery reaches
the outer world.   Satire and mysticism are thoroughly
mixed.   When Lyone dies of an electric shock, for example,
her subjects exert their soul power (in conjunction with a
kind of electrical circuit made up of a super-metal,
terrilium) to bring her back to life.   White is crowned
king and promises to make commercial treaties with the U.S.
and Britain, although maintaining Atvatabarian institu-
tions.   In a prefatory note Julian Hawthorne attacks the
realism represented by Zola and Tolstoi, suggesting the
future of fiction lies with works of the "imagination" like
Bradshaw's novel.

092.   Brebner, Percy [James].   The Knight of the Silver Star.
New York: Fenno, 1907.

Originally published as The Fortress of Yadasara in England
by Warne (1899): the first-person narrator, Clinton Verrall, discovers the medieval kingdom of Drussenland in the
Caucasus Mountains.   It is inhabited by descendants of the
last crusaders.   The storyline centers upon his rescue of
the Princess Daria from the villainous Count Vasca.   They
return to live in England, accompanied by Captain Dennis
O'Ryan, who had found Verrall in the mountains.

093. Breckenridge, Gerald. <u>Radio</u> <u>Boys</u> <u>Seek</u> <u>Lost</u> <u>Atlantis</u>. New
York: Burt, 1923.

A juvenile lost race novel, perhaps its most important
element is a prefatory note suggesting that Atlantis was
the continent from which all civilization arose. All known
civilizations, either in America or the Mediterranean
basin, were its colonies. Jack Hampton, Bob Temple, and
Frank Merrick join Mr. Hampton in an expedition which
discovers the Atlantean city, Athensi, in the Atlas Mountains. Most of the story is devoted to the rescue of Bob,
who is kidnapped to participate in the annual tournaments.
The Americans help a youthful group rebel successfully
against the Oligarchy, a ruling class, who have enslaved
the people.

094. Brereton, Captain F[rederick] S[adleir]. <u>The</u> <u>Great</u>
<u>Aeroplane</u>; <u>A</u> <u>Thrilling</u> <u>Tale</u> <u>of</u> <u>Adventure</u>. London: Blackie &
Son, 1911.

A juvenile in the episodic manner of Verne: the young
inventor, Theodore Brown, and his companions, George and
Harvey, fly his new aeroplane made of an alloy of aluminum
and an unspecified metal. They go to Canada, where they
thwart efforts of various sinister spies attempting to
steal the secrets of the plane. Then they go to Africa to
help Frank Rutley look for a mine of black diamonds.

095. Brinsmade, Herman Hine. <u>Utopia</u> <u>Achieved</u>; <u>A</u> <u>Novel</u> <u>of</u> <u>the</u>
<u>Future</u>. New York: Broadway, 1912.

In 1960 after fifty years in Australia Tom Harrington
returns to America. He goes to Vermont, where he eventually marries a childhood sweetheart. The real interest
of the narrative, however, is utopian speculation. The era
of the common man has arrived in America. New York, now
with a population of 20,000,000, serves a great megapolis
because of the United Aero Company. Everything is powered
by electricity. One main reform advantageous to individual
health is a vegetarian diet. Tirades against both the use
of meat and tuberculosis are included. The concept of the
single tax is upheld. The working day is only five hours.
An airplane wreck in Maryland allows Tom to see the extent
of rural development. The Community Hall has transformed
the life of the farmer, for it provides not only a meeting
place, but a social and educational center. Harrington
reveals that the failure of socialism in New Zealand proved
that it was a dream incapable of success.

096. Brooks, Byron A[lden]. <u>Earth</u> <u>Revisited</u>. Boston: Arena,
1893.

Herbert Atherton dies of an incurable kidney disease. He
revives as a younger man, Harold Amesbury, who has been ill

after falling from an electric cycle. His memories of the nineteenth century are regarded as illusions during illness. Manhattan has been entirely abandoned to warehouses, offices, and the wholesale business. Brooklyn has become part of the greater city of Columbia, which has been transformed into a suburban utopia through electricity and aluminum. Co-op trusts have made this financially possible. The city owns the land; man, his home. Communication has been established with Mars. There are no churches or denominations; Sunday has become a "day of joy and good works." The liquor saloon is branded as the enemy of the people, keeping them in poverty. Immigration has been restricted. Extremely topical, the narrative celebrates technology, urbanization, and a practical Christianity. The plot line involves marital confusion. Although the protagonist awakes to find his wife, he finally marries another woman.

097. Brown, Joseph M[ackey]. Astyanax; An Epic Romance of Ilion, Atlantis and Amaraca. New York: Broadway, 1907.

This is one of the most extravagant fictional reconstructions of prehistory. Astyanax, the son of Hector, survives the Trojan War, which he suggests originated because the Greeks did not want to pay tariff to Troy (Ilion). Grown up, he leads the remnant of the Trojans first to Egypt briefly and then to Atlantis. He and his people narrowly escape the volcanic destruction of that continent. They then sail westward to Mexico, where he falls in love with a royal princess who is kidnapped by the king of Anahuac (Mexico). With the aid of the Incas and others, he defeats the Anahuacans, weds the princess, and thus rules a mighty empire.

098. Bruce, Muriel. Mukara. New York: Henkel, 1930.

In addition to dedicating the novel to Colonel P.H. Fawcett and his son, Bruce suggests in a preface that she has built the narrative, in part at least, on notes which Fawcett left before disappearing in 1925. A manuscript dated 1753 leads John Kirby, his son Richard, and two companions to the discovery of the city of Mukara in the interior of Brazil. Its people are pure Aryan, descendants from the lost continent of Mu, as are the ruling countries of the outside world. The other races are "accidental survivors" of the same cataclysm which drowned Mu and caused the biblical flood. There is a strong mystical element, and much is made of a powder--radium?--which can cause both life and death. The Kirbys help the Princess Clia marry Nubti, the lineal descendant of Osiris. Those who would prevent that marriage attempt to force the wedding of Richard and Clia. He foils this by calling out the name, Maura [McLeod], who is in London and whom he loves. She is psychic and is aware of his danger. He is initiated into

the mysteries of Mukara and given the name Anatza. The
Kirbys leave the city, but their companions remain. At the
end John Kirby's note implies that he is returning to
Mukara and hopes to master the mysteries which will en-
lighten the world. He feels that civilization is nearing a
crisis and needs such spiritual truths.

099. Bruere, Martha Bensley. Mildred Carver, U.S.A.. New
York: Macmillan, 1919.

This seems to be one of the most feminist books of the
period. Martha Carver, a wealthy socialite, must serve a
year in the universal draft (Universal Service) as a member
of the 42nd unit, doing agricultural work in the Mississippi valley. She learns, for example, to drive a tractor.
All of this, together with increased knowledge of the
common people, brings her to reject her social class. Nor
does she marry a good working man, John Barton. She wants
to do something that will bring about better food production. Most important for celebration of agriculture and
a distinct attack on class distinction.

100. Bryce, Lloyd. A Dream of Conquest. Philadelphia: Lippincott, 1889.

This brief novel becomes a parody of the future war motif
as it uses the framework of a war between China and America
to satirize many aspects of American political and social
life. One cannot be certain how deeply Bryce is concerned
with American unpreparedness and Chinese immigration. Wang
Chi Poo, a second class mandarin, loves an American woman,
Mrs. Percival T. McFlusterer, despite the fact that "Meli-
can woman all foot and all tongue." The Committee of
Twelve advises her to go with Wang Chi Poo to end the war.
Yet Bryce introduces such items as a "Pneumatic Dynamite
Gun" and has some of the Eastern coastal cities attacked.
At the end there is the suggestion that all has been a
dream.

101. Bull, Lois. Captive Goddess. New York: Macaulay, 1935.

An illustration of the decline of the lost race novel: on
the island of Artocos off the coast of Aden, Tommy Drew, a
flyer, finds a primitive tribe in the mountains who worship
a white goddess. She is Antoinette Beatty, daughter of an
Englishman long dead. The villainous Sultan of Artocos
wishes to marry her. The storyline concerns the efforts to
rescue Antoinette. The Sultan, believing that he is the
god Mithras who flew near the sun, is killed in a plane
crash. Antoinette is reunited with Buddy Whitaker, who
loves her, while Tommy is to marry an American woman flyer.

102. Burgess, [Frank] Gelett. The White Cat. Indianapolis,
In.: Bobbs-Merrill, 1907.

A transitional novel imitiative of Robert Louis Stevenson:
the villain, a doctor, hypnotizes the heroine in order to
summon up her evil alter ego. He wants to marry her so
that he can control her fortune. Much attention is given
to hypnosis, but none is given to psychological theories.

103. Burland, Harris [pseud. of John Burland Harris-Burland].
The Princess Thora. Boston: Little, Brown, 1904.

In London, the first-person narrator, Edward Silex, an
eccentric millionaire, meets John Silver, supposedly a book
dealer, and his ward Thora de Brie. Silver dies. Silex
finances a large expedition to reach the North Pole. On
the ice when they meet the Count Thule de Brie, Thora
reveals that the purpose of the expedition is to restore
her to the throne of Asturnia, which lies beyond the
barrier of ice. It is a feudal kingdom peopled by the
descendants of Norman French who fled the wrath of Henry I
in 1105. She says that some five years earlier Thule de
Brie and Silver, actually the Lord Argenteuil, saved her
when her father was deposed. They made their way to
London. Restored to her throne, she is to marry Sir Guy de
Marmorel. Only then do she and Silex acknowledge they love
one another. In disguise, Thule de Brie challenges her
right to rule; he must fight Sir Guy and does, killing him
and being badly wounded. At that point Thora reveals that
she is in reality Sybil Hartington, who looked enough like
the Princess to be her twin and was substituted for her by
John Silver. As long as Silver lived she maintinaed the
delusion, but now she must reveal the truth and surrender
the throne to de Brie. This allows her to marry Silex, and
together they set out for England.

104. Burroughs, Edgar Rice. At the Earth's Core. Chicago:
A.C. McClurg, 1922.

Originally serialized in All-Story (April 1914): David
Innes, a youthful mine owner, and Abner Parry, inventor of
an "iron mole" to serve as an "underground prospector,"
accidentally penetrate the 500-mile crust of the Earth,
emerging in Pellucidar. Burroughs' adaptation of Symmes'
inner world. Lighted by a small sun and knowing only
eternal day, Pellucidar is an endless prehistoric jungle in
which beast-men and savage animals struggle for survival.
The plot develops along two main lines: first, Innes and
Parry are captured by Sagoths and taken to the city of
Phutar, the capital of the ruthless, dominant Mahars, a
race of reptiles entirely female which reproduces parthenogenetically. Innes steals the book which describes sci-
entifically their method of reproduction; without it they
are doomed. Secondly, when first captured, Innes saves

Dian the Beautiful, Princess of Amoz, from Hooja, the Sly
One. He does not know that fighting triumphantly for her
means that she is his mate, his slave; by seeming to reject
her, he alienates her. Hooja escapes and kidnaps Dian;
this initiates a search ending only after Innes kills
Jubal, the Ugly One, whose attentions drove her from Amoz.
Innes and Dian marry in what he calls "The Garden of Eden."
Together with friendly Sarians, they plan a revolt against
the Mahars, but Innes must return with the mole to the
surface to obtain necessary books. Dian is to accompany
him, but Hooja substitutes a Mahar for her. Innes does not
realize this until he reaches the surface. The story is
framed by the note of a young Englishman who encounters
Innes in the Sahara.

105. Burroughs, Edgar Rice.   The Beasts of Tarzan.   Chicago:
A.C. McClurg, 1916.

Originally serialized in All-Story Cavalier (1914): Rokoff
and Paulvitch kidnap Tarzan's infant son Jack, intending to
have him raised by cannibals. They lure Jane and Tarzan
aboard the ship Kincaid and abandon Tarzan on Jungle Island
close to the coast of Africa. With the aid of jungle
animals, especially the ape Akut, Tarzan sets out in
pursuit of the villains. The plotline involves a number of
escapes as well as occasions when Tarzan and Jane narrowly
miss one another along the Igambu River. Rokoff is killed,
while Paulvitch is forced to flee into the jungle. The
denouement turns upon the fact that Paulvitch has double-
crossed Rokoff.

106. Burroughs, Edgar Rice.   The Cave Girl.   Chicago: A.C.
McClurg, 1925.

Combines "The Cave Girl" serialized in All-Story (1913) and
"The Cave Man" serialized in All-Story (1917): Waldo
Emerson Smith-Jones, an effete member of the upperclass
sheltered by his mother, is swept overboard onto a tropical
island in the Pacific, where a primitive race long separated from the rest of mankind dominates. His love for
the beautiful Nadara inspires him to become a fierce
warrior whom Nadara names Thandar. After a suitable number
of flights and rescues, when his father's yacht comes in
search of him and the lovers are saved from an earthquake,
any objection to their marriage is erased by the disclosure
that Nadara is the daughter of the Count and Countess Crecy
born on the island on the night of her mother's death after
the wreck of her parents' yacht marooned the Countess on
the island.

107.   Burroughs, Edgar Rice.   The Eternal Lover.   Chicago: A.C. McClurg, 1925.

   Originally published in All-Story (March 1914): Burroughs' treatment of the familiar theme of reincarnated lovers.   On the African estates of John Clayton--with Tarzan, Jane, and their baby son present--the narrative concentrates upon Virginia Custer, who is terrified of earthquakes and dreams that she lives in a primitive world of cavemen.   An earthquake opens a cave where "Nu of the Niocene" survives.   She is the reincarnation of his ancient love, Nu-Tal, and as Virginia, she decides in his favor.   A new quake transfers them to Nu's era.   The action is then dominated by Nu's hunt for a sabre-tooth tiger in order to prove his manhood and worthiness as her lover.   The implication at the end of the book that all has been Virginia's dream is counteracted by the discovery of a cave containing the head of a sabre-tooth tiger and the skeleton of a caveman.

108.   Burroughs, Edgar Rice.   The Gods of Mars.   Chicago: A.C. McClurg, 1918.

   Originally serialized in All-Story (1913): in 1886, twenty years after his original journey, John Carter once more wills his transmigration to Barsoom.   Together with Tars Tarkas, he undertakes the rescue of Dejah Thoris, who has undertaken a pilgrimage to the Valley of Dor, where Martians go to die.   In doing so, he reveals the falseness of the religion of the Therns and the Goddess Issis, for the country is inhabited by a kind of plantmen who devour the pilgrims.   But Dejah Thoris has been taken by the Black Pirates of Barsoom, and John Carter must invade their underground city.   With the aid of his son, Cathoris, he defeats the Pirates, but the novel ends as Dejah Thoris, Thuvia, and Phaidar are locked in a cell in the revolving Temple of the Sun.   A year must pass for the cell to rotate once so that Carter knows whether or not Dejah Thoris has survived.

109.   Burroughs, Edgar Rice.   The Land of Hidden Men.   New York: Ace, 1963.

   Originally serialized in Blue Book (1932) and published as The Jungle Girl (1932): in search of ruined Khmer cities in Cambodia, Gordon King, a physician, is aroused by the sensuous, primitive beauty of Fou-tan, whom he saves from a tiger.   She fled into the jungle to escape becoming the concubine of Lodivarman, the leperous king of Lodidhapara.   She is the daughter of the ruler of Pnom Dhek.   The cities have long been at war.   The plot devolves into a series of captures and escapes until King cures Lodivarman, who actually suffered a severe dermititis from eating too many mushrooms.   King then saves Fou-tan's father left for dead by the treacherous Bharaka Khan, who tries to force mar-

riage upon Fou-tan.   King kills Bhakara at the wedding
ceremony, and when Fou-tan offers herself to him, he
becomes the groom.   As her father dies, he proclaims King
the ruler of Pnom Dhek.

110. Burroughs, Edgar Rice.   The Land That Time Forgot.
Chicago: A.C. McClurg, 1924.

A trio of novelettes originally published in Blue Book
(1918): through a series of misadventures following the
torpedoing of the ship on which they were sailing to
France, Bowen Tyler and the actress Lys La Rue--and a mixed
crew of British and Germans--take the submarine U-33 to the
prehistoric, cliff-enclosed island of Caspek.   Supplied
with oil from a crude refinery, the German commander, Von
Schoenvorts, abandons them.   The primitive peoples of
Caspek are at various stages of evolution; once Tyler
suggests that Lys has learned to speak to Neanderthal man.
Several times he rescues her from cavemen who desire her;
finally he and Lys "plight [their] troth beneath the eyes
of God" and settle in the land of the Galus.   Tyler puts
his manuscript in a thermos and throws it into the sea.   In
the second part, after finding the manuscript and taking it
to Tyler's father, Thomas Billings takes a small plane to
Caspek to search for the couple.   After a crash, he discovers the "half-naked little savage," Ajor, and falls in
love with her.   Repeatedly he refers to her as a beautiful
"animal."   After a similar series of rescues, they find Lys
and Tyler, now a chief of the Galus.   Although that couple
goes home, Billings remains behind with Ajor.   In the third
part, the Englishman, Bradley, encounters the Weiroos, a
horrible, winged, man-like species (there are hints of
vampirism), but he, too, finds a primitive beauty, Co-Tan.
Finally all three couples are married aboard a waiting
yacht and return to California.   The novel is most interesting for Burroughs' speculation that each species,
beginning as eggs, undergoes the entire cycle of evolution.

111. Burroughs, Edgar Rice.   The Monster Men.   Chicago: A.C.
McClurg, 1929.

Originally published in All-Story (November 1913): Burroughs adapts the Frankenstein theme to a jungle setting.
On an island near Borneo Dr. Maxon's experiments produce
only beast-men.   The reader infers that his servant, Sing,
has destroyed vat 13, but Number Thirteen seems a success
though initially mindless.   Trained, he helps the other
beast-men escape into the jungle; only he survives, as
Bulan, the mighty warrior.   Maxon's daughter Virginia has
been pursued by such villains as Dr. van Horn, her father's
assistant, and one of the beast-men.   After suitable
captures and escapes, Virginia declares her love for Bulan;
their marriage is made possible because he recovers from
amnesia and reveals that he is Townsend J. Hope, Jr., who

has followed Virginia from the first time he saw her in a
train station in Ithaca. Sing verifies his story.

112. Burroughs, Edgar Rice. The Moon Maid. Chicago: A.C.
McClurg, 1926.

Three novelettes published in Argosy All-Story (the first
in 1923; the others, 1925): perhaps Burroughs' most extravagant narrative in that its protagonist, Air Admiral
Julian, recounts his adventures in three future incarnations. The introductory frame is dated 10 June 1967,
marking the first radio communication with John Carter of
Barsoom. Moreover, after a half century warfare has ended,
and the Anglo-Saxon race is triumphant throughtout the
world. There is universal disarmament except for the
International Peace Fleet. As Julian V, the protagonist
tells of the first space flight (2025) intended to reach
Mars but sabotaged by Lieutenant Commander Orthis so that
it lands on the moon. Julian V falls in love with Nah-
ee-lah, princess of the city-state Laythe; unsuccessfully
they resist the conquest of the Kalkars and flee to Earth.
The second part picks up Julian V as Orthis and the Kalkars
invade an Earth made even more helpless by the stop of
scientific progress in 2050. After he and Orthis are
killed in a final battle, Julian IX pictures an Earth
dominated by the Kalkars (who are communist) and a revolt
that is crushed by the oppressors. The third part, told by
Julian 20th, shows an America reverted to a primitivism
resembling the culture of the original American Indians.
This permits Burroughs to praise the nomadic culture. A
final successful revolt is sealed when Julian 20th marries
Bethelda, a descendant of the Or-Tis tribe.

113. Burroughs, Edgar Rice. Pellucidar. Chicago: A.C.
McClurg, 1923.

Originally serialized in All-Story Cavalier (1915): an
initial framing device leads to the telegraph wires which
David Innes planted in the Sahara. Their message makes up
the main story. Upon returning to the inner world, he
faced two problems; first, to find the kingdom of Sari;
second, to rescue Dian the Beautiful from Hooja the Sly
One. After passing through many lands, he does rescue Dian
from Hooja. All of the lands that Innes conquers he unites
in a federation, but so vast is Pellucidar that much of its
area remains unexplored and unknown. One of the more
unique features of the novel is the manner in which David
Perry, especially, has tried to bring civilization to the
inner world, establishing observatories and a railway.
Innes and Dian rule the Federation as the novel ends.

114. Burroughs, Edgar Rice. _Pirates of Venus_. Tarzana, Ca.:
Burroughs, 1934.

Originally serialized in _Argosy_ (1932): Jason Gridley,
persuaded to return to the outer world aboard the 0-220
instead of hunting for von Horst, now introduces Carson
Napier, with whom he has communicated telepathically after
Napier flew to Venus. Parachuting into the kingdom of
Vepaja, Napier learns that the remnants of the Vepajans
long ago fled to this forested island because they were
driven from a mighty empire by a laborer named Thor, who
preached class hatred and sought to destroy the cultured
class. (Except for _The Moon Maid_, this novel presents
Burroughs' most explicit attack on Communism.) The Vepajans have a longevity serum, but as a result they must
limit the number of their children. He falls in love at
first sight with Duare, the only daughter of the ruler,
Mintep. Because she is not yet twenty, he is forbidden
even to speak of her. Captured by bird-men, he is kept
aboard a seagoing ship and becomes part of the Soldiers of
Liberty, an anti-Thorist group. They capture a larger ship
on which Duare is a prisoner, but hardly is she released
before a Thorian spy, Vilor, sent to steal the secret of
the longevity serum, kidnaps her. Once again Napier must
save her. He learns that she loves him but sends her to
safety as he himself is captured and taken to the kingdom
of Noobol. The narrative ends abruptly. This is the first
of five novels dealing with Carson's adventures. Apparently Burroughs delayed using Venus as a setting because
Otis Adelbert Kline had made use of it.

115. Burroughs, Edgar Rice. _A Princess of Mars_. Chicago: A.C.
McClurg, 1917.

Originally serialized as "Under the Moons of Mars" in
All-Story (1912): trapped by Apache Indians, John Carter
first finds himself somehow free from his body and then
wills his transmigration to Mars (Barsoom). Captive of the
Tharks, a giant, six-armed, savage green people, Carter
impresses them by his physical acts (he can leap great
distances because of the difference in gravity); he especially impresses Tars Tarkas, who eventually becomes
chief of the Tharks. When Dejah Thoris, Princess of Helium
(and a representative of the noble red people of Barsoom),
is captured, Carter rescues her. Separated from her, he
fights his way to Helium, where he helps win a war. He
marries Dejah Thoris; for nine years they remain happy, but
when the atmosphere machine begins to fail, he attempts its
restoration. From stress and lack of oxygen, he becomes
unconscious and awakens in the cave in Arizona. He has no
idea what occurred on Mars. Because Carter usually fights
with the sword, one finds the Barsoom series of eleven
novels a principal source of the "sword and sorcery" motif
made popular by such later writers as Robert E. Howard.

116.   Burroughs, Edgar Rice.   The Return of Tarzan.   Chicago:
A.C. McClurg, 1915.

   Originally serialized in New Story (1913): in a series of
incidents in Paris, Tarzan incurs the enmity of Alexis
Paulvitch and Nikolas Rokoff and is tricked into a duel
with Count DeCoude (his wife, Olga, Rokoff's sister, is the
first of many women who cannot resist Tarzan; in this case,
because he has renounced Jane, he is lonely).   His attitude
toward the Europeans contrasts sharply with the sincere
liking Tarzan has for Kadour ben Saden and his men during a
brief mission in the Sahara.   The Russians knock Tarzan
overboard on a ship bound for Cape Town.   A flashback
indicates that Cecil Clayton knows Tarzan is Lord Greystoke.   He wants to marry Jane quickly, but she puts him
off; they go on a year-long cruise, after which they will
be married, but they are shipwrecked and end up in Africa.
Tarzan swims ashore.   Then occurs one of those sequences in
which he celebrates the primitive life over civilization.
After helping the Waziri against slavers, he becomes their
chief, and they lead him to Opar, the last colony of
Atlantis.   The high priestess, La, falls in love with him.
Thus he escapes, but he returns later with the Waziri to
secure a vast fortune in gold.   Opar becomes the source of
Tarzan's wealth.   He saves Jane and Clayton from a lion.
Oparians kidnap Jane, but he saves her from sacrifice.
They return to camp where the dying Clayton admits that he
has wronged them both and reveals that he knows Tarzan is
Lord Greystoke.   Lieutenant D'Arnot and his ship arrive on
the scene; once aboard Tarzan and Jane are married as they
go to England.

117.   Burroughs, Edgar Rice.   The Son of Tarzan.   Chicago: A.C.
McClurg, 1917.

   Originally serialized in All-Story Cavalier (1915): after
ten years Paulvitch is rescued from the jungle and returns
to London, where his trained ape Ajax (actually Akut)
performs in a music hall.   When Paulvitch attempts to
kidnap Jack, Akut kills the Russian.   The boy and ape flee
to Africa.   Jack resolves to return to England, but cir-
cumstances force him into the jungle.   Quickly he becomes
Korak the Killer, seeming to forget his youthful past.
Meanwhile, in an act of vengeance, Arabs abduct Jeanne
Jacot, daughter of an officer of the Foreign Legion.   After
three years Korak rescues her, and they become companions
until blacks capture her.   She ends up at the African
cottage of "Bwana" and "My Dear" (obviously Tarzan and
Jane).   Now a lovely sixteen, Meriem, as she has been known
since her abduction, is sought after by various villainous
men, including the Hon. Morison Baynes, who says he cannot
now marry her.   Pursuits and captures ensue, with both
Korak and Bwana following her.   Korak rescues her, but
Tarzan must save the two of them.   Father and son immed-

iately recognize one another. Jack/Korak and Meriem are
married, and General Jacot appears to identify her, calling
her a princess in her own right.

118. Burroughs, Edgar Rice. Tanar of Pellucidar. New York:
Metropolitan, 1930.

Originally serialized in Blue Book (1929): Jason Gridley
picks up radio signals from Abner Perry. The message makes
up the main storyline of the book. Sometime in the past
pirates from the outer world entered Pellucidar through a
northern polar opening. Their descendants, the Korsars,
continue acts of piracy on the oceans of Pellucidar. The
novel ends with David Innes a prisoner in the dungeons of
the Korsars, although Tanar has wooed and won the beautiful
Stellara.

119. Burroughs, Edgar Rice. Tarzan and the City of Gold.
Tarzana, Ca.: Burroughs, 1933.

Originally serialized in Argosy (1931): in the Abyssinian
valley of Onthar Tarzan finds Cathne, the city of gold,
whose nobles raise prides of man-hunting lions for sport.
In addition to his prowess in the arena, he becomes involved in palace politics. He rejects the advances of the
half-crazed, beautiful Nemone, Queen of Cathne. Consequently he is to be run down by the lion Belthar, whose
life Nemone feels is closely tied to hers. When Jadbal-ja,
the Golden Lion, kills Belthar, thereby saving Tarzan, the
queen commits suicide. Nemone's passion for Tarzan seems
the most erotic of any of the pagan jungle queens he
encountered.

120. Burroughs, Edgar Rice. Tarzan and the Jewels of Opar.
Chicago: A.C. McClurg, 1918.

Originally serialized in All-Story-Cavalier (1916): Lieutenant Albert Werper, a Belgian renegade, and Achmet Zek
plan to kidnap Jane and demand ransom. When his business
affairs collapse, Tarzan must go to Opar to seek more
treasure. Hurt in an earthquake, he suffers amnesia. La
again expresses her love for him and releases him. There
follows a passage in which he celebrates primitive life.
The storyline becomes an involved series of captures and
escapes. Tarzan's home is burned, Jane is repeatedly
caught, the villains fall out, an Abyssinian--Abdul Mourak
--gets into the struggle to obtain the gold the Waziri have
brought back from Opar, and Werper has a pouch of jewels he
took from Tarzan. Werper reveals all to Tarzan, who thus
recovers from his amnesia in time to help the Waziri set
things right. Although Werper disappears, his body and the
pouch of jewels are finally found. Opar also figures in
the plots of Tarzan and the Golden Lion (1923) and Tarzan

the Invincible (1931), in which La leads her priests out of Opar in an attempt to recover a sacred knife.

121.   Burroughs, Edgar Rice.   Tarzan and the Lion Man.   Tarzana, Ca.: Burroughs, 1934.

Originally published in Liberty (1933-1934): this novel contains Burroughs' most notable satire, although he did not take full advantage of its potential. The B.O. film studio plans to shoot a spectacular in the Ituri Forest, with Stanley Obroski--who could be Tarzan's twin--as a jungle lord raised by a lioness. A coward, Obroski is captured by natives who attack the safari; Tarzan rescues him and leaves him to be sent to the coast. The film people mistake Tarzan for Obroski, and he sets out to rescue the two actresses, Naomi Madison and Rhonda Terry, who have been taken to the unknown city called London on the Thames. There dwells a race of English-speaking gorillas who are ruled by Henry VIII and have taken identities from that period. They have been created by a mad Victorian scientist--called God--who has determined their heredity by stealing the deathless genes from persons buried in Westminster. He speaks of Lamarck, Darwin, and Mendel as acquaintances. After suitable (quick) rescues, Tarzan discovers a beautiful girl, Balza, who is a genetic freak, so to speak, of the experiment. She returns to Hollywood with the company. A year later, as John Clayton, Tarzan visits Hollywood. Balza has been transformed into a starlet; hired as an extra, Tarzan is fired for killing a valuable lion which had gone berserk. He hastens back to Africa.

122.   Burroughs, Edgar Rice.   Tarzan and the Lost Empire.   New York: Metropolitan, 1929.

Originally serialized in Blue Book (1928-1929): Tarzan searches for the young archaeologist, Eric van Harben, in the Wiramwazi mountains. He finds two Roman cities, Castrum Mare and Castra Sanguinarius, now at perpetual warfare although founded as a single city in 98 A.D. when Sanguinarius fled up the Nile to escape the Emperor Nerva. Thought a barbarian chief of Germania, Eric remains captive in Castrum Mare, where he woos the lovely Favonia. Tarzan manhandles the hated ruler of Castra Sanguinarius and saves Delicia, daughter of Don Splendidus, from the emperor's son. A prisoner, Tarzan performs heroically in the arena. Aided by the timely arrival of the Waziri and local tribesmen, he leads a revolt that unites Delicia and her Roman lover and places her father on the throne. He then quickly rescues Eric and Favonia from the turmoil following the assassination of the ruler of Castrum Mare by Eric's faithful black servant. The narrative ends so abruptly that one is not certain Eric remains with his beloved.

123. Burroughs, Edgar Rice. <u>Tarzan</u> <u>at</u> <u>the</u> <u>Earth's</u> <u>Core</u>. New York: Metropolitan, 1930.

Originally serialized in <u>Blue</u> <u>Book</u> (1929-1930): going to Africa, Jason Gridley persuades Tarzan to go with him aboard the dirigible 0-220 through the polar opening to rescue David Innes from the Korsars. Although Tarzan finds himself lost in the vast jungles, he does eventually rescue David Innes. He has also been instrumental in saving Jana, the Red Flower of Zoram, whom Gridley loves. Together they head for Sari to ask David Innes' help in setting up an expedition to search for Lieutenant Von Horst, lost from the 0-220. Tarzan returns to the outer world. The adventures of Von Horst, including his love (and rescue) of the lovely La-Ja make up the storyline of the next Pellucidar novel, <u>Back</u> <u>to</u> <u>the</u> <u>Stone</u> <u>Age</u> (1937).

124. Burroughs, Edgar Rice. <u>Tarzan,</u> <u>Lord</u> <u>of</u> <u>the</u> <u>Jungle</u>. Chicago: A.C. McClurg, 1928.

Originally serialized in <u>Blue</u> <u>Book</u> (1927-1928): amid typical jungle adventures, in the Valley of the Sepulchre, Tarzan discovers the city of Nimmur, whose inhabitants are descendants of shipwrecked crusaders loyal to Richard the Lion-Hearted. He helps to defeat the efforts of King Bohon, ruler of the City of the Sepulchre, to kidnap Princess Gunialda. His efforts to rescue the American, James Blake, come to naught, for Blake, who loves Gunialda, remains in the valley.

125. Burroughs, Edgar Rice. <u>Tarzan</u> <u>of</u> <u>the</u> <u>Apes</u>. Chicago: A.C. McClurg, 1914.

Originally published in <u>All-Story</u> (October 1912): the orphaned son of Lord Greystoke and Lady Alice, raised in the heart of Africa by great anthropoid apes (a species existing only in Burroughs' imagination), Tarzan epitomizes the brute/primeval man portrayed by such writers as Jack London and Frank Norris. This novel emphasizes his education. Not only does he master his environment, but his native intelligence allows him to teach himself to read. Moreover, after he has nursed Paul D'Arnot back to health, that naval lieutenant takes him to Paris and quickly turns him into a sophisticated gentleman. Earlier having defeated Terkoz and become leader of the anthropoid apes, Tarzan abandons them. He falls in love with Jane Porter, saving her from Terkoz and taking her into the jungle. Persuaded that he is dead, Jane returns to America with her father and Cecil Clayton, who holds the title Lord Greystoke. Although Tarzan follows her to her mother's farm in Wisconsin and saves her from an unwanted marriage, Burroughs manipulates the plot so that she becomes engaged to Clayton. She has misgivings about Tarzan's background, but "the primal woman" in her is not so attracted to the civilized Tarzan as to the "stalwart forest god" she had known. When he proposes to her, she acknowledges her love for him but feels bound by her commitment to Clayton. The narrative ends abruptly when Tarzan learns that fingerprints prove that he is Lord Greystoke. He conceals this information from Jane and Clayton.

126. Burroughs, Edgar Rice. Tarzan the Terrible. Chicago: A.C. McClurg, 1921.

Originally serialized in All-Story (1921): Tarzan follows Jane to the Congo Free State, where he finds that she has escaped and that a German force headed by Lieutenant Erich Obergatz, who loves Jane, has gone after her. Tarzan finds the prehistoric kingdom of Pal-ul-don, peopled by two races, the Waz-don, covered with black fur, and the Ho-don, covered with white fur, both races having tails. He goes to the city of A-lur, where Jane is held captive; both the king and high priest want her, but she escapes into the jungle and survives on her own. Princess O-ol-a and the beautiful Pan-at-lee figure briefly in the novel as Tarzan becomes the god of the Ho-don (this explaining the absence of a tail). Tarzan, Jane, and the now-crazed Obergatz are taken prisoner and are about to be executed when Jack, Korak the Killer, rescues them. He comes directly from the Argonne front. He, Tarzan, and Jane ride a triceratops out of Pal-ul-don and decide to rebuild the African estates.

127. Burroughs, Edgar Rice. Tarzan the Untamed. Chicago: A.C. McClurg, 1920.

Originally published in Red Book (March 1919) and combined with "Tarzan and the Valley of Luna" serialized in All-Story (1920): returning from Nairobi, Tarzan finds his estates destroyed by German troops. He finds a woman burned to death whom he identifies as Jane because of a ring. For a time he fights with the British against the Germans in East Africa. He becomes involved with the British flier, Harold Percy Smith-Oldwick, and a girl who is a double agent (for the British), Patricia Canby. After crossing a desert, Tarzan finds the lost city of Xuja, peopled by a race so ingrown that they are all mad; they also participate in a lion cult. Smith-Oldwick and Patricia Canby turn up as prisoners, but all three are rescued by British troops. Tarzan learns that Jane is alive, a captive of the Germans. Granted the previous existence of Opar, Xuja still serves as the prototype of the lost cities whose exotic, isolated cultures became the major narrative framework of so many subsequent Tarzan stories.

128. Burroughs, Edgar Rice. Thuvia, Maid of Mars. Chicago:
A.C. McClurg, 1920.

Originally serialized in All-Story Cavalier (1916): already
mentioned in The Gods of Mars and The Warlord of Mars,
Thuvia is identified as the princess of Ptarth. Promised
to Kulan Tith, a man whom she does not love, she is abducted by Astok, Prince of Dusar.   The main storyline
involves the successful efforts of Cathoris, son of John
Carter and Dejah Thoris, to rescue her. The significance
of the novel lies in the creation of the city of Lothar,
whose inhabitants--only a few men who have survived--are
capable of transforming thoughts into material beings.
Their greatest accomplishment is the creation of the Bowmen
of Lothars, who defeat their enemies, a tribe of green
barbarians.   Cathoris must twice rescue Thuvia from the
rulers of Lothar before they return to Helium, where they
are married.

129. Burroughs, Edgar Rice. The Warlord of Mars. Chicago:
A.C. McClurg, 1919.

Originally serialized in All-Story (1913-1914): Dejah
Thoris and Thuvia survive the ordeal in the Temple of the
Sun only to be kidnapped by two therns so that the rescue
must begin again. By the end of the novel John Carter has
bested most of the known city-states and kingdoms of Mars
so that he is given the title Jeddak of Jeddaks, Warlord of
Mars. This is the last of the original trilogy. Hereafter
John Carter and Dejah Thoris will remain in the background,
while other protagonists rescue the women they love.

130. Burroughs, Joseph Birkbeck. Titan, Son of Saturn; The
Coming World Emperor. Oberlin, Oh: Emeth, 1905.

This is neither fantasy nor sf; indeed, it is not fiction.
Warning of the coming of the Antichrist--who will be
defeated at Armageddon by Christ--it is nothing more than a
diatribe which insists that the Bible is "the word of God"
and denounces the theory of evolution.

131. Bywater, Hector Charles. The Great Pacific War; A History
of the American-Japanese Campaign of 1931-1933. Boston: Houghton Mifflin, 1925.

Amusingly, some libraries catalogue this as history instead
of fiction.   It is presented as an expository, analytical
study rather than dramatized in terms of individual characters and scenes.   To prevent the rise of a leftist
government, Japan increases aggression against China and
launches a propaganda attack against the United States. In
the ensuing war, American naval forces defeat the Japanese,
the Chinese occupy Manchuria, and Japan surrenders Sakhalin
to Russia to prevent her from entering the war. After the

defeats at sea Japan surrenders. Much attention is given
to military technology and strategy. Air warfare is not
especially emphasized, although some fifty American planes
do appear over Tokyo.

132. Cairnes, Captain [William Elliot]. The Coming Waterloo.
Westminster: Constable, 1901.

In 1903 war breaks out between England and France. Russia
masses troops at strategic approaches to India, while
Germany and Austria become allies of Britain. The main
action centers upon a British army invading France and
fighting until an armistice is declared. Cairnes introduces machine guns and suggests that in the war of the
future the "highly-trained few" will be able to annihilate
the "half-trained multitude" because of the advances made
in armaments.

133. Cameron, Commander [Verney Lovett]. The Queen's Land; or,
Ard al Malakat. London: Sonnenschein, 1886.

In Aden an old Jewish rabbi tells the first-person narrator
of a "civilized but unknown" country to the south of
Abyssinia. The resultant safari provides a view of Africa
as it works its way to Tebaza in the Kingdom of Saba, where
there are horsemen in armor. King Solomon once visited the
city. The narrator releases the queen from a trance she
has long been in. The narrator studies the old lore with
the aid of the rabbi, while his companion marries a beautiful girl and returns to England.

134. Candler, Edmund. The Dinosaur's Egg. Edinburgh: Blackwood, 1925.

The first-person narrator tells the story of his wife
Angela's godfather, Uncle Bliss, emphasizing his children's
reactions to him, especially of the girl Irene. The novel
provides a gentle satire of the British African explorer/
colonial official type. The narrative abounds with al-
lusions to Don Quixote, including references to Castles in
Spain and tilting with windmills. Bliss' aide, Staff, is
called Sancho Panza. Bliss purchases a dinosaur egg on
sale in America, quests for a pterodactyl, and shoots a
"fabulous monster" in an equatorial swamp--whose body is
never found. Other references suggest that Candler is
having fun with the whole of romantic fiction of the
period.

135. Carew, Henry. The Vampires of the Andes. London: Jar-
rolds, 1925.

Professor Humphrey Stevenson receives news from Peru
suggesting a lost city and making much of the girl Quiti,
the last descendant of the reigning Inca. A second letter

provides an account of Will Wootton, who finds the city of
Aztlan, a remnant of Atlantis. There is a society based on
the legend of vampires because of the existence of blood-
sucking birds. Will and Quiti fall in love.

136.   [Carrel, Frederic]. 2010. London: Laurie, 1914.

The year is 2010 after a new Renascence. London has been
transformed; an advanced technology, including aircraft,
exists. Caesar Brent, a genetic engineer, has created new
forms of animals and wishes to control nature. Victor
Veitch leads the opposition against Brent's wish to experiment with people, especially children, to advance man's
mental powers. Racism is very much present; the American
negro, Sylvanus Strong, praises Brent, who has whitened his
skin. In the East the woman Khadija Khayat threatens war,
hoping to conquer Europe. A comet strikes the Earth,
causing widespread destruction. The survivors ask Brent to
be President of the Council governing the Federated States
of Europe. He marries Constantia Deane. Veitch appears
again to form the League of Good to oppose Brent, under
whose leadership man has learned to control nature.
Khadaji appears in London as Mariam Zend and joins the
League. A new plague strikes, killing Brent's son and
rendering Western men sterile. Brent has a substance
which, if released in the atmosphere, would destroy all
mammals. Oriental forces attack in a great fleet of
airships, and there is fighting in London and England.
Brent, however, not only discovers a remedy for the disease
but reverses it so that it destroys Oriental women, including Khadaji, who has gained entry into his home and
laboratory; she is the first to die from his new formula.
These are but the high points in one of the more sensational novels of the period. Obviously, after the defeat
of Khadaja, "the reign of lasting happiness commenced."

137.   Carruth, [Fred] Hayden. The Adventures of Jones. New
York: Harper, 1895.

The first-person narrator (Jones) tells a series of tall
tales to Jackson Peters. All of them are spoofs on scientific advances and the literary treatment of popular
motifs. For example, he stores electricity in cats to form
a new type of motor, and he crosses the honeybee with the
firefly so that the new breed of bees will work all night.
He invents submarines having wings. He also satirizes the
journeys into Africa and the Arctic.

138.   Casey, Patrick and Terence. The Strange Case of William
Hyde. New York: Hearst's International Library, 1916.

The first-person narrator tells of his adventures somewhere
among the Pacific Islands. He goes by river through a
mountain into a crater where lies Jallan Batoe, "another

Lhassa."   At one time Genghis Khan's Tartars were there, but he finds no men--only beautiful women.   The Tartars were wiped out by the Dyaks, who now consider the area sacred.   He becomes involved in a triangle--a beautiful "golden woman" and the brunette priestess Lip-Plak-Tengga. Because of his appearance, he is thought to be a reincarnation or manchild of the Khan.   Eventually he is forced to flee, abandoning the golden woman who is killed by a "Monster Man," more Orang-Outang than human.   Now he is a beachcomber and wants to return to the city.   For its period this is one of the most erotic lost race novels.

139.   Casparian, Gregory.   An Anglo-American Alliance; A Serio-Comic Romance and Forecast of the Future.   Floral Park, N.Y.: Mayflower, 1906.

In a "Foreword" the author asks for Universal Brotherhood and asserts that his narrative is an allegory of the friendship between Britain and the United States.   It focuses upon the girls--Aurora Cunningham, only daughter of the Secretary of Foreign Affairs for Great Britain, and Margaret MacDonald, daughter of a senator from Wyoming. With the help of the scientist, Dr. Hyder Ben Rabba, Margaret undergoes an operation which changes her by physical and mental metempsychosis into a man.   As Spencer Hamilton, she declares her love for Aurora; they marry, and Hamilton becomes the Viceroy of the African Commonwealth. The other interesting aspect of the narrative is a long chapter recording briefly the significant event(s) of each year of the twentieth century, ranging from the volcanic eruption of Mount Pelee in Martinique in 1902 to discussions of Balloons and Airships (1921), Uniform Divorce Laws (1923) and the Discovery of the North Pole (1931).   The Anglo-American alliance occurred in 1925-1926.   A significant decline in Germany under a socialist regime led to an exodus of Teutons to many other parts of the world.

140.   Chamberlain, H[enry] R[ichardson].   6,000 Tons of Gold. Meadville, Pa.: Flood and Vincent, 1894.

Two men are given 6,000 tons of gold by Indians in South America.   This upsets the world's financial structure, and there are threats of war until the formation of a Board of Trustees (having representatives from each major nation) decides to expend the money on "works for the general benefit" of mankind instead of permitting private gain.

141.   Chambers, Julius.   "In Sargasso"; Missing, a Romance; Narrative of Capt. Austin Clark, of the Tramp Steamer "Caribas," Who, for Two Years, Was a Captive among the Savage People of the Seaweed Set.   New York: Transatlantic, 1896.

As narrator, Clark tells of finding a race of castaways in the Sargasso, an area as large as Texas, who are descen-

dants of the mixture of negro women from slave ships and
Spanish and Portugese men. He goes into great detail about
the Sargasson manners and customs, calling them "scrupu-
lously honest."   Although he must fight through a revolution, the main interest of the storyline is the love
between Clark and Fidette, whose mother was a Louisiana
Creole. They eventually escape. Perhaps the most interesting portion of the narrative is a chapter concerned with
the "New Woman" in Sargasso, for Fidette and a friend had
undertaken the "laudable task" of "ameliorating the condition of women" among the Sargassons.

142.   Chambers, Robert W[illiam].   The Gay Rebellion.   New York:
D. Appleton, 1913.

Originally published, at least in part, as A Matter of
Eugenics in Hampden Magazine (1911):   a light, episodic
comedy aimed at the suffragette movement.   Curtis Langdon
and William Sayre are sent to write a newspaper story about
the disappearance of four handsome young men in the Adi-
rondacks.   They learn that at the instigation of the
Central National Female Franchise Federation a number of
beautiful young women have founded the New Race University
and Masculine Beauty Preserve there in the mountains.   On
the basis of "cold blooded scientific selection," these
young women--whose ideal is the cult of the cavewoman--
intend to kidnap eugenically perfect young men in order to
found a more perfect race.   As usual, however, the heart
prevails over science when Sayre and Amourette and Langdon
and Ethra Leslie fall in love at first sight.   Two further
episodes involve Lord John Marque and Lady Diana Guernsey
and Professor Betty Challis and the Governor of New York.

143.   Chambers, Robert W[illiam].   The Green Mouse.   New York:
D. Appleton, 1910.

Through a stage prop which he uses as a magician--a green
mouse--William Augustus Destyn meets Ethelinda Carr, one of
three beautiful triplets.   They fall in love.   He persuades
her wealthy father to finance the development of a machine
which captures psychical currents and is thus able to match
the man and woman who are soul mates.   After a demonstra-
tion works for the second of the girls, her father sponsors
Green Mouse, Ltd., whose motto is "Wedlock by Wireless."
The third daughter, Flavilla, goes against science; she
loves Henry Kingsbury, who first sees her garbed as a
mermaid.   They forsake "machine-made bliss" for the va-
garies of the heart.

144.   Chambers, Robert W[illiam].   In Search of the Unknown.
New York: D. Appleton, 1904.

The episodic narrative takes as its protagonist Harold
Kensett, who serves as general superintendent of the water-

fowl department of the Zoological Gardens being built at
Bronx Park.   Always sent somewhere in search of exotic
animals, he falls in love with every pretty girl he meets.
In a prefatory note Chambers writes of the "urgent need"
for more "nature books" devoid of any fiction and relying
on fact, and he hopes that this volume will "inspire
enthusiasm for natural and scientific research. . . ."
Kensett first goes to Black Harbor, where Burton Halyard
offers a pair of giant auks for sale.   The auks and their
chicks are lost overboard when Kensett tries in vain to
kill a humanoid creature having gills who is known as the
"Harbor Master."   He next goes to Graham's Glacier in the
Hudson Mountains of Canada after mammoths.   Miss Susan
Smawl, Professor of Natural History at Barnard College,
temporarily head of the Zoological Gardens, and the beautiful Professor Dorothy Van Twiller follow him into the
wilderness.   From a lake the head and arm of a woman emerge
briefly to warn the researchers away.   At the International
Scientific Congress at the Paris Exposition in 1900, he
helps Countess Suzanne d'Alzette hatch the eggs of an ux;
scientists and statesmen must sit on the eggs until they
hatch because a strike in New York prevents the French
workers from maintaining the proper level of steam heat.
Finally, he is sent to Florida to seek a thermosaurus.   The
light tone of the book makes it memorable, for throughout
Chambers is having fun with two themes: young romance and
science.

145. Chambers, Robert W[illiam].   Police!   New York: D.
Appleton, 1915.

Chambers resumes the misadventures of a protagonist who
searches for exotic animals and falls in love with every
pretty girl he meets.   This time it is Percy Smith, Curator
of the Department of Anthropology at Bronx Park.   The
episodes involve a new, three-eyed species of man in
Florida, a half dozen young women who pretend to be cave
women, mammoths frozen into the ice of Baffin Land, a mile-
long worm and the eggs of an exotic butterfly.   The girls
range from several waitresses to beautiful women scientists
and aged suffragettes.   But this volume does not have the
same light touch as In Search of the Unknown.

146. Chambers, Robert W[illiam].   The Slayer of Souls.   New
York: Doran, 1920.

Chambers combines a tirade against the Bolshevists and all
leftist terrorists with the plot of a secret Oriental cult
of devil-worshippers and magicians led by the Hassani to
seize control of America and the world.   They can take over
the minds of individuals and are responsible for a new
plague (influenza).   During the years of World War I,
Tressa Norne was their prisoner and learned their secrets.
She returns to the United States, marries a member of the

Secret Service, Victor Cleves, and finally kills the leaders of the Orientals by occult means. This is the most sensational of Chambers' narratives and obviously gives expression to private concerns.

147. Chambers, Robert W[illiam].   Some Ladies in Haste.   New York: D. Appleton, 1908.

A student of mental suggestion since hypnosis cured him of smoking, William T. Manners undertakes an experiment. Choosing five "very imperfect" acquaintances of his and giving them personal qualities which he thinks they lack, he also wills that the "first five ornamental young girls" who pass the Lenox Club on Fifth Avenue marry the men. So well does the experiment work that he loses his fiancee. Public clamor and the failure of his business drive him to upstate New York, where he meets the fashionable young woman whom he willed to get rid of her servants and lead a bucolic life. They fall in love.

148. Chancellor, J[ohn] W[alter].   Through the Visograph Boston: Christopher, 1928.

In the Big Bend of the Rio Grande the narrator and his companion find the visograph, an instrument which permits them to view events taking place ten million years ago. It is an extravagant history of the kingdoms of Ut and Milino and tries to attain to religious allegory. It ends with a sign that God has created and destroyed the world as it was then. The most interesting aspect of this ending is that planets near the Earth move so that it is left in isolation.

149. Channing, Mark. King Cobra. London: Hutchinson, 1933.

Published in America by Lippincott (1934): Diana Lindsay is kidnapped by the outlaw Alam Khan--King Cobra--and her father, the British resident, is killed. Alam Khan takes her to his stronghold, the Valley of the Palace of Mirrors. Colin Gray follows and kills Alam Khan. When an earthquake seals the valley, he and Diana escape through subterranean passageways where they find the twelfth century tomb of Prester John.

150. Channing, Mark. The Poisoned Mountain. London: Hutchinson, 1935.

Dedicated to F. Yeats-Brown, this is more nearly straight adventure than sf or fantasy. As Major Colin Gray and Diana Lindsay honeymoon in the Kuen-Lin Himalayas, they must investigate the anti-British activities of the Bengali, Lall Behari, whose base is near the volcano Guari-Jan, from which emanates a poisonous gas called the Blue Breath. Separated by an avalanche, Diana is hypnotized by

Behari, who proclaims her a goddess. Sir James Carnforth, a former scientist, has obtained a half ton of crystals to produce the gas. With the aid of a British secret agent, Creighton, and the beautiful native girl, Parvati, Gray overcomes Behari; bombing planes cause volcanic action and the Blue Breath encompasses his stronghold. Only Gray and Diana escape; they are picked up by a British aviator.

151. Channing, Mark. White Python. London: Hutchinson, 1934.

Published in America by Lippincott (1934): in London Colin Gray has a vision of a serpent and a woman. Despatched to Tibet by the Foreign Office, he undertakes the rescue of Piers Bryan, a world-famous flier who crashed during a solo flight across the Himalayas. She is held prisoner by a strange, sightless race living in an underground world. They are led by the beautiful Gynia, described as a lamia and somehow tied to a giant white python. Infatuated with Gray and jealous of Piers, Gynia would sacrifice the American girl to the python. Gray destroys the snake and rescues Piers as the underworld is destroyed by earthquake. Piers declines his love; he returns to the military in India.

152. Chapman, S[amuel] E. Doctor Jones' Picnic. San Francisco: Whitaker & Ray, 1898.

Dr. Jones invents a 200-foot diameter aluminum balloon, The Silver Cloud, enabling him to travel to the North Pole. With this journey as a narrative frame, as a doctor he develops several cures of diseases, including one for cancer. Although Jones is critical of society, especially the "great money kings," and calls for social reform, his achievements give the narrative a lighter touch which the utopian attacks do not have. At one point he refers specifically to Ignatius Donnelly's Caesar's Column; despite his own invention, he does criticize the growing reliance upon machines. However, after being received as a hero after his return from the pole, he begins to make plans to set out for the south pole.

153. Chappell, George S[hepard]. Through the Alimentary Canal with Gun and Camera; A Fascinating Trip to the Interior. New York: Stokes, 1930.

The introduction is by Robert Benchley. Chappell parodies the fantastic voyages by taking a journey through the digestive system. Others of his parodies include The Cruise of the Kawa: Wanderings in the South Seas (1921), Sarah of the Sahara: A Romance of Nomads Land (1923) and My Northern Exposure: The Kawa at the Pole (1925). The last of them is Dr. Traprock's Memory Book, or Aged in Wood (1930), presented as a biography of his intrepid explorer.

154. Chavannes, Albert.   In Brighter Climes; or, Life in
Socioland; a Realistic Novel. Knoxville, Tn.: Chavannes, 1895.

Chavannes states that this is a history of the life and
marriage of Charles Morril and Mary Lenard, who live in a
country "under social conditions very different" from those
in America.   He places Socioland in Africa because the
Mormons have "pre-empted" the only site available in the
U.S. and because he objects to the Moon or Mars "as a
dwelling place for earthly beings." Although he gives some
notice to property reform and has the commonwealth handle
all trade, most attention goes to sexual matters.   Women
have gained full equality with men, prostitution does not
exist, and there is no stigma attached to illegitimate
births. Marriage is a free contract between equals. After
Morril's wife has two children, the main storyline concerns
his affair with a young woman, Rose Mansfield, who is
something of a flirt. When Mary learns of this, the couple
is brought closer together, and they realize that monogamy
is the "best form of sexual association" at the present
stage of civilization.

155. Chesney, Sir George [Tomkyns].   The Battle of Dorking; or,
Reminiscences of a Volunteer.   Edinburgh: Blackwood, 1871.

Published anonymously in the May 1871 issue of Blackwoods:
a surprise attack by Germany in 1875 easily defeats an
unprepared Britain despite the courage of a volunteer army.
This 64-page pamphlet established the basic form of the
future-war motif.   A participant acts as narrator and
pictures the invasion in minute detail. One should turn to
I.F. Clarke for the most complete account of the story's
impact and the popularity of the motif it created.   It
rivaled the impact of Bellamy's Looking Backward on the
popular imagination. Nor should one forget that it appeared at an appropriate psychological moment; surpris-
ingly, Germany had just defeated France. Thus The Battle
of Dorking could play upon the fears of a society, both
European and American, which regarded a major war as
inevitable.

156. Chester, George Randolph.   The Jingo.   Indianapolis, In.:
Bobbs-Merrill, 1912.

Making use of all the established conventions, The Jingo
presents the recovered manuscript of Jimmy Smith, an
American salesman shipwrecked in the Antarctic.   On the
island of Isola he finds a Greek race which has preserved
its culture throughout the centuries.   Much of the storyline deals lightly with the love story of Jimmy and Princess Bezzanna (Betsy Ann), but more attention is given to
Jimmy's introduction of the commonplaces of American life
into the society. When a German aviator lands because of
engine trouble, Jimmy recalls the dangers of imperialism

and has the island declare itself a repubic and a colony of
the United States.   As well as satirizing the romanticism
of the lost race motif itself, Chester chides America for
its materialism and growing jingoism.

157. Chester, William L.   Hawk of the Wilderness.   New York:
Harper, 1936.

Originally serialized in Blue Book (1935-1936): the narrative frame presents James Munro, an anthropologist and
authority on the American Indian, who journeys into the
Arctic to verify evidence he has obtained regarding the
origin of the Amerinds.   The main storyline, set in the
continent of Nato'wa, homeland of the Indians, centers upon
the character of Kioga, the Snow-Hawk.   After his parents
are killed in a raid on the Shoni village where they had
been accepted, Kioga was first raised by Mokuyi, the
Amerind companion of his father.   Driven into the wilderness by jealous youthful companions who actually cripple
him for a time, Kioga is adopted by the she-bear, Yanu.
Not only does he recover his physical strength, but he
gains a cunning and knowledge surpassing that of the Shoni.
The tribal elders offer him a place on the Council, and he
unites the Kindred Shoni Tribes.   Beth Kendle, her brother,
and Munro discover him, and he finally returns to San
Francisco with them.   Although he loves Beth, he chooses to
return to Nato'wa, and the novel ends with the note that
Beth and Munro have gone back in search of him.   One series
of short stories and two other novels were published in
Blue Book but did not see book publication until DAW
editions in the 1970s: Kioga of the Wilderness (1936,
1976); One Against the Wilderness (1937, 1977); and Kioga
of the Unknown Land (1938, 1978).

158. Chesterton, G[ilbert] K[eith].   The Napoleon of Notting
Hill. London: Lane, 1904.

Chesterton attacks the concept of progress and the as-
cendancy of science, specifically referring to Wells.
Projecting a London some eighty years in the future, he
finds it to be much as it is at the turn of the century.
The main storyline concerns the efforts of young King
Auberon to grant all of the boroughs charters which will
make them essentially medieval cities.   Chesterton believes
that society can avert catastrophe only by re-emphasizing
local allegiance and the universal ideas held during the
Middle Ages.   His emphasis is upon the tie of the individual to the smaller community.

159. Chetwode, R.D.   The Marble City, Being the Strange Adventures of Three Boys.   London: Sampson Low, Marston, 1895.

Much in the manner of Jules Verne: three brothers (Bob,
Harry, and Jack) are shipwrecked on a Pacific island.

Captured by natives, they are taken into the interior to the city of Alsico. The most unusual twist is that the young priestess, Airee, who aids them, suffers briefly from smallpox. They are allowed to leave in a canoe and are picked up by a ship.

160. Childers, Erskine. The Riddle of the Sands; A Record of Secret Service Recently Achieved. London: Smith, Elder, 1903.

One of the outstanding examples of the future-war motif, the novel caused a sensation when confiscated in Germany. Instead of the usual portrayal of armies in conflict, Childers presents the novel as a problem in detection. The first-person narrator discovers the German plan for massing the necessary ships for a surprise invasion. He presented the manuscript as though he were editor. The novel was reprinted during the threat of invasion in World War II.

161. Childs, Edward Earle. The Wonders of Mouseland. New York: Abbey Press, 1901.

The introduction explains that the author wanted to find Marvin Lampson, who had disappeared in the South Seas; after three years he turns up and tells the story of his adventures to the author, though he insists that the location of Mouseland be kept secret. It is obviously an imaginary voyage to such a kingdom as Gulliver visited in order to devise a means of criticizing society. The first-person narrator tells how he was captured by tiny ships and taken to the city of Klangsdown in the kingdom of Halloway. The mice have knowledge of the outside world and have a technology. Lampson becomes a citizen, but leaves after they have been defeated by the Iripys, the "Indians of Mouseland."

162. Chipman, W[illiam] P[endleton] and C[harles] P[hillips]. An Aerial Runaway; The Balloon Adventures of Rod and Tod in North & South America. Boston: Lothrop, 1901.

A juvenile adventure begins with the rescue of the two little girls whose team of horses runs away. The boys undertake a balloon flight to Mount Roraima in Venezuela, where they discover a city peopled by descendants of the Incas called the Antalcans. After a series of jungle adventures, they return to the United States, bringing with them the youthful Prince Admaxla, who enrolls with them two years later in a "well-known" Polytechnic School, where they will all learn to be engineers.

163. Christopher, Edward Earl. The Invisibles. Akron, Oh.: Saalfield, 1902.

The first-person narrator, Castleman, tells the story of Jean Valdermere, who once saved Castleman's life in India.

He learns that Valdermere, who has a highly scientific mind, represents a society, the Invisible Hand, which is devoted to the overthrow of the Czar, because Russia is the cruelest nation on Earth. The headquarters of the society is in a series of caverns near Chattanooga. In the caverns is a giant and some two thousand warriors, the remnants of an ancient race. Castleman wonders whether they are related to the Mound Builders. The society is building a submarine to attack the Russian navy. Part of the story is concerned with the love of Castleman for Mlle. Marie de Tavenier. They escape when a gas explosion destroys the caverns and the society.

164. Clemens, Samuel Langhorne [see Mark Twain].

165. Clock, Herbert and Eric Boetzel. The Light in the Sky. New York: Coward McCann, 1929.

After seeing the same woman several times on the Western Front and in Paris, the first-person narrator is drugged and awakens in a strange city. A man identifying himself as Juan Velasquez, companion of Cortez, greets him. The narrator finds himself in the city of Atzlan in a great cavern beneath Mexico, which is inhabited by Aztecs who fled Cortez. Tizoc, the brother of Montezuma, is the ruler. The narrator recognizes the woman whom he has seen as Princess Tinemah, daughter of Montezuma. Supposedly the narrator has been selected for sacrifice because he has in him the blood of Cortez; the sacrifice is to inaugurate the Aztec conquest of the world, something made possible because of the weapons Tizoc has developed from light. However, the end of the novel becomes clouded with mysticism. Tizoc does not want war; he wishes to release the soul of the narrator so that it can journey to other worlds and discover the nature of afterlife. As the experiment starts, Tizoc is killed by his son, Prince Naguma. As the narrator and Tinemah escape, the city and cavern are destroyed by the spirit of Tizoc. Much is made of the eighth color--invisible--being love. In the epilogue the narrator wonders whether or not "a Supreme Being is building life into a nobler and more God-like form."

166. Clowes, [Sir] William Laird. The Captain of the "Mary Rose"; A Tale of Tomorrow. London: Tower, 1892.

Once again France defeats Britain, with emphasis upon warfare at sea and the new ships. The usual criticism about the lack of expenditure to ensure readiness is present.

167. Clowes, [Sir] William Laird and Alan H. Burgoyne. The Great Naval War of 1887. London: Hatchards, 1887.

Published in St. James Gazette (1887): France defeats Britain because of the suddenness of attack and because of Britain's highly inefficient methods of mobilization. The authors also criticize the Admiralty and War Office for not spending enough money over the years to assure an adequate defense.

168. Clowes, [Sir] William Laird and Alan H. Burgoyne. Trafalgar Refought. London: Nelson, 1905.

The authors portray what might have happened had Lord Nelson lived at the present time. All of the historical battles are refought in dreadnaughts and, of course, Britain wins. However, the authors conclude that the topedo is a failure and that the ram is not effective. As always, guns and the gunners will win naval battles. For vividness the story is told by a first-person narrator.

169. Cobb, Weldon J. A Trip to Mars; or, The Spur of Adventure. New York: Street & Smith, 1901.

Intended for a juvenile audience: young Frank Edison, "the nephew of a learned savant," assists Nikola Tesla as he tries to communicate with Mars by means of an apparatus which outshines the sun. The novel contains no mysticism nor social criticism; as with most juveniles, it relies upon a capture-and-escape plot to sustain the reader's interest.

170. [Colburn], Frona Eunice Wait. Yermah the Dorado. San Francisco: Doxey, 1897.

As Frona Eunice Wait, the author combines reference to Atlantis with a portrait of pre-Columbian America, in which the highly civilized tribes worship a god whose principles are those of Christianity. The novel becomes a hodgepodge of mysticism, with references to astrology, Gnosticism, various of the Oriental religions, and Theosophy. Yermah comes among the people as a teacher. Both Yermah and the tribes are Aryan.

171. [Cole, Cornelius]. California Three Hundred and Fifty Years Ago; Manuelo's Narrative, Translated from the Portugese, by a Pioneer. San Francisco: Carson, 1888.

This is more a pseudo-historical novel of early California than a lost race novel. Supposedly it is based on a manuscript recently found in Evora, Portugal. A Spanish ship lands in San Francisco harbor; when its crew goes inland, they are attacked by Indians. One wounded member is left behind; eventually he marries an Indian woman and becomes chief of the Yono tribe. A reference to Drake (1579) implies that this event took place earlier.

172. Cole, Cyrus. The Auroraphone; A Romance. Chicago: Kerr, 1890.

In the Rockies the narrator, S.I. Karbun, and his companions meet Gaston Lesage, who has developed a device (something akin to both telephone and telegraph) but as yet has failed to communicate with other worlds. During a strong aurora borealis, his signals are picked up by a scientist on Saturn, Rulph Bozar, who then takes command of the narrative. He describes the origin of the solar system, but he gives most attention to the religion Certology—introduced long ago by the prophet Creeto—which has as its core the concept of the oneness of the universe. Slavery, warfare among humans, and fierce competition for money have been done away with. The advanced technology has developed "dummies" [robots], which had been used by men and boys as opponents in war games to relieve "human pugnacity." The latest models, however, have been programmed to recharge their own "electrometer"; now the dummies have gone on strike and the threat of a terrible war between man and machine threatens. His narrative ends soon after he suggests that nation and individual alike must learn from this threat the need to engage in "manual labor" daily. His narrative is framed by the love story of Karbun and Rose Pardee, daughter of Karbun's host.

173. Cole, Robert William. The Death Trap. London: Greening. 1907.

A coalition of European powers led by Germany soundly defeats Britain and occupies the British Isles. Noteworthy both for the detail in which Cole portrays the ruthlessness of the occupation and for the introduction of guerilla tactics, suggested by the Japanese. Cole criticizes government, civilians, and military alike.

174. Cole, Robert William. The Struggle for Empire; a Story of the Year 2236. London: Stock, 1900.

Historically important as one of the first accounts of interstellar war, the novel concentrates upon the struggle between Earthmen and aliens from the planet Kairet of the Sirian system. The Sirians destroy fleet after fleet until James Tarrant invents an Electro-Ednogen force which nullifies gravity and thus annihilates the Sirians—but only after they have bombed London, the capital of the Solar System. The protagonist, Lieutenant Alec Brandon, marries Celia Herbert, who nursed him through his wound. His former fiancée, a British beauty, weds Tarrant and thus becomes the ruling Princess of conquered Kairet. Of equal importance is the introductory chapter describing an idyllic world ruled from London and celebrating the Anglo-Saxon race.

175. Collier, John. Full Circle. New York: D. Appleton, 1933.

Published as Tom's A-Cold; A Tale (1933) in England by Macmillan: the scene is projected to 1995 after Britain has been devastated by a series of unspecified wars, and the people have fallen to the level of barbarism. The plot follows two lines of development: the first deals with the efforts of young Harry to replace the aged Chief; the second results from Harry's leading a group of raiders against a tribe living in the ruins of Swindon. He has fallen in love with Rose, a girl he has seen there. He captures her during the raid; they seem to fall in love until he accidentally kills her brother. She is killed when her tribe attacks Harry's group. Full Circle was one of the most successful post-holocaust novels between the wars and exerted influence on subsequent writers. Its literary quality is high, and its tone attempts to remain optimistic in that mankind can rebuild, though with Rose's death the implication is strengthened that life will remain harsh.

176. Collingwood, Harry [pseud. of William Joseph Cosens Lancaster]. The Log of the "Flying Fish"; A Story of Aerial and Submarine Peril and Adventure. London: Blackie, 1886.

The first of a series of juveniles involving a machine that is both airplane and submarine. Highly Vernesque, it presents a series of conventional incidents in Africa and the Arctic.

177. Collins, Gilbert. The Starkenden Quest. New York: McBride, 1925.

Also published in Britain by Duckworth (1925): a manuscript in the family tells how in the past Wulf Starkenden journeyed to the East and acquired a gem (an "eyestone") and an old compass. Now after Marah Starkenden disappears, her father hires John Crayton to seach for her. He and Gregory Hope follow her trail into Indo-China, where they are captured by dwarfs and imprisoned in caverns in the interior. They are to be sacrificed, as is Marah, who is also a prisoner. The dwarfs are led by Marah's brother Jacob, whose mind is controlled by an old priest, the Undying One. When Crayton and Hope kill the old priest, Jacob regains his mind and leads them to freedom. Marah and Hope are infatuated. The dwarfs are the Ktawrh, remnants of the ancient Khmer people; much is made of the dying out of ancient races, direct reference being made to the ancient glories of Angkor-Wat.

178.   Collins, Gilbert.   The Valley of Eyes Unseen.   New York:
McBride, 1924.

> Also published in Britain by Duckworth (1924): fleeing
> China, Robert Mirlees joins an expedition bound for Tibet.
> It finds a valley populated by descendants of Greek sol-
> diers led by Alexander the Great.   When the expedition's
> leader is regarded as a reincarnation of Alexander, civil
> war occurs.   Mirlees is forced to flee the valley alone,
> using man-made wings to take him over the mountains.

179.   Colmore, G. [pseud. of Gertrude Renton Weaver].   Priests
of Progress.   New York: Dodge, 1908.

> A thin storyline centering on the love of a girl who wants
> to become an artist but instead marries a doctor holds
> together what is really a debate on the nature of science,
> emphasizing especially medical science.   It becomes a
> violent attack upon vivisection, not only because of its
> brutality but because the doctors who use it become callous
> and indifferent.   The climax is the formation of an inter-
> national league to combat vivisection.   The real issue lies
> in the assertion that love and the preservation of the
> spirit are more important than the material body and
> science.

180.   Colomb, Rear-Admiral P[hillip Howard] and others.   The
Great War of 189-.   London: Heinemann, 1893.

> Originally written at the suggestion of the editor of Black
> and White and serialized in that magazine in 1892: written
> by a group of high ranking naval officers, Charles Lowe,
> long-time correspondent in Berlin, was the only civilian to
> participate, although many of the incidents are presented
> as newspaper despatches.   An Anglo-German alliance fights
> against a combination of French and Russians; the battles
> engulf the continent from the approaches to Paris and the
> Riviera to Vladivostok.   Fighting begins after an attempted
> assassination in the Balkans embroils Serbia and Bulgaria.
> It was translated into German (1894) and proved successful
> there.

181.   Colver, Alice Ross.   The Red-Headed Goddess.   New York:
Dodd, Mead, 1929.

> This is not a lost race story as it has sometimes been
> called.   Lorraine Kirk and Dirk Leslie, bored with fash-
> ionable life, crash aboard his plane in northern Arizona in
> Navajo lands.   They must live primitively in an idyllic
> valley protected from the desert; in doing so, they dis-
> cover their love for one another.   Because he is injured,
> she must go for aid.   She enters a kiva during a ceremony
> and is thought to be the wife of the sun.   Dirk tries to
> cross the desert and fails.   They are aided by the Indian,

Silver Tongue, who sends a telegram to her father, a
senator who must investigate rumors of Indian unrest,
especially because of the discovery of oil on Navajo lands.
The novel becomes a harsh criticism of the injustice the
government has shown in dealing with Indian affairs.

182. Comstock, Sarah. The Moon Is Made of Green Cheese.
Garden City, N.Y.: Doubleday, Doran, 1929.

This novel should not be considered science fiction or
fantasy. Beginning with the announcement that John Kingsbury has won the Fordyce prize in astronomy, it flashes
back to trace his life and that of a close friend, another
astronomer, Brian Shedlock. It thus becomes a not-too-deep
psychological study of the two men, its principal question
being which of them is a failure. Kingsbury wins the award
and recognition; Shedlock wins the three women they have
loved.   On a perfect night for photography, Shedlock
forgets to take his turn at the Whipple Observatory and so
any pictures that might have been taken are lost.   When
they go on an expedition to Winged Arrow Island in the
South Pacific, other members of the staff ask Kingsbury to
assume authority when a crisis occurs.   Shedlock resigns,
takes a place on Wall Street, and is financially ruined.
Like Sinclair Lewis' Arrowsmith, this novel seems an
example of science in literature rather than sf.

183. Connington, J. J. [pseud. of Alfred Walter Stewart].
Nordenholt's Million. London: Constable, 1923.

In a reflective narrative, the first-person narrator, Jack
Flint, recalls the famine caused by Bacterium diazotans,
which destroyed the nitrogenous content of the soil,
reducing it to sand.   It began in Regent's Park but devastated the world.   Douglas Nordenholt seized dictatorial
powers, setting up a colony of five million people in the
Clyde valley.   Although one effective sequence deals with
the collapse of London, the novel is most important because
of Nordenholt's deliberate use of propaganda to break down
the structure of society outside of his colony and his use
of psychological weapons.   He emphasizes the "breaking
strain" of humanity and the individual.   His colony survives, but one of the greatest dangers to it occurs after
the food supply and survival are assured.   The stress of
the ordeal has brought the population to the edge of
collective hysteria; a religious revival begins, but is
ended after The Reverend John does not ascend to heaven and
is killed by machine guns when he would turn his wrath
against Nordenholt and destroy the colony.   His methods are
ruthless and alienate his niece, Elsa Huntingtower, whom
Flint loves.   Nordenholt's death brings them together.   The
final portion of the narrative deals with the period when
Flint is leader of the colony.   The development of atomic
engines revolutionizes the society even more than he and

Nordenholt had expected. Society prospers but not in the manner Nordenholt had dreamed. (The only other colony specifically named was founded by Kiyotomo Zade in the Kobe shipyards.)

184. Conquest, Joan. Leonie of the Jungle. New York: Macaulay, 1921.

Also published in Britain by T. Warner Laurie (1921): the entire story is the battle for the soul of Leonie Hetth, whose native Ayah insists that the goddess Kali took possession of the child's soul when she was an infant. Jan Caxson loves her, but she is finally released from any spell which afflicts her by the love and protection of Madhu Krishnaghar, an Indian prince who also loves her. An earthquake destroys the temple of Kali, Madhu dies, and she is free to return to Devon with Caxson.

185. Conquest, Joan. The Reckoning. New York: Macaulay, 1931.

Also published in London by T. Werner Laurie (1931): Professors Kev and Linkoff discover a "life enervating" molecule in a special fibre found in the Dolomites. Through their aid Clara Wean has a baby girl, to be named Crystal Smith. A month later the laboratory blows up, destroying the scientists and their secret. Crystal does not learn of her scientific origin until she is in her late teens. The entire issue, as Conquest puts it, turns upon whether or not Crystal has a soul. Significantly, neither of her parents had a shred of honour or decency; therefore, she surrenders to temptation. She illicitly loves a Spanish torero. In the Atlas Mountains she is aboard a train attacked by locusts. She is injured and then suffers from peritonitis. She dies in surgery, where it is discovered that she has no reproductive organs. By implication, at least, this proves her Satanic nature. In some ways the science is a side issue to an attack upon the new woman, contraception, and the whole of current morality.

186. Conrad, Joseph and Ford Madox Hueffer. The Inheritors. London: Heinemann, 1901.

The first-person narrator, Etchingham Granger, member of an old family and an author, tells of his encounter with a young woman who says that she is from the Fourth Dimension and insists upon calling herself his sister. She; Charles Gurnard, a politician; and Fox, editor of the Hour, are Dimensionists, the next stage of mankind who will appear and take control of the world from humanity. Most attention is given the woman, for this is essentially a love story, albeit unrequited. She suggests that the Dimensionists will be cold, self-seeking, merciless individuals; the implication is that they will be ruthless capitalists. The storyline concerns the failure of the government to gain backing for the infamous Duc de Mersch's railroad across Greenland. Here occurs the first problem: the authors refer both to Polar regions and to the inhuman treatment of blacks. All of the essential action is off-stage; the narrative is trapped within the subjectivity of the narrator. None of the science nor the sketch of the nature of the Dimensionists is given adequate attention. The novel may be read as an attack upon such individuals as Cecil Rhodes and King Leopold of Belgium.

187.   Converse, Frank H.   In Search of an Unknown Race.   New York: Street and Smith, 1901.

Originally published as Van; or, In Search of an Unknown Race by the United States Book Company (1891): Van Briscoe, the protagonist, goes up the Amazon River in search of his uncle and Robert Martin, who possessed a dozen of the finest diamonds. Although the storyline involves a number of captures and escapes, Van does find a city near the volcanic peak, Escomada; its people are related to the Incas and an even older race which at its height equalled Europe. The people now resemble "the highest type" of Spanish or French Creole. Among them Van finds Ninanda, the daughter of his uncle and thus his cousin. Flores is a young rival who causes Van trouble, including the theft of the money-belt containing the diamonds. His uncle and Ninanda return to the United States, and he follows them. His uncle plans to marry an old love with his daughter's full consent, and the implication is that Van and Ninanda will also marry.

188.   Cook, William Wallace.   Adrift in the Unknown.   New York: Street & Smith, 1904-1905.

The first-person narrator, a newspaperman, reports how four capitalists--Gilholly, Popham, Meigs, and Markham--are lured to the home of Professor Quinn, which is a spaceship, and are taken to the planet Mercury. The plot becomes a foolish series of captures and escapes in the kingdoms of Baigadd and Baigol in the interior of the planet. When they escape and return to Earth--Quinn is left behind--they have reformed and work for the good of the people. The Mercurials, as the narrator calls them, are small and only grotesquely humanoid.

189.   Cook, William Wallace.   Around the World in Eighty Hours.   New York: Chelsea House, 1925.

Because of its date, this novel is more a straight adventure story than sf. John Mornung, a "Napoleon of finance," believes that progress is synonymous with speedy transportation and communication along regular routes. David Whitley pilots a special plane around the world in exactly eighty hours despite the efforts of sundry adversaries, especially a rival capitalist.

190. Cook, William Wallace. Cast Away at the Pole. New York: Street & Smith, 1904.

The first-person narrator, Captain Salis of the U.S. Navy, is obsessed by his desire to reach the North Pole. His scientist companion, Professor Preeble, wishes to prove two theories: first, the meteoric origin of the aurora borealis; secondly, the failure of the human mind north of the Arctic circle because of stress. A whirlwind blows them into the kingdom of Nyll, which has a tropical climate though it is twenty-three miles from the pole. The warmth is caused by the friction of the Earth turning on the pole; later they actually see "the great spindle itself." Cook manipulates a conventional storyline to prove Preeble's second theory. When they escape from captivity aboard a balloon, Salis imagines that he has brought the Princess Ylma with him. Recovering consciousness, he learns that he had to be helped aboard the balloon and left the princess behind, though once aboard the balloon he spoke as though she were present. One of the notable satires both of Arctic exploration and the lost race motif.

191. Cook, William Wallace. The Eighth Wonder; or, Working for Marvels. New York: Street & Smith, 1906-1907.

A scientist who has been cheated out of his inventions by the oil trusts attempts to gain revenge by cornering the electrical supply of the country. To do this, he intends to attract every particle of electricity to the giant electro-magnets he has set up in the Black Hills. He can do this because there is just so much electricity in the world which is used over and over again. Instead of stopping the flow of electricity, his magnets cause the axis of the Earth to begin to shift. Branded a "world-wrecker," troops are sent against him. In the end the government rights the wrongs done him with retirement and a pension. The youthful narrator is given a government job and marries the "girl of his choice."

192. Cook, William Wallace. Marooned in 1492, or, Under Fortune's Flag. New York: Street & Smith, 1905.

Percival Tapscott desires to plant a colony of skilled artisans in the Middle Ages in order to bring the period modern technological wonders. Trenwyck and Blinkers volunteer to help him. The actual time travel is achieved through the use of a drug. Their plans are complicated by Professor Byngs, who insists that the drug was stolen from him, and by Baron von Lauderbach, who wishes to discover America for the Kaiser. They arrive in Spain in 1492, and after various confusions momentarily bring Columbus back to

the nineteenth century. Finally, Blinkers is marooned and
will sail with Columbus, but the others are safely back in
New York.

193.   Cook, William Wallace.   A Round Trip to the Year 2000; or,
A Flight Through Time.   New York: Street & Smith, 1903.

Accused of bank robbery and pursued by the detective Jasper
Kinch, Everson Lumley permits Dr. Kelpie to undertake an
experiment, to fly a time coupe to the year 2000.   Kelpie
is too tied up with mundane matters to undertake the experiment himself, and by accident Kinch accompanies Lumley
aboard the coupe.   This assures that the storyline is
dominated by a series of incidents in which Lumley avoids
capture, as well as escaping the marriage proposal of the
ardent Miss Tibijul, daughter of the Explainer.   Lumley
discovers "The Nineteen Hundred Colony," sponsored by the
Century Trance Amusement Company and made up of utopian
writers who have arrived in the year 2000 primarily through
suspended animation and are marooned there.   He also learns
that his book, The Possibilities of the Subconscious Ego,
is responsible for the development of robots (Cook calls
them Muglugs) who make up the entire labor force.   The
Muglug Trust, which has built a statue to Lumley, is the
most powerful of the Trusts which dominate the society.   He
also finds a document written by Gabriel Osborne which
explains that Osborne hypnotized Lumley and made him commit
the robbery; thus Lumley is cleared.   Cook also makes the
point that robots who lessen the work load are a blessing;
those who eliminate it, a curse.   When the Head Center, the
man who controls the Muglugs by subconscious rays, weakens,
the Muglugs run amok, destroying one another but not
harming people.   Lumley returns to the year 1900 to write
his book.

194.   Copley, Frank Barkley.   The Impeachment of President
Israels.   New York: Phillips, 1912.

Despite public pressure, including that of the jingoistic
newspapers, President Israels refuses to declare war on
Germany.   He is then impeached, but eventually his position
is sustained.   Copley emphasizes the natural and scientific
basis of moral law.   Like so many of his contemporaries, he
suggests that the next step in evolution will bring about
the perfection of the human soul.

195.   Corelli, Marie.   The Young Diana.   New York: Doran,
[1918?].

Published in England by Hutchinson (1918): to escape a
humdrum life as a spinster living with bickering, pre-
tentious parents who simply use her and thrown over by a
fiancé in India, Reginald Cleve, Diana May fakes her own
drowning.   With the aid of a suffragette friend, she goes

to Geneva in answer to an advertisement of the scientist, Feodor Dimitrius, who seeks a "mature woman" to aid him in his work. At one point he refers to their relationship as that of a vivisectionist and his animal; at another, she is his electric battery. Within a year she is transformed into a young girl of great beauty. As a side effect, however, she loses much of her emotional involvement. Dimitrius' mother declares that she is no longer human. When she returns to England, no one recognizes her; every man, including Cleve and her father, desires her sexually. Corelli uses this narrative frame to discuss the role of women in society; at one point she speaks of humanity as "cruel, destructive" and calls love "merely sex-attraction." Diana does feel some regret at the outcome, but this is more than compensated for by her social criticism. The aged Professor Chauvet dies and makes her his heiress; she lives in Paris, where she is the "reigning beauty" of society. "She feels neither love nor hate." For the tone of its criticism (satire) this novel comes as a surpise, especially from this author.

196. Cory, Charles B[arney]. Montezuma's Castle, and Other Weird Tales. Boston: Author's Edition, 1899.

This is a group of weird tales, told realistically by and large, in which the oddities of the old Southwest come into play. In "Montezuma's Castle" the first-person narrator tells how he and a Mexican companion go to Montezuma's Castle, a cliff dwelling, to search for relics. His helper knocks down the ladder; the narrator shoots him and finally works his way down the cliff. "The White Tanks" recalls Bierce in that a practical joke is played on a half-breed Mexican Indian. He thinks that he has been bitten by a rattlesnake (whose fangs have been removed) and is frightened to death. "An Aztec Mummy" concerns the practice of faking relics. In "The Elixir of Life" the narrator plans to wait to see if a friend lives to be one hundred and fifty before he himself takes a wonderful powder obtained in the Far East.

197. [Coverdale, Henry Standish]. The Fall of the Great Republic. Boston: Roberts, 1885.

After the Civil War the United States becomes a haven for all the undesirables from Europe, especially socialists, nihilists, and Irish exiles. The Irish plan a number of brutal crimes, including an attempt to kill the Queen and her cabinet. Various socialist societies provoke strikes and riots in such cities as Wheeling, Pittsburgh, and Chicago. Hard times occur as a result between 1882 and 1887. By 1887 two-and-a-half million Americans are unemployed. On July 18 workers lay down their tools and demand both an eight-hour-day and a 50% increase in wages. Fighting results. When their embassies are attacked,

Britain, France and Germany declare war, and their forces occupy the United States. Recounted by a first-person narrator in 1895, this narrative is prepared for the Board of European Administration in the Province of New York. It implies that a new spirit of independence is beginning to take form and may lead to further revolution. This is significant as an early dystopia.

198. Cowan, Frank. _Revi-Lona; A Romance of Love in a Marvelous Land_. Greensburg, Pa.: Tribune, 188?.

In a prefatory statement Cowan outlines the basic story of the novel: a Pennsylvanian journeys to the South Pole, discovers a temperate land inhabited by prehistoric creatures, and peopled by the remnants of an ancient continental race. It is a purely communistic state, "a perfect but petticoated paradise," where beautiful women govern "little and learned men," and where love has been suppressed for ages. Given to drink and promiscuity, the first-person narrator makes love to each of the twenty-five women who make up the governing council. The resultant jealousy and rivalry lead first to suicide and murder and then to civil war. He also brings with him such diseases as smallpox, measles, and syphilis, which decimate the population. A series of natural catastrophes, including a flood, destroys the land itself. His wives--including his favorite, Nada-nana--and many children are frozen to death aboard the ship he arrived on. He is picked up by another ship and returned to America. _Revi-Lona_ if far more than a satire on the communistic state; it must also be read as an attack upon the societies portrayed in the lost race motif, as well as a comment upon the actual effect of the impact of America and Europe upon the islands of the South Seas.

199. Cowan, James. _Daybreak; A Romance of an Old World_. New York: Richmond, 1896.

In _Daybreak_ the protagonist and his companion explore both the moon and Mars. To solve the problem of transportation, the moon falls from the sky, coming to rest in the Pacific basin. Once the protagonist reaches its surface by balloon, some force repels it from Earth and it becomes a temporary satellite of Mars. He finds the moon now dead, though once a fertile planet. On Mars, a utopian civilization in advance of Earth exists, though none of its technology is described in detail. The Martian Thorwald takes the defense of Christianity one step further; he asserts that Christ was incarnated on Mars as well as Earth. In a prefatory note Cowan declares that Christ must be incarnated on every world.

200. Cox, A[nthony] B[erkeley]. The Professor on Paws. New York: Dial Press, 1927.

> Also published in Britain by Collins (1926): Professor Dulverton theorizes that one can transfer the brain cells of someone just dead to another being and have them work. Professor Ridgeley is thus transformed into a small black cat. He can speak, learns to dance, and likes to be clothed. Soon, as a cat, he begins to have lapses of memory when the operation wears off. Professor Cantrell marries Ridgeley's daughter Marjorie. At the end they sit before the fire; the cat lies by the fire near them with its kittens.

201. Cox, Erle. Out of the Silence. New York: Henkle, 1928.

> Originally published in Australia by E.A. Vidler (1925): in Australia an archaeologist, Alan Dundas, finds a vault in which three survivors of an ancient, advanced civilization have been placed in suspended animation. With the aid of a medical friend, Barry, he revives the woman, Earani, and falls in love with her. Barry is afraid of her; she begins to take over Australia preparatory to taking over the world. Marian, a woman who loves Alan and of whom he had been fond, knifes Earani, killing her. Dundas commits suicide in order to be with her, but first he destroys all artifacts of the ancient civilization.

202. Craig, Alexander. Ionia; Land of Wise Men and Fair Women. Chicago: Weeks, 1898.

> Helen Musgrave, a wealthy widow, hopes to turn Chingford, Surrey, into an ideal village. Her son meets a Greek named Delphos, who tells him of Ionia, an isolated valley in the Himalayas. Founded by the Greeks, mostly Athenian, at the time of Alexander, its only entrance was sealed shut by dynamite about 1575 to avoid the threat of Mongol invasion. It was anti-Semitic; when Jewish bankers controlled all its money, laws were passed so that Jews could not marry. They died out. Most of the laws are still those passed by Timoleon, an early philosopher-king. Eugenics rule; marriage is strictly controlled; inheritance is limited; all private transactions are cash; wholesale business must operate on a monthly cycle. No rakes are allowed, and its women are pure, although the "social evil" is regulated. Women who "sacrifice" themselves to the community are regarded as "public benefactors" and are given comfortable accomodations as well as maintenance when they grow old. Musgrave and Delphos travel to the valley. Electricity is the source of all power, but none of the advanced technology is described. Education is not uniform but is granted to the highest extent that the individual child warrants. The novel closes with the suggestion that labor unions restrict invention lest it deprive the workers of

labor.   The suggestion is made that perhaps the time has come to be concerned about quality, not quantity.   A final salute is given America as the country where the golden age of dreams may become a reality.

203.   Craig, Colin [pseud. of Henry Spencer Booth].   A Suitor from the Stars.   Baltimore, Md.: Thomas & Evans, 1928.

Dedicated to Hugo Gernsback, "Author, Editor, and Scientist": the author explains that Baird told him the story some years ago in a camp in the Cascades.   After asserting that science has a great future when it goes beyond materialism to be concerned with matters of the spirit, Baird introduces the mysterious Professor Alexandrei, an archaeologist, who becomes head of the department at the university and wishes to marry Baird's cousin, Kathleen, who is unreceptive to him.   One night Baird awakens to find that the body of a colleague, Smith, has been possessed by Prince Kiromar of the planet Sotherion somewhere near the nebula of Orion.   Ten thousand years ago he loved Princess Atheia; while he and other volunteers went in search of the central world of the universe which is the abode of the "ULTIMATE WILL," an arch criminal, Atheopher, escaped and kidnapped her.   Kiromar has traced them to Earth, where he believes Atheopher has imprisoned them in the flesh. Kiromar expects the warrant for Atheopher's arrest momentarily.   Kathleen has suddenly agreed to marry Alexandrei, but when the wedding comes, she has disappeared.   Among her effects is a likeness of Kiromar; by implication, then, she was Atheia.   Kiromar has explained that Earth has served as a penal colony for those who have violated the Law of Cosmic Harmony.   The author implies that Baird himself may have returned to Sotherian.

204.   Cram, Ralph Adams.   Black Spirits and White; A Book of Ghost Stories.   Chicago: Stone & Kimball, 1895.

The only notable story is "The Dead Valley"; Olof Ehrensvard and his companion Nils go into the mountains one night and find a small valley filled with an ashy white, slightly phosphorescent fog.   Their dog dies.   Three weeks later both are ill with a fever.   Olof returns alone to find a great dead tree surrounded by a wilderness of small bones.

205.   Crawford, Isabell C.   The Tapestry of Time.   Boston: Christopher, 1927.

Another pseudo-historical fantasy involving the sinking of Atlantis: when King Lumnos of Atlantis ignores Astrellon's warning that the continent is about to be destroyed, Astrellon takes his followers to Peru, where they found a great city.   The high priest, Memhota, experiments with the atom, already harnessed by Astrellon, and brings about the sinking of Atlantis.   King Lumnos is rescued by a prince of

Crete, and they develop the village of Athros into a city.
Thus does the culture of Atlantis survive. Once again the
theme is that love remains the key to life. Egypt and
Greece are gone, but in the Peruvian heights the remains of
a temple still exist.

206. Crawford, T[heron] C[lark].   The Disappearance Syndicate
and Senator Stanley's Story. New York: Reed, 1894.

Both stories originally appeared in Cosmopolitan: Arthur
Livingstone, a journalist, learns of a series of disappearances of wealthy men throughout the world. A friend
suggests that a syndicate must exist to promote such
disappearances. Through Mortimer Mortimer, an adept
hypotist, he learns that a secret society exists which
wishes to eradicate crime and poverty. Some of its members, however, have left the original society, act in self
interest, and are responsible for the major crimes in
Europe. Livingstone becomes a member of the Circle of
Light. Senator Stanley tells his own story; he is possessed and made to act philanthropically, though despising
those whom he benefitted. He has a contempt for the public
and its wishes. He dies suddenly after voting against the
ouster of Senator Backus. Transformed into a blue man-
drill, he kills himself. "Napoleon Wolff" deals with a
newspaperman who wishes to keep watch on public figures so
they cannot do evil. He is aided by Wolff, who also
develops an airplane powered by anti-gravity.

207. Crawley, Rayburn.   Chattering Gods.   New York: Harper,
1931.

With his wife Joan, Ned Shackleton returns to the valley of
creeping men looking for the yellow ape, while Frank
Merrington searches for a chemical which will revolutionize
the world. Ned finds Sergius Marakoff's daughter Marnia,
who has been left in the care of the Russian peasant, Igor,
and has the yellow ape as a companion. Igor knows that
Marakoff has set up some kind of experiment, but beyond
thinking that it will somehow "test civilization" does not
know its nature. Marnia is attracted to Ned, who makes
love to her, thus alienating Joan. Marnia leads Ned into
the valley to the ruins of an ancient temple containing a
vast amount of jewels. The black apes of the inner valley
(the creeping men because they sometimes walk upright) go
berserk and pull down the ruins of the temple onto themselves. Marnia and Ned are trapped underground but are
rescued. Igor is killed. Joan finds a letter from Marakoff to Ned, in which Marakoff asserts that one of his
experiments is to test Ned's pride and honor; he insists
that Marnia will cause Ned to be unfaithful to Joan. Joan
destroys the letter before Ned sees it, but Ned confesses
that he was unfaithful. They are reunited, for he rejects
his passion for Marnia.

208. Crawley, Rayburn. The Valley of Creeping Men. New York:
Harper, 1930.

> Dr. Sergius Marakoff experiments with a yellow gorilla.
> When he is murdered, the gorilla disappears, as do a sum of
> money and all of Marakoff's notes regarding his psycho-
> logical experiments attempting to link the workings of the
> human mind to those of the lower animals. Ned Shackleton,
> an American scientist, is trying to gain access to the
> valley to find the gorilla, while Frank Merrington looks
> for a new chemical (he believes the valley to be rich in
> radium). His sister Joan (Jo-John) arrives, declaring that
> she sees no reason men should have a corner on adventure.
> She and Ned fall in love. Instructions from Marakoff tell
> Ned to seek the yellow ape, but the action breaks off.

209. Cromie, Robert. The Crack of Doom. London: Digby, Long,
1895.

> In a prefatory note Cromie says that he has assembled the
> story from notes given him by the narrator. Arthur Marcel,
> a doctor, is the first-person narrator. He tells the story
> of Herbert Brande, a physicist who believes that there is
> no real order in nature and that the world is a mistake.
> He has the ability to achieve the transmutation of metals
> into gold. He and a colleague, Grey, who has gone to
> Labrador, plan an experiment which may destroy the world
> because it involves atomic power. Brande does succeed in
> blowing up an island as well as a French fishing fleet.
> Marcel returns to London with a friend, Edith Metford, but
> he has no money and is not sure whether or not Brande did
> have the power or was simply mad. The secret, of course,
> dies with Brande.

210. Cromie, Robert. El Dorado. London: Ward, Lock, 1904.

> Much time is spent characterizing Dr. Maurice Whitmore,
> Alexander Mackenzie, and Marie Reinitz, who will undertake
> an expedition up the Amazon to find a lost city which once
> housed the first civilization of the world even before
> Babylon. Julius Kleinpaul joins them. After a detailed
> account of their journey, they arrive at the "Eden of the
> West" and begin excavations where protagonist Reinitz once
> worked. They discover gold, but Kleinpaul goes to the
> Brazilian government. A ship stops them as they sail, but
> they face down the confrontation and depart for England.
> Reinitz wants the gold to sponsor a United States of South
> America. There is the suggestion that Whitmore and Marie
> are in love.

211. Cromie, Robert. For England's Sake. London: Warne, 1889.

> England defeats Russia, who has tried to take over India.

212. Cromie, Robert.   From the Cliffs of Croaghaun.   Akron,
Oh.: Saalfield, 1904.

     This is the American title of El Dorado.

213. Cromie, Robert.   The Next Crusade.   London: Hutchinson,
1896.

     In an introductory note Cromie asserts that when he wrote
     For England's Sake, he did not "foresee" that hostilities
     would be renewed on a vaster scale on another continent;
     the action of this novel takes place soon after that of the
     earlier one.   After Turkish atrocities in Albania and
     Macedonia, Austria vows to drive Turkey from Europe, al-
     though conflict does not begin for a year. The nations of
     the Balkans and Great Britain join Austria, while Russia
     sides with Turkey, hoping to get Constantinople for her-
     self. At one point British destroyers and transports fight
     German torpedo boats. The Balkan nations are incorporated
     into the Austrian Empire, while from "Constantinople on the
     east [to] Gilbraltar on the west, the Mediterranean was at
     last a British lake."   Despite the attention to military
     matters, much of the narrative is a love story, primarily
     between Lieutenant Cameron and May Winton.   As an added
     touch, Cameron discovers that her supposedly dead sister
     did not die until recently when she served as a British
     agent, as did her half-Greek daughter, Janita.

214. Cromie, Robert.   A Plunge Through Space.   London: Warne,
1890.

     By the use of a Steel Globe developed by Henry Barnett, he,
     Alexander MacGregor, and their party journey to Mars.   For
     a time there seems to be nothing there but shifting sand,
     but they discover the City of Delight, capital of an
     advanced utopian civilization.   Dr. Profoundis becomes
     their tutor, and they learn that the peninsula of Lagrange,
     where the city is located, is much like Great Britain,
     especially in that through its soldiers, merchants, mis-
     sionaries, and colonists it had become the leader of a
     "consolidated and enlightened people."   Much of the story-
     line concerns the love of Durand for the fair Mignonette,
     daughter of Dr. Profoundis.   When they leave Mars, she
     comes aboard as a stowaway and inadvertently damages the
     air tanks.   When they realize that they may make it to
     Earth if their number is one less, Mignonette throws
     herself into space.   By increasing their speed to 100,000
     miles per minute, they barely make it, but Durand, maddened
     by the loss of Mignonette, blows up the ship with Barnett
     aboard it.   This ending remains unique for the period.
     Jules Verne wrote a single-page introduction praising
     Cromie.

215. Crosby, Edward Harold. Radiana. Boston: Ivy Press, 1906.

When the protagonist, Amory, attempts suicide, Dr. Groebel saves him; he will make the young man his heir, but insists he change his name to Harry Merwin and do his bidding. He is sent to Chicago to the home of Alexander Douglass; he is questioned and would be made a prisoner, but Katherine Grey, Douglass' niece, intervenes. She tells him Groebel has developed a small dynamo which can stun a man. When Groebel takes a trip, Stillman, a secret service man enters, saying he is after Douglass, a counterfeiter. When Katherine's father died, Douglass tried to find a secret which he thought her father had. On a yacht at Newport they encounter a submarine; Douglass takes Merwin prisoner and asks for Groebel's secret, suggesting Germany would pay well for it. Stillman rescues Merwin, and Douglass is drowned. Groebel's secret is that he can produce radium, which is capable of increasing one's life span. Douglass has used him, obtaining radium from him and killing his son. Merwin and Katherine have fallen in love. Groebel opposes the marriage, but he kills himself experimenting with a new formula. Merwin and Katherine wed.

216. Crosby, Ernest. Captain Jinks; Hero. New York: Funk & Wagnalls, 1902.

This is a hilarious satire of militarism and American imperialism. Sam Jinks' parents buy lead soldiers for him as a birthday present. This begins a chain of events which take him through "the John Wesley Boys Brigade" and East Point to the Cubapines. Germany also comes in for attack (Tutonia). Jinks fails to become a successfuul candidate for the presidency, largely because he discriminates against some of the women's groups, especially in the eastern part of the country, by not kissing them all. The novel ends with a scene in which he plays with his toy soldiers.

217. Cross, Victoria. Martha Brown, M.P., A Girl of Tomorrow. London: Laurie, 1935.

In a novel presenting the most complete reversal of sex roles of any in the period, women rule and have brought peace to the world. Martha tells her husband James that a woman has her own life to live, her own aspirations to fulfill. He has the house to care for and the three children she "sacrificed four years . . . practically" to give him. Her England knows no unemployment or dole (workers are exported to the empire); society is vegetarian; the air is clean; there is no prostitution, but there is free love. Martha has a brief, passionate affair with an Italian artist, Matteo, and an old lover Gerald Kingsley turns up. An American, Bruce Campbell, begins a kind of courtship. He saves her when Gerald tries to shoot her. In an ending that seems to deny most of what has gone on before, "the magnetic current" of Campbell's will drowns "all resistance" to him. She goes with him so that in a sense romantic love triumphs.

218. Cruger, Mary. <u>Hyperaesthesia</u>. New York: Fords, Howard, Hulbert, 1886.

Dr. Frank Hilton is tortured by the memory of the death of his fiancée, to whom he was engaged after a brief shipboard flirtation. Ten years later the girl's mother haunts him, pretending that she is the girl's ghost. Hilton and his patient, Clare Ashton, who suffers from physical hyper-aesthesia, undergo much stress. The haunting ends only after another doctor investigates and proves the girl dead. A transitional story, the novel has some importance because it links physical and mental illness and because Hilton treats Clare Ashton wtih hypnosis.

219. Crump, Irving. <u>Mog the Mound Builder</u>. New York: Dodd, Mead, 1931.

Crump wrote this book in response to the request that he tell the story of an American prehistoric boy to match those of his European, Og. Mog-an-ah must search for his father who has disappeared, or at least he must return his body to be placed in the village mound. In addition to various encounters with animals, this means that he must brave the Algonquins. He finds his father a prisoner of the Algonquins and rescues him, although this results in a battle between the Long Heads, Mog's people, and the Algonquins, who include Shawnees and Ojibways.

220. Crump, Irving. <u>Og of the Cave People</u>. New York: Dodd, Mead, 1935.

The action begins with young Tao, who allows the fire to go out. Left to find his own food that day, he is captured by Flatheads but kills a giant lizard which has terrorized them. The leader asks Og and his people to help kill a monster living in the mist. They do. Subsequent adven-tures involve hunting mammoths and conducting war against the Red Beards.

221. Crump, Irving. <u>Og--Son of Fire</u>. New York: Dodd, Mead, 1922.

Og and two wolf cubs are marooned by a fire which has devastated the valley. From this he learns the use of fire and so assumes authority. He undergoes the usual adven-tures of a youthful caveman. Most interesting is an element of racism: captured by the tree people, a kind of ape man, he learns that their skin is black. They are a different race, one that is thousands of years behind Og and his people and will remain so throughout history.

222. Crump, Irving. Og, Son of Og. New York: Dodd, Mead, 1965.

This is the last of Crump's prehistoric stories; he says that what he has done for one generation of readers, he hopes to do for another. Og, the young protagonist, has been stolen from the Cave People by the ape band. He escapes during the confusion following the killing of his protectors (the female who has substituted him for a babe she lost) by other members of the band. His adventures are typical of such a narrative: the taming of wolf cubs, encounters with mammoths and sabre tooth tigers. A Flat-head saves him from a giant octopus, and together with a second Flathead, they overcome the evil medicine man who leads the Red Beards. Og shows his companions how to make fire. They are reunited with his people after an avalanche almost kills them.

223. Cruso, Solomon. The Last of the Japs and the Jews. New York: Lefkowitz, 1933.

This novel must qualify as probably the worst example of racism during the period. Written as future history, it is dedicated to "the Caucasian Race, the white Aryans," who died in world-wide battle 1980-1985. In 1942 the capita-list nations combined against the Soviets and soon overran all of Russia. Kiril I was named Czar and was admired as much as Mussolini. In a terrible storm the Pacific "swal-lowed up" Japan, leaving no survivors. At a 1962 banquet the Russain ambassador (who was then assassinated) sug-gested that all Asiatics should go where the Japanese went. By the end of the 1960s war between the West and the East begins (the Nanking Republican Government--Kuoming-tang--has been overthrown by Mongols). Great battles rage. Eleven million Jews are systematically killed in their sleep, European white armies are annihilated, and America, although she fought valiantly, is overwhelmed. Apparently at some point around 1985 the American Indians took command of the western hemisphere. Despite the apparent annihi-lation of almost everyone, in 2490 Indian armies are on the alert to repel any white invaders. Incidental in this slaughter is a love story between a Chinese prince and the daughter of a Mexican ambassador; she retreated to a convent.

224. Cummings, Ray[mond King]. Brigands of the Moon. Chicago: A.C. McClurg, 1931.

The first-person narrator, Gregg Haljan, is aboard the spaceship Planetera, which is seized by Martian pirates under the command of Miko--with aid from traitors. The

Martians hope to steal radium from the Grantline Treasure Camp on the Earth's moon. Haljan causes the ship to crash. After a long siege the Martian effort ends when Haljan kills Miko in single combat. Mao, Miko's sister, loved Haljan and kills herself after defeat. Haljan is in love with Anita Prince, although he was also attracted to the Venusian dancer, Alta Venza, who dies during battle.

225. Cummings, Ray[mond King].   The Girl in the Golden Atom. New York: Harper, 1923.

This novel fuses two of Cummings' novelettes originally published in All-Story: "The Girl in the Golden Atom" (1919) and "The People in the Golden Atom" (1920). The narrative opens as Rogers, the "chemist," tells a group of friends that in an atom of his mother's wedding ring he has discovered a sub-atomic universe in which a beautiful woman lives. Before their eyes he uses a chemical which reduces his size; after forty-eight hours he returns to tell of his love for the Princess Lylda. He returns to her. (The first novelette makes up the first eight chapters of the novel.) After five years his friends also enter the sub-atomic world. Much of this portion of the story centers upon the love of "the very young man" and Aura, the sister of Lylda. The main action involves the villainous Targo, who seizes power and rules the Oroids; to prevent his acquistion of the size-changing drugs, the Earthmen, with Lylda and Aura, return to this world and spend their first Christmas in upper New York state.

226. Cummings, Ray[mond King].   The Man Who Mastered Time. Chicago: A.C. McClurg, 1929.

While experimenting, for a moment the Chemist is able to see far into the future; he watches a beautiful young girl struggling against a man who tries to kiss her. Loto, the son of Rogers and Lylda, discovers how to cross time; he finds the girl but must return without her. The second time that he goes, he rescues Azeela from Toroh, but Toroh's barbaric hordes seize control of Orleen, the city which her father rules. Her father releases thunderbolts (by implication atomic energy) which destroy the city and all in it. Loto and Azeela return to New York City.

227. Cummings, Ray[mond King].   The Sea Girl.   Chicago: A.C. McClurg, 1930.

In 1990 some of the Pacific volcanoes become active and the ocean levels begin to recede. Jeff Grant, the narrator; Dr. Plantet, an oceanographer; and his daughter Polly and son Arturo go to Micronesia to investigate. After an interlude between Arturo and a mermaid whom he calls Nereid, Arturo does report that a race, the Gian, seek to conquer the world. Nereid's people, the Middge, who live even deeper, are also threatened with destruction. The narrator and the Plantets descend into the kingdom of the Gian. Their queen, Rhana, loves Jeff and thinks he loves Nereid. Jeff overcomes the plot of Rhana to release a plague upon the surface; she dies as the Middge destroy her kingdom in a series of explosions. They, too, disappear, although plans to search for them are mentioned. Jeff and Polly and Arturo and Nereid are in love.

228. Cummings, Ray[mond King]. <u>Tarrano, the Conqueror</u>. Chicago: A.C. McClurg, 1930.

The first-person narrator, Jac Hallen, is nearby as the President of the Anglo-Saxon Republic is assassinated. This is the first killing as Tarrano takes control of all the governments of Earth. Hallen goes to Dr. Brende, who has discovered a way to make humanity immortal. A message from Venus, sent just before it falls to Tarrano, warns of his threat. He desires the immortality elixir as well as power. Hallen goes to Venus and aids the Princess Maida, who leads resistance. Tarrano kidnaps the Lady Elza, Brende's daughter, and she must be rescued. Tarrano destroys much of the capital city with a poisonous black cloud. Eventually he is defeated and exiled. Hallen and Maida are lovers.

229. Cummins, Harle Owen. <u>Welsh Rarebit Tales</u>. Boston: Mutual, 1902.

At least two stories suggest the influence of Ambrose Bierce. In "The Fool and His Joke" the protagonist wagers that he can disinter a corpse at midnight and stay with it until morning in a haunted house. He dies of fright. In "The Man Who Was Not Afraid" the protagonist bets that he can enter a mausoleum and take a string of pearls from the throat of a recently deceased woman. By error he opens the coffin containing the body of a tramp mutilated by a train. Discovered in the morning, he is quite mad as he plays with parts of the tramp's body. The Frankenstein theme forms the basis of "The Man Who Made a Man," while a device is developed in "The Space Annihilator" which can instantaneously transport objects long distances.

230. Dail, C[harles] C[urtis]. <u>The Stone Giant; A Story of the Mammoth Cave</u>. New York: Neely, 1898.

The iron box near the Stone Giant in Mammoth Caves produces the manuscript memoirs of Wymorian, once king of Atlantis, described as the first of the world's republics. Essentially this is another of the pseudo-historical novels of prehistory. What makes it different is that Wymorian and his people go through the caverns connected with Mammoth Cave and find a world inside the Earth. When the crops which produce the Elixir of Life die in a drought, Wymorian leaves the kingdom to his children and travels upward toward Mammoth Cave. As he feels death approaching, he writes his memoirs; after death his body turns into the stone giant.

231. Dail, C[harles] C[urtis]. Willmoth, the Wanderer; or, The Man from Saturn. Atchison, Ks.: Haskell, 1890.

The nameless first-person narrator (presumably Dail) gains Willmoth's confidence and thus is given an account of his travels on Saturn, Venus, and Earth. A hatred of the church and a belief in progressive evolution seem the dominant themes. On Saturn his native city, Eathmon, houses a vegetarian, polygamous society. There, too, he finds a land of giant apes involved in tribal wars; a gluttonous race, the Tlakes, who remind him of humanity; and the fragile "Rosemen," who drink attar of roses and live for thousands of years. In one subterranean kingdom he discovers the beautiful Zea, who becomes his bride and traveling companion. On Venus, queen Onana tells him that once the men of her kingdom competed and waged war, but now the women rule; they also do the courting. He encounters the black Ophars, who enslave a dwarf race of whites as laborers and field hands. On Earth he helps the Tarths, man's giant predecessors, by breeding them, but earthquakes destroy all but a single "first man" who presents revised accounts of the events of Genesis. Exploring Mammoth Cave, he finds a kingdom within the Earth. He travels both with Zea until she dies and is buried on an asteroid that plunges into the sun, and with the astronomer Elwer, who invented the "flying chair" as a convenient vehicle. Throughout the work giantism is a condition of barbarism. Willmoth is virtually unique among extraterrestrial visitants in that both on Saturn and Venus, especially, he praises the pleasures of sexuality.

232. Dake, Charles Romyn. A Strange Discovery. New York: Kimball, 1899.

Dake's novel provides a possible conclusion to Edgar Allan Poe's The Narrative of Arthur Gordon Pym. Its English, first-person narrator finds Pym's companion, Dirk Peters, dying in Bellevue, Illinois. Befriending Doctors Castleton and Bainbridge, who are treating Peters, the narrator and doctors interrupt the narrative frequently with discussions of the Romantic movement in literature, American politics and economics, the current state of medical practice, and a summary of Poe's story for those who have not read it. Bainbridge is the one who tells Peter's story. After Pym and Peters penetrate the veil, they find the city of Hili-li, inhabited by citizens of the Roman empire who fled the barbarian invasions of the fourth century. One ship reached the Antarctic. They represent the height of Greco-Roman culture; though mentally advanced, they have made no

practical application of their knowledge.   Pym falls in
love with Lilama; so great is their devotion that "the
episode of Romeo and Juliet sinks into insignificance" when
compared to it.   After parental objection, kidnapping by a
rival suitor Ahpilus, and an attack by barbarians, they
marry.   Within months occurs "the strange thermal phenomenon" which occasionally devastates the city; the winds
shift so that a combination of a hurricane and a blizzard
strikes Hili-li.   The city is unprepared.   Pym goes in
search of food and fuel, while Lilama is among those who
freeze to death.   After her death the Hili-lites permit
Pym, highly depressed, and Peters to depart in a small
boat; they are picked up by a ship which takes them to
Montevideo, where they separate and never see one another
again.

233. Daniel, Charles S.   Ai; A Social Vision.   Philadelphia:
Miller, 1892.

This may be read as a parody of the utopian novel.   In 1950
Alice and Enid Hamilton (twins) marry the Burr brothers and
stir up Philadelphia's fashionable society.   Alice becomes
a medical adviser to the poor, especially children, while
Enid draws up plans for a tenement.   Ai, a social worker
who is elected an Episcopal bishop, advocates various
reforms, but he dies before any are effectively carried
out.   Members of all denominations join together at his
funeral.   Yet he has said that "man is an animal" and can
be improved only by the "principles of Natural Selection."
He means eugenics and breeding.

234. Davenport, Benjamin Rush. Anglo-Saxons, Onward; A Romance
of the Future. Cleveland: Hubbell, 1908.

Delighted because the victory over Spain in 1898 opened "a
new vista of . . . grandeur and glory" to the United
States, the novel focuses upon the career of John Morrison
as he rises through the ranks to become first general and
then president.   He helps defeat a European coalition which
attacks Halifax; later as the commander of Federal troops
stationed in Argentina to defend that country against the
threat of Italy, he defeats the enemy there.   His daughter,
Helen, becomes the heroine of a rebellion at Montevideo,
which is defeated.   Not only does Morrison make treaties
with the nations of South America, but he is also instrumental in bringing about an alliance between the U.S. and
Britian.   This occurs only after British and American
forces defeat a combination of Turkey and Russia; the
fighting in the Middle East becomes something of a crusade.
The storyline during that portion of the novel focuses upon
George Howard, a graduate of V.M.I., who assumes command of
the forces.   For a time he falls under the spell of the
"magnetic sexuality" of Princess Vera Gourkoff, a "Northern
Venus," who is at the heart of the conspiracy joining

Turkey and Russia. But Howard survives temptation to marry
Helen Morrison.

235. Day, Oscar F[ayette] G[aines]. The Devil's Gold, The
Story of a Forgotten Race. Chicago: Morrill, Higgins, 1892.

Day receives a manuscript from Captain Harold C. Starkey
given him by a friend aboard his ship bound for China.
Starkey suggests that he himself later explored the kingdom
in the mountains of southeast Oregon. Jilted by Bernice
Crawford, Harlow S. Ritchie and his friends travel across
the Isthmus to California and there translate a message on
a flask which leads them to gold. They penetrate a system
of caverns, are isolated there by a dynamite blast but
first find the largest mass of virgin gold the world has
ever known, and then emerge into the valley kingdom of
Nahaeco and the city of Sharrai inhabited by the Dumachas.
Perhaps the distinguishing feature of this pastoral society
is that it limits population. The "brilliant dark beauty"
of Princess Nanona is celebrated, but the novel is more
noteworthy because of its criticism of the fickleness of
women as illustrated by the jilting of Ritchie.

236. Dean, Frederic Alva. The Heroines of Petoséga. New York:
Hawthorne, 1889.

In a "Key to the Novel" Dean explains that the action takes
place some thirty centuries ago: the city of Petoséga and
island of Effelda (now Mackinac Island), the nation of
Zoatia in what is now the South Pacific, and "heroic
Athens." Another pseudo-history, this narrative dwells
upon the threat to Petoséga of the barbarian Monhegans and
a new glacial age. They are apparently of Grecian origin,
and a surviving couple returns to Greece.

237. DeCamp, Etta. Return of Frank Stockton; Stories and
Letters Which Cannot Fail to Convince the Reader that Frank
Stockton Still Lives and Writes through the Instrumentality of
Miss Etta DeCamp. New York: Macoy, 1913.

A minor item noteworthy only for its emphasis on mediumship. She suggests that a book by William T. Stead brought
automatic writing to her attention in 1909.

238. de Madariaga [y Rojo], Salvador. The Sacred Giraffe,
Being the Second Volume of the Posthumous Works of Julio Arceval. New York: Harper, 1931.

Originally published by Hopkinson in England (1925): this
manuscript edited by a friend of the author regrets that
the first volume, Notes on England, must wait. Arceval
disappeared mysteriously "in the sea" in 1920. The narrative projects a society in 6922 in which women are dominant
and men care for the families. The white race and Europe

are legendary, for the black Ebonites are the race portrayed. Calling the sexes "natural adversaries," the
author proposes that while physical strength belongs to
men, both the forces of mind and will belong to women. If
control of public life is given to men, women "evolve" so
that they lose the qualities of leadership.

239. DeMille, James. A Strange Manuscript Found in a Copper
Cylinder. New York: Harper, 1888.

At the outset the novel echoes Poe and Symmes. Reputedly
the manuscript of an English sailor, Thomas More, shipwrecked in the Antarctic in 1843, More reports how he is
swept through subterranean caverns to a temperate land at
the South Pole. He falls in love with the maid, Almah, a
sentimental love story complicated by the queen, Layelah,
who seemingly loves More. Some of the narrative analyzes
the Kosekin society, which is antipodal to that of the
outer world in that poverty, squalor, and death are most
highly regarded. (If DeMille intended to achieve a social
satire, he failed.) A series of hunting episodes encounter
various prehistoric monsters, ranging from giant birds akin
to the dodo to a dinosaur akin to the triceratops and a
sea-serpent. At the end More and Almah will rule the land.
What makes the novel unique, however, is its framing
device; DeMille opens the novel aboard a becalmed yacht
near the Canary Islands. Its owner, Lord Featherstone, and
his companions fish More's manuscript out of the sea and
read it. At three points they interrupt the reading to
speculate about the validity of its contents; once they
debate whether it is a sensational novel or a scientific
romance. Thus a variety of scientific and technical data
are introduced. This technique makes notable an otherwise
imitative romance which attacks nineteenth century materialism.

240. [De Morgan, John]. "Bess." A Companion to "Jess." New
York: Munro, 1887.

The weakest parody of Haggard: in London Captain Henry
Waldo Adair encounters Captain John Neil, an old friend.
Neil has married Bessie Croft, whose sister Jess is dead.
Adair receives and edits the memoirs of both Niel and Bess.
Against a thin background of the Transvaal dominated by the
villainous Frank Muller, who wishes to marry Bess, the two
narratives tell of a triangle. Bess loves Niel, who has
proposed to her; Jess loves Neil and tells him so. When
Bess is apparently to be forced to marry Muller, Jess kills
him and dies in Niel's arms. Bess marries Niel, knowing
that he loves Jess, and of course their daughter is named
for the deceased sister. Allan Quatermain is a friend of
Neil's and proposes to Jess, but is rejected.

241. De Morgan, John. "He," A Companion to "She". New York:
Munro, 1887.

> Published in England by Longman (1887) and attributed to
> John Lang and Walter H. Pollock by the British Museum: John
> Theodosius Aristophano and Captain Fjord acquire an old
> manuscript from the time of Khung-fu-Tsze [Confucius]
> telling of the settlement of an island to which "He the
> Mighty," a white man, comes to represent the god Tabu. The
> two travel to a Pacific island, Rapa Nui, where they are
> given native women as wives. Then the principal actions of
> Haggard's novel are parodied. Alethea, a marble goddess,
> comes alive to woo Theo and reject He; the founder of
> Theo's family was Kallikrates. She dies; He perishes in a
> column of fire. Though the reader recognizes the obvious
> parody, part of its success comes from the straight,
> serious tone which the author has captured.

242. De Morgan, John. It. New York: Munro, 1887.

> Aristophano and Captain Fjord join Quatermain, Good, and
> Sir Henry Curtis in Africa to search for the kingdom of
> Oph. They find it ruled by Shebina, who gives herself in
> marriage to Sir Henry; he remains with her as King Incubu.
> Aristophano is loved by the native Queega, who dies. They
> also encounter the Homonos, the missing link. At one point
> Aristophano, the narrator, refers to his adventures with
> Fjord on the island of Rapa Nui. The narrative has much
> the same tone as He.

243. De Morgan, John. King Solomon's Treasures. New York:
Munro, 1887.

> The first-person narrator, Arthur Montmorency, and Jack
> O'Brien undertake a journey to Africa to find Solomon's
> treasures. Aboard ship Montmorency falls in love with the
> queenly Nyassa Balkis, one of whose guardians is the banker
> Novarro. Because he is poor, he will not ask for her hand.
> The narrative then becomes a travelogue as they encounter
> various tribes and wonders, including the ruins of the
> Queen of Sheba's palace and Solomon's triumphal arch.
> Their man Medjid falls in love with a Troglodyte girl,
> Shagaffa, and marries her on their return. Conveniently
> Navarro has a daughter named Nyassa, whom Jack marries.
> The discovery of a crystal statue proves that Montmorency's
> Nyassa is indeed the descendant of Solomon. Of them all
> this is the least obvious parody; its tone is straight and
> serious, while none of its discoveries blatantly satirizes
> Haggard, as do He, It, and King Solomon's Wives. In New
> York the International Book Company published an edition of
> this novel, undated. That edition names as additional
> parodies the titles "Ma" and "Pa."

244. De Morgan, John (as Hyder Ragged). King Solomon's Wives; or, The Phantom Mines. New York: Munro, 1887.

Published in England by Vizetelly (1887) and attributed variously to Andrew Lang or Sir Henry Charles Biron: the first-person narrator, Ananias Quarterman, with his companions, Sir Harry and Captain Noegood, venture to Africa in search of the mines of the Great King. His native servant is named Umbugs, while two others, Joss and Boss, are immediately killed by an elephant and a lion. They go into the kingdom of Twosh, who gives up his throne to Umbugs. Sir Harry has ridden a tricycle across the desert. In a cavern within a mountain they find effigies of Solomon's "seven hundred wives and three hundred ----," together with a pyramid of wedding cakes. They return to England in the balloon of Dr. Carlyon, who had fallen over "the biggest waterfall in South America and discovered a new city." Direct reference is made to Jules Verne, whom Umbugs has not read. When Captain Noegood does not marry the native girl, Fullarder, she sues him for breach of promise and collects "heavy damages." This is a broad burlesque rather than a skilled parody; yet references to such matters as Tennyson's "Locksley Hall" suggest that the author could have been British.

245. de Pereyra, Diomedes. The Land of the Golden Scarabs. Indianapolis, In.: Bobbs-Merrill, 1928.

Charles Sherwood and Eulogio Alba, two engineers of the All Ores Corp., land in Rio and begin a search that takes them across the Matto Grosso and up the Amazon River. The novel's significance lies in its wealth of realistic detail. They finally arrive in a valley full of gold; it holds descendants of the Incas living exactly as did their ancestors. Alba returns, taking enough gold to reimburse the company ten times over for its expenses. They wish to keep the valley a secret. Sherwood is known as Quilla-Aullo. Ima Sumac is the beautiful native woman.

246. d'Esme, Jean (pseud. of Jean d'Esmendard). The Red Gods ("Les Dieux Rouges"); A Romance. Trans. from the French by Moreby Acklom. New York: Dutton, 1924.

An introductory note suggests the idea for the novel originated in a passage in an official French report, "Les Jungles Moi," dated 1912. A later note says that the manuscript was discovered among the personal effects of Captain Jacques Bressand, who was killed on the Western Front in 1917. The narrative frame for the story itself is a dialogue in the opium den of Tsen-Tai between Bressand and Pierre de Lursac. From Saigon Lursac travels to Post 32, the third attempt the French have made to establish a base in the unexplored mountains of Moi (located in Laos). Wanda Redeska, sister of the commandant at Post 32, accompanies Lursac. They find a stone age race and a Khmer temple. More importantly, they find Father Ravennes, who has collected fossils, including a quarter of a skull, which he asserts comes from the ancient, equatorial continent, Gondwana. The priest dies; Wanda and her brother disappear; Post 32 is destroyed; and Lursac ends up in Saigon being cared for by the Sisters of Mercy. Released, he begins his conversation with Bressand.

247. Dessar, Leo Charles. A Royal Enchantress; The Romance of the Last Queen of the Berbers. New York: Continental, 1900.

Sometimes identified as a lost race novel, this should be classified as a pseudo-historical fantasy. Dessar asserts that he drew upon a brief passage in Gibbon describing Cahina, the beautiful Prophetess Queen of the Berbers. The narrative concentrates upon her reign, dated at the end of the seventh century, about 697.

248. Dickberry, F. (pseud. of F. Blaze de Bury). The Storm of London; A Social Rhapsody. London: Long, 1904.

Just as Lord Somerville attempts suicide, a strange electrical storm strikes London. Not until the end does the reader learn that Somerville experiences a dream-vision in which all clothing has vanished from London. Thus the distinction between social classes has disappeared. The satire is essentially comic, for without clothes, individuals no longer know the proper way to behave. Much is made of how hygiene has improved the human condition. An American Seer says that soon man will be able to read "the inner souls" of his fellow creatures; this will mark the next stage in advancement. This, too, may be part of the satire, for as the Seer is about to reveal his method publicly, Somerville awakens. He did wound himself, and Gwen Towerbridge has nursed him; consequently, she has heard all of his remarks during a convalescence of several months while he was unconscious. The doctor thinks him insane; Gwen shares his ideals resulting from the vision.

249. Diehl, Mrs. A[lice] M[angold]. Dr. Paull's Theory. New York: D. Appleton, 1893.

Published the same year in Bristol by Arrowsmith: a transitional novel, the narrative is essentially a love story involving the concept of reincarnation. After Dr. Hugh Paull's wife dies and as he becomes famous, at least two young women seem to be reincarnations of his wife. When the second young woman, Mercedes, dies, she sends him a note asking him to come to her; he dies.

250. Dieudonné, Florence Carpenter. Rondah; or, Thirty-Three Years in a Star. Philadelphia: Peterson, 1887.

The narrative is presented from four points of view. Roy Lee, Isabel, Regan Farmington, Father Renaudin, and Rondah are transported to a small world passing close to the Earth. They survive, although as the world goes farther into space because of the effect of the gravity of such planets as Jupiter, they must hibernate for a twenty-year, wintry period. Its inhabitants are huge birds, although apparently of vegetable origin. Although Regan calls them monsters, he also asserts that if there were a god he would not people all worlds alike. At one point Roy seems to kill Regan, but he does not die. The third narrator--the "historian"--tells of seeing the Earth, including Atlantis, from which he rescued a few survivors so that mankind might survive. They are granted visions of future wonders. The novel becomes increasingly mystical and concludes that "save for the clog of sin," there is no limit to what mankind may accomplish. "Man yet shall chain the stars; shall drive the harnessed worlds." One infers that the characters (and readers) are taken to the essentially primitive world in order to dramatize, or make vivid, the idea of inevitable progress from the very formation of the worlds through the incomparable future.

251. Dixon, Thomas. The Fall of a Nation; A Sequel to The Birth of a Nation. New York: D. Appleton, 1916.

Serialized in the National Sunday Magazine (1915-1916): with the aid of many German-American citizens, the Kaiser's fleet and army launch a surprise attack which overwhelms the U.S. The nation is conquered and occupied. Uniquely for the period, American science and scientists do not save the country. After several years of occupation each member of a secret society of American women "dates" and kills a German officer or soldier, while their menfolk--described as "rough riders" from the West--attack the ammunition dumps and communication centers. Once free, America develops its military forces. A second unique feature of the narrative shows the failure of an international peace conference sponsored by the U.S. The European nations partition both Africa and Asia.

252. Dodge, H[oward] L[ewis]. Attraction of the Compass; A Romance of the North, Based upon Facts of a Personal Experience. Long Beach, Ca.: Dove and Courtney, 1912.

The first-person narrator gives an account of his journey to Alaska; he is accompanied by a Norweigan girl, Minnie, who is looking for two lost brothers. When he is injured, she saves him. They become lost and pass through a mountain rich in gold and iron to find an unknown city, Tyron, in a valley which is tropical in climate (including banana trees). There is a second city, Kyron; both were founded by Norweigan pirates fleeing from justice. Although the narrator confesses his love for her, Minnie marries the prince of the city. The narrator must give her in marriage. He does, but the experience turns his hair white. There is the suggestion that he goes into delirium. Without adequate explanation, he ends up in British Columbia. Although he strikes a rich claim, he dies; the manuscript of his journey to the north is found in a clothes bag. This is one of the more unsatisfactory examples of the lost race motif from the period.

253. Donnelly, Ignatius (as Edmund Boisgilbert). Caesar's Column; A Story of the Twentieth Century. Chicago: Schulte, 1890.

In 1988 a revolution occurs because the developments in technology fulfilled the Marxist prediction by splitting society into an elitist oligarchy and an impoverished working class. Civilization collapses, but the protagonist, Gabriel Welstein, takes some machines and people to Africa, where he hopes that a new socialistic state will eventually encompass the world. New York had been turned into a wondrous city by the new technology. Donnelly insists that technology is the only means of attaining utopia; the fault lies in its control by a small group who have no concern for the populace.

254. Donnelly, Ignatius. Doctor Huguet. Chicago: Schulte, 1891.

By transmigration, the narrator, a southern doctor, finds himself in the body of a black. The novel provides the angriest criticism of racism during the period.

255. Donnelly, Ignatius. The Golden Bottle; or, The Story of Ephraim Benezet of Kansas. New York: Merrill, 1892.

A prefatory note refers to the "great political struggle" going on in the U.S. But to read this novel as no more than a utopian forecast based on free coinage and paper money is to catch only its most superficial level of criticism. Part of its basic storyline is the love of Ephraim and Sophie Hetherington, both of whom have been victims of mortgages foreclosed on their parents' farms. Ephraim early declares that the Earth cannot be the work of God but must be the "clumsy handiwork" of lesser spirits. An old man calling himself "THE PITY OF GOD" gives Ephraim a bottle capable of changing base metals into gold. A Woman's Cooperative Association is formed to improve their working standards and assure them a fair return for their work; The Brotherhood of Justice is also formed. More importantly, Ephraim founds a great city at the mouth of Great Egg Harbor River (New Jersey), to be powered entirely by electricity. He offers free power to all manufacturers who will agree to a cooperative plan. He becomes president representing the Peoples Party. He offers to help the people of Europe. This brings about warfare; Canada joyfully accepts occupation within a month; Ireland is freed; and Europe is overcome, the final battle being with Russia. He establishes a world-wide Universal Republic, its capital in the Azores. Waking from his dream, he confronts a figure who tells him that the universe "is nothing but work" and that there is no afterlife, only "one eternal now."

256. Dooner, Pierton W. Last Days of the Republic. San Francisco: Alta California, 1880.

Presented as a future history, this novel chronicles the conquest of the U.S. by Chinese. The trouble begins because the Trusts which control California (the Six Companies) allow unrestricted immigration of Coolie labor. When white laborers try to curtail the flow of cheap labor, the Courts and Congress join the Companies against them. Labor forms its own militia and attacks Chinatown; it is defeated. Cooperating with the Chinese government, the Trusts begin to make contracts for Coolie labor east of the Rockies. The race struggle begins after such southern states as South Carolina try to resist; after several years of fighting, famine reinforces a war of extermination. The U.S. is destroyed as a nation. Chinese success is aided in part because its soldiers (imported as laborers) intermarry with the "daughters of America." Also the American black "disappeared, perished" as the Chinese took over the South in particular.

257, Dorrington, Albert. The Radium Terrors. London: Nash, 1912.

A scientist and a journalist combine forces to recover radium stolen by a sinister Oriental who anticipates Sax Rohmer's Fu Manchu. A beautiful woman doctor uses some of that radium to achieve miraculous cures of such maladies as blindness. Some of her cures go awry.

258. Doughty, Francis Worcester. Mirrikh; or, A Woman from Mars; A Tale of Occult Adventure. New York: Burleigh & Johnson, 1892.

A trip to an advanced city on Mars is almost incidental to a love story mixing together the Orient and Mars. In Cambodia in 1870 the wife of the first-person narrator, George Wylde, deserts him. This leads to a passage denouncing marriage as "slavery" for both partners. However, Wylde meets Mirrikh, an adept from Mars, and rescues a beautiful Asiatic girl from a whipping. In Tibet he meets Mirrikh and the girl again. She is a member of an unknown

mountain people, although apparently educated in Philadelphia for ten years. After a trip to Mars she is killed
in a fall, but is transformed into the Martian woman who
has declared herself to be the narrator's soul mate. The
lamasery in Tibet serves as a haven providing bodies for
the souls of those visiting Earth from many different
planets; moreover, the farther from the sun a planet is,
the more "refined and intellectual" are its people.

259. Douglas, Theo [pseud. of Mrs. H.D. Everett]. Iras; A
Mystery. New York: Harper, 1896.

Also published in Britain by Blackwood (1896): a strange
mixture of hypnosis and Egyptology, the narrative shows how
authors of the period combined the supernatural (occult)
and science. The reflective narrative of Ralph Laverham,
the story recounts his ill-fated marriage to an ancient
Egyptian princess. Told that her husband will not be of
her land or generation, the princess agrees with the
priest, Savak, to enter a state of suspended animation. If
her lover appears, she will marry him; if not, she will
somehow revive so that Savak can marry her. Hardly does
Laverham acquire her sarcophagus before he begins having
hallucinations in which he sees Savak. Revived, the
princess falls in love with Laverham and marries him. They
flee to Scotland. As she becomes weaker, he falls into a
delirium, finally losing consciousness. After recovering
from the illness, he learns that he was found embracing a
mummy. He must prove whether or not she ever lived. The
evidence is contradictory. The persons met during the
early stage of their trip to Scotland remember her; those
during the later stage, only that he was alone and ill. He
discovers that her mummy wears a wedding ring, but her
modern clothes were never worn. The novel closes with a
passage reaffirming a belief in the occult.

260. Dowding, Henry Wallace. The Man from Mars; or, Service
for Service's Sake. New York: Cochrane, 1910.

During a tour of France and Italy, especially Rome, Morris
Dunraven, the first-person narrator, learns of Mars from
General Moraine.

261. Doyle, Sir Arthur Conan. Danger! and Other Stories. New
York: Hurst, [1918].

Published in Britain by John Murray (1918): the title
story, "Danger!" (The Strand, July 1914) warns of the
threat to England brought about by submarine warfare. Its
first-person narrator commands the eight submarines of "one
of the smallest Powers in Europe"; his narrative dramatizes
the effect of attacking the merchant marine instead of the
royal navy. The food supply is cut off, prices become

inflated, and rioting occurs in the Midlands as well as London. Britain surrenders. The narrator closes the story with a warning about food production and, declaration favoring a Channel tunnel. "The Horror of the Heights" presents the fragmentary manuscript of the narrator. He flies his plane to the height of 43,000 feet and discovers various creatures, among them a kind of giant airborne jellyfish. He fears they will attack him. An appended note states that wreckage of his plane was found scattered across the countryside.

262.   Doyle, Sir Arthur Conan.   The Great Keinplatz Experiment, and Other Tales of Twilight and the Unseen.   New York: Doran, 1919.

In "The Great Keinplatz Experiment" Professor von Baumgarten, a celebrated anatomist, wishes to found an exact science of mesmerism and spiritualism. He wants to know if one can separate the body and soul/personality. He exchanges bodies with Fritz von Hartmann, a roustabout student in love with his daughter, Elisa. The exchange is successful, but neither personality seems aware of it so that each is subjected to the role of the other. The experiment must be reversed. No one believes it took place. In "The Los Amigos Fiasco" the attempt to electrocute Duncan Warner gives him "enormous nervous energy" so that he will not die--either by hanging or shooting. Electricity is equated with life.

263.   Doyle, Sir Arthur Conan.   The Land of Mist.   New York: Doran, 1926.

Professor George Challenger is less important than in the other novels in which he appears; primarily he plays the skeptic, although at the end he is convinced, as his companions learn that it is possible to communicate with the dead. It thus becomes evident that man is a part of a universal order.

264.   Doyle, Sir Arthur Conan.   The Lost World.   London: Hodder & Stoughton, 1912.

When Professor George Challenger, eccentric zoologist, is challenged regarding his supposed discoveries on a previous trip to South America, he leads an expedition to the plateau Roraima in Venezuela. His companions include the skeptical Professor Summerlee; Lord John Roxton, wealthy sportsman and explorer; and Edward D. Malone, reporter for the Gazette and first-person narrator. They discover the remnant of a prehistoric world, where dinosaurs exist side-by-side with early Homo sapiens and a tribe of apemen. Challenger and Roxton lead the cavemen in a final victory over the apemen. The group returns to London, but their photographic negatives are lost. Challenger then releases

a pterodactyl which escapes into the London night. Doyle
delights in the material, giving almost as much attention
to Challenger and the initial quarrel as to the journey
itself. Its success ranks with that of the earlier novels
of Sir. H. Rider Haggard, although it differs in tone from
those earlier works.

265. Doyle, Sir Arthur Conan.   The Maracot Deep.   New York:
Doubleday, 1929.

Also published by Murray in England (1929): to prove his
belief that extreme pressure does not exist in the ocean
depths, Professor Maracot and two companions--an oceanographer and a mechanic--begin to descend into the Atlantic
in a tank which Maracot has designed. At 1700 feet a giant
crab-like creature cuts their hawser line with its claws.
They plunge to the bottom--some five miles down--where they
discover the descendants of Atlantis living in a domed
city. Although a love story plays a part in the narrative,
Doyle recalls the tradition of Verne in that he describes
many undersea wonders. The trio finally return to the
surface by means of a "vitrine ball" (a kind of plastic)
and a gas lighter than hydrogen. Although Doyle declares
that nature is cruel, his mysticism becomes apparent in a
lengthy scene, a confrontation between the three explorers
and "the lord of the dark face," who must be regarded as
Satan.

266. Doyle, Sir Arthur Conan.   The Poison Belt.   London: Hodder
& Stoughton, 1913.

A sequel to The Lost World in that the same characters are
assembled, this narrative stems from Challenger's discovery
that the Earth is about to pass through a deadly cloud of
interstellar gas. Challenger's party isolates itself in a
hermetically sealed room supplied with oxygen. The next
morning they emerge to find themselves apparently the only
survivors. After a tour of desolated London, the world
comes alive, having been caught in a cataleptic spell
brought on by the gas. The language of the final chapter,
emphasizing as it does the "very special fate" reserved for
that generation and the changed perspective brought on by
the experience, seems highly ironical in view of the fact
that it was, so to speak, written on the eve of World War
I. Like Wells, Doyle emphasizes the idea that mankind has
been given a second chance--an idea recurrent in British
treatment of the catastrophe motif during the period. In
view of the novels after the war, Doyle may have made the
last hopeful statement of that belief in a second chance.
Notice, too, that this catastrophe is not man-made.

267. Drayton, Henry S[hipman]. In Oudemon; Reminiscences of an
Unknown People. New York: Grafton, 1900.

   Drayton's novel is almost essay-like as it advocates a
   state based upon the principles of Christian Socialism.
   Oudemon itself is the deliberate experiment of men who
   entered the South American jungles a century ago; a natural
   catastrophe isolated it physically from the rest of the
   world. They have made great accomplishments in various
   fields of science. In addition to a mastery of telepathy,
   they have discovered a marvelous gas which powers their
   "goalone" cars, "aerolot" flying suits, and a tube-like
   weapon, the "impeller," as well as having a variety of
   industrial uses. Despite this technological progress, the
   people of Oudemon idealize the natural man; like Emerson,
   the narrator is told, they believe in the inherent goodness
   of man. The religion of the society is simple and funda-
   mentalistic, based solely on biblical teachings. The love
   affair between the narrator and a pretty maid provides a
   conventional storyline. One incident involves the discovery of a semi-collapsed balloon of an Arctic explorer;
   another, the discovery and killing of a "relic of the
   Miocene."

268. Duhamel, George. America the Menace; Scenes from the Life
of the Future. Trans. from the French by Charles Miner Thomp-
son. Boston: Houghton Mifflin, 1931.

   After a visit to America Duhamel returns to France to warn
   that American materialism threatens the finer civilization
   of Europe. His criticism ranges from automobiles and
   bathrooms to movies and sports. American critics did not
   so much object to his criticism as they did to his "surly"
   manner.

269. Dunn, Waldo H[ilary]. The Vanished Empire; A Tale of the
Mound Builders. Cincinnati, Oh.: Clarke, 1904.

   This pseudo-historical romance of prehistory idealizes the
   civilization of the Mound Builders. Description of the society submerges a thin storyline. It includes an "Historical Appendix," which gives diagrams, discussions of
   present theories regarding pre-Columbian America, and a
   bibliography of scholarly books.

270. Dwyer, James Francis. "Breath of the Jungle". Chicago:
A.C. McClurg, 1915.

   Set in the jungles of the East, these short stories remind
   one somewhat of Conrad in that many of them deal with the
   theme of the deterioration of a white man who has come
   under the influence of the jungle. Perhaps the most
   notable story is "The Soul Trapper," in which a beautiful
   native woman sings to a man in order to save his sanity

after he has gone mad in the jungle. "The Phantom Ship of Kirk van Tromp," a variation of the Flying Dutchman theme, contains a savage fight among the innumerable rats aboard the ship.

271. Dwyer, James Francis. The Spotted Panther. Garden City, N.Y.: Doubleday, Page, 1913.

In Borneo Red Templeton, Chico Morgan, and Lenford--the first-person narrator--search for the Great Parong of Buddha, an almost legendary sword stolen from a Buddhist temple by Portugese in the fifteenth century. Its possession could cause the Orient to rise and, for example, drive the British from India. A beautiful native woman, Nao, the Golden One, guides them, but they must keep it away from the savage Dyak, who is called the Spotted Panther. This typifies the adventure stories which have always been associated with (sometimes mistaken for) the fantasy early in this century. There is a strong element of racism in it as the three fight for "the white race and America." Similarly, there is the theme that "Aggressiveness is life itself."

272. Dwyer, James Francis. The White Waterfall. New York: Burt, 1912.

A prefatory note speaks of the mysteries of the islands of the Pacific, but a scientific expedition interested in the strange stone structures on a remote group of islands serves as no more than a backdrop for a love story between the first-person narrator, Jack Verslun, and the Junoesque Edith Herndon.

273. Eames, Frederick. The Two on Galley Island; A Thrilling Tale of the Sea. New York: Collier, 1893.

In 1861 Arva Lake and Wilson Arkley sail from Boston to Calcutta, where they are to be married. In the Indian Ocean the ship burns and sinks; Arva and Paul Keene find an island which has recently risen from the bottom of the sea. She finds mammoth bones, and they find an old ship containing gold Roman coins. They are rescued and are married; the suggestion that they may return to explore the island is negated by the implication that it has sunk again. A variation of the shipwreck motif in Charles Reade's Foul Play, this novel contains much more of the materials of early fantasy and sf than the basic love story usually bothers with.

274. Edson, Milan C. Solaris Farm; A Story of the Twentieth Century. Washington, D.C.: published for the author, 1900.

Edson declares that "Agriculture is the true basis of industrial and commercial success." The spread of co-op farm communities brings about a utopian America. The competitive system is declared evil; standardization becomes a central theme. Besides elaborate nurseries, there is a matrimonial school, although marriage between the races is not tolerated. "The Human Creed"--an oath of allegiance to humanity--emphasizes physical health, cleanliness, and temperance, as well as "purity in thought, word and deed." There is also an element of spiritualism in the novel, as well as an attack upon the pollution which affects the cities.

275. Edwards, Gawain (pseud. of George Edward Pendray). The Earth-Tube. New York: D. Appleton, 1929.

The Asians, ruled by the evil Tal Majod, tunnel through the Earth, building the city Tiplis on an artificial island in the south Atlantic; they build a causeway between the city-island and attack Montevideo with huge tanks. Later as they press northward into Mexico, they bomb such cities as New York, Philadelphia, and Washington with gold in an attempt to disrupt the American economy. Meanwhile the protagonist, King Henderson, a young scientist, gains access to Tiplis, where he learns that liquid air will destroy both the metal of the tunnel and the tanks. Aided by an American girl, Diane, whose parents were tortured to death by Tal Majod, he escapes. After Houston has been burned and the Asians approach New Orleans, the American air force destroys the column of tanks and thus wins victory. In its description of the Asians, the novel is extremely racist, but they are early described as "unknown tribes" from somewhere in the interior. They live by science, and their nation is far more important than the individual.

276. Egbert, H. M. See Rousseau, Victor.

277. Ehrmann, Max. A Fearsome Riddle. Indianapolis, In.: Bowen-Merrill, 1901.

Also published in England by Stevens & Brown (1901): a character named only "the judge" begins the story of Professor Whitmore, who taught mathematics in 1883 at Rose Polytechnic Institute in Terre Haute. His companion is "a colored attendant" named Blanchard. The following autumn after the judge finds that Whitmore has been eating less and less, Whitmore is found dead. Morphine and a hypodermic needle are found among Blanchard's possessions, and he is accused of killing Whitmore with chloroform. Blanchard has disappeared. In 1887 a doctor finds him and is told that he is crazy. Blanchard then relates the story of Whitmore's experiment intended to prove the subjectivity of time. He changes his eating habits and asks Blanchard to wake him earlier and earlier until he should be awakened at the moment he should go to sleep. Blanchard follows instructions. Whitmore starts to awaken and then dies; Blanchard flees, disguising himself because he knows the police are after him. Now as his own death approaches, he tells the story. The question regarding the relationship of time and mathematics remains open. At the outset, although the judge called it "a case of life," he said it would be as "strange" as a story by Haggard or Doyle.

278. Ellis, Edward S.   The Huge Hunter; or, The Steam Man of the Prairies. New York: Beadle and Adams, 1882.

Originally published as one of Irwin's American Novels (1865): the humpbacked, dwarfed, brilliant son of a St. Louis mechanic (deceased), Johnny Brainerd invents a coal-powered steam man. With the aid of a trapper, Baldy McSquizzle, to keep the invention a secret, Johnny crates up the steam man and takes him to Independence; to avoid curious onlookers, he tests the steam man on the prairie. He proves a fine buffalo hunter and Indian fighter, but when he runs out of fuel, Johnny, Baldy, and their companions must hide him. They have discovered gold. To save themselves from Indians, they fire up the steam man once more and he is destroyed when he collides with a wall of boulders the Indians have built to entrap the protagonists. Johnny ends up at one of the finest schools in the country. The steam man was not constructed to move in reverse, nor could he be used during rainy weather.

279. Ellis, Edward S.   Land of Mystery. New York: Lovell, 1889.

A young American, Fred Ashman, leads a group of friends into the Matto Grasso, where they find the Murhapa tribe near the Xingu River. The implication that a lost race is somehow involved exists because the king and his daughter, Ariel, have fair complexions. Two whites, Waggaman and Burkhardt, have tried to persuade the tribe to kill all other intruders. The storyline is essentially one of pursuit and escape. At stake is a monstrous cavern filled with gold and diamonds. As Fred and Ariel escape, she is wounded by a poisoned arrow, but conveniently carries the antidote. Now she and Fred, wealthy, are happily married.

280. Elmore, Ernest.   The Steel Grubs. London: Selwyn & Blount, 1928.

At Dartmoor the protagonist, a prisoner, finds a meteorite containing the eggs of an alien insect. When they hatch, the grubs eat the iron bars of his cell so that he escapes. He threatens industrial Britain, hoping to overthrow the old order and establish himself as a Lenin. As the system begins to collapse, British science discovers both a preparation which protects iron and steel and an insecti-cide. The climax comes when Communists try to storm the laboratory before the antidotes can be produced in adequate amounts to destroy the grubs.

281.   Emerson, George Willis.   The Smoky God.   Chicago: Forbes, 1908.

Emerson cuts both plot content and description of the utopian society to a minimum as he draws from mythology, the observations made by Arctic explorers, and recent scientific writers to support his belief that a Symmesian inner world was the Edenic homeland of the human race. Except for giantism and longevity, it is a conventional utopian society; the only mechanical device is a kind of mono-rail train.   Its natives worship the small sun which heats and lights the inside world, but at one point Emerson suggests that the sun is the incandescent top of a strange pillar whose nature is not explained.   The protagonists are Norse fishermen who enter the northern opening but exit by the southern.

282.   England, George Allan.   The Air Trust.   St. Louis, Mo.: Wagner, 1915.

The chemist Herzog, long the tool of the "ruthless" capitalists, Isaac Flint and Tiger Waldron, is commanded to perfect a device to remove the oxygen from the air so that the Trust can control even the breath of humanity.   Herzog plans to do this by enlarging the method used to release nitrogen from the air in the process of manufacturing fertilizer.   A by-product is free oxygen. ·Herzog perfects the device.   Kate Flint breaks her engagement with Tiger Waldron and falls in love with an "honest" socialist agitator, Gabriel Armstrong.   A revolution which establishes a "people's state" succeeds just before the plan to remove the oxygen from the air is completed.   Flint and Waldron die from an overdose of ozone.

283.   England, George Allan.   Darkness and Dawn.   Boston: Small, Maynard, 1914.

Originally serialized in All-Story: in 1920 a great explosion rips the Earth, forming a new, dark moon.   After an unspecified number of centuries Allan Stern, an engineer, and Beatrice Kendrick, a secretary, revive in the ruins of New York.   The first book, "The Vacant World," focuses upon their exploration of the wilderness that was the eastern U.S. and their escapes from monstrous, subhuman creatures who are compared unfavorably to Neanderthal and Pithecanthropus.   At the end they confess their love and dream of an ideal world.   "Beyond the Great Oblivion" records their discovery of the great abyss in mid-America from which the new moon was torn.   In it are a primitive, albino people who vaguely recall legends of the former world and name themselves "Merucaans."   Stern finds a

battered biplane, carries the albinos to the surface, and
becomes their chieftain.   "The Afterglow" traces his
attempts to build a new civilization. By 2930 he has built
an astronomy observatory and established a newspaper; some
years later in the last chapter, he speaks of a train, and
a plane from California carries the mail.   They have
created their ideal world.

284.   England, George Allan. The Flying Legion. Chicago: A.C.
McClurg, 1920.

A millionaire and an accomplished scientist, world-weary
after the war, the protagonist, known only as The Master,
gathers about him a number of ex-fliers also bored with
peacetime life.   After stealing an advanced plane--called
the Eagle of the Sky--he leads them to Mecca, where they
seize a number of religious artifacts, and then flies into
the deserts of Arabia to an unknown city carved from a
mountain of gold.   They offer the artifacts in return for
treasure.   The Moslems attack the Legion and overwhelm it.
Only The Master and "Captain Alden" survive.   Alden has
early been identified as a beautiful woman.   A year later
he offers her The Great Pearl Star, a sacred gem.   Their
love is thus sealed.

285.   England, George Allan. The Golden Blight. New York: H.K.
Fly, 1916.

Deploring the control international bankers have on society, the physicist John Storm develops a "radiojector"
capable of turning gold to dust.   His ultimatum is rejected; a conflict between him and the "Blackertons," hired
to kill him, results.   He triumphs in a scene at the U.S.
Treasury--the last place in the world where a supply of
gold exists--when he turns his radiojector on his pursuers,
loses control of it, and watches as his opponents are
buried in a flow of molten gold.   His victory is hollow,
however, for it is learned that the effect of the radiojector on gold is only temporary.

286.   Enton, Harry. The Steam Man of the Plains. New York:
Tousey, 1896.

First serialized in The Boys of New York (1876):   later
retitled Frank Reade and His Steam Man of the Plains.
According to E.F. Bleiler (The Frank Reade Library, 1:viii)
this is the first of four Frank Reade stories by Endon, all
of them involving the same formula--a young inventor and
sundry adventures, often on the frontier.   See the entry
for Lu Senarens, who wrote most of the Frank Reade stories.

287. Ewald, Carl.   Two-Legs.   Trans. from the Danish by
Alexander Teixeira de Mattos. New York: Scribner, 1906.

Not the obvious caveman story implied by the title: a
beast-fable in which the animals tell how mankind, Two-
Legs' descendants, came to dominate the Earth.   The lion,
for example, protected Two-Legs and his wife when they came
naked into the forest.   Not complimentary of mankind.

288. Ewers, Hanns Heinz.   Alraune.   Trans. from the German by
S. Guy Endore. New York: Day, 1929.

John Braun, a university student who leads a rather loose
life, is about to be disinherited by his uncle, Jacob ten
Brinken.   He suggests that ten Brinken, a famous biologist,
conduct an experiment.   By artificial insemination ten
Brinken mates a Berlin prostitute with a crazed sex-killer.
The child, Alraune, is an incarnation of evil.   Old ten
Brinken, her guardian, succumbs to her and commits suicide.
Braun, now an archaeologist who has gathered artifacts from
around the world, falls in love with her; she drains his
energy as though she were a kind of vampire.   She dies
accidentally.   For Ewers she is "the final archetype of all
womanhood . . . sex and sex only," Mother Earth.   The
Sorcerer's Apprentice (John Day, 1927) has importance only
in that Braun hypnotizes his mistress and loses control of
her.   It can be read only as an attack upon religion.   Both
novels were printed in Germany before World War I.

289. Eyton, John [Seymour].   Jungle-Born.   New York: Century,
1925.

Published in England by Arrowsmith (1924):   in India apes
steal a child, and he becomes Nanga, a creature of the
jungle.   Piri Ram's daughter, Parmala, steals a tin box
filled with money and jewels.   She loses it in the jungle.
The narrative becomes the love story of Nanga and Parmala;
it attempts to salute the primitive innocence of the jungle
preferred to civilization.   It is presented in a simple
style as though it wants to be a fable, but it is too
imitative, too thin to be fully effective.

290. Fairman, Henry Clay.   The Third World; A Tale of Love and
Strange Adventure.   Atlanta, Ga.: Third World Publishing Co.,
1895.

A prefatory note explains that the tale is the manuscript
of the sole, unnamed survivor of the Franklin expedition.
A Norweigan discovered the manuscript and two bodies in a
cave in Greenland in 1859.   Saved by the Eskimo, Loolik,
who died of fever and was buried in the cave, the first-
person narrator discovers a city buried in the ice and
passes through a long cave in which there are a number of
petrified bodies.   He enters the kingdom of Polaria, whose

chief city is Hiawana; it is in the extinct crater of a volcano at whose center is a bottomless abyss, the pole itself. He does not identify the lost race except as being of "Adamic blood," though "they have no account of our common first ancestors." Named Wanhama by the king, he returns from the ice-encased city with part of the treasure of their ancestors, including the lost crown which he bestows upon the king. The central storyline focuses upon his love for the Lady Noona of Damauna, though it brings him the enmity of Prince Bambana. At one time Noona is named as Bambana's wife; however, when the king goes through the ceremony of betrothal between Noona and Wanhama, Noona would remain engaged rather than be married. They do finally marry, and his son, William, is the first blonde born in Polaria. At Noona's request he writes of his adventures; the final entries are brief passages of a diary. He leaves it in the cave where he finds a body of a Polarian. But he returns to Noona.

291. Farrère, Claude (pseud. of Frederic Charles Bargone). Useless Hands. Trans. from the French by Elizabeth Abbot. New York: Dutton, 1926.

Supposedly written about the year 2130, the narrative first pictures the world of James F. Machead Vohr, Governor of the American Siturgic Monopoly, which controls all of the wheat for the three Americas ruled by the monopoly. In a society in which the machine dominates, the latest development is the creation of mechanical hands which will replace whatever laborers still exist. The latter part of the novel focuses upon Block 216, where Pietro Ferrari leads a strike against Vohr. The strikers are annihilated by a weapon that literally disintegrates them. An added element of melodrama has Eva Machead Vohr, daughter of the Governor, the lover of Ferrari. She is also destroyed; because of the trouble, Vohr is replaced by Ralph Athole. The principles of Darwinian law are adhered to by the rulers. The novel is significant in the post-war era because of its emphasis upon machines replacing men.

292. Fawcett, E[dward] Douglas. Hartmann the Anarchist; or, The Doom of the Great City. London: Arnold, 1893.

The first-person narrator, Stanley, an English socialist who does not believe in "barricades," tells the story of the fanatic Hartmann. Having failed to kill the German Crown Prince when he visited London in 1910 (although wreaking great havoc), Hartmann fled the country. Now in the 1920s, having mastered the art of flight (a grey substance decreases the weight of the machine to be lifted), Hartmann returns in the airship Attila. He first sinks a British "battle-ship" and then bombs London. He hopes to bring about a socialist revolution throughout Europe and has recruited some international colleagues to act as part of the crew. When he faces mutiny and realizes that the range of his destruction is not so great as he anticipated, he destroys himself and the Attila. Stanley implies that his decision to do so was helped by a message from his dying mother calling on him to reform. Stanley marries Lena Northerton, who has nursed Mrs. Hartmann and earlier inherited a fortune of 5000 pounds.

293. Fawcett, Edgar. The Ghost of Guy Thyrle. London: Ward, Lock & Bowden, 1895.

An Oxford student who has become fascinated with the work of the Society for Psychical Research tells the story of Thyrle to a doctor whom he consults. Thyrle finds a drug which separates the spirit from the body so that he is able to go on three journeys, one to other worlds. Perhaps the most significant idea in the book is that parallel evolution may not exist. However, because of the narrative frame, Thyrle's story may be interpreted as an hallucination. The student kills himself, the implication being that only then can Thyrle cross into the world of the dead.

294. Fawcett, Edgar. Solarion. Philadelphia: Lippincott, 1889.

Published only in the September 1889 issue of Lippincott's Magazine: Brookstayne, an American staying in Switzerland, tells the story of Kenneth Rodney Stafford. The narrative combines three actions. An introverted youth, Stafford studies in Germany and masters the field of electricity. He falls in love with Celia Effingham, who marries Caryl Dayton. Instead of destroying the book of Conrad Klotz when that genius dies, Stafford uses its theory to increase the intelligence of the dog Solarion until they are able to converse. Stafford gives Celia Solarion as a gift in order to know the details of her relationship with Dayton. Solarion falls in love with Celia; in a jealous rage and disgusted by the idea that the dog should love the woman, Stafford tries to kill Solarion. The dog attacks him, destroying half his face, though Stafford lives. This must remain one of the most original treatments of the Frankenstein theme during the period. The conversations between Stafford and Solarion recall Mary Shelley's novel in centering upon the loneliness of the creature and the Faustian qualities of Stafford.

295. Fenn, George Manville. The Young Inventor. New York: Street and Smith, 1892.

In England conventional adventures beset Lance Distin, Fred Gilmore, Aleck Macey, and Vane Lee as they develop a mechanical means of powering a small boat.

296. Fezandié, Clement. Through the Earth. New York: Century,
1898.

     Serialized in St. Nicholas Magazine (1898):   this novel
celebrates technology.   Dr. James Giles, a renowned engineer, wishes to build a tunnel from New York to Australia
to facilitate transportation between the countries.   He
sees this as the first of many tunnels (tubes).   He develops giant drilling augurs, and the tube itself is made
of a new metal, carbonite; it can be protected with refrig-
erating agents capable of a temperature of -425F.   The car
will be a tapered cylinder twenty feet long, fifteen wide.
For a fee of one hundred pounds, a boy of sixteen, William
Swindon, volunteers to be the first passenger. Destined to
be a mechanical engineer, he had to withdraw from college
when his father died; his mother lost what little money was
left; and his most recent employer has failed. Chief among
his adventures is the experience of free fall.   Despite
Giles' calculations, the heat at the center of the Earth is
so great that melting does occur and plans for the company
are abandoned.   But young Swindon becomes wealthy because
the Universal Press Association pays him one hundred
thousand dollars for exclusive rights to his story.

297. Field, Marlo. Astro Bubbles. Boston: Four Seasons, 1928.

     Essentially an attack upon the modern scientific concept of
the structure and nature of the universe, the narrative is
primarily interesting because of its date and its variation
on Symmesian theory.   Dr. Harlan Sargent leads an expedition into Antarctica past the Ross Sea.   He discovers
another world, where the woman Arjhail becomes the critic
of the modern world.   Sargent is flown back to the base at
the Ross Sea by the people of Cielo, but he is not believed.   The novel ends with the announcement that a scientist, Perry Helion, has discovered that the world is a
cylinder and that humanity lives on the inside with the
oceans flowing down the center.   The central theme is that
the human soul is held back from further advancement
(already attained by the people of Upper-Earth) by the
"extensive development of science."   Man has not been an
ally of nature.

298. Finger, Charles J[oseph]. The Spreading Stain; A Tale for
Boys and Men with Boys' Hearts.   Garden City, N.Y.: Doubleday,
Page, 1927.

     The first-person narrator, Joseph Graham, is told that he
has no imagination. He reports how Wayne Thorndyke and a
man named Webster develop a "Wonder Weed Killer" to be used
along railroad tracks. It goes out of control killing the
microorganisms on which the growth of plants depends.   It
becomes a blight which spreads throughout the world; in
fifteen years time only a few areas in the Arctic or sub-

Arctic survive. Then abruptly the narrator explains that
he has written a "romance about a microbe" to prove that he
does have imagination. Yet the implication that all is but
a figment of his imagination is dulled by his final suggestion that although he could have given the story any
ending he wished, he "set down things as they were."

299. Flammarion, Camille. Omega; The Last Days of the World.
Trans. from the French. New York: Cosmopolitan, 1894.

In the twenty-fifth century a comet threatens to collide
with Earth. Instead of dramatizing the event, Flammarion
presents series of essay-like discussions of its effects,
as well as including reference to numerous religious events
and previous threats to Earth. The comet merely skims the
Earth but becomes the most memorable event in history. The
last chapters describe the final death of the world from
cold millions of years in the future. In the last two
glass-domed cities of the world, Omegar and Eva are united
briefly before their deaths. She has a final vision of
Jupiter as a bounteous world. The spirit of Cheops comes
for them to take them to Jupiter, which is now ready to be
the heir of all "human achievement." But even that world
must end, although a new universe will come into being.
Those souls who had gained immortality "continued to live
forever in the hierarchy of the invisible psychic universe." Moreover, the visible universe is only the brief
outward manifestation of "the absolute and eternal
reality." Thus does Flammarion add his to the other voices
preaching a form of Theosophy. The copyright is held by
J.B. Walker; since no translator is specifically named, he
may well have done the translation.

300. Fleming, A[ndrew] M[agnus]. Captain Kiddle; A Fantastic
Romance. New York: Alden, 1889.

The young first-person narrator is hired to record Captain
Kiddle's adventures. The ship Boreas is frozen in the
Arctic ice and eventually wrecked. They discover a valley
with a temperate climate; giantism is the rule, from the
prehistoric people resembling Patagonians to the trees
dwarfing California's redwoods. The fountain of youth and
sea serpents are introduced, but after building a ship and
loading it with twenty tons of gold, Kiddle returns south-
ward. The narrator flies south on the back of a giant bird.

301. Fletcher, Lawrence. Into the Unknown; A Romance of South
Africa. London: Cassell, 1892.

At best a poor imitation of Haggard, this novel becomes a
tirade against Mormons who live in East Utah, a section of
South Africa. Alfred Leigh and Dick Grenville, together
with the Zulu Myzukulwa, rescue Dora Winfield. Another
girl, Rose of Sharon, who calls herself Queen of the

Mormons though she has been imprisoned by the villainous
Holy Three, joins them. They discover large amounts of
gold. Rose is killed by the Mormons. Leigh becomes Lord
Drelincourt when his father and older brother are killed;
he marries Dora. Grenville, who loved Rose, threatens to
exterminate Mormons but remains in Africa.

302. Foley, Charles. Kowa the Mysterious. Trans. from the
French by William Frederick Harvey. London: Everett, 1909.

Basic to the novel is a sharp criticism of American materialism and the manners of the wealthy. The narrative is
viciously racist, primarily attacking the Chinese. Jacques
Bermond becomes secretary to the millionaire Carl Stone,
while his fiancée, Janine (Ninette) Flory, becomes the
companion to Stone's beautiful wife Evelyn. As they
disembark from a liner, the elderly Chinese, Tao, is
discovered smuggling handguns and carbines. In the city of
Kowa, where Chinese immigration has reached "epidemic"
proportion, Stone pays ransom to release the foreman of one
of his factories from the Chinese. Evelyn Stone and Janine
disappear. Bravely Jacques follows them into a great
subterranean grotto where the Chinese have built an
elaborate city beneath Kowa. Tao is Governor of the city.
An earthquake figures in a highly melodramatic climax.
While the emphasis is upon an attack of the Chinese (all
American women have a "horror" of them), Blacks are
dismissed as "a bestial, lazy race," and the American
Indian is virtually exterminated by an organization which
has given them smallpox-infected blankets.

303. [Forbes, Alexander]. The Radio Gunner. Boston: Houghton
Mifflin, 1924.

In 1937 war breaks out between the United States and the
"Constantinople Coalition," which controls the entire
Mediterranean basin and plans to dominate the world. The
protagonist is Jim Evans, a physicist, whose main effort
concerns the development of radio equipment to detect the
presence of enemy ships, especially submarines. There is
some criticism of senior naval officers who will not use
the new equipment, but the major problem is to ferret out
traitors and spies. The final battle is a two-hour naval
engagement. Aircraft have no significant part in the
battle because there has been no development of military
aviation.

304. [Ford, Dougulas Moret]. A Time of Terror; the Story of a
Great Revenge (A.D. 1910). London: Greening, 1906.

Against a background criticizing the rise of socialism and
the presence of increasing numbers of aliens (although the
Japanese are praised), the main thrust of the plotline
concerns the appearance of a German fleet off Plymouth and

the eventual defeat of the Kaiser's forces. Something of a hodgepodge.

305. Forester, C[ecil] S[cott].   The Peacemaker.   Boston: Little, Brown, 1934.

Unhappy in marriage, Edward Pethwick, a teacher of mathematics, begins an affair with the daughter of the headmaster, Dorothy Laxton, who is a pacifist. His genius leads him to develop a magnetic device which stops all engines. Spurred on by Dorothy, he calls for the complete disarmament of England and threatens to use the device to halt all traffic. He adopts the name Peacemaker. Suspecting his identity, his jealous wife reveals his identity to a mob. He destroys his machine and his notes and dies at the hands of the mob.

306. Forrest, Aston.   The Extraordinary Islanders; Being an Authentic Account of the Cruise of the "Asphodel", as Related by Her Owner. London: Everett, 1903.

Three friends join Forrest in a world-cruise. Somewhere near Australia a storm strands them on the island of Rectinia, whose inhabitants have no ankles or feet and a thumb and one broad finger, though their brains are three times the size of man's. A series of dialogues with King Tumarkine involves God, science, and evolution; the Rectinians worship reason and restrain the physical appetites. Leaving one friend on the island, the others travel aboard the repaired Asphodel to the nearby islands of Scrumpolon and Melanoon. The Scrumpolonians esteem the emotions and give themselves to the artistic spirit. They are without morals, and the females mix coyness and lasciviousness. Forrest's artist friend remains on Scrumpolon, while the other two sail for Melanoon, where the Owowkoods are obsessed with a strict religion. Forrest returns to England alone, where another friend, Dr. Andrew Fareland, has succeeded in liquifying sin. The narrative obviously is a satire of the imaginary voyages of the period and weakly echoes the tradition of Swift's Gulliver.

307. Forster, E[dward] M[organ]. "The Machine Stops" in The Eternal Moment. London: Sidgwick & Jackson, 1928.

Originally published in 1909: among the earliest attacks upon Wells, this story remains one of the classic dystopian prophesies. Thousands of years in the future humans live singly in hexagonal cells of honeycomb structures beneath the surface and are entirely dependent upon the automated machine which controls the worldwide subterranean environment. Kuno asks his mother, Vashti, to visit him though this requires a two-day air flight. Even the light of the sun is repulsive to her. Vashti learns that Kuno is threatened with "homelessness" because he has visited the

surface.   On the surface he was attacked by a monstrous
white worm which did kill the young woman who came to his
aid.   As the machine breaks down, Kuno and Vashti realize
that this means the end of civilization, but Kuno holds out
the hope that humanity will continue because of those few
who do live on the surface.

308. Frank, Waldo. Chalk Face. New York: Boni & Liveright,
1924.

John Mark, a young psychologist, undertakes an experiment
using himself as a subject to discover the various facets
of his own personality. He is in love with Mildred Fayn,
but his parents refuse to give him financial support if he
marries her, while she cannot decide between him and Philip
LaMotte.   He has an hallucination in which he sees a
handsome young man murdered.   He learns soon that LaMotte
has been killed by a man with a chalk white head.   His
parents are killed in a car accident by the same chalk-
faced man.   John is wealthy.   In a dream sequence he
encounters the man, who attempts to draw him down into a
lime pit.   Mark escapes, spraining an ankle; when he
wakens, he finds that he has an injured ankle. He decides
that he has somehow separated his will from the rest of him
and thus has committed the murders.   When he confesses to
Mildred, she abandons him.   The ending suggests the possibility that he may be mad.

309. Frankau, Gilbert. The Seeds of Enchantment; Being Some
Attempt to Narrate the Curious Discoveries of Doctor Cyprian
Beamish, M.D., Glasgow; Commandant Renée De Gys, Annamite Army;
and the Honourable Richard Assheton Smith, in the Golden Land of
Indo-China. London: Hutchinson, 1921.

De Gys tells his two friends the legends both of French
aristocratic adventurers who came to Indo-China at the end
of the French Revolution and of the white woman beyond the
mountains.   N'Gang, the Chinaman who has supported every
native revolt against the French, tells them of the kingdom
of Harinesia deep in the interior.   The three of them find
the Flower Folk, who are the descendants of De Gys' French-
men, but who have become completely Asiatic, particularly
because of their addiction to opium.   De Gys, in particular, loves a number of Asiatic women, beginning with the
girl Melie.   The three are rescued by Nak, the Elephant,
and return to Hanoi and Saigon.   Their story is not
believed.

310. Franklin, Edgar (pseud. of Edgar Franklin Stearns). Mr.
Hawkins' Humorous Adventures. New York: Dodge, 1904.

The narrative concerns the misadventures of Hawkins, whose
inventive genius produces such wonders as the pumpless pump

and the auto-aeromobile. They all fail. The treatment is comic rather than satirical.

311. Friel, Arthur O[lney]. The King of No Man's Land. New York: Harper, 1924.

Continues the adventures of Knowlton, McKay, and Ryan in the mountains between Peru and Ecuador. José Martinez establishes his capital in ancient, unknown ruins and says that the Indians who call themselves Sumataras--"the White Ones"--are remnants of a lost, scattered people. Dave Rand marries the beautiful Nuné, long a captive of the Jiveros. He forsakes civilization in favor of the primitive jungle life, suggesting that he prefers to live as did his pre-historic ancestors.

312. Friel, Arthur O[lney]. Mountains of Mystery. New York: Harper, 1925.

The final adventure of Knowlton, Ryan, and McKee in the Andes Mountains.

313. Friel, Arthur O[lney]. The Pathless Trail. New York: Harper, 1922.

The first of the Knowlton, McKay, Ryan adventure stories: far up the Amazon the three find Dave Rand, who has lived in the jungle for some five years after he was wounded in the head and suffered amnesia. They find with him José Martinez, who has been outlawed by the Peruvian government.

314. Friel, Arthur O[lney]. Tiger River. New York: Harper, 1923.

Knowlton, McKay, Ryan, and Rand go up the Tiger River between Ecuador and Peru. They find there Flora Almagro, whose family has long mined gold using drugged Indians as slaves. José Martinez remains in the area to be king of the "White Indians" as the others depart with a vast quantity of gold. The enemy is the Jivero Indians.

315. Fuller, Alvarado M[ortimer]. A.D. 2000. Chicago: Laird & Lee, 1890.

By deliberate experiment, with the aid of friends, Junius Cobb places himself in a state of suspended animation. He awakens in the year 2000 to find a United States which dominates the North American continent and is governed by a single political party, the American Party. Much techno-logical progress has been made. Niagara Falls has been harnessed so that electrical power is cheap; the Gulf Stream has been diverted so that the climate is milder. In 1916, however, near Pittsburgh "a hugh melting of aluminum bronze" flowed into an abandoned natural gas well; its heat caused a kind of subterranean chain reaction causing much of the Mississippi-Missouri-Ohio basin to be transformed into a Central Sea. This disaster turned American attention from gas to electricity and led finally to the development of the ultimate energy, lipthalite vapor. A thin storyline allows Cobb to be reunited with his nineteenth century sweetheart, Marie Colchis, daughter of a scientist; she had been placed in suspended animation on Guadaloupe Island in the Pacific.

316. Fuller, Frederick T. Beyond the Selvas; A Vision of a Republic That Might Have Been--and Still May Be. Boston: published for the author, 1929.

Less than a hundred pages, the narrative has significance because of its date; a first-person narrator describes a Christian Socialist community located in the Amazon valley. The narrative does assert that "self seeking competition" remains one of the basic motivations of man. At the end he is arrested for sedition and imprisoned.

317. Fuller, Sam[uel Michael]. Test Tube Baby. New York: Godwin, 1936.

Eleanor Garrison raises her son to be a scientific genius. At twenty-five James Garrison is experimenting with rabbits to produce an embryo in a test tube. Inside the laboratory he is a "machine"; outside, an extremely high-strung young man. Patricia Douglas, a beautiful coed, falls in love with him when he lectures to her school on chemistry. Although he dates her, he remains platonic, at one time discussing Darwin and evolution. In Palisades Park, however, he picks up a prostitute, Peggy Argyle. Through her he becomes acquainted with the criminal, Augie Wallace, and proposes that they undertake a twenty-five million dollar robbery. During the day he successfully performs heart surgery; at night because he "must have an outlet" for his nervous energy, he hangs out with Augie and Peggy. For two months he conducts a "Jekyll-Hyde existence." At last he rapes Peggy; when Augie comes to his lab, Jimmy shoots him. The novel ends in a trial scene in which he accuses his mother of being insane because she raised him so strictly. She agrees. After being found not guilty, he exits the courtroom, his mother on one arm, Patricia on the other.

318. Futrelle, Jacques. The Diamond Master. Indianapolis, In.: Bobbs-Merrill, 1909.

Like Serviss' Dr. Syx, the protagonist approaches the syndicate controlling the diamond market and announces that he has an unlimited quantity of flawless stones. He promises to destroy them if the syndicate buys a hundred million dollars worth of diamonds from him at half the current price per carat. He outwits the police investigation until the heroine's father, Professor Kellner, is killed (by a wandering tramp). Only after further investigation do authorities learn that Kellner produced the diamonds synthetically by heating brown sugar in an electric furnace and at a certain temperature bombarding it with a special naval-type gun. The secret, of course, dies with Kellner.

319. Futrelle, Jacques. The Thinking Machine. New York: Dodd, Mead, 1907.

"The Thinking Machine" is the name given to Futrelle's detective, Professor S.F.X. Van Dusen, who made his first appearance in "The Problem of Cell 13" (1905). In 1973 E. F. Bleiler edited Best "Thinking Machine" Stories for Dover. They should not be regarded as science fiction or fantasy.

320. G.H.P. [George Haven Putnam]. The Artificial Mother. New York: Putnam, 1894.

A brief note suggests that the narrative was written twenty-five years earlier. Annoyed by the fussing of his baby twin sons, their father, Tom, the first-person narrator, manufactures a robot and dresses it in his wife Polly's clothes. The babies are satisfied; she wrecks the robot in taking them from it; and the narrator wakens from a dream.

321. Gaillard, Stephen. The Pirates of the Air; A Tale of Modern Adventure. Chicago: Rand McNally, 1915.

Tom Baldwin, reporter for the Chicago Courier, tells how he and the distinguished aviator, William Grahame, search for the mysterious black airplane which has bombed numerous American cities and then looted the banks. They fight the plane over the Cumberland Valley and are forced down. Grahame escapes, but Tom wakens in the Cave of the Condor, where he finds Bogdan Vankovich, a Russian working with an international Brotherhood of revolutionaries who rob the rich and give to the poor of the world. Tom also meets Theodora Bagdansward, the orphaned daughter of noble Russian parents. Grahame becomes the narrator. Before Tom left Chicago, Beatrice Cameron refused his proposal of marriage. She is carried off by Cecil Colmslie, seemingly the leader of the Brotherhood. Grahame follows them to the valley of the Orinoco, where the pirates have their base in a volcano crater. Tom resumes his narration. Vankovich, who perfected the planes and found the Orinoco base, is poisoned by members of the Brotherhood who have lost their ideals. An earthquake destroys the base, and the pirates' plane falls in a lake of fire. Papers prove that Theodora is a Russian princess, but she loves Tom. Grahame settles for Beatrice.

322. Gale, Zona. <u>Romance</u> <u>Island</u>. Indianapolis, In.: Bobbs-Merrill, 1906.

This narrative possesses a quiet, idyllic quality absent from other novels relying heavily on plot action. It is the love story of St. George and Olivia Holland. Her father has been taken to the island of Yaque somewhere in the eastern sea; its inhabitants are descended from Phoenicians who settled it in 1050 B.C. Her father is made its king; despite the offer of a royal marriage, Olivia chooses St. George. Together they leave the enchanted isle.

323. Gann, W[illiam] D. <u>The</u> <u>Tunnel</u> <u>Thru</u> <u>the</u> <u>Air</u>; <u>or</u>, <u>Looking</u> <u>Back</u> <u>from</u> <u>1940</u>. New York: Financial Guardian, 1927.

The novel declares that the Bible is a "wonderful book" which contains all scientific laws. Deeply religious, Robert Gordon had a father who was an army captain, a mother who was a great student of the Bible. In 1930 Japan destroys the American fleet by air attack; Spain and Mexico bomb many major American cities. Soon England, Germany, Italy, Austria, and Russia join the alliance against the U.S. Through a device that uses light and radio waves American science develops a vacuum (tunnel) machine through which American planes can fly without being seen or heard. There is a Radium Ray acting like a radar device, as well as sleeping gas. Robert Gordon, now supreme American commander, defies the alliance's call for a surrender which would partition U.S. territory. After preparing himself spiritually, Gordon bombs and spreads the sleeping gas throughout the major cities of the alliance. The nations of the alliance surrender; in New York City a conference of all nations is held in 1932. Gordon is called the greatest man since Christ. The U.S. will retain all weapons, including a machine that can be built to destroy every living soul on Earth. Gordon tells the assembly that the victory was God's will. He asks that all live in brotherhood. He marries a childhood sweetheart, Marie Stanton, in "the new city, the City of the Lord, which is the capital of the United Kingdom of the World."

324. "Ganpat" (pseud. of Martin Louis Alan Gompertz). <u>Harilek;</u> <u>A</u> <u>Romance</u> <u>of</u> <u>Modern</u> <u>Central</u> <u>Asia</u>. Edinburgh: Blackwood, 1923.

Also published by Houghton Mifflin (1923): Ganpat presents the manuscript of an old friend, Harry Lake, but will not vouch for its authenticity. Lake, Alec Forsyth, and John Wrexham have the diary from 1822 of Wrexham's great-uncle. It tells of a kingdom somewhere across the desert in mountains north of India. They undertake the venture. Lake rescues Aryenis, who takes them to her father Kyrlos, patriarch of the Blue Sákae. The remainder of the narrative stresses the growing love of Harilek (as she calls him) and Aryenis and the civil war between the Blue Sákae and the Shámans, seemingly a Mongol race which, guards the single gate to the extensive valley.   The Sákae are a people of Nordic stock driven from Central Asia in the first century B.C. by the Chinese; their culture was made more complex by the arrival of Father Basil and a Greek group in the 5th century.   After victory over the Shámans, the novel ends with the wedding of Harilek and Aryenis.

325.   "Ganpat" (pseud. of Martin Louis Alan Gompertz).   Mirror of Dreams; A Tale of Oriental Mystery.   London: Hodder & Stoughton, 1928.

Also published by Doubleday, Doran (1928):   John Oxley and Tom Carrouthers find the City of Vision in the mountains north of India.   Its people guard the Mirror of Dreams and other artifacts of ancient peoples.   Carrouthers meets Dhyan, a white woman of whom he has dreamed.   When a Tibetan revolutionary tries to seize them and the city, they escape toward India with Dhyan.

326.   "Ganpat" (pseud. of Martin Louis Alan Gompertz).   The Voice of Dashin; A Romance of Wild Mountains.   London: Hodder & Stoughton, 1926.

Also published by Doran (1927):   while searching in Tibet for Janet Fraser, Louis Kervers rescues Danushya, a prince of the so-called People of the Hand, whose Norse ancestors fled into the mountains.   Regarded as part of the ful- fillment of a prophecy, Kervers helps Danushya and his people retake their ancient City of Fairy Towers from Tibetans.   Danushya becomes the king, while Kervers and Janet return toward India.

327.   "Ganpat" (pseud. of Martin Louis Alan Gompertz).   Wrex- ham's Romance, Being a Continuation of "Harilek".   London: Hodder & Stoughton, 1935.

This narrative centers on the love stories of Wrexham and Shaīsta and Henga and Fréiné.   Shaīsta's half brother, Durza, would join a revolt led by Zorlas, who is attracted to Shaīsta.   The revolt fails; the lovers are united in a peaceful kingdom.   Harilek and Aryenis figure in the background.

328.   Gardner, Marshall B.   A Journey to the Earth's Interior; or, Have the Poles Really Been Discovered?   Aurora, Il.: pub- lished by the author, 1920.

An essay instead of a novel, the narrative should be noted solely because it argues so late for the concept of an inner world, although specifically disavowing Symmes' theory.

329. Garland, Hamlin. The Shadow World. New York: Harper, 1908.

One must regard this narrative as a fictionalized account of Garland's experiences with psychical research; yet one hesitates to call it a novel because, for example, there is nothing resembling a conventional plot. It divides itself into two parts. The first records a miscellany of incidents involving spirit writing, poltergeists, and spirit voices. The second presents a series of dialogues between a skeptical scientist and Garland. He concludes that he is ready to "go wherever science leads" and hopes that life here "is but a link in the chain of existence."

330. Garland, Rufus Cummins. Zaleá: A Psychological Episode and Tale of Love. Washington: Neale, 1900.

Major Byrne and a detective, Edward Sanford, investigate the murder of a wealthy Frenchman, Paul Dumons, in Washington. Three years earlier Byrne's fiancée, Marie Chantelle, had been murdered in New Orleans; he is convinced that a woman killed both Marie and Dumons. In New Orleans Sanford consults with a "trance medium," Lawson, who is also a scientist. After much discussion of psychology, dreams, and Christianity, Lawson will not reveal his findings until Sanford has heard La Fontaine in the opera the next evening. She confesses. In reality she is Zaleá Gonzales. After plighting her troth with Dumons, she learns his parents have arranged his marriage to Marie Chantelle. Zaleá goes to Havana and has "little Paul" with her. After studying music in Paris, she kills Marie; she kills Paul when she learns that he is to have dinner with the daughter of the ambassador. As she dies, she sees Paul and Marie beckoning to her. A year later at her grave Lawson reveals to Sanford that he has had a message from her. The crime was committed by her baser self; she admonishes him to practice a "broad, true, and human Christianity."

331. Gayton, Bertram. The Gland Stealers. London: Herbert Jenkins, 1922.

The first-person narrator, George Barnett, tells the story of wealthy Charles Henry Hadley, aged 95, who learns of Professor Serge Voronoff's theory of rejuvenation through the transplanting of glands. After reference to du Chaillu's account of gorillas, Hadley acquires the needed gorilla, and the operation is successful. Enthusiastic, he decides to offer the chance of rejuvenation to other old men (there is a contest with twenty-one winners) as well as to an old sweetheart, Sally. Barnett reports that they learn that the transplant of glands is not the secret of rejuvenation.

332. Genone, Hudor (pseud. of William James Roe). Bellona's
Husband; A Romance. Philadelphia: Lippincott, 1887.

Genone presents himself as the editor of a manuscript sent
him by Archibald Holt. His wife believes that Holt is
completely demented. Holt reports that a Professor Garrett
invents a flying disc made of the metal hydrogenium in
order to fly to Mars. As editor, Genone deletes all of the
technical details and arrangements for the trip from the
manuscript. On Mars they encounter several beautiful
women, but the description of Mars suggests that the narrative is intended as a satire of the societies discovered on
such journeys. Yet the narrative does involve itself in
the question of the nature of God--". . . energy, infinite
. . ."--and belief.

333. Genone, Hudor (pseud. of William James Roe). Inquirendo
Island. New York: Putnam, 1886.

The first-person narrator departs from Far Rockaway to land
upon an unknown island. The narrative becomes a satire of
the society which he finds there; its god is Mathematics.
Among the denominations are the Multipliers and the
Decimals. He attends the church of Saint Complex Fraction.
Finally, with Marjorie Mayland, whom he has found on the
island, he returns to Far Rockaway just as a funeral
service is being held for him. In a prefatory note Genone
trusts that despite his satire, "full reverence" for "the
truths of God's universe" will be found in the writing.

334. George, W[alter] L[ionel]. Children of the Morning. New
York: Putnam, 1927.

After a tidal wave sweeps a city on the coast of Venezuela,
some of the children are placed aboard a ship, but it sinks
and leaves them on a desert island some forty miles off the
coast. By following them as they grow up, George comments
upon human nature and society. He explains their individuality in terms of temperament and natural selection; only
after they grow somewhat older do those traits which
separate man from beast begin to appear. Essential is the
discovery of agriculture. Sadism is a part of human
nature, as he illustrates through the character of "Arry."
On the other hand, they never discover "romance" because
"nothing was forbidden." There is implication of at least
one case of homosexuality. Tsail is aggressive and steals
the girls from others. Warfare reduces their number to
twenty-three. Finally an American warship discovers them
and takes Dzon and Elnor from the island. In many ways the
novel anticipates such a work as Golding's Lord of the
Flies.

335. Gernsback, Hugo. Ralph 124C41+; A Romance of the Year
2660. Boston: Stratford, 1925.

Originally serialized in Gernsback's magazine, Modern
Electrics (1911-1912):   more than any other novel of the
period this is filled with descriptions of mechanical
"gadgets" which have helped transform the future.   Gernsback sketches a federated world government based on socialistic principles. The storyline concerns Ralph's love for
Alice 212B 423. With the aid of Fernand 600 10, the real
"other man" proves to be the Martian, Llysanorh CK 1618,
who kidnaps Alice and takes her into space. Ralph pursues
him in a ship that appears to be a comet threatening Mars.
He kills Llysanorh, who knifes Alice so that Ralph's
supreme action must be to restore his beloved to life. He
does. The novel is really a celebration of him as a superb
scientist. Incidentially, just before a description of
wondrous New York City in 2660, Gernsback includes reference to a petrified animal standing on a pedestal at
Broadway and 389th Street: it memorializes Pete, the last
horse to die in harness in New York, 19 June 2096.

336. Gerrare, Wirt (pseud. of William Oliver Greener).   The
Warstock; A Tale of Tomorrow. London: Greener, 1898.

After inventing the Sterrygraph--better than telegraph--the
wealthy American, Robert Sterry, and the invalid genius,
Willie Redhead, offer it to Britain.   Rebuffed by the
government, Sterry decides to establish an industrial
community where he and others like him can pursue invention
and production without restriction or interference.   His
group, calling themselves "Isocrats"--"people who take a
serious view of life"--found the Commonwealth of Cristallia
somewhere in southern Morocco. They make no use of black
labor; they hope colonists will come from the U.S. and the
English Midlands and North, but they do guard their
secrets. Their first development comes from the use of the
metal Iltydium. After they successfully repel an American
ship, the Oklahoma, the U.S. recognizes the Commonwealth.
Germany causes the greatest trouble; finally, through
treachery, forces from the German colony, Pieterstadt, take
the city, but as the Isocrat leaders abandon the bombarded
city, Redhead, who is mortally wounded, sets into action an
unknown machine he has worked with.   Not only does it
destroy the city, but its signals explode all of the
munition dumps in middle Europe. Germany must capitulate;
Cristallia is rebuilt.   Various love stories flavor the
action. The British government is suspect because it wants
no independent nations in Africa.

337. Gibbons, [Raphael] Floyd [Phillips].   The Red Napoleon.
New York: Cape & Smith, 1929.

Gibbons becomes a first-person narrator as he recalls the
effort of Karakhan of Kazan to conquer the world.   Asia
drives out European imperialism; North Africa rises against
Europe's domination.   Gibbons is assigned to Moscow.   After
Stalin's assassination (November 1932), Karakhan assumes
total power.   The killing of the USSR ambassador in Warsaw
results in the invasion of Poland.   Much of Eastern Europe,
as well as Communist Germany, joins his forces.   They sweep
through Italy and France; Paris is occupied April 3, 1933.
Japan seizes the Philippines; the Churchill government in
England falls.   Asiatic forces invade Mexico, the Pacific
Northwest, Nova Scotia, and the St. Lawrence valley.   By
Christmas 1934 Boston falls.   Early in 1936 Margot Denison,
whom Karakhan has kept with him, gives Gibbons vital
information which he takes to St. Louis, the American
capitol.   On March 4, 1936, begins the naval Battle of
Jamaica; the victory of the Windward Passage cuts Karakhan's supply lines.   A great air battle follows along the
Canadian border.   But cutting the supply lines assures
Karakhan's defeat.   Margot is revealed as Princess Victoria
Louise.   She marries an American and is elected to Congress
from Saskatchewan after a 1937 plebiscite makes Canada part
of the U.S.   A United States of Europe is also formed.   One
of Karakhan's generals had declared that this was a war
against "race prejudice and capitalistic greed."   Karakhan's troops had fathered children of mixed races throughout Europe and America.   The novel becomes the most noteworthy denunciation of racism during the period.   Gibbons
is with Karakhan, exiled to Bermuda, as he finishes this
book in 1941.

338. Giesy, J[ohn] U[lrich].   All for His Country.   New York:
Macaulay, 1915.

Japan attacks Mexico and California; the Japanese-Americans
treacherously aid them so that much of California is
occupied.   New York City is bombed, and the American fleet
destroyed.   Meade Stillman has invented an "aero-destroyer," an advanced ship powered by radium.   As the Americans
retreat into Utah, they call for devastation of the coastal
areas and guerilla warfare.   Using the aero-destroyer and
magnetic bombs, Harold Darling annihilates the Japanese
fleet, but he is killed.   Stillman loves and will marry
Bernice Biddy Gethelde.   A secondary plotline involves J.C.
Gotz, Congressman from Chicago, who warns against spending
too much money on armaments, cheated Stillman's father, and
seeks to control the aero-destroyer before it is patented.
The novel is vehemently anti-Japanese.

339. Gillmore, Inez Haynes (pseud. of Inez Haynes Irwin).
Angel Island. New York: Holt, 1914.

> Somewhere in the remote Pacific five men survive a ship-
> wreck and are stranded on an unknown island. They range
> from Frank Merrill, a college professor to whom women mean
> nothing, to Ralph Addington, a salesman who is a libertine.
> Even before they realize that they may be marooned for
> months, Addington complains about the absence of women.
> Honey Smith, a typical man to whom everyone, including
> women, are attracted, asserts that he woke in the night and
> saw a large bird and heard a woman's voice. They become
> aware of large birds flying in the distance--a survival
> from prehistory, says Merrill. They plan to capture one;
> the discovery that they are winged women elicits a spectrum
> of responses--from Pete Murphy's declaration that they are
> angels to be worshipped and Bill Fairfax's earnest asser-
> tion that they should be cherished and protected to Honey's
> idea that they should "josh and jolly" the girls and
> Addington's "contemptuous" remark that they are "females"
> to be tamed and subjugated. The women are differentiated,
> from the dark Chiquita to the serious Julia. Thus does
> Gillmore dramatize a fable exploring the complete gamut of
> male-female relationships. The men use clothes and mirrors
> to capture the women. Romantic love is followed by a
> dissipation of interest; fatherhood sparks a new interest
> briefly, but then the men build a camp where they can be
> alone. They have clipped the wings of the women so that
> they can neither fly nor walk. The baby girl Angela has
> wings but is not allowed to fly. The climax occurs after
> the women try desperately to fly away. Undoubtedly this is
> the most successful symbolic presentation of the period
> concerning the relationship of men and women.

340. Gilman, Charlotte Perkins. Herland. New York: Pantheon,
1979.

> Originally published in Forerunner, which Gilman edited
> (1915): she suggests that women should and could be the
> moving force capable of transforming society. In the nar-
> rative three young men discover a sylvan utopia somewhere
> in the east of Canada, where for some 2,000 years women
> have reproduced by parthenogenesis; they have limited popu-
> lation so there is no want. The maternal instinct serves
> as the center of their values. The three young men are
> allowed to marry, but Gilman skillfully uses them to
> dramatize the basic attitudes of men toward women in her
> society. Terry Nicholson exemplifies the thorough chauvi-
> nist, insisting that women "love to be mastered." Jeff
> Margrave represents Southern gallantry and romantic love;
> he places women on an inhuman pedestal. The first-person
> narrator, Vandyck Jennings, understands that the so-called
> feminine charms are totally artificial, evolving only to
> please the men in a male-dominated society. His wife

reminds him that the women of Herland are mothers and people, not housekeepers. The three are forced to leave the society because of Terry's treatment of his wife. Together with Gillmore's Angel Island, Herland remains the most convincing and complete statement regarding the equality of women written during the period.

341. Gilson, Barbara (pseud. of Charles Gilson). Queen of the Andes. London & New York: Warne, 1935.

Norma Mansfield, a comely schoolgirl, accompanies her uncle and Professor Chatterton in a search for Inca treasure. Separated from them, she is taken through a subterranean passage to a city on the shores of a lake within the crater of Coquichima. A blonde, Norma seems to fulfill the vision of the girl Zoma, a Virgin of the Sun, who had seen the god Chasca on his way to Cocquichima. For a time she is worshipped despite the displeasure of the high priest, Villac Ima. Eventually her uncle and Professor Chatterton make their appearance. They find the treasure; Norma reveals that she is mortal; the high priest apologizes; and the explorers are permitted to leave.

342. Givins, Robert C[artwright]. A Thousand Miles an Hour. Chicago: Maclear and Marcus, 1913.

Leonora Loveday, an "exceedingly pretty" and accomplished aeronaut, and Professor Childs, an "authority on atmospheric conditions," are among the party of six who fly the airship, Bermuda. It lifts off vertically (powered by a spiral screw capable of lifting thirty tons) and supposedly is capable of flying beyond the range of gravity (said to be forty miles). Professor Childs gives no explanations of his theories and methods. Once aloft the airship seems to maintain itself while the Earth turns beneath it; Childs suddenly realizes that the screw will not take hold once they pass beyond the atmosphere into space. This celebration of flight is interrupted by such affairs as a "jinrikisha" tour through Japan and a series of brief dramatizations in flight during which the Japanese Empress gives Leonora a string of pearls. And, of course, her father's death leaves Leonora unexpectedly wealthy (real estate in Chicago) through the aid of the millionarie Huntington, who has financed the building of the ship.

343. Gleig, Charles. When All Men Starve, Showing How England Hazarded Her Naval Supremacy, and the Horrors Which Followed the Interruption of Her Food Supply. London: John Lane, 1898.

Germany lands troops in Africa and declares that no further British troops may enter the Transvaal. France and Russia demand that Britain evacuate Egypt and move their navies. The British Mediterranean fleet is defeated. Britain has no food supply so that there is rioting and rebelling. The

Wimbledon Massacre involves the death of 6,000 policemen. There are no government, no parliament, no police. The narrative ends at night as revolutionaries dance around a fire while the palace burns.

344. Glossop, Reginald. The Orphan of Space; A Tale of Downfall. London: MacDonald, 1926.

Professor Carl Donop Schlater, "the greatest perverted scientist of all time," supplies the weapons for Endikoff the First, the Dictator of the Trinity--Russia, Germany, and China. They plan on world conquest, using the air-planes manufactured in subterranean factories beneath the Urals and spreading a plague through France, Britain, and Spain. Late in the novel Endikoff reveals that the rays which Schlater and others have been experimenting with are causing sterility among his soldiers. Their plans for conquest are overcome by Ronald Drake and Li Hwang-hai, the latter of whom communicates while in a trance with the spirit of an ancestor. An element of mysticism muddies the thematic current when he seems to communicate with the living spirit which is the Earth; that spirit declares itself an "Orphan of Space, Outcast of the Constellations" because its inhabitants practice war. Britain develops an antidote for the plague. Drake, Li Hwang-hai, and Yu-Tseng, another scientist, destroy Moscow--Endifkoff's capital--with an atomic bomb. Li cries out that "War will be no more" as a "ruddy glow" brightens the night. That final chapter is called "Holocaust."

345. Godfrey, Hollis. The Man Who Ended War. Boston: Little, Brown, 1908.

An unknown scientist delivers an ultimatum: if the major powers do not disarm immediately, he will begin sinking a ship from each navy. The first to go is the American Alaska. James Orrington, a newspaperman; his scientist-friend, Tom Haldane; and Haldane's sister Dorothy, who is his lab assistant, try to learn the identity of the man. After two German ships disappear in Portsmouth, they search the floor of the harbor and find the bodies of the German crews--with all traces of metal vanished. This proves their deduction that some radioactive force which decom-poses matter is the force the unknown scientist uses. They devise a wireless device to try and find him. Only after a battle between the British and German fleets in the Channel, during which ship after ship disappears, do the nations sign a disarmament agreement. Only then after they return to New York, where Orrington and Dorothy are to be married, does a submarine surface. The man who ended war dies a victim of the radioactivity; his secret dies with him.

346. Goldsmith, John Francis. President Randolph as I Knew Him; An Account of the Historic Events of the 1950's and 1960's, Written from the Personal Experience of the Secretary to the President. Philadelphia: Dorrance, 1935.

Presented as though written in 1970, this is the political biography of David Randolph, who is elected president in 1956. He demands that a plank of his platform denounce the growth of chain stores, newspapers, and banks; an advocate of private capitalism, he nevertheless believes that there is no "material difference" between huge monopolies and communism. Both enslave the common man. In his inaugural address he pledges himself and his administration to work toward ending all war. In the spring of 1957 a Convention of nations meets in New York City to act upon his suggestion; he has proposed a constitution similar to that of the U.S. which would empower the United Nations to act upon all international matters. The news that Germany has discovered a new and terrible method of chemical warfare accelerates the acceptance of the proposed constitution. Much of the remainder of the book documents the congressional debate accepting that constitution as the twenty-fourth amendment and the subsequent ratification by the states. The first Parliament of the U.N. meets in Brussels in 1961. Its test comes in 1964 when it brings charges against Nicolas Padski for ordering Polish forces to invade Germany. He is found guilty and sentenced to death. A special appendix contains the nine articles of the U.N. constitution.

347. Graham, P[eter] Anderson. The Collapse of Homo Sapiens. London & New York: Putnam, 1923.

Writing in 1920, the anonymous first-person narrator, a deeply religious man, explains that he wished to live 2,000 years in order to understand the flow of events. Instead, a cosmic (though mortal) intelligence gave him a glimpse two centuries into the future. The Kentish landscape had reverted to wilderness, man to a furtive, monkey-like animal. Horrified yet given a second view, he learns from William Cecil that interminable wars between nations and races as late as 2085 destroyed civilization throughout the world. He journeys with Captain Billy Hart up the Thames to the one village remaining; to its west a lengthy (miles-long) palisade keeps out the savages. Hart's daughter Bessie tells him that insanity is their heritage because war and suffering broke even the stoutest individuals; fear, not reason has prevailed. Even Christianity, though extant, is questioned. From Dr. Turnbull, the archivist, he obtains the manuscripts of the first Dr. Turnbull and his wife, giving their separate accounts of escapes from Glasgow when an invading "coloured army" sacked the city. From a magazine he learns of an attempted revolution by Nihilists in London even before that invasion. Finally, the manuscripts of Lord and Lady Scarlett report their flight from Yorkshire to the Thames. Bessie tells him that he must go because the people fear him and think he is causing the bad weather and the deaths of their swine and cows. He awakens in Kent, but he clutches the notes he made from Turnbull's records.

348. Grant, Robert; John Boyle O'Reilly, J.S. of Dale, and John T. Wheelright. The King's Men; A Tale of To-Morrow. New York: Scribner, 1884.

Twenty years before the opening of the story a peaceful revolution deposed George V, who became an exile holding court in Boston. An elective Senate had replaced the House of Lords; O'Donovan Rourke, "that good-natured Irishman," had been elected president, but he was subsequently over-thrown by Radicals. Emigration; the bankrupcy of the landed classes; the cheap labor of the Chinese (after the Americans abandoned a protective policy in 1889); and Russian seizure of India had all contributed to Britain's demise. Once this background is sketched, the authors impose a storyline that is little more than court intrigue. The attempt of Loyalists to return the King at the battle of Aldershot is defeated, primarily through Mrs. Oswald Carey, who is a spy as well as the King's mistress. The young Loyalist, John Dacre, is executed by a firing squad, and his beloved Mary Lincoln dies of a broken heart. At his death he sees that he was wrong to support the King. Similarly, although Geoffrey Ripon is a prisoner, he escapes to Boston and denounces the King. He marries the American heiress, Maggie Windsor. One laments the waste of a background having such potential on so dated a storyline. The one notable sf gadget is a gun that shoots electric bullets which electrocute those they hit.

349. Granville, Austyn [W.]. The Fallen Race. New York: Neely, 1892.

In the Australian Outback Dr. Paul Clifford and the aborig-ine, Jacky Jacky, sole survivors of an expedition, discover a strange race of circular beings called the Anonos. As first-person narrator, Clifford explains how they are taken to the city of Anono, where a young woman, Azuela, rules as goddess/queen. Falling in love with her, he learns that she is the daughter of American explorers who vanished some eighteen years earlier. He teaches her the precepts of Christianity, and during the next five years under his tutelage the Anonos make great progress, especially in the "useful arts." An Anono woman, Alalah, is infatuated with Clifford; through her he learns of a conspiracy against Azuela. He defeats the conspirators and grants them amnesty. He and Azuela, married, rule for a time as king and queen. The kingdom has steam engines and flourishing towns. For a long time no government, police, jails, or

lawyers have existed; divorce is unknown.   After telling
his story, he returns to Azuela and their children.

350. Gratacap, Louis P[ope].   The Certainty of a Future Life on
Mars. New York: Irving, 1903.

The plot concerns the successful attempt of the narrator,
Dodd, to communicate via wireless with his deceased father
who has been reincarnated on Mars.   Not only is the elder
Dodd the scientific equal of an Edison or Tesla, he also
has concluded that the human soul goes through a number of
reincarnations on successive spheres, each time moving to a
higher plane nearer perfection.   Electricity dominates the
socialistic Martian society, although mechanical invention
is discouraged unless it aids astronomy.   One form of electricity, which nullifies gravity, is used to cast evil
souls into the abyss of space.   One of the most mystical sf
novels of the period.

351. Gratacap, Louis P[ope].   The End; How the Great War Was
Stopped; A Novelistic Vagary. New York: Benton, 1917.

The first-person narrator, Alfred Lupin, has a sister,
Gabrielle, who has visions.   The Germans come in a "whirlwind of destruction."   By the spring of 1915 the Dead come
to Lupin's house to speak with his sister; his house
becomes a rendezvous for "the spirits of the dead."   As
preparations begin for a last savage struggle in the spring
of 1917, Gabrielle is told that the dead are going to
appear to stop the war.   Such action will reveal the
presence of God; this is a traditional mysticism.   A
radiance begins, a voice like that of God proclaims the
brotherhood of man, and the troops of all armies are
overcome.   Gabrielle dies but says that she will always be
with Lupin.   The war ends; there is peace in Europe; the
armies "succumbed in terror" before the incursion of the
dead and the revelation of God.

352. Gratacap, Louis P[ope].   The Evacuation of England; The
Twist in the Gulf Stream. New York: Brentano's, 1908.

Alexander Leacraft, an Englishman in Washington in the
spring of 1909, reports how the building of the Panama
Canal has caused a catastrophic series of earthquakes and
volcanic actions (Mt. Pelee) throughout the Caribbean.
Cuba and other areas begin to rise.   The Gulf Stream is
diverted into the Pacific.   He is in Edinburgh in November
when storms devastate Iceland, Scotland, the Faroe Islands,
and northern Europe.   In February the House of Commons
orders the evacuation of England.   Most survivors emigrate
to Australia, where English society is revived and broaden-
ed.   Alaska and British Columbia also benefit.   Women have
gained a more equal status in the new lands.   Leacraft
praises Wells by name and salutes the strength and vitality

of the United States despite some characteristics of its wealthy and middle classes.

353. Gratacap, Louis P[ope]. The Mayor of New York; A Romance of the Days to Come. New York: Dillingham, 1910.

Helen Lorimer, extremely wealthy, is the beautiful woman who wishes to bring the Pope to the United States. Much of her property is burned by revolutionaries. She wishes to have the socialists defended so that much of the storyline concerns the trial of the accused. Also the brilliant young mayor of New York courts her, as does the Catholic scholar, Amato. The Mayor is killed when he breaks up a serious attempt at revolution. Amato marries her, and the Pope does come to America.

354. Gratacap, Louis P[ope]. The New Northland. New York: Benton, 1915.

North of Cape Barrow the narrator and his companions discover Krocker Land, whose people are of a mixed Hebraic-Eskimo stock, although nothing is said of their origin. The narrator falls in love with one of the women and learns from her that radium is the source of all the society's power, although the society is not mechanized. The suggestion is made that the valley in which Krocker Land is located is the crater from which the Earth's moon was torn. The identification of the small stationary sun in the valley as a mother-lode of radium launches a debate as to the advisability of informing the outside world of the existence of so much radium, thereby, in all probability, starting a "radium rush" which will destroy the "lost race." The decision is made that radium will so benefit the world that it must be informed. The narrator sets out with the news, while his commander, Bjornson, remains as the new king. Hopefully his rule will ease any transition resulting from the discovery.

355. Gratacap, Louis P[ope]. A Woman of the Ice Age. New York: Brentano's, 1906.

Announcing that prehistoric man needs "rehabilitation," Gratacap recounts the love story of the woman, Lhotto, and the man, Oggo. The main threat to them other than the climate is Lagk, who kidnaps her. Gratacap places the scene in the Sierras because 30,000 years ago the climate there was much like that of the Great Rift Valley in Africa. They die in the desert.

356. Graves, C[harles] L[arcom] and E.V. Lucas. The War of the Wenuses. Bristol: Arrowsmith, 1898.

Making direct reference to Wells and his novels, the authors parody The War of the Worlds. The women of Wenus land in London in their Crinoline bubbles. They are irresistible to men who are devastated by their Mash Glance. The Wenus women wish to subjugate the men. Thus, the opposition must be launched by the women. The first-person narrator is supposedly Wells himself, but references are made to "Jools Werne" and Grant Allen. Much of the success of the parody lies in its style and use of detail ridiculing Wells's attempt at verisimilitude.

357. Green, Fitzhugh. <u>ZR Wins</u>. New York: D. Appleton, 1924.

America's new dirigible, <u>ZR-5</u>, enters an international competition to fly across the Polar Sea. Lieutenant Bliss Eppley is certain that a polar continent exists and that somewhere on it are the descendants of the Norse colony in Greenland during the eleventh century. Thorne Welchor (really a Russian agent, Velchorski) attempts to sabotage the <u>ZR-5</u>. When the ship is damaged, Bliss and Scotty McAlford cross the ice to discover Norsemen in a heated valley which is compared to Iceland or Yellowstone. Hroar Holgrimson, leader of the tribe, relates its history. His daughter Kristina is kidnapped by Olaf, but is saved from him and a herd of mammoths when the Viking Eric causes an avalanche. Bliss and Scotty find a platinum mine, a lake of oil, and the only helium gas mine in the world. When Welchor flies to the colony accompanied by Joan Beckett, whom Bliss loves, and her father the admiral, Welchor's further villanies are defeated, and <u>ZR-5</u> appears in time to rescue everyone from the threat of a volcano. The new land is to be a national park in order to protect both the Norsemen and its natural wealth.

358. Greene, John O. <u>The Ke Whonkus People; A Story of the North Pole Country</u>. Indianapolis, In.: Vincent, 1893.

Captain Sampson De Lilly journeys to the North Pole, where he finds an ancient race of people. Fortunately the son of one of Sir John Franklin's people can act as interpreter. Most of the narrative is given to the history of the people, which goes back some 11,000 years. Almost two centuries ago they established a republic; they are largely governed by a belief in reason and science, although the old religion still exists. Eugenics and equal political rights for men and women are also stressed.

359. Greenlee, Maccowan. <u>The Lure of the Purple Star</u>. Washington, D.C.: Macdaniel, 1912.

The first-person narrator, Harry Hardwick, finds a manuscript in a bottle put out from the sinking <u>Titanic</u>. It declares that Toth-Ra-Sen, greatest of the Egyptian Esoterics, discovered a powder which annihilates time, but it was stolen when the Israelites fled Egypt. The narrator follows the leads put forth by a French Egyptologist in the manuscript and finds the powder in some ruins. Its vapors transport him back to biblical times. This becomes a love story of him and Rose of Sharon against the Hebrew background.

360. Greer, Tom (pseud.?). A Modern Daedulus. London: Griffith, Farren, Okeden, & Welsh, 1887.

John O'Halloran learns to fly by strapping wings to his shoulders and steering with his body. When his father first asks that he use his invention to aid the Irish against England, he declares that his invention is for peace. He flies to London and lands atop Nelson's Monument, causing panic in the crowd. In County Donegal near his home an extensive eviction is planned; when the Irish resist, English soldiers subdue them. The Home Secretary offers O'Halloran a hundred thousand pounds to use his device against the Irish, for rebellion has broken out. He refuses, is imprisoned, but escapes. In Ireland he trains fifty men to fly such wings; armed with five-pound dynamite bombs they bomb the English soldiers holding the Castle in Dublin. Later the rebels occupy Belfast, and he and his men destroy the English ships in Belfast Lough. Although he aids the Irish, who now occupy all Irish soil, he dreams of using his invention for peace. Several times the aid of Americans against the English is strongly suggested.

361. Greg, Percy. Across the Zodiac; The Story of a Wrecked Record. Edinburgh: Trübner, 1880.

The eccentric Colonel A-- found a manuscript after he saw what he believed to be a meteor crash on a Pacific Island. He shows it to a friend (presumably Greg). The first-person narrator recounts in great detail his flight to Mars, making use of a form of antigravity (apergy) as a means of locomotion. The Martian (or Martial) society is an advanced one, making great use of electricity. Its history dates from something more than 13,000 years ago when it became a world state; its present government is a monarchy which came about after the failure of communism. Its philosophy is dominated by a dogmatic positivism which makes any questioning of science a heresy. Perhaps most important, there is no sexual equality; women are regarded as less intelligent than men. Polygamy is practiced, and the narrator's first marriage (a two-year contract) is with Eveena, daughter of his host. Only a woman, however, may acquire a divorce. Much of the novel is subsequently given over to the narrator's marital problems, for he ends up with six wives, four given him by the Prince. Significantly, Eveena expects to be treated badly, for compassion/ love seems to be a quality the Martians lack. His kindness creates an enemy, Endo Zampta, who finally kills Eveena and her father. The narrator flees to Earth. Greg was to influence subsequent writers in diverse ways; thus perhaps the most important feature of this novel is its early date.

362. [Gregory, Jackson] (as Quien Sabe). Daughter of the Sun. New York: Scribner, 1921.

Essentially a straight western adventure story: at a town on the Mexican border Jim Kendric gambles and loses to the beautiful Zoraida Castelmar, who claims to be the last descendant of Montezuma. Captain Fernando Escobar kidnaps and holds the American girl, Betty Gordon, for ransom. The storyline concerns Kendric's discovery in a subterranean chamber of a rich treasure--gold and pearls--presumably Montezuma's, and his rescue of Betty Gordon. Though left somewhat ambiguous, Zoraida and one of her men, Ruiz Rios, die by falling into a pit in the treasure chamber. Kendric learns that Zoraida had earlier claimed that he was the only man she loved. But he, Betty, and the treasure return to the U.S. aboard the ship Half Moon.

363. Gregory, Jackson. Ru the Conqueror. New York: Scribner, 1933.

The evil medicine man Urg kills Ru's father and would take his sister, Little Blue Flower. Ru saves her but must flee into exile. Thus begins a set of conventional incidents, including the pursuit of Dawn Maiden of the Forest people, as well as the fight with Red Stag, who becomes Ru's friend. He finally fights with Urg, who drowns in a flood; Ru becomes headman.

364. Gregory, Owen. Meccania; The Super-State. London: Methuen, 1918.

The Chinese tourist, Ming Yuen-Hwuy, visits the continental nation of Meccania--commonly acknowledged to be a portrait of Germany. He learns that the "false ideals" of Liberty and Democracy, as well as the overly ambitious aims of socialism, have been replaced by a ruthless totalitarianism.

365. Griffith, George (pseud. of George Chetwynd Griffith-Jones). The Angel of the Revolution; A Tale of the Coming Terror. London: Tower, 1893.

Serialized in Pearson's Weekly (1893): in 1903 Richard Arnold invents an air-ship and is persuaded to join the Brotherhood of Freedom, a group of international anarchists known as the Terrorists. Arnold loves Natasha, the daughter of Natas, a Jew once imprisoned by the Tsar, Alexander Romanoff. When Natasha is captured by the Russians, Arnold rescues her, blowing up several fortresses in the process. As the Terrorists build a fleet of air-ships in the valley of Aeria in Africa, Franco-Russian

forces attack Germany, Britain, and Austria. With the use
of dirigible balloons and poison gas, the Franco-Russian
forces soon sweep the Continent. They are aided when some
Russian traitors steal one of the Terrorist air-ships and
use it against the German and British fleets. A long-
planned revolution occurs in America, and the Terrorists
proclaim an Anglo-Saxon Federation. But England is more
afraid of the Terrorists. Only after England is invaded
and swept by famine, while London is beseiged, does the
King join the Anglo-Saxon Alliance. The Terrorist fleet
wins easily, and it also brings to an end a war between the
Moslems and Buddhists. After six months' war in 1904,
peace comes to Earth at last, but the Terrorists assume all
powers of government and keep their weapons. Tsar Alexander Romanoff is marched to Siberia, where he dies of a
broken heart. Arnold and Natasha are married.

366. Griffith, George (pseud. of George Chetwynd Griffith-
Jones). The Great Weather Syndicate. London: White, 1906.

Arthur Arkwright, an engineer and geologist, discovers a
method to combine the elements to create an "atmospheric
disintegrator" by which he can control the weather of the
world. In love with Eirene Hockley, he forms a partnership
with her father, the World Weather Syndicate. Unfortu-
nately Falkner Merindin of South Africa, with the aid of
the American engineer Alfred Harkness, also has a plan to
control weather. His syndicate would dam the Arctic Ocean,
thereby causing an accumulation of ice which would tilt the
axis of the world and change the flow of the Gulf Stream to
the detriment of Britain and Europe. To convince the
British, Arthur causes snow to fall in London on July 6.
Merindin also loves Eirene so that much of the center of
the narrative becomes a pursuit after Oscar Merindin and
Baron Osbert de Venderle kidnap both Eirene and Arthur's
sister Clarice. During the pursuit he learns of the plans
of the Kaiser to bring about war. Once the girls are
rescued, he tries to establish communication with the
Kaiser, who will not listen to him. The result is that he
manipulates the climate of Germany and at the battle of
Brocken, one of his weather stations, defeats the German
army. Clarice loves Ralf Forman, a socialist, who proves
to be a relative of a noble family. The Kaiser proves
friendly once his idea of conquest is stymied, and he gives
away both Clarice and Eirene at their weddings. The
Merindin threat fades away after the failure to kidnap the
girls.

367. Griffith, George (pseud. of George Chetwynd Griffith-
Jones). A Honeymoon in Space. London: Pearson, 1901.

Originally published in Pearson's Weekly (1900) as "Stories
of Other Worlds": after the American genius Rennick
developed "R force," a form of negative gravity, Lord

Redgrave financed and built the Astronef. He abducted
Zaidie Rennick and her female companion from the ocean
liner St. Louis; her father now dead, Zaidie had been on
her way to Europe to enter a marriage arranged by her
unscrupulous uncle. She admits her love for Redgrave, and
they marry; at the wedding breakfast aboard the Astronef as
it hovers above the dome of the Capitol, her uncle agrees
and gives her a check for five million dollars payable when
she returns from her honeymoon. Before these pleasantries
can take place, however, Redgrave delivers a proposed
Anglo-American treaty which prevents war with Russia and
France and participates in an election campaign--"sound men
. . . sound money." Then he and Zaidie tour the planets of
the solar system. The moon was once inhabited; Venus is a
young world; a Martian fleet attacks them but is repulsed.
Ganymede is the site of the finest civilization they find;
a handsome race lives there simply in glass-domed cities.
Griffith advocates the idea of the survival of the fittest,
as well as his more jingoistic and racist themes. The idea
of the supremacy of the Anglo-Saxon peoples is the cornerstone of his thinking.

368. Griffith, George (pseud. of George Chetwynd Griffith-
Jones). The Lake of Gold; A Narrative of the Anglo-American
Conquest of Europe. London: White, 1903.

Serialized in the U.S. in Munsey's Argosy (1902-1903):
aboard the air-ship he has developed Gillette Morgan and
Sheila Kingston discover a lake of gold in a volcanic
crater in South America. This permits them to form the
Kingston-Mervin Mining and Prospecting Syndicate. They use
the vast amount of gold to break the American Trusts (the
Food Trusts hold out longest). They revolutionize American
society so that there is complete freedom of contract
between capital and labor; lock-outs and strikes become
penal offenses. With British friends, they consult with
the King of England and kidnap the Kaiser in order to bring
about a new Anglo-Saxon Alliance among the U.S., Britain,
and Germany. Once again France and Russia are the primary
villains; they and all powers outside the alliance must
give up all warlike development. At the end a torpedo
starts an earthquake which causes the lake of gold to
disappear, but not before the aims of the Alliance have
been realized. This is the only one of Griffith's works
published during his lifetime in the U.S.

369. Griffith, George (pseud. of George Chetwynd Griffith-
Jones). Olga Romanoff; or, The Syren of the Skies. London:
Tower, 1894.

Serialized in Pearson's Weekly (1893-1894) as The Syren of
the Skies: in 2030 after 125 years of peace and technological progress under socialism, the Aerians (as the
Terrorists are now known) return sovereignty to the nations

of Europe. Olga Romanoff tries to restore the Russian monarchy. She tricks Alan Arnold, son of the president of Aeria, and keeps him drugged for five years, learning all of the Aerian military secrets. In her lair in the caverns beneath Mt. Erebus (Terror) in the Antarctic, she builds a fleet of air-ships. Unaccountably she releases Alan and his friend Alexis, who help defeat her attack on the Aerian base at Kerguelen. She makes a pact with Khalid, ruler of the Moslems, and eventually marries him. Their armies sweep Europe, for the Aerians withdraw when they learn that a comet known as the Fire Cloud will strike the Earth. Alan tries to arrange a truce; Olga will not believe the threat. The Aerians build a series of caverns beneath their valley and partially flood it. Millions go mad as the comet approaches, and Olga keeps on with her war. After the comet comes, Olga and Khalid, wounded, retreat to her lair; Alan and his wife Alma go to her. Half crazed, Olga mistakes the corpse of Khalid for that of Alan and confesses that she has always loved him. She drops dead. Griffith minimizes the threat of the comet. He also incidentally mentions that the Aerians have acquired the power of vril, the force Bulwer Lytton used in his novel, The Coming Race.

370. Griffith, George (pseud. of George Chetwynd Griffith-Jones). Valdar the Oft-Born. London: Pearson, 1895.

Serialized in Pearson's Weekly (1895): like Phra the Phoenician, Valdar lives through a number of reincarnations which permits Griffith to write an episodic, pseudo-histor-ical novel. Valdar first fights for Armen, City of the Sword, against Nimrod of Ninevah. He is a warrior during the reign of Cleopatra and Caesar, a Viking, a Crusader with Richard the Lion-Hearted, a sailor against the Spanish Armada, and finally a soldier against Napoleon. In each incarnation he loves Ilma but loses her. One speculates that in such a work as this, one finds the beginnings of what became the sword-and-sorcery motif.

371. Griffith, George (pseud. of George Chetwynd Griffith-Jones). The World Peril of 1910. London: White, 1907.

Incorporates much of "The Great Crellin Comet" from Pearson's Weekly (1897): the Irishman, John Castellan, invents a combination submarine-aeroplane which he gives to the Kaiser to use against the British. Francis Erskine commands the cruiser Ithuriel; his second in comman, Denis Castellan, brother of John, has developed a new explosive shell. France and Germany attack Britain; Portsmouth, Dover, and London are bombed. The British have developed an aerial fleet which defeats Germany; the Kaiser sur-renders. But the astronomer, Gilbert Lennard, has sighted a comet which threatens to destroy the Earth. With the aid of American money and know-how, a great cannon is built in

Bolton, a mine shaft serving as its barrel. The shot deflects the comet so that it does not strike the Earth. John and his ship are destroyed, and Erskine marries his sister, Norah, whom he rescued at the beginning of the novel when she appeared to be drowning.

372. Grisewood, Norman R. Zarlah the Martian. New York: Fenno, 1909.

Through experiments with electricity and the conduction of sound, the first-person narrator communicates with the Martian, Almos. Mars has discovered radium and observed Earth for 700 years. The narrator, Harold Lonsdale, transmigrates to Mars, though his body remains on Earth. He falls in love with Zarlah, and they return to Earth. No significant addition is made to the portrayal of Martian civilization except that Mars considers unhappiness a disease.

373. Grogan, Gerald. A Drop in Infinity. London and New York: Lane, 1915.

As the novel progresses an ambiguous tone develops so that one cannot be certain whether or not this is a satire of the field, the main characters are mad, or it is a straightforward narrative. Jack Thorpe goes to Polytack in Cornwall. There he meets an old friend, Marjorie Matthews, who is engaged to Captain Angus Crawley. In a cave a stranger--called Hubble Bubble--sends them through a gateway to another world, which Thorpe refers to as Arcadia. At least once he returns to the present, but he willingly goes back to what he calls Marjorieland. The narrative concerns their efforts to survive and their meetings with a variety of people. At one point Thorpe refers to passing through the fourth dimension; at another he calls this his "frivolous book." One group joining him asserts they have been aboard a ship sunken by a Japanese submarine, but they have escaped the "Yellow Peril." One gathers that Hubble Bubble sends various persons into this world, sometimes as an act of vengeance, sometimes not. He refers to his colony in the world. Various quarrels occur, but there is no single dramatic storyline. This must be regarded as one of the first alternate world stories.

374. Groner, Augusta. Mene Tekel; A Tale of Strange Happenings. "English version by Grace Isabel Colborn". New York: Duffield, 1912.

A native of Vienna, Augusta Groner created the detective Joseph Muller, whom contemporary reviewers compared favorably to Sherlock Holmes. In this novel he plays a subordinate role to the Swedish scientific genius, Professor Clusius, who has discovered an unexplained method of recapturing photographically the persons and events which

have impressed themselves in the past on a given surface.
He attempts to help his friend, Lord Tannemore, an archaeologist, prove that certain Babylonian and Assyrian artifacts in the British Museum are forgeries. In the process
he hopes to learn how these ancient people lived.

375. Gwinn, D. Howard.   The Gold of Ophir.   London and New
York: Neely, 1898.

The first-person narrator and his friend join the wealthy
Lena Upton on a trip along the Colorado River, where they
discover parchments which tell the story of the lost tribes
of Israel.   The narrative becomes more of an essay than a
dramatization. Hoping to found the nation of Ophir, the
Tribes reached the Gulf of California and established their
first temple and village at Palenque in the State of
Chiopas, Mexico.   The narrator suggests that the Tribes
provided the first Inca, and that their mixture with the
native peoples explains finally the mysteries of the pre-
Columbian American civilizations. The narrative ends as he
and Abner, after their long researches, return to modern
America to develop their great industrial cooperative
plans.

376. Haggard, Sir H[enry] Rider.   Allan and the Ice-Gods; A
Tale of Beginnings. London: Hutchinson, 1927.

Also issued in America by Doubleday, Page (1927):   after
Lady Luna Ragnall's death, although he gives away the money
she left him, Allan Quatermain keeps the Taduki herb.   He
and Good inhale its vapours, and he dreams of a previous
incarnation as Wi, the Hunter, a member of a nameless band
of cavemen during an oncoming Ice Age. His mate is Aaka,
though he is enchanted by the mysterious Laleela, called
the Witch of the Sea.   The vision closes as they flee the
glaciers; he is alone upon the ice and sees a woman throw
herself from the canoe.   One cannot be certain it is
Laleela. When he awakens, Good informs him that he was a
comrade, Moananga.   They praise Wi for having a higher
spiritual development than his contemporaries and for
trying to establish laws. Quatermain suggests that Laleela
may have been Lady Ragnall, for they were both priestesses
of the moon. The last passages allow both men some mystical speculations.

377. Haggard, Sir H[enry] Rider.   Allan Quatermain, Being an
Account of His Further Adventures and Discoveries in Company
with Sir Henry Curtis, Bart., Commander John Good, R.N., and One
Umslopogaas. London: Longmans, Green, 1887.

This is the novel which established the basic enduring form
of the lost race motif.   Quatermain is the first-person
narrator as he and his companions search beyond "Mt. Kenia"
for a mysterious white race. On a high tableland they find

the war-like Zu-Vendis, who have lived there on the shores
of Lake Mitosis for a thousand years.   Not African, by
implication they may have been Persian in origin.   They are
governed by twin queens, the blonde Nyleptha and the dark
Sorais.   Curtis falls in love with Nyleptha; Good with
Sorais. When Nyleptha rejects the priest Natas and Good
spurns Sorais, civil war results.   But Quatermain and
Nyleptha's forces win the battle of the Pass, although they
must save Nyleptha from a final plot.   Umslopogaas dies
defending the stairs of the palace.   Sorais kills herself,
while Quatermain dies of his wounds.   Curtis marries
Nyleptha and reigns as her consort; they have a son.   Much
of the effectiveness of the narrative arises from Haggard's
rich detail.   This storyline became the standard of the
motif, one of the most popular forms within the field at
the turn of the century.   Often stressing the themes of
neo-primitivism and the rejection of urban-industrial society, it expressed the complex interests in geology, archaeology, anthropology, and exploration.

378. Haggard, Sir H[enry] Rider.   The Ancient Allan.   London:
Cassell, 1920.

In Africa Allan Quatermain allows Lady Luna Ragnall to
persuade him to inhale the vapours of the Taduki herb.   He
dreams of himself as Shabaka in Egypt during the period of
Persian domination.   Lady Ragnall is Amada, a priestess of
Isis.   Although they are in love, the vision ends before
they can marry.   The novel shows an ever greater mysticism
on Haggard's part.

379. Haggard, Sir H[enry] Rider.   Ayesha; The Return of She.
London: Ward, Lock, 1905.

Also issued in New York by Doubleday, Page (1905):   Leo
Vincey and L. Horace Holly journey to the mountainous,
central Asian kingdom of Kaloon.   After trouble with its
ruler, they find sanctuary in a temple at the Sacred
Mountain, where Ayesha is reincarnated as the priestess,
Hesea.   She reveals her identity after a sequence of
visions takes them as far back as ancient Egypt.   Holly
survives to tell the story, for he implies that the spirits
of Leo and Ayesha are joined forever.

380. Haggard, Sir H[enry] Rider.   Benita; An African Romance.
London: Cassell, 1906.

Issued in New York by Longmans, Green as The Spirit of
Bambatse; A Romance (1906):   this exemplifies Haggard's use
of Africa without Ayesha or Allan Quatermain.   Benita
Clifford joins her father in the high-veld of the Transvaal.   A love story provides a framework, but the principal
interest lies in a journey to the ruins of the fortress,
Bambatse, built by an unknown people, though Haggard

implies that they were Phoenicians. The descendants of that race, the Makalanga, now dwell there. The main action involves a search for gold hidden by early Portugese, a siege by warring Matabele, and the mesmeric transfer of souls between Benita and her namesake, who had been the daughter of a Portugese commander.

381. Haggard, Sir H[enry] Rider. Heart of the World. New York: Longmans, Green, 1895.

James Strickland loves Maya, princess of the City of the Heart, where those who believed in Quetzal remained instead of going to the north to become the founders of the Aztec nation. The narrator, Ignatio, wants to have all of the Indians rebel against the ruling Spanish Americans. It retains most of the conventions of Haggard's treatment of the lost race motif: intrigues and feuds, the city's destruction, and the death of Maya.

382. Haggard, Sir H[enry] Rider. King Solomon's Mines. London: Cassell, 1885.

With this novel Haggard discovered Africa, drawing upon his personal knowledge. Quatermain is the first-person narrator as he, Curtis, and Good search for Curtis' brother and the lost diamond mines of Solomon. They enter the land of the Kukuanas, where they become embroiled in warfare, having discovered that their companion, Umbopa, is the rightful heir to the throne. Once they have overthrown the tyrant, Umbopa forces the woman Gagool to lead the three to the mines. She dies as a result of her own treachery, and after escaping from Solomon's subterranean tomb, the three return to civilization. Haggard's Africa competed with the polar areas for more than two generations as the favorite setting for explorations among unknown people in an unknown land. The novel has remained in print since its first publication.

383. Haggard, Sir H[enry] Rider. She: A History of Adventure. London: Longmans, Green, 1887.

In Ayesha, She-Who-Must-Be-Obeyed, Haggard created the prototype of the mysterious, exotic woman who enchanted and bewitched American and European explorers for at least two generations. Supposedly immortal, She rules a colony of Egyptians in the Valley of Kor, awaiting the reincarnation of her lover, Kallikrates, whom she long ago killed. He seems to come to her in the person of Leo Vincey. Before they can marry, Leo must enter the same "Flame of Life" which Ayesha has used so often. She enters it to prove its power; she withers and dies. He is distraught. L. Horace Holly is his companion and first-person narrator. Her dark beauty with all its complexities--including the sensual and the mystical--has undoubtedly contributed lastingly to the portrayal of women in popular fiction.

384. Haggard, Sir H[enry] Rider. <u>She</u> <u>and</u> <u>Allan</u>. New York: Longmans, Green, 1921.

To learn whether or not his dead wife survives after death, Allan Quatermain seeks a sorceress in the interior. He comes to the Valley of Kor, where Ayesha tells him her story and offers him immortality. He cannot accept. She takes him into the spirit world so that he can speak to his wife, but he believes that it is an hallucination. Before leaving Kor, he helps Ayesha defeat some rebels.

385. Haggard, Sir H[enry] Rider. <u>When</u> <u>the</u> <u>World</u> <u>Shook; Being</u> <u>an</u> <u>Account</u> <u>of</u> <u>the</u> <u>Great</u> <u>Adventures</u> <u>of</u> <u>Bastin,</u> <u>Bickley</u> <u>and</u> <u>Arbuthnot</u>. London: Cassell, 1919.

Those critics regarding this novel as Haggard's closest approach to science fiction do so by emphasizing his use of the myth of Atlantis. Shipwrecked on an unknown island in the South Pacific, the wealthy Arbuthnot and his companions find Lord Oro and his daughter, Yva, in suspended animation in a cavern which the natives fear. A priest in Atlantis, Oro caused its sinking because the world had become evil. He will bring another Deluge if he finds the world still evil. He compels Arbuthnot to take him to Europe, where they witness the devastation of the First World War. His attempt to bring another catastrophe fails when Yva inter- feres; she is consumed by the light rays which give Oro his power, but before she dies, she confesses her love for Arbuthnot, who dies soon after returning to England. By implication he has seen Yva and knows that he will be united with her. A number of flaws mar the narrative. Bastin and Bickley exist solely to argue morality with Oro. It contains much talk and little action. The death of Yva, of course, reminds one of Ayesha.

386. Haggard, Sir H[enry] Rider. <u>Wisdom's</u> <u>Daughter;</u> <u>The</u> <u>Life</u> <u>and</u> <u>Love</u> <u>Story</u> <u>of</u> <u>She-Who-Must-Be-Obeyed</u>. New York: Doubleday, Page, 1923.

Published in London by Hutchinson (1923): this is Ayesha's biography, so to speak. Born the daughter of an Arabian chieftain, she flees to Egypt, where she becomes a Priestess of Isis. She falls in love with a Greek priest, Kallikrates. When the Persians conquer Egypt and defile the Temple of Isis, Ayesha brings about their death by sorcery and goes to the Valley of Kor. She becomes queen of the once-mighty race and bathes in the Flame of Life to become immortal. In a fit of jealous rage she kills Kallikrates and, lonely, must hope for his reincarnation.

387. Hahn, Charles Curtz. The Wreck of the South Pole; or, The Great Dissembler and Other Strange Tales. New York: Street & Smith, 1899.

When George Wilding was shipwrecked in the Antarctic, he found a hut and directions to travel south. He discovers a beautiful woman, Winnifred, who dwells in the city of Theon. After meeting another woman named Winnifred, who does not know the first, he learns that the entire society are adepts in "all of the intricacies of the occult sciences." Supposedly the two women are manifestations of the same soul because the spirit can free itself from the human body. A group wishes to "wrench" the pole so that the climate will change throughout the world. The so-called Odylic force--not explained--destroys the group to a man. Wilding sails north. None of the other tales is notable.

388. Haines, Donal Hamilton. The Last Invasion. New York: Harper, 1914.

Tom Blakesley and his friend Jack confront forces (called simply the Blues) invading the United States. The enemy dirigibles have guns. After the usual defeats, the proper equipment and reinforcements enable America to persevere. In Haines' judgment even trained fighting men cannot conquer a great nation, and war is more than terrible or expensive; it is "useless."

389. Haldane, Charlotte [Burghes]. Man's World. New York: Doran, 1927.

Originally published in England by Chatto & Windus (1926): the narrative begins after the death of Mensch, a kind of prophet responsible for the shape of society. The scientists are in control, but most important is the work of the geneticists, for population is strictly controlled. Women who have been selected to be mothers breed in some of the most beautiful spots of North America, Australia, and Europe. Other women, sterilized, devote themselves to professional careers. The storyline centers upon Christopher, an incurable romantic, in love with Nicolette, who is to have a child by another man.

390. Haley, Harry F[ranklin]. Immortal Athalia. Philadelphia: Dorrance, 1922.

In Peru searching for rubber, Wilder MacDonald joins Professor Drexel of New Haven and his nephew to seek an ancient city ruled by a mythical queen. They find the Inca city of Loretto, governed by the sorceress Athalia. The conventional difficulties with the high priest occur; Athalia destroys the city and herself in an earthquake. MacDonald dies at sea, the implication being that he and

Athalia will be united in the spirit world.   Athalia
declares that MacDonald is an incarnation of her lover
Ollantry. The imitation of Haggard seems obvious.

391. Hall, G[ranville] Stanley.   Recreations of A Psychologist.
New York: D. Appleton, 1920.

In a collection of stories dating as early as "Getting
Married in Berlin" (1881), only "The Fall of Atlantis"
merits any attention. Hall uses the decline of that civilization as a basis for criticism of present society. He
suggests that education should be immediately valuable, and
feels that divorce is too easy, marriage too circumspect.
He also advances the dispersion theory, as well as speculating about Lemuria.

392. Hall, Owen. Eureka. London: Chatto & Windus, 1899.

James Lockhart becomes the executor of his neighbor Ambrose
and thus comes into possession of a manuscript. Ambrose is
the first-person narrator. His friend, Dr. Mackenzie, had
the theory that Alexander's Greeks were in India. They go
to a monastery and discover "The Diabasis of Anaxagoras,"
which proves the theory but also asserts that a group
sailed eastward from India. Following the clues in this
second manuscript, Ambrose and Mackenzie find a ruined city
and a statue of Apollo in Australia. Penetrating farther
into the interior, they find the city of Atalka. Ambrose
gains the enmity of the priest Ephialtes and he and Mackenzie pass themselves off as dieties, but he also wins the
love of Princess Eureka, last descendant of Anaxagoras.
Although Ephialtes and Mackenzie both die, Ambrose and
Eureka leave the city and go into the desert. She dies
there, promising Ambrose that they will be united after
death.

393. Hamilton, Cicely [Mary].   Lest Ye Die.   New York:
Scribner, 1928.

Originally published as Theodore Savage; A Story of the
Past or the Future in England by Parsons (1922) and reissued there by Jonathan Cape under the new title (1928):
modern civilization is destroyed in England by another war;
there is a return to barbarism. The Eastern powers are
triumphant. Rationing is not successful, and the small
villages are dominated by women. Hamilton suggests that
"wars of the air and the laboratory" have destroyed the
distinction between soldiers and civilians. Moreover, she
suggests that if man must fight like an animal, he should
first kill off his scientists. There is also a stress upon
orthodox religion. Theodore Savage, the protagonist,
survives the fall of the modern state and becomes a citizen
in one of the small communities governed by women. He is
admitted only after he assures them that he was never a

scientist or engineer. He wonders whether or not a remnant
of civilization exists anywhere.

394. Hancock, H[arrie] Irving. At the Defense of Pittsburgh;
or, The Struggle to Save America's "Fighting Steel" Supply.
Philadelphia: Altemus, 1916.

Third in the Conquest of the United States series for a
juvenile audience: although the government has fled from
Cincinnati to St. Louis and Ohio is occupied by the
Germans, Captain Howard and Captain Prescott fight val-
iantly in the mountains east of Pittsburgh. At the end the
Army of the Alleghenies is still holding out.

395. Hancock, H[arrie] Irving. In the Battle for New York; or,
Uncle Sam's Boys in the Desperate Struggle for the Metropolis.
Philadelphia: Altemus, 1916.

The second volume of the Conquest of the United States
series for a juvenile audience: the date remains 1920.
Thirty-eight thousand men have been lost in the costly
Connecticut and Massachusetts campaigns; now the lines
stretch from Yonkers southeast to Long Island Sound.
Hancock makes use of Dick Prescott, whom he had followed
through West Point. Tom Reade wishes for an airplane which
could carry a six-inch gun. Much of the German infantry
makes use of motorcycles. Philadelphia has fallen, and
Dick knows of a retreat to Pittsburgh.

396. Hancock, H[arrie] Irving. The Invasion of the United
States; or, Uncle Sam's Boys at the Capture of Boston. Philadelphia: Altemus, 1916.

The first in the Conquest of the United States series for a
juvenile audience: Lieutenant Dick Prescott is the central
protagonist. In 1920 a German fleet attacks after a declaration of war the evening before. The Gridley High School
boys make an appearance, headed by cadet captain Albert
Howard. Since he invented a long range camera, he goes
aloft with Prescott in an airship. Darrin and Dalzell,
whom Hancock followed through Annapolis, are reported dead
aboard a submarine after the defeat of the navy. The
Japanese situation is a threatening one.

397. Hancock, H[arrie] Irving. Making the Stand for Old Glory;
or, Uncle Sam's Boys in the Last Frantic Drive. Philadelphia:
Altemus, 1916.

Fourth in the Conquest of the United States series for a
juvenile audience: by 1921 Dick Prescott has command of
the entire Thirty-eighth United States Infantry. He is now
a Lieutenant Colonel. They are still dug in before Pittsburgh, though the enemy outnumbers them two to one. A
great sea battle takes place, and American submarines

destroy much of the German fleet. They are aided by troops from Brazil, who thank them for the Monroe Doctrine. Tom Reade's air force now outnumbers the Germans. The Americans are finally victorious in an infantry battle so that the Germans in western Pennsylvania and Ohio surrender; and the east coast cities are given up. Both Darrin and Dalzell have survived. America has learned that in times of peace it must prepare for war. The use of characters from his other juvenile series reinforces the effect upon an audience familiar with the characters. The fighting is very outdated, but Hancock does go into detail throughout all four books.

398. Harben, Will[iam] N[athanuel].   The Land of the Changing Sun. New York: Merriam, 1894.

Marooned by a balloon accident on an island in the Arctic, Henry Johnston and Charles Thorndyke are taken by an underwater craft to the kingdom of Alpha in a great cavern beneath the Earth's surface. No ordinary utopian society, Alpha's people are descendants of men who discovered gold in its tunnel entrance and chose to live there to avoid the restrictions that would be put upon them by government and society (as well as the disastrous effect of releasing so much gold into the world economy). Through the use of electricity and geothermal power, they have created a perfect climate as well as an artificial sun. They have become obsessed with eugenics and exile anyone with a physical defect, however slight. The king (a hereditary position) denounces the practices of medical science in the outer world. The main storyline centers on the love of Thorndike and Princess Bernardino. Johnson is exiled; he must be rescued. The climax occurs when a breakthrough of the ocean threatens to engulf the volcanic fires which warm the cavern. Temporarily controlled, this accident still means that Alpha must be evacuated because the heat of the volcanoes is eating away the roof which protects Alpha from the ocean.

399. Harper, Vincent.   The Mortgage on the Brain, Being the Confessions of the Late Ethelbert Croft, M.D. New York: Doubleday, Page, 1905.

Dr. Pablo Yzanga attacks both orthodox religion and orthodox concepts of personality; he has developed a method by which he can alter personality. Ethelbert Croft is the first subject of Yznaga's experiment which applies radio-energy to the brain centers. Croft is transformed from a shy, introverted youth to a social lion. In that role he searches Europe for the vanished heroine, whom he and Yzanaga have promised to cure of an emotional insecurity which demands love and affection. When Croft finds her, he begins a flirtation, forgetting that he must return her to the laboratory. In time his colleagues find and cure them both. Although Yzanga attacks the concept of a fixed ego and declares that personality is the result of constantly changing forces upon the combination of cerebral and nervous conditions at any one time, he does not reduce man to a mechanism; instead, he insists that the "incandescent fibre" within the brain is but a segment of a "universal all-life."

400. Harris, J. Henry. A Romance in Radium. London: Greening, 1906.

Ma-Myliita, whose race has wings, wishes to visit Earth in order to find out what has become of her fellow Murani, immortals who had previously visited Earth and with one exception had not returned. She is radioactive and can spend only a limited time on Earth. Harris uses this background to explore the nature of love and the power of women. She wonders if the Murani loved the women of Earth and stayed, thereby surrendering their immortality. She falls in love with Professor Fonblanque but returns to her planet. He is found dead.

401. Harris, W[illiam] S[huler]. Life in a Thousand Worlds. Cleona, Pa.: Holzapfel, 1905.

The author, a minister, declares that there must be innumerable solar systems throughout space, each serving in its own way some universal plan. There is no real story-line, for he is content to describe the societies on the moon, the planets of Alpha Cenaturi, and Polaris. He finally views Heaven, which houses creatures from many systems, all of whom are united by love.

402. Harris-Burland, J[ohn] B[urland]. The Gold Worshippers. New York: Dillingham, 1906.

The uncle of the first-person narrator has a gadget which changes all metals to gold. He obtained it in Asia, and the Chinese who possessed the secret try to regain the device. The uncle disappears, and the narrator fights off the villainous Orientals. Much of the narrative's concern is with the love story of the narrator, Drew, and the girl, Mary Playle.

403. Harrison, T[homas] Milner. Modern Arms and a Feudal Throne; The Romantic Story of an Unexplored Sea. New York: Fenno, 1904.

John Allison, a native of New Zealand, and his companion, Charles Desmer, a physician and postgraduate of Johns Hopkins, are shipwrecked in the South Pacific. Although it remains somewhat ambiguous, the implication is that they have entered a Symmesian world. On the shores and islands of an inland sea several thousand miles long and five or

six hundred miles wide, they find Spanish and English
colonies at war with one another.   Allison loves the
Princess Alice.   After a revolution she assumes the throne.
The Spanish are also defeated.   A volcano erupts, causing
earthquakes which seal the passage through which they have
come.   The novel has all of the conventions and reads like
a medieval historical romance.

404.   Hastings, George Gordon.   The First American King.   New
York & London: Smart Set, 1908.

Thomas Kearns, head of the secret service in New York City,
and Walter Stuart Dean, a professor at the University of
Chicago who has been dismissed because of his book on
political economy, are placed in a state of suspended
animation by Dr. Raoul Jaquet.   (He believes that were man
to hibernate, nature would cure many ills, especially those
of the stomach.)   When Jaquet is killed by a lightning
bolt, they remain asleep for seventy-five years from 1900
to 1975.   They awaken to find a society that has such
things as automobiles and automatic shaving devices.   Most
importantly, they find themselves in the Empire of the
United States ruled over by William the First.   The Empire
includes much of Central America as well as the Philippines
and Japan.   The remainder of the narrative becomes a
vehicle for criticizing the democratic process.   The emphasis suggests that the accumulation of private capital late
in the nineteenth and early in the twentieth centuries
created a class structure resulting from the scramble for
wealth and "its ostentatious fooleries."   The result was
the creation of an aristocracy and a monarchy.   With the
aid of airplanes, however, Kearns and Stuart aid the
triumph of a socialist revolution.

405.   Hastings, Milo [Milton].   City of Endless Night.   New
York: Dodd, Mead, 1920.

Originally serialized as Children of "Kultur" in True Story
(1919): by 2041 the forces of the United World State have
entered into an "endless war" with the remnant of Germany,
a vast underground city-fortress beneath Berlin.   There the
Germans are impregnable because they have a ray which
destroys the oxygen-carrying capacity of the blood.
Because the first-person narrator is interested in the
abandoned potash mines near Stassfurt, he accidentally
gains access to the subterranean city and passes himself
off as a chemist, Karl Armstadt, who looked exactly like
him and had died in the accident.   From Dr. Ludwig Zimmern
he learns how completely the German society is controlled
by eugenics.   He refers to the "Black Utopia of Berlin" as
a combination of strict mechanistic automation and riotous
personal license.   He learns that the development of the
food supply is essential to the continued existence of the
city-fortress.   He is made head of the protium works, which

will produce synthetic food. Through his conspiracy, however, the stalemate is ended and Berlin surrenders. He reveals himself as Lyman de Forrest of Chicago, and he is in love with Marguerite, the daughter of Zimmern. The novel violently attacks German militarism and the concept of perfecting the German race; all others, of course, are "mongrel" races. This has importance as an early dystopia, certainly, but it also marks the high tide of anti-German feeling at the period of the First World War.

406. Hatfield, Frank (pseud. of John Stevens). The Realm of Light. Boston: Reid, 1908.

Also published in London by Arthur F. Bird (1908): in a prefatory note Stevens asserts this is Hatfield's manuscript. Hatfield and his companion Hum venture to Africa, first discovering the Masgninas and then, on a mountain plateau, the kingdom of the Zoeians. Its people are an ancient race advanced technologically (using solar energy, for example), but their importance lies in their spiritual development. Hatfield denies modern materialism; the Zoeians are the "living exponents" of divine truth and reality as it was expressed in Christ. Both protagonists marry women from the Zoeians and establish a happy "colony" in Maine. A Mrs. Durand, who has psychic powers, reinforces the basic theme.

407. Hatfield, Richard. Geyserland; Empiricisms in Social Reform. Washington, D.C.: Richard Hatfield, 1908.

In a volume that is more like an essay than a novel, Hatfield advocates Marxism, trying to show its relationship historically and philosophically to Christianity. More importantly, he argues for an Arctic land-bridge connecting the American and European continents, although he emphasizes that it was probably in the temperate or tropical region. To support his contention, he cites Joseph Alphonse Adhemar and dates the last false rotary motion of the Earth--the last shifting of its axis--as 9262 B.C. (the date occurs on the cover but not the title page). Such a shift would explain the biblical deluge and perhaps account for the disappearance of the Missing Link (a species thrown suddenly into the Arctic and unable to survive). The narrative is presented as the record of Adam Mann, an English sailor shipwrecked in 1638 while trying to seek the Northwest Passage. His record has been recently found in Holland by Mark Stubble, who edited it. The thin storyline concerns the love of Adam and Evrona, whose people, the citizens of Geyserland, are "a fragment from some wreck of antediluvian cultured people" marooned in the new Arctic. As Adam prepares to reach the mainland and England, Evrona begs him to stay, but he must go because his beloved awaits him at home.

408. Hatton, Joseph.   The White King of Manoa.   New York:
Fenno, 1890.

The narrative is bitterly anti-Catholic and anti-Spanish as
it deals with Sir Walter Raleigh's voyage to the Orinoco.
Raleigh is treated as though he were a tragic hero.   But
the protagonist is youthful David Yarborough, who is like a
son to Raleigh.   On the Orinoco he disappears and eventually finds the Golden City of Manoa, where he falls in
love with Zarana Peluca, the Inca's daughter, and marries
her.   He becomes king.   When the Spanish first appear, he
defeats them, but eventually they conquer the city.   They
burn Zarana at the stake as a heretic, and David destroys
the city.   He returns to England, where he marries his
childhood sweetheart, Lucy Withycombe, and lives happily
ever after.

409. Hawthorne, Julian.   The Professor's Sister; A Romance.
New York: Belford, Clarke, 1888.

Although Ralph Merlin declares that science will enable man
to do many things, including visiting other planets and
communicating with other varieties of mankind, the novel is
dominated by mysticism.   In Dresden, Conrad Hertrugge,
scientist and student of the occult, protects his fragile
sister, Hildegarde, from their foster-mother, the sensuous
Catalina.   Widowed, she loves Ralph Merlin, but he rejects
her advances because he loves Hildegarde.   On one occasion
Conrad appears suddenly to save Hildegarde from falling
over a cliff although he is miles away in a laboratory.
Hildegarde seems to die suddenly from an incurable disease.
Conrad takes her body into his laboratory.   Ralph goes to
Africa, where the spirit of Hildegarde guides him to
safety.   Back in Dresden, he learns that Catalina gave
Hildegarde deadly bacteria.   Conrad kept his sister in a
state of suspended animation (a trance) as long as Catalina
endangered her.   That risk no longer exists.   Conrad
revives Hildegarde; she and Ralph marry; but the disease
does kill her.   Ralph dies soon after.   The novel serves as
a vehicle for various ideas of the period about spirit and
matter and the nature of the universe.

410. Hayes, Jeff W.   Portland, Oregon A.D. 1999, and Other
Sketches.   Portland, Or.: Bates, 1913.

The first-person narrator is visited by a woman supposedly
in her eighty-sixth year.   She describes Portland as it
will be in 1999.   The most interesting aspect of the book
is her use of names and places existing in 1913.

411. Hazard, R.H. The House on Stilts. New York: Dillingham, 1910.

   The first-person narrator is shipwrecked on the island of
   Gabrielle in the Caribbean. His father was on an expedition lost some ten years ago, but the narrator is actually
   after the thief Varney. He must also rescue the heroine,
   Norelle Pierson. The Yellow Queen (quadroon) practices
   voodoo and keeps the natives on the edge of rebellion. A
   monastery exists in the mountains (it is the house on
   stilts) apparently founded by Aztec refugees fleeing
   Cortez. They keep their dead somehow electroplated in a
   giant cavern. Natives attack the monastery and it is
   destroyed. The Yellow Queen wants the narrator; she is
   rejected; so she throws herself into the volcano, Mt.
   Lazarre, when it erupts, apparently destroying much of the
   island. This exemplifies those novels which cloak a pure
   adventure story with a few tattered conventions of the lost
   race motif.

412. Hepworth, George H[ughes]. The Queerest Man Alive, and
Other Stories. New York: Fenno, 1897.

   The first-person narrator and Dr. Rem Budd, a noted surgeon, visit a dime museum and see their reflections in a
   carnival mirror. This leads Budd to tell a tale of a man
   in Colorado who was stretched and shrunken to various
   lengths. Important only as an example of the tall tale
   using the sf narrative frame.

413. Hermann, Louis. In the Sealed Cave. New York: D. Appleton, 1935.

   Published in England by Williams & Norgate (1935): the
   novel is presented as though it were based on a hitherto
   unknown manuscript of Lemuel Gulliver coming down to the
   present through the family of Ithiel Samways, a citizen of
   Natal, South Africa. The present editor refers at length
   to the Moustierian culture of the Dordognes area of France,
   for the premise is that Gulliver encountered Neanderthal
   man. Most of the narrative is devoted to the description
   of their society. Gulliver is rescued from the island by a
   trading brig, but the final implication is that the colony
   was destroyed because Gulliver's common cold had the effect
   of an epidemic. Significantly, the novel is subtitled "A
   Scientific Fantasy."

414. Hernaman-Johnson, F[rancis]. The Polyphemes; A Story of
Strange Adventures Among Strange Beings. London: Ward, Lock,
1906.

   Presented as though written a quarter century after the
   events of 1912, the narrative of Dr. John LeGallienne
   recalls the war between the Polyphemes, giant ants, and the

British.   First contact came in 1910 when the ship Britannia accidentally came across the islets west of South
America inhabited by the Polyphemes.   In 1912 when a
British fleet comes into the area because of an ultimatum
to warring South American countries, the Polyphemes attack
several of the ships.   Because they control an unknown
energy, X Magnetism, they are able to fly.   London and
various cities are bombed, while Azotine, a poison, is put
in British waters and kills anyone who drinks it.   Le-
Gallienne is taken prisoner to the islets.   Thus he gives
an account of the Polypheme society.   They worship the
moon, and most of them soon revolt against their cruel
priests.   As three gunboats come to the islands, an earthquake or volcano destroys the islands and all the Polyphemes.   While a prisoner, LeGallienne discovers his
beloved Marjorie Tremayne, who in a show of temper had
married Reginald Crawford and thus had been aboard the
Britannia.   Crawford takes LeGallienne's place and is
sacrificed to the moon.   The love story is particularly
insipid, but there is a faint echo of Wells as the narrator
speaks of man's frailty.

415.   Herrick, Robert.   Sometime.   New York: Farrar & Rinehart,
1933.

Cast at least a thousand years into the future, the narrative describes what happened to humanity after a new Ice
Age drove people from Europe and North America.   The scene
is New Khartoum.   An expedition does go to the North
American continent, but there is no sustained, dramatic
storyline.   The principal changes that occurred involved a
mixing of the races and an abandoning of the false ("pruri-
ent") modesty which marred the late Christian era.   Sexuality is much more open, and women are equal to men.   The
most bitter criticism is directed toward American urban society.   Little is left besides "Rockpiles."

416.   Heuston, B.F.   The Rice Mills of Port Mystery.   Chicago:
Kerr, 1892.

Concerned primarily with the Pacific Northwest, this narrative seems to have been overlooked in most bibliographies.
It speaks of the "Chemical Age" taking up the line of development from the mechanical arts and invention in the
late nineteenth century.   It makes specific reference to
aluminum.   It concerns itself with the last industrial
ocnflict.   The major food has become rice, and the Atlantic
Coast protects cheap rice.   The key to the economy is free
trade.   Finally, the vice president casts the deciding vote
when the Senate is in a tie.   Utopia is achieved.

417. Hile, William H.   The Ostrich for the Defense.   Boston:
Ellis, 1912.

Anne Newman tells Peter Rutledge to seek truth, study man,
and dedicate himself to the new age of brotherhood.   In
Africa he finds an unknown tribe whose white queen is
widely respected.   Her society is utopian because it does
not fear poverty.   Hile wants to emphasize the need for co-
operatives, and an appendix announces that the first co-
operative store opened in Rochedale, New York, sixty-eight
years earlier.

418. Hilliers, Ashton (pseud. of Henry Marriage Wallace).   The
Master-Girl; A Romance.   New York & London: Putnam, 1910.

Within the framework of a nameless professor who makes the
discovery of a campsite, the narrative gives the conventional treatment of cavemen a new twist.   Dêh-Yān, sixteen
years old, mates with Pul-Yun and stays with him when he
breaks his leg.   When they return to his tribe, the so-
called Sun-disc people, Pul-Yun takes part in a spear-
throwing contest.   Dêh-Yān introduces the bow and arrow.
She becomes chieftainess and forms a special force of women
archers.   She also introduces the worship of the moon among
the women especially.   During her reign every man has two
wives.   Yet when Pul-Yun dies, she immolates herself.

419. Hilton, James.   Lost Horizon.   London: Macmillan, 1933.

Rutherford, an English diplomat, gives the unnamed narrator
a manuscript based on Rutherford's conversations with Hugh
Conway some time after the latter's disappearance; later
the two speculate about Conway's story and fate.   In 1931
during an attempt by Conway and three companions to escape
war-torn Baskul, their plane is hijacked and crashes deep
in Tibet near the mountain Karakal (the Blue Moon).   Only
youthful Charles Mallinson is eager to leave.   In a series
of dialogues Conway learns that the High Lama is a Capuchin
Friar, Father Perrault, who came to the valley in 1734 when
he was fifty-three.   Through yoga and drugs he and the
other monks have gained longevity.   Outsiders who stray
into the valley are detained in order to enrich the life of
the lamasery; because no one has come since the war,
Conway's plane was deliberately brought to the valley,
though Conway himself was unknown.   Depressed by the war,
Conway and Father Perrault discuss the dangers facing
civilization, the coming Dark Ages.   Before the High Lama
dies, he tells Conway that he must assume leadership.
Conway accepts.   Sometime in the nineteenth century the
beautiful, eighteen-year-old Manchu girl, Lo-Tsen, strayed
into the valley.   Platonically, Conway loves her.   He
leaves Shangri-la only after learning that Lo-Tsen will
accompany Mallinson; Lo-Tsen has "eyes only" for the youth.
As the frame resumes, Rutherford reports that Conway

arrived at Chung-Kiang in China accompanied by the "most old" woman the Chinese doctor had ever seen. Leaving Rutherford, Conway disappeared, heading into the northwest from Bangkok. Lost Horizon must be regarded as a variation of the lost race motif; beyond that, it has importance because of the pessimism of the dialogue between Conway and Father Perrault. Despite the "most old" woman touch, the ambiguity seems deliberate; the ability of Conway to regain Shangri-la, uncertain at best.

420. Hilzinger, J[ohn] Geo[rge]. The Skystone; A Romance of Prehistoric Arizona. New York & London: Neely, 1899.

An introduction gives extravagant praise to the prehistoric ruins in Arizona. The ensuing narrative echoes most of the conventions of pseudo-historical romances of prehistory.

421. Hinton, C[harles] H[oward]. Scientific Romances; Second Series. London: Sonnenschein, 1896.

Influenced by Abbot, Hinton wrote extensively about the fourth dimension. He published An Episode in Flatland (1907) and a series of essays, Scientific Romances: First Series (1888). In this volume he comes closer to orthodox science fiction than elsewhere. The heroine of "Stella" has been made invisible by a deliberate experiment, while "An Unfinished Communication" implies that life after death permits one the freedom to move in the fourth dimension.

422. Hodder, William Reginald. The Daughter of the Dawn; A Realistic Story of Maori Magic. Boston: Page, 1903.

Also published in London by Jarrold (1902): because Hodder has an interest in the Maori, he is given the manuscript of Wanaki to edit. A firm of London solicitors asks Dick Warnock (called Wanaki by the Maori) to search for an heiress, Miriam Grey, who disappeared eighteen years earlier. With the aid of Kahikatea, who will not give his English name, Warnock seeks an old chief, Te Makawawa, and learns of a legend dating far back to the time when New Zealand was part of a now-submerged continent. At that time the goddess Hinauri, daughter of the dawn, ruled a great city with a doctrine of love. He finds Grey and his daughter Crystal. After he also discovers a mountain honeycombed with caves in which are statues of many ancient gods, including Hinauri, the novel becomes a mystical struggle between the ancient forces of good and evil. Crystal is the reincarnation of Hinauri. Reunited with her mother, she dies but only after proclaiming her message of love. Kahikatea, who loved her and was loved by her, returns to England to spread her doctrine. Miriam Grey and her husband also return to England briefly, but Warnock/Wanahi is killed by lightning because he revealed the ancient secrets.

423. Hodgson, William Hope.   The Boats of the 'Glen Carig.
London: Chapman & Hall, 1907.

> The first-person narrator, John Winterstraw, recounts the
> horrifying adventures of those who survive the sinking of
> the Glen Carig in the eighteenth century in an area re-
> sembling the Sargasso Sea. First they come to an island
> where they are attacked by seemingly carnivorous plants
> which have human and animal shapes embedded in them. After
> fighting various sea monsters, they arrive at a second
> island; throughout the remainder of the narrative they
> fight off what they call "Weed Men," a kind of giant slug.
> Aboard one of the derelict ships, they find Mary Madison,
> with whom Winterstraw falls in love. They finally escape.
> Like Bierce and Jack London, for example, Hodgson's
> strength lies in the verisimilitude of his detail; he makes
> even the most terrible seem feasible because of his tone.
> Unlike Poe and James, there is no question of the nar-
> rator's being mad. Hodgson regarded this as the first
> novel of the trilogy dealing with "borderlands," though no
> explicit reference is made to that concept by Winterstraw.

424. Hodgson, William Hope.   The Ghost Pirates.   London:
Stanley Paul, 1909.

> Also published in New York by Reynolds (1909): the first-
> person narrator, Jessop, sails aboard the Mortzestus, bound
> for the South Pacific and Cape Horn. He learns that the
> ship has a bad reputation, and mysterious accidents occur.
> It sails through one of those "borderlands" into a world of
> mist. Jessop sees phantom ships, and finally the crew is
> overwhelmed by an attack whether of the ghosts of pirates
> or strange beings from the other world, one cannot be
> certain. Jessop is the sole survivor and is picked up by a
> ship which had long seen the Mortzestus but could raise no
> signal. Effective because of Hodgson's skill with rea-
> listic detail of sea life, it lacks the power of The House
> on the Borderland.

425. Hodgson, William Hope.   The House on the Borderland.
London: Chapman & Hall, 1908.

> In a remote area of Ireland two English sportsmen sense
> that their campsite is permeated with the feeling of fear,
> of evil.   Amid ruins near a pit-like depression, they
> discover a manuscript. Its first-person narrator--an
> unnamed man living with his sister and dog--seems over-
> whelmed by terror. The reading given the novel depends on
> whether one sees the manuscript as the record of a fear-
> crazed man obsessed with evil or of an individual somehow
> able to transcend his physical being and attain cosmic
> visions. In either case the novel has importance for two
> basic reasons. First, Hodgson suggests that certain places
> on Earth either intersect with or coexist with another

world (or dimension). Through these areas (borderlands)
men may pass from world to world. So may various manifestations of evil, in this case "swinish" creatures who
besiege the house and finally kill the narrator. Secondly,
the narrator has a complex vision (or is actually present
at) the death of the Solar System when the Earth and the
dead sun are consumed by a great green sun, one of three
cosmic forces which appear. Although primarily concerned
with horror and evil in a way anticipating H.P. Lovecraft,
the novel anticipates the concept of alternate worlds.
This is the second book of the trilogy, certainly the most
complex and effective in its evocations of a man desperate
in a universe dominated by evil forces/beings.

426. Hodgson, William Hope. The Night Land. London: Nash,
1912.

Certainly Hodgson's longest and most extravagant novel: a
strange first chapter dealing with the love of a girl whom
he marries and who dies in childbirth leaves one unsure
whether the narrator is projected into the future, or in
that future briefly recalls a previous existence. Millions
of years in the future a remnant of mankind dwells in an
enormous metal pyramid, the Great Redoubt, surrounded by
darkness (the sun has long been dead) and monstrous forces
of evil. Their energy comes from tapping the "Earth
Current"--apparently a kind of electrical force--without
which they will be destroyed. The narrator receives
telepathic signals from the girl, Naani (a reincarnation of
the woman in the first chapter?), who lives in a second
Redoubt under savage attack by evil, monstrous forces. He
goes and rescues her. Much of the narrative is given to
his various encounters as he travels by foot to the second
Redoubt and returns with Naani, one of the few survivors,
to the Great Redoubt. She is killed, but the Current in
the Redoubt revives her. In Supernatural Horror in
Literature, Lovecraft complicates any interpretation by
asserting that the narrative deals with the dreams of a man
in the seventeenth century. He has high regard for that
portion dealing with the narrator's quest outside the
Redoubt. In its concern with horrific detail and evil, it
makes one think of Lovecraft.

427. Hoffman, Franz. The Treasure of the Inca. Trans. from
the German by John Frederick Smith. Philadelphia: Lutheran
Board of Education, 1870.

When a German farmer's crops are destroyed by hail, he and
his son emigrate to Peru. There they become obsessed with
stories of the Inca's treasure. The native Matteo guides
them, and when they find treasure, they attempt to kill
him. He seals them in the chamber with the treasure. The
novel's major importance lies in its date.

428. Holt-White, W[illiam Edward Bradden]. The Man Who Stole the Earth. London: Fisher, Unwin, 1909.

> With the aid of Joe Langley, inventor of an airship (four propellors), the Englishman John Strong hopes to bring peace to the world. In love with Princess Diana, daughter of King George II of Balkania, he asks the King to abdicate in his favor and allow him to marry Diana. When George II refuses, Strong builds the Victor, a ship which carries twenty men and innumerable steel shells. Soon he has bombed the city of Bomberg, capital of Balkania; kidnapped Diana, taking her to his base in the Ring of Nissa in the Carpathian Mountains -- so called because of an impenetrable ring of glaciers; and issued an ultimatum to the world asking their aid (Britain is excepted). Further bombing of the capital brings its surrender and Diana's return. The King, losing all sense of honor and love, hoists Diana into a balloon and flies to Paris pursued by Strong in the Victor. Then begins a series of decisive actions: he bombs the casino at Monte Carlo; kidnaps the infant son of the Czar; bombs Potsdam and arranges an aerial dual with the Kaiser. By now Diana opposes her father who would marry her to Prince Luwdig of the neighboring Balkan state of Sylvania. Strong continually laments the bloodshed he is causing; however, he persists and declares repeatedly that he will steal the world (become its ruler because he has the airships). He literally drops the bombs (with deadly accuracy) by hand. Ultimately his three ships defeat the Kaiser's three ships; the two declare their friendship, and the Kaiser offers to give the bride away at the wedding. Strong declares that he will be Dictator of the World (America will "fall in line" once Russia and Germany no longer resist him). This must be read to be believed; it is not a parody of the future war motif.

429. Hopkins, Jeune (pseud. of Squire D. Hopkins?) (as by Vic St. L.). The Mysterious Hunter; or, The Last of the Aztecs. Chicago, Jeune Hopkins, 1892.

> A prefatory note suggests that the Aztec empire was "the peer of Spain" at the time of its conquest by Cortez. The first-person narrator is traveling in Arizona in order to write about the land. He is given a manuscript by an old man. It concerns the ruins at Monte Diablo and asserts that they are the artifacts of some prehistoric race which has been exterminated. The narrator and his companion encounter a beautiful young woman, Aweta, who in turn tells her story. She is one of the last who has Aztec blood. The use of a story within a story becomes confusing, especially since reference is made to Geronimo. The idea of the prehistoric race, though really only touched on, is the element giving the novel importance.

430. [House, Edward Mandell].   <u>Philip</u> <u>Dru</u>, <u>Administrator</u>; <u>A</u> <u>Story</u> <u>of</u> <u>Tomorrow</u>, <u>1920-1935</u>. New York: Huebsch, 1912.

A 1920 graduate of West Point, Philip Dru is almost blinded when he and Gloria Strawn are lost in the southwestern desert. He then begins a career aimed at social reform, while Gloria tries to obtain donations from the wealthy. Five years later Senator Selwyn of the corrupt Selwyn-Thor political machine selects James Rockland as presidential candidate. Thor's secretary reveals the corruption to the press, and the machine calls out troops so that there cannot be an honest election. Wisconsin, Minnesota, Iowa, and Nebraska form the nucleus of states who oppose the eastern machine. (All states west of the Mississippi are numbered among the opposition.) Dru, who has become Rockland's opposition, becomes the general of the army which defeats Selwyn's machine in a civil war that lasts for a single battle. Dru establishes himself as Administrator of the Republic. A new constitution limits the power of the president and elects senators for a life-long term. Women are given the franchise. Canada welcomes union with the U.S., and after a brief war with Mexico, the Central American states are united and admitted to a U.S. which stretches from the Arctic to the Panama Canal. The reforms are conventional for the period, although Dru wishes to reform the method of burial, advocating cremation. During the battle of Elma, which he won, he watched over the battlefield on horseback. Many comparisons are made between the corrupt Selwyn organization (the East) and the post-Civil War North. However, Selwyn becomes Dru's friend and tells his life story. Dru and Gloria sail into the Pacific sunset after he has governed for seven years and resigns before a new election. House was an adviser to Woodrow Wilson.

431. Howells, William Dean.   <u>Between</u> <u>the</u> <u>Dark</u> <u>and</u> <u>the</u> <u>Daylight</u>. New York: Harper, 1907.

As a framework for his short stories dealing with the supernatural, Howells creates a group of men who dine together. Each one in turn tells a story which involves him personally (or a friend) with some ghostly encounter. One member of the group is the psychologist, Wanhope, who explains each story in terms of the theory of the period. In each case he suggests that the ghost represents some concern that the individual feels. Like Bierce, he dramatizes fear. The protagonist of "The Angel of the Lord" is afraid of death; believing that a tramp he meets is the angel of death, he runs after the tramp and kills himself in a fall. The protagonist of "Though One Rose from the Dead" becomes obsessed with the idea that his dead wife will return to him. He plunges into the surf and accidentally drowns himself when he thinks he hears her voice calling to him.

432. Howells, William Dean. Questionable Shapes. New York: Harper, 1903.

This collection of stories introduces the psychologist Wanhope.

433. Howells, William Dean. Through the Eye of the Needle; A Romance. New York: Harper, 1907.

So long as Aristides Homo remains in the United States, the novel retains the vividness and realism of A Traveler from Altruria. When he and his American friends leave New York City and go to Altruria, he simply portrays another utopian society.

434. Howells, William Dean. A Traveler from Altruria; A Romance. New York: Harper, 1894.

Originally serialized in Cosmopolitan (1892-1893): Howells reverses the usual narrative technique of the utopian novelists in that he brings Aristides Homo to America to comment directly upon society as he witnesses it. He is particularly critical of slavery, class inequality, and the American emphasis upon competition. He asserts that Altruria is "the first Christian commune" since Christ. Significantly, the inhabitants of Altruria voted to bring about a socialist utopia. Electricity supplies all of the country's energy and actually does all the work except for handicraft from which the people gain aesthetic pleasure. Howells seems indebted to many sources for his ideas.

435. Hoyt, Francis Deming. The Coming Storm. New York: Kennedy, 1913.

In 1910 both George Stuart and Herman Villard have espoused the doctrines of Marx and Engels. The novel issues a warning because of the growth of socialism in the U.S. during the past decade, yet it also discredits most of the leaders (and organizations like the I.W.W.) of the working class. The storyline involves the attempt to blow up the Express Building on 23rd Street. It fails. George is converted to Catholicism and marries Gertrude Drayton. At the end of the novel he takes his first communion and realizes how much that action means to the devout Catholic.

436. Hungerford, Margaret Wolfe. The Professor's Experiment. London: Chatto & Windus, 1895.

The protagonist, Paul Wyndham, a barrister, learns of the experiment. The professor uses an anesthetic known to the Indians of South America to induce a deathlike trance in an eighteen-year-old girl. It succeeds. He is afraid that he has killed her; (he speaks of pride in his belief and thus

faintly echoes Dr. Frankenstein). She revives and talks to
Wyndham. But the professor dies.

437. Huxley, Aldous. Brave New World. London: Chatto &
Windus, 1932.

Brave New World remains one of the classic early dystropian
novels. Its forecast of the regimented life in the era
After Ford needs no plot summary here. Two points should
be emphasized. First, the thematic center of the novel
lies in the dialogue between John Savage and Mustapha
Monde. Secondly, it provides one of the few examples where
a future totalitarian state keeps the people under control
through pleasure instead of fear.

438. Hyne, C[harles] J[ohn] Cutcliffe [Wright]. Empire of the
World. London: Everett, 1910.

This must be read as a parody of the future war motif.
Amid hysteria over the threat of war when Germany buys Phos
Island from Greece as a possible coaling station, John
Byrn-Scarlett, M.P., sinks a torpedo boat, the Z-7, in the
Thames and the Kaiser Charlemagne in the Kiel Canal. He
proclaims that he has a "New Force" and soon calls himself
Imperator Mundi. He later sinks another German ship in the
Baltic, but he also sinks a Channel Boat which would carry
Lady Laura Deeping, whom he thinks he wants to marry, to
Ostend so that she could marry Count von Stalheim, am-
bassador to Britain. He destroys some 500 miles of the
Atlantic Trust Cable and silences the British press by
threatening to destroy their presses. All of these things
happen offstage. The main storyline deals with his poverty. He has returned from Mexico with claims verifying
six rich mines, but he can make no money from them. Lady
Deeping says she will marry only for money. Hamburg
revolts against the Kaiser, Italy recognizes him as World
Emperor, a U.S. candidate for president becomes his lieutenant, and Germany breaks up the federation into the old
states. He says that the Empire works because people want
peace, and everyone knew that Germany would attack at least
one of the Western powers. Raines of the Uganda Development Syndicate suggests Scarlett form Golconda of Mexico
Ltd. He does, becomes rich, and marries an American, Mary
De Foe, a millionairess from Chicago. The novel attacks
the few millionaires who control the finances of Europe,
and it is both violently anti-German and anti-Semitic.

439. Hyne, C[harles] J[ohn] Cutcliffe [Wright]. The Lost
Continent. London: Hutchinson, 1900.

Originally serialized in Pearson's Magazine (1899) without
the introduction; published in New York by Harper (1900):
the first-person narrator has some fun with an established
convention as he reports how he and Coppinger discover a

manuscript in a cave in the Grand Canary. He damages the
wax tablets. What is left is the fist-person narrative of
Deucalion, for twenty years viceroy of Yucatan. He is
summoned to Atlantis by Phorenice, the queen and self-
proclaimed goddess, who recalls Rider Haggard's Ayesha. He
marries Phorenice, but loves Naïs, daughter of the priest
Zaemon. Atlantis seethes with revolt; the battles and
intrigues of the queen take up much of the manuscript.
Naïs must be buried alive, but is kept in suspended animation. An Egyptian colony is referred to, and Deucalion
learns that Yucatan has been overrun by little hairy men
from the West, whom he regards as subhuman. As the priests
cause earthquakes which sink the continent, Deucalion and
Naïs escape aboard the Ark of Mysteries. He destroys
earlier manuscripts of Life and Death, which Phorenice
sought. Mammoths, cave tigers, and saurian monsters all
dwelt in Atlantis. The novel established many of the
conventions governing the presentation of Atlantis.

440. Jackson, Ambrose Lester. When Shiloh Came. New York:
Oglivie, 1899.

This novel exemplifies those listed in some bibliographies
which might therefore be mistakenly considered science
fiction. The narrative dwells upon an imaginary kingdom,
the Valley of Hesydrus, somewhere in the East. It deals
with the adventures of Carmyhl, who has just reached
maturity and sets out on his first quest--to do away with a
renegade ruler. The novel becomes concerned with religious
matters and ends with the Wise Men coming to Bethlehem to
witness the birth of Christ.

441. Jackson, James W. A Queen of Amazonia. London: Walker,
1928.

The first-person narrator, together with Sir Falcon
Richardson, Dr. Robert Sanderson, and other companions,
penetrates deep into South America; on a high plateau they
come upon the kingdom of Verstae inhabited by two races in
different cities. The whites are descendants of Vikings;
their capital is the city of Temanée whose queen is Cettys.
The other race, the Sayans, is identified at least once as
descendants of Aztecs. Warfare between the two races
develops; the Vikings are annihilated, and many of the
women and children poison themselves to escape the Sayans.
The narrator, Richardson, and the few who survive take
Cettys and her crown jewels to England. There is no love
story. Perhaps the most original touch occurs when Dr.
Sanderson removes Cettys' appendix.

442. James, Henry. The Ghostly Tales of Henry James. New Brunswick, N.J.: Rutgers University Press, 1948.

Although James does not make explicit reference to science, his contribution to the evolution of the traditional ghost story is highly significant, especially in those stories which present the supernatural as a manifestation of a disordered mind. His most famous tale, of course, remains "The Turn of the Screw," where the ambiguity is so perfect that one cannot know for certain whether the spirits of Peter Quint and Miss Jessel are is real or a delusion of the governess' imagination.

443. Jane, [John] Fred[erick] T[homas]. Blake of the "Rattle-snake"; or, The Man Who Saved England; A Story of Torpedo Warfare in 189-. London: Tower, 1895.

In 189- Britain becomes embroiled in a war with France and Russia. The narrative is told by a first-person narrator, Bouvier, who is the sole survivor of the last battle of the Rattlesnake. He concentrates on close detail on a number of naval engagements, admitting that he is particularly interested in the decisive fighting of the torpedo boat flotilla instead of the whole war. At one point they ressue the ship Valetta, whose passenger, Lucy Monckton, daughter of General Monckton, is Blake's fiancée. She remains aboard ship for awhile and sees the base on the Holy Isle, near the Isle of Arran. Blake's flotilla costs the enemy some forty ships within a week, and in the final victorious battle, he loads the Rattlesnake with dynamite, thereby taking two enemy ironclads to the bottom with him as well as damaging another. Miss Monckton haunts his tomb before she dies, for both Blake and her father died during the same battle. At one point the narrator suggests that Britain expected Germany to come to her aid.

444. Jane, [John] Fred[erick] T[homas]. The Incubated Girl. London: Tower, 1896.

Two men--Blackburne Zadara--an Egyptologist--and Meredyth Wilson--find an egg in a temple devoted to Isis. Following instructions given on a papyrus, they incubate the egg in a laboratory. From it comes a baby girl whom they name Stella. Wilson is pleased that they have not produced a Frankenstein. An immediate eighteen-year time lapse occurs. Zadara condemns modern women and asserts that women like Stella will replace the "new woman." He wishes to raise her by a strict moral code. Much of the potential is lost because the book does become a harangue against modern morality. One does not know what to make of Stella, for she rejects Wilson's son and takes Susan Riley as a companion. She becomes something of a public figure and voices Jane's basic themes.

445. Jane, [John] Fred[erick] T[homas]. <u>To Venus in Five Seconds</u>, <u>Being an Account of the Strange Disappearance of Thomas Plummer</u>. London: Innes, 1897.

> The first-person narrator, a medical student, Thomas Plummer, loves a woman doctor, Zumeena. She reveals that she is descended from ancient Egyptians and takes him to the planet Venus. Finding that he and other humans are to be subjected to experiments, he tries to escape. This causes a final battle between the humans on Venus and the Thothens, an intelligent species of giant insect.

446. Jane, [John] Fred[erick] T[homas]. <u>The Violet Flame</u>; <u>A Story of Armageddon and After</u>. London: Ward, Lock, 1899.

> The first-person narrator, Lester, tells the story of the comic-looking Professor Mirzarbeau, who believes that the Earth and Solar System are thinking entities, that people are merely molecules of that being, and that all objects are merely different arrangements of hydrogen atoms. He develops a purple ray by which he is able to communicate with Earth, the brain of the Solar System, he asserts. The ray annihilates objects like Waterloo Station and reduces people to toy-size statues. Dornton is his accomplice. When people, including Landry Selina Baker, a millionairess from Chicago, scoff at his ideas, he becomes angry and proclaims himself the Beast of Revelation. He got the idea from the fact that the real war is being fought between the financiers/stock exchanges of London and the second "London" built in the Euphrates valley, which he calls Esdraelon (another Hebrew word for Armageddon). He panics London into accepting him as ruler. When the government tries to dig a tunnel beneath his lab in order to blow it up, they fail, but he accidentally kills himself in his ray. The comet which he said that he and Earth had decided to use to destroy the world does come, causing vast floods and upheavals. Only Lester and Landry survive as a new Adam and Eve. The story is written for their children. One cannot be certain what the object of Jane's attack is; certainly he is striking out at international financiers; for example, peace prevails because it upsets the stock markets of the various capitals to have the "long-expected bogie" --a war--take place.

447. Janvier, Thomas A[llibone]. <u>The Aztec Treasure-House</u>; <u>A Romance of Contemporaneous Antiquity</u>. New York: Harper, 1890.

> Janvier's protagonist, Professor Thomas Palgrave, occupying the Chair of Topical Linguistics at the University of Michigan, is working on a book, <u>Pre-Columbian Conditions on the Continent of America</u>. Obtaining certain hitherto unknown manuscripts, he organizes an expedition to find a lost valley of Aztecs. He undergoes the usual hazards of a jungle expedition; he finds the valley in time to take part

in a civil war. His companion, Friar Antonio, meets an Aztec warrior in the arena in an attempt to gain the release of his friends. Unresisting, he meets his death after having preached to the Aztecs. He fails to convert them, but his death brings about such natural phenomena as a fireball which destroys all the pagan shrines in the city. Palgrave proclaims this event a miracle and escapes during the ensuing confusion. Several times he refers to Stephens and LePlongeon.

448. Janvier, Thomas A[llibone]. In Great Waters. New York: Harper, 1901.

This is a group of short stories and should not be confused with the novel In the Sargasso Sea.

449. Janvier, Thomas A[llibone]. In the Sargasso Sea. New York: Harper, 1898.

The first-person narrator, Stetworth, takes passage aboard a freighter to get to Loango in Africa. When he discovers that it is a slaver, he refuses to participate; he is thrown overboard and is picked up by a ship, which encounters a fierce storm. He is abandoned and drifts into the Sargasso Sea. Except for a brief talk with a murderer who dies, he encounters only a cat. He makes his way out aboard a small boat. What makes the novel unique is that the narrator is entirely alone throughout his experience; he simply describes what he sees and does.

450. Jeffries, [John] Richard. After London; or, Wild England. London: Cassell, 1885.

The novel is divided into two parts: "The Relapse into Barbarism" and "Wild England." Despite a first-person narrator, no specific catastrophe is named as bringing about the end of modern England. A vast exodus from Britain did take place; within thirty years most of the country had reverted to forest, although the area of London was a fetid swamp. A great central lake fills most of the midlands, and only bushmen, gypsies, and a few walled towns remain. The first part is simply descriptive; the second shapes itself around the odyssey of Felix Aquila, a native of Thyma Castle, as he travels around the shores of the great lake. He finally returns to bring his beloved Aurora to live with him among a band of shepherds whose leader he has become. The second part is told from a third-person omniscient point of view focusing upon Felix. The early date seems important because it emphasizes a desire to be rid of urban, technological civilization. After London stands with the works of Hudson and William Morris in rejecting modern, scientific times long before any disillusionment caused by the First World War set in.

451. Jensen, Johannes V[ilhelm]. The Long Journey; Fire and
Ice. Trans. from the Danish by A. G. Chater. New York: Knopf,
1923.

   Published in London by Gyldenal (1922): this is the first
   of several volumes whose central theme concerns "tracing
   the long journey from primeval chaos to modern civilization." Its premise suggests that mankind originated in the
   northern latitudes of Scandinavia; thus his first struggle
   was to survive the last glaciation. It seems safe to say
   that Jensen worked on a more epic scale than any of the
   earlier writers dealing with cavemen. In his prefatory
   note he declares that the Ice Age was of paramount importance. Those who stayed in the north grew into modern
   humanity, while those who fled to the south remained "naked
   jungle folk" whose descendants still live in "their primitive state in the tropics." In this assertion may be seen
   something of the myth which fed the concept of a "pure"
   Aryan race (variously located) and the inferior peoples of
   the remainder of the world.

452. Johnson, George Lindsay. The Weird Adventures of Professor Delapine of the Sorbonne. London: Routledge, 1916.

   Through a series of seances the professor changes his views
   toward spiritualism. The main storyline ends with two
   marriages--Delapine and Renée, Marcel and Violette, and
   includes a coup at the tables in Monte Carlo.

453. Johnson, Owen [McMahon]. The Coming of the Amazons; A
Satiristic Speculation on the Scientific Future of Civilization.
New York: Longmans, Green, 1931.

   First-person narrator, John Bogardus, a graduate of Harvard
   and Oxford, first introduces his wife, Ernesta, who is a
   leader of the women's movement; then he allows Professor
   Sachaloff to hypnotize him into a cataleptic trance. That
   action takes place in November 1929. He awakens in 2181 to
   find a society dominated by women. Scientific progress
   includes automatic machinery, airplanes, and the prolonga-
   tion of life. There is a ratio of one man to twenty-five
   women; however, the women control reproduction genetically,
   and he learns that the young men between ages twenty and
   thirty-five are kept as pampered darlings to be used as
   breeders. The most bitterly satiric sequence is the
   "Promenade of Young Males"; they are to be chosen for
   breeding. One of the Amazons points out that he is simply
   witnessing a reversal of sex roles. He has Acquilla and
   Dianne as his guides, but no love story develops, for he
   wants to promote a rebellion among the men. The climax of
   the narrative comes with his trial when he denounces the
   society for its lack of humor and the loneliness it causes
   the individual. An appended note suggests that he wrote
   the narrative during an eight-month period while he was

confined in an asylum; it speaks of his fear of women and
his desire to warn his fellow men of the danger of "feminist progress."

454. Johnstone, D[avid] Lawson. The Mountain Kingdom; A
Narrative of Adventure. London: Sampson, Low, 1888.

Dedicated to Jules Verne: the first-person narrator, young
Douglas Dalziel of Airth, had an uncle, Alistair Douglas
Dalziel, who disappeared in the East some twenty years
earlier. With his companions, Eric Trevanion and Eric's
East Indian cousin, Henry Lee, Douglas decides to journey
eastward. The legend of a city like an El Dorado in the
Kingdom of the Smoking Mountains in Tibet attracts them.
Lee's man, Sirikisson Teli, a Ghoorka, verifies the legend.
Aboard ship they are joined by an older man, G. Graham
Edwards, who proves troublesome once they start inland.
They lose their equipment and animals in a landslide. They
journey down a Mysterious River; they meet Dadchierka Caen,
adviser to Timrac, King of Kisnia, a temperate area like
Italy.   Parchments tell of soldiers of Alexander the
Great's army intermarrying with the natives.   After an
assassination attempt on Timrac, they become involved in a
civil war concerning the heir to the throne. They are on
the side of young Pellas; Edwards sides with the older
Asoka. Timrac is killed and Asoka wins, but only after
they learn that Dadchierka is Douglas' uncle. They flee to
England, taking Pellas with them.

455. Johnstone, D[avid] Lawson. The Paradise of the North; A
Story of Discovery and Adventure Around the Pole. London:
Remington, 1890.

In his will Randolph Torrens leaves a large bequest to his
daughter, Edith, to explore the Arctic north of Nova
Zembla. Captain James Sneddons agrees to use his ship; Dr.
Felix Lorimer, a "savant of the day," joins them, as does
his brother Cecil, who is betrothed to Edith.   Near a
volcanic mountain they find what they call Torrens Land,
"an Arctic Switzerland," and winter in Ft. Lorimer. They
discover the young warrior, Eyvind, whose country is called
Isloken and capital city Hjalnord. With Eyvind's aid they
reach the North Pole. The ruling people are Icelandic.
Cecil declines the hand of Sigrida, daughter of King Aleif,
and the English party makes a "dash for liberty."   They
succeed, and Cecil marries Edith, who did not accompany
them on the voyage. The first-person narrator is Geoffrey
Oliphant, a member of the party.

456. Johnstone, D[avid] Lawson. The White Princess of the
Hidden City, Being a Record of Leslie Rutherford's Strange
Adventures in Central America. London: Chambers, 1898.

> During a revolution in Salvatierra in Central America,
> Leslie Rutherford meets Don Gaspar O'Driscoll, who tells
> him that he closely resembles a young woman who saved
> O'Driscoll from Indians in the back country of Nicaragua.
> She wore a ring bearing the crest of the Leslies. Ruther-
> ford tells of a manuscript in the family recounting the
> adventures of Gavin Leslie in the seventeenth century.
> Leslie and O'Driscoll go into the interior. There is
> legend of a city near Monte del Diablo. On a lake they
> find the city Oyalapa. Leslie meets the fair Chiatapua,
> who is related to him. Gavin found the city and married
> Khalama, princess of the city, and apparently member of a
> white race. They become involved in a civil war with the
> chief, Adano, a suitor for Chiatapua's hand. They regard
> Rutherford as an incarnation of his ancestor whom they
> deified. The white race is descended from people in
> Yucatan. Chiatapua loves Leslie; he agrees to stay until
> she is killed by Adano's brother. Then he and O'Driscoll
> depart.

457. Jones, Claude P. and A. L. Sykes. Quick My Rifle. New
York: Cortlandt, 1907.

> The heroine, an American taken at birth by natives, be-
> lieves herself to be an incarnation of Kubla Khan and frees
> Tibet from China. The protagonist, an American balloonist,
> arrives on the scene in time for this to become essentially
> a love story.

458. [Jones, Jingo, M.P.]. The Sack of London by the Highland
Host; A Romance of the Period. London: Simpkin, 1900.

> Aroused by a Punch cartoon caricaturing some Highland
> leader, Sir Yachin Tash, head of the House of Clachan-
> fooash, gathers the Chieftains to rebel. Sir Rory Mac-
> kenzie of Castle Gorach becomes their commander. Inci-
> dental is the hasty love story of Miss Lucy Walters and
> Jonathan Granville, an unsuccessful American claimant.
> With their army based in Hampstead Heath, the Chieftains
> destroy many important buildings with a dynamite plus x
> charge, but while London is devastated, their plot fails.

459. Kane, James J[ohnson]. Ilian; A Psychological Tale of the
Civil War. Boston: Little, Brown, 1888.

> A Boston professor seduces a beautiful Southern girl; when
> she dies in childbirth, she curses him and all his des-
> cendants. Their illegitimate daughter, Ilian, becomes the
> instrument of the curse when she persuades the professor's
> legitimate son, Adrien, to betray the North and spy for the

South. She loves Adrien and marries him, but they never
live as man and wife, for recurrent hallucinations warn her
to hate him. After he dies, she learns they are related
and revels in her emotional horror at having come so close
to incest. Kane does refer at various times to hypnosis
and "psychic exaltation" induced by drugs.

460. Kelly, James Paul. Prince Izon; A Romance of the Grand
Canyon. Chicago: A. C. McClurg, 1910.

A geologist/archaeologist leads an expedition, including
two young women, into the Grand Canyon, where they are met
by Prince Izon, leader of a group of Aztec warriors.
Though he is friendly, they are attacked by other Aztecs,
who slaughter everyone but the explorers and Prince Izon.
Their captors take them to the Red City; Izon is to be
sacrificed to the pagan gods. At the last moment warriors
from Izon's city rescue them. There is something of a love
story, as well as some mysticism growing out of the Aztec
religion.

461. Kelly, Teague M. Mucca Scob; or, Threads of Prehistoric
and Present History, Concatenated. Oakland, Ca.: The Author,
1885.

Near the Klamath River on "16 day of February, Era of
Science, 284," the first-person narrator encounters a
caveman, Mucca Scob, who lived there some 20,000 to 50,000
years earlier. That life in the Firelands was his last
incarnation; he has lived on several planets, all of whose
people are of a higher order than those of Earth. A brief
story tells how Susser took fifty-five male and fifty-five
female infants and mated them, the tallest to shortest, as
though seeking an average. Mucca Scob was mated to Sai
Criff. The book is more philosophical than story. It
stresses that all Indians are on the way to extinction.

462. Ker, David. The Lost City; or, The Boy Explorers in
Central Asia. New York: Harper, 1885.

The tone of the narrative reminds one of Henty: three
boys--Tom, Bill, Ernest--fresh from Rugby School end up
near the Afghan city of Tashkent. A series of battles and
escapes involve the English against Persians and Afghans.
A Professor Makaroff wants to find a lost city; by crawling
through a narrow passage--a water conduit?--they find the
ruins of what appears to be a Greek city in a narrow valley
between high cliffs. The discovery makes quite a stir in
the "learned circles" of St. Petersburg.

463. Kinross, Albert.   The Fearsome Island; Being a Modern Rendering of the Narrative of One Silas Fordred, Master Mariner of Hythe, Whose Shipwreck and Subsequent Adventures Are Herein Set Forth.   Chicago: Herbert S. Stone, 1896.

> Published in Bristol by J. W. Arrowsmith: Kinross poses as editor of a manuscript found among a "mass of ancient documents" in the Town Hall Center.   Fordred encounters a variety of horrors associated with a castle on the deserted island of Don Diego Rodriguez.   Because the apparently supernatural events involve a technology in advance of the sixteenth century--a sword that sweeps across a room, spears that fall from a ceiling, noxious gas, and a kind of power boat--some individuals have classified the novel as science fiction.   But Fordred meets a "Hag of the Turret," whom he calls a witch, and apparently the ghost of her father, Don Diego.   From the beginning Fordred's imagination, as would be appropriate to a Renaissance mariner, is colored by superstition.   Thus the tone of the novel is more Gothic than science fictional.   In addition, a naked savage, named Esau, recalls Crusoe's man Friday.   Fordred finally escapes (by the power boat) and returns to England. Well written, the novel gives a good psychological portrait of the protagonist.

464. Kip, Leonard.   Hannibal's Man, and Other Tales.   Albany, N.Y.: Argus, 1873.

> Near Heidelberg the first-person narrator and his beloved Ursula find a Carthaginian in a glacier.   He revives and identifies himself as one of Hannibal's men.   He would go to Carthage but returns in two months.   The narrator and ancient warrior finally fight one another for Ursula's hand.   The Carthaginian's leap sends him into a crevasse. A number of references are made to archaeology, and the narrator asks science to believe his story.

465. Kipling, Rudyard.   "With the Night Mail" in Actions and Reactions.   New York: Doubleday, 1909.

> The Aerial Board of Control (A.B.C.) governs the world because aviation has completely changed the order of things.   The story centers on the flight of Postal Packet 162 from London to Quebec.   Dirigible balloons use the air currents to aid their flight.   Everything is controlled by the smooth flow of "traffic and all it implies."   To emphasize the future nature of the tale, Kipling concludes with supposed excerpts from the magazine in which the story was presented as a factual account: ads, letters to the editor, and inquiries about lights, missing aircraft, and weather. "As Easy as A.B.C." (1912) portrays the effort of the District of Illinois to break away from the Aerial Board of Control in 2065.   The rebellion is put down, but the most important implication suggests that a relatively few people

are now spread out across the world. With a few exceptions, the growth of urbanization has been ended because flight makes it possible for people to scatter to the four corners of the world and still remain in communication with one another.

466. Kirk, Eleanor (pseud. of Eleanor Maria Ames). The Christ of the Red Planet. New York: Publishers, 1901.

Highly mystical: the protagonist of this narrative, a woman, encounters Christ on Mars.

467. Kirk, Hyland C[lare]. When the World Grows Young; A Romance. New York: Dillingham, 1888.

This is a portrait of the city of Bridgburg in a mining area of the American West. Cast into a utopian future, it shows the perfection of man "mentally, morally, and physically." Each person's job is regulated to give variety in order to facilitate good health; travel and relaxation are emphasized. Buildings are warmed by hot water from the interior of the Earth, while air conditioning results from bringing air down from the 25,000 foot level by a device combining balloons and flexible tubes. Schools instruct both boys and girls to attain "endless life."

468. Klette, C[harles] H[erman] B[runo]. The Lost Mine of the Mono. New York: Cochrane, 1909.

Against a western background, the chief concern of the narrative is to indulge in a lengthy discussion of the soul and "the continuity of purpose" throughout nature and the universe. The suggestion is made that somewhere along the line "moral law" has been broken and things are not as they were. While it argues for the divinity of man in God's universe, it also asserts that there was no such place as a single Eden but rather the appearance of men in many places and many times. Everything is in the "complete control" of God. The first-person narrator and his friends discussed these matters years ago around a campfire; they did, incidentally, discover a lost mine.

469. Kline, Otis Adelbert. Call of the Savage. New York: Clode, 1937.

As an act of revenge because Georgia Adams married Harry Trevor when Dr. Bracken was in Africa, the scientist kidnaps their infant son, Jan, and raises the boy with an old female chimpanzee, Chicma. He also teaches the boy to respond violently to the phrase, "Mother! Kill!" Jan and Chicma escape his stockade, but they are captured by Santos and an accomplice who wish to put Jan in a sideshow. After a series of accidents and storms, Jan and Chicma end up in the jungles of Venezuela. He rescues Ramona Suarez and

returns her to her foster-parents who--one learns later--
found her as an infant aboard a boat. Jan and Chicma are
captured by armored warriors riding triceratops. They are
taken to a mysterious valley and befriend Koh Kan, whose
people live in the city Temuhan and worship Quetzalcoatl,
but are always at war with a white people who live in the
city of Samsu. The latter group is related somehow to an
ancient Pacific continent and to Egypt through the worship
of Osiris. Periodically Jan rescues Ramona over the years
when she returns from school; periodically he lives in the
valley. His parents, Santos, and Bracken all search for
him. He learns that Ramona is a princess of Samsu; Bracken
makes one last effort to have Jan kill his parents. This
must be one of the most overplotted novels of the period as
Kline imitates Burroughs. Retitled Jan of the Jungle
(1966).

470. Kline, Otis Adelbert. Maza of the Moon. Chicago: A. C.
McClurg, 1930.

When Ted Dustin and Roger Sanders fire a projectile at the
moon from the Galapagos Islands, the moon's dominant
people, the P'an-ku, a yellow race, bombard Earth's cities.
Ted sees the image of Maza, a white girl, on the moon, and
he flies there alone in a small vehicle of his invention.
He learns that ages ago the moon was devastated in a savage
war with Mars. The white Martians came to Earth; so later
did the Oriental races who are descendants of the P'an-ku.
Ted allies himself with Maza's people. The P'an-ku
threaten Earth with a cold ray, while Roger leads a space
fleet armed with a degravitor. Earth triumphs, and Ted and
Maza are married. Not only does this novel recall Jules
Verne, but it adapts the yellow peril motif.

471. Kline, Otis Adelbert. The Planet of Peril. Chicago:
A. C. McClurg, 1929.

A victim of ennui, Robert Ellsmore Grandon of Chicago is
kidnapped by Dr. Morgan and offered the opportunity to
change bodies with a man who is slave on the planet Zorovia
(Venus). He accepts. He leads a revolt that fails and
crosses swords with Rogi Destho, a villainous noble who
covets the throne and person of the beauteous blonde,
Vernia, ruler of the kingdom of Reabon. In a last minute
switch she tricks Destho by signing a proclamation declaring that she marry Grandon and share the throne with
him. Destho lunges forward, but Zueppa, an enemy of his,
stabs him fatally. Vernia proves to be Grandon's "wonderful little woman."

472. Kline, Otis Adelbert.   The Port of Peril.   Providence,
R.I.: Grandon, 1949.

Robert Grandon sets out to find Harry Thorne. Almost as
soon as he leaves, Vernia is kidnapped by the pirate San
Thoy. No sooner does she escape from him than they are
both captured by the Toad People. Thus begins a series of
threats to her virtue and rescues which unify the friends
and add the kingdom of Mernerum to the allies of Reabon.

473. Kline, Otis Adelbert.   The Prince of Peril.   Chicago:
A. C. McClurg, 1930.

In the opening of The Planet of Peril, Dr. Morgan had
mentioned a Mr. Thorne, who was to exchange bodies with a
man on Zorovia (Venus).   This is the story of Borgen
Takkor, born on Mars, who lived as Harry Thorne for a
decade and then became Prince Zinlo of Olba on Venus. The
friend of Vorn Vangal, who had originally communicated with
Morgan, Zinlo rescues Princess Loralie of Tyrhana, but when
his father dies, the treacherous Taliboz takes the throne
and kidnaps Zinlo and Loralie. After he escapes, with the
aid of Vorn Vangal, Zinlo regains the throne and weds
Loralie, the most beautiful woman on three planets.

474. Kline, Otis Adelbert.   Tam, Son of the Tiger. New York:
Avalon, 1962.

Copyright 1931 by Popular Publications: in Burma the child
Tam is taken by/accompanies the white tiger, Leang. When
he grows up he becomes part of a titanic war involving the
old Hindu gods, whose domain is a huge subterranean world.
Lozong, a pious lama, acts as his teacher. He rescues the
lovely Nina, and the plot dissolves into a series of
captures and rescues until he fights and destroys Siva.
The lovers are united. Along the way Major Charles Evans
recognizes Tam as his son.

475. Knapp, Adeline.   One Thousand Dollars a Day; Studies in
Practical Economics. Boston: Arena, 1894.

A group of short stories which are pro-labor and anti-
capitalist: the most memorable piece is "The Discontented
Machine." A mammoth cutter and shaper is developed which
will replace twenty-five per cent of the laborers in the
boot and shoe trade. One owner wants to develop a machine
which will totally replace labor. The machine stops and
informs its operators that it is being overworked, has gone
on strike, and asks for wages.

476. Knoblock, Edward.   The Ant Heap; A Novel.   New York:
Minton, Balch, 1930.

The first novel of an American playwright, this narrative
splits down the middle.   The first-person narrator, the
orphan Tim, gives a vivid account of his uncle's experiments in "the Barn" as he seeks to create a new race
combining characteristics of plant and animal to replace
humanity.   He denounces the individual and thinks of the
ant as a kind of ideal.   To save his cousin Stephen from
seeing the monsters--and perhaps being experimented upon--
Tim kills the specimens.   His uncle sends him from the
farm.   Tim goes to London, where he suffers various pri-
vations during the first war.   He becomes acquainted with
the Callendar family, which has given up its position of
wealth to help the masses.   Tim is thoroughly indoctrinated
with pro-Labor, reformist ideas.   His uncle and Stephen
both die.   He returns to the farm and in the last pages
gains the love of Joyce Callendar, a suffragette.

477. Knowlton, J[ames] A[lbert].   Origin.   Boston: Eastern,
1900.

Beginning with a reference to Noah and his ark, this narrative provides another pseudo-historical account of the
Western hemisphere.   In the character of Mantu, Knowlton
may have tried to suggest the origin of Manitou.   It does
not sketch the fabulous kingdoms of some of the other
American prehistories.

478. Knox, Ronald A[rbuthnot].   Memories of the Future, Being
Memoirs of the Years 1915-1972, Written in the Year of Grace
1988, by Opal, Lady Porstock.   London: Methuen, 1923.

Also published in New York by Doran (1923): Knox passes
himself off as editor.   This is the autobiogrqphy of an
aristocratic lady whose father gained a title for his
services to Lloyd George's government.   After 1928 titles
were sold.   Its main concern is with social changes,
especially those which brought about equal rights for
women, but the lasting impression is one of continuity
rather than radical change.   One must praise the gossipy,
informal tone maintained throughout.   Lady Opal studied at
Oxford, where she was the first president of the Union.   By
1944 business took her to the States, which had settled the
war debt for a number of titles which the U.S. sold off.
Lord and Lady Massachusetts were often her hosts, while she
married Wilson J. Harkness of Connecticut, who "appeared in
the Honours List as Wilson Lord Porstock."   Indian Home
Rule had been granted in 1938, and an Anglo-American
entente had been in force since the 1930s.   Her husband set
out in a helicopter for France in 1963 and vanished.   She
breaks off the narrative in 1972 on the eve of a war with
an unspecified enemy; without naming the enemy, she asserts

that after three years it ended in a limited victory which expresses British ideals. At the close she wishes that she could write the imaginary reminiscences of a granddaughter as of 2050.

479. Kummer, Frederic Arnold. The Earth's Story; I. The First Days of Man, as Narrated Quite Simply for Young Readers. New York: Doran, 1922.

He expresses thanks to Dr. William K. Gregory of the American Museum of Natural History. He suggests that the book is not intended as a "strictly" scientific work but as "a romance," for only in that manner can one gain the interest of young readers. He advises parents that the book is intended for ages 5 to 15. God tells Mother Nature to prepare Earth for Man. The early forms are ape men: Ma and Ra. Tor makes pottery. Whenever Mother Nature wants man to think, she sends him some kind of trouble. The volume includes the use of fire and the development of the first canoe.

480. Kuppord, Skelton (pseud. of J. Adams). A Fortune from the Sky. London & New York: Nelson, 1902.

Against a background of a threatened war between France and England, Fred Gurleigh goes to London. Soon he becomes the assistant of Professor Wellingham of Russell Square. He tells of having discovered a tremendous power derived from electricity--panergon--and is afraid that it will fall into the hands of Blaise Frisaine, a former assistant who might give it to the French. With it Wellingham could write on the sky. Fred sees its advertising potential and for four hours uses the device to advertise pills across the British skies. A side effect occurs; an aroma makes everyone nauseated. Laws are passed so that such an ad cannot occur again. Fred goes to the U.S., strikes a business deal, and returns to England aboard the S.S. Laurentia. He and his companion, Mr. Boosterbeg, discover everyone else aboard the ship is dead. Scores of vessels suffer the same fate, and along longitudinal lines deaths occur also in France, Spain, and New Zealand. The British Channel fleet itself has its personnel die. The lines of force come from a seven-foot model of Wellingham's machine. He is found dead, and Frisaine warns about the machine. Fred takes care of it, and an ultimatum bringing war to an end throughout the world takes effect. The machine becomes the ultimate weapon; Fred, the one man army to maintain peace.

481. Lamarre, Joseph. The Passion of the Beast. Boston: Stratford, 1928.

The first-person narrator, William St. Clair, tells of meeting Armand Dumesnil in Paris. He accompanies Armand to his country estate where he meets his father, a famous

explorer, and his sister Yvonne. They are dominated by a
giant gorilla, Melek, whom they captured in Africa. Melek
once saved the father's life. They ask St. Clair to leave;
he recovers consciousness to find himself bound to Armand,
who is dead. He returns to Paris and brings Edmund Pelle-
pont back with him. They search for Yvonne and her father;
both the father and Melek die. But as he dies, Melek, the
gorilla, gazes at Yvonne and licks her hand. This is
certainly a reworking of Beauty and the Beast, and it
anticipates King Kong.

482. LaMaster, Slater. <u>Cupid</u> <u>Napoleon</u>. Boston: Humphries,
1934.

In a prefatory note LaMaster declares the novel to be a
caricature of the "golden age of propaganda" in which
society lives. It must be regarded as a parody, at least
in retrospect. N.B. Luckett agrees to fly a special plane
invented by Le Faire to the moon. He lands on the property
of Professor Basil Oom, an alienist, whose only clients are
women. He permits them to assume classical identities and
act out their fantasies. Oom passes Luckett off as a
"beautiful spirit" wandering among the planets. Oom calls
him Cupid but returns him aboard the ship to New York,
where he leaves Luckett to burn in the ship. He escapes
and says that he has been to the moon and is in love with a
young woman he met there, Josephine D'Aubrey. Josephine
comes of age and inherits a large estate, which includes
all of the Kingdom of Oom. She meets Luckett; they are in
love and marry. Oom brings his public career to an end.
The parody is essentially silly and misses a great deal of
its potential.

483. Lamb, Harold. <u>A</u> <u>Garden</u> <u>to</u> <u>the</u> <u>Eastward</u>. Garden City,
N.Y.: Doubleday, 1947.

This is the last of three novels Lamb wrote which may be
associated with the lost race motif. Immediately after
World War II in Cairo, Jacob Ide buys a bronze statue
reputed to be some 7000 years old. It leads him to the
mountains of Kurdistan. He hopes to find further samples
as well as a clue to the people who produced it. There he
renews acquaintance with the woman, Michal Thorne, who has
survived the war in Cairo as best she could. Their love
affair provides a thin storyline for a discussion of
ancient Kurdistan as the Edenic homeland from which civilization arose. Soviets attempt to take over the area after
their archaeologists have come searching for ancient
artifacts. Ide must report to Washinton, but he returns to
Michal.

484. Lamb, Harold. The House of the Falcon. New York: D. Appleton, 1921.

This blends together the Indian Northwest Frontier with the idea of a lost city, Yakka-Akir, guarded by the Sayaks, an ancient group outlawed by orthodox Mohammedans. The main storyline involves the kidnapping of Edith Rand by the Vulture, a leader of slave caravans, and her rescue by the Sayaks. The love story is between her and Donovan Khan, an Englishman.

485. Lamb, Harold. Marching Sands. New York: D. Appleton, 1920.

Captain Robert Gray leads an American expedition into Mongolia to the Gobi Desert to find the lost city of Sungan peopled by the Wusun, a white race. Arminus Delabar, the scientist sent with him, proves to be a traitor and an agent of Wu Fang Chien, the Buddhist leader. Gray meets the expedition of Sir Lionel Hastings and his niece, Mary. Sir Lionel is killed by Wu Fang's men and Mary taken prisoner in Sungan. Gray finds the city, and he learns that the Wusun, who date back to the days of Kubla Khan at least, are captives of the Buddhists. They regard Mary as a White Queen, and side with her and Gray against Wu Fang. After a final battle Mary and Gray escape.

486. Lamszus, Wilhelm. The Human Slaughter-House (Scenes from the War That Is Sure to Come). Trans. from the German by Oakley Williams. New York: Stokes, 1913.

Also published in London by Hutchinson (1913): attacks supporters of militarism who would suppress both facts of warfare and human suffering. Suggests that war waged with picric acid and electric wires cannot be described in traditional idiom of past warfare. Description of a terrible, general war.

487. Landis, S[imon] M[ohler]. The Social War of the Year 1900; or, The Conspirators and the Lovers! A Lesson for Saints and Sinners. Philadelphia: Landis, 1872.

This is another of the narratives where a thin storyline guards an extreme mysticism. The Second Advent of Christ establishes a new Eden.

488. Lane, Jeremy. Yellow Men Sleep. New York: Century, 1919.

The mysterious Oriental, Chee Ming, has brought the drug koresh to San Francisco and sold it. Con Levington joins with the explorer, Andrew March, whose wife and daughter disappeared in Asia some years ago. They penetrate into central Asia and find Chee Ming in control of Tau Kuan, the Empire of the Yellow Sun, supposedly older than the Tower

of Babel. Eventually Chee Ming and his Empire are destroyed, but more importantly, Con and March find March's
daughter, Helen, who has been subjected to koresh and never
told that she was white. Although her mother is dead, the
two men bring Helen back to America and, of course, break
her drug habit.

489. Lane, Mary E. Bradley. Mizora; A Prophecy. New York:
Dillingham, 1890.

Serialized in the Cincinnati Commercial (1880-1881): the
first-person narrator, Vera Zarovitch, a Russian noble-
woman, is given a life-sentence in Siberia. After escaping
and living for a time with Esquimaux, she sails alone
across an unknown sea into a Symmesian inner world. She
fins Mizora, a feminist utopia, far-advanced technologically. Chemistry is the foremost science, producing all
foodstuffs so that animals and birds are extinct. Genetic
engineering has eliminated all dark complexions; the women
are uniformly handsome blondes. Lane's anger focuses upon
the nineteenth century's use of women and children for
cheap labor. She insists that universal education is
necessary for culture to advance. Beating children leads
only to psychological as well as physical harm. Not until
the second part of the narrative does Vera learn that the
women have reproduced parthenogenetically for 3,000 years.
At that time a general regarded as a national hero [Grant?]
tried for a third term; that, together with corrupt politicians, led to civil war in which the "race" of men almost
exterminated themselves. Women took control of government
to escape the ensuing anarchy. For a hundred years they
forbade men to hold office; by then men were extinct.
Wauna serves as her guide and returns to America with her;
she is appalled at the conditions, tries to reach Mizora
but dies, with Vera mourning beside her. Vera can only
write this manuscript found among her private papers and
lament what man has done to woman.

490. Langford, George. Kutnar, Son of Pic. New York: Boni &
Liveright, 1921.

To gain Pic's secret regarding weapon-making, Gouch, a
villainous cave-man from the north of Spain, kidnaps
Kutnar. Pic's wife is dead; he pursues Gouch with Hairi,
the Mammoth, and Wulli, the Rhinoceros. Eventually Gouch
is killed and Kutnar rescued.

491. Langford, George. Pic the Weapon-Maker. New York: Boni &
Liveright, 1920.

In a prefatory note Henry Fairfield Osborn says the author
may have idealized the cavemen as Cooper idealized his
Indians, but he thinks Langford correct in that qualities
of human mind and character had to be present from the

beginning. Langford identifies the people as being of the Mousterian culture of the Dordogne area of France and calls them the last of the Neanderthal men. The companions of Pic are Hairi, the Mammoth, and Wulli, the Rhinoceros. An Ice Age is approaching. The majority of the narrative concerns Pic's efforts to find better flint to work into arrowheads and tools. He finds the means of working flint (a bone), mates, and has a son so that he can no longer travel with the animals.

492. Lanza, Clara [Hammond] and James Clarence Harvey. Scara-baeus; the Story of an African Beetle. New York: Lovell, Coryell, 1892.

Thematically, this is another narrative which complains about the materialism of the day. The storyline rather awkwardly combines two main threads: first, a murder story involving the ability to photograph images on the retina of the eye, as well as photographs of the past; secondly, a hunt for treasure in Africa. Harold Davedge is the individual obsessed with photography, while Martin H. Laird finds the ruins of an ancient kingdom. Paul St. Martin provides the bridge in that he flees from Davedge but drowns at sea. The scarabeus is an ancient sacred gem which various persons try to steal.

493. Lath, J.A. (pseud.?). The Lost City of the Aztecs; or, The Secret of the Hidden Crater. New York: Cupples & Leon, 1934.

In Arizona Dick Daniels, son of a rancher, and Ralph Hudson, son of an archaeologist, find an old book telling of a city of Aztecs in the southern part of the state. Senor Porfiaz Rodriguez, a neighbor, steals the book, but they have a note written in code. They find a city inside a mountain near Yucca Peak. Rodriguez is the High Priest of the Sun God. They become involved in a factional battle, and eventually Tulah and Mahtl blow up the tunnels leading into the mountain and take their people to Mexico. The boys return with genuine artifacts which they sell at a good price and deposit the money in a "college fund."

494. Laurie, André (pseud. of Paschal Grousset). The Conquest of the Moon; A Story of the Bayouda. London: Samson, Low, 1892.

This is a strange mixture of African imperialism and exploration of the moon. General Gordon, the Mahdi, and Khartoum are all part of the background as "the all-power-ful Kaddour" plots to overthrow the British. With the aid of M. Kersain, the young astronomer, M. Norbert Mauny, is to establish a scientific station on the tableland of Tehbali in the desert of Bayouda (Sudan). Meanwhile a group in London headed by Costerus Wagner, forms Luna Company, Ltd. to explore the moon. They increase the magnetic power of the Earth so that the moon is attracted close enough to gain its surface. While Gertrude Kersain is kidnapped by Kaddour, the scientific experiment gets under way as Mauny and his friends turn the Peak of Tahbali into a giant magnet. When the moon and Earth make contact, there is an explosion which blows Mauny and his party, including Gertrude, onto the surface of the moon. Gertrude discovers a giant excavation and staircase which lead to colossal buildings proving that millions of years earlier, when the Earth was still incandescent, the moon was inhabited by Selenties, who had tremendous knowledge. The Earth eclipses the sun. All in all they spend twenty-nine days on the moon and then parachute to Earth. Although Norbert and Gertrude are betrothed, no one will believe that the group was on the moon.

495. Laurie, André (pseud. of Paschal Grousset). The Crystal City. Boston: Estes & Lauriat, 1896.

Also published in London by Sampson, Low (1896): lost at sea west of the Pillars of Hercules, Rene Caondal encounters an old man and a girl in a grotto. Unconscious he surfaces and finds that he has a ring. After much speculation about an Atlantic continent, he joins the yacht Cinderella, which will sound the Atlantic shoals, and invents a submersible vehicle so that he can explore underwater. He encounters a crystal city and learns of the gradual sinking of the continent of Atlantide from the dying Charicles. Rene marries the young girl, Atlantis, and brings her back--together with a fortune of pearls--but builds her an undersea villa because she longs for her old home.

496. Laurie, André (pseud. of Paschal Grousset). New York to Brest in Seven Hours. London: Sampson Low, 1890.

The central storyline concerns the manufacture and shipment of Pennsylvania oil from New York to Brest in an underwater pipeline. When it fails at first because of friction, Niagara is harnessed to push the oil through. Raymond Frézols is the young French inventor; the heroine is Madge Curtiss, daughter of an oil magnate. Among the hazards to be faced are the efforts of Peter Murphy to blow the pipeline with nitroglycerin and the desire of LeComte de Kélern to marry Madge. Raymond must transport himself through the tube in order to interrupt a forced wedding. Kélern killed Madge's father. Although the project is momentarily halted, Raymond will build again.

497. Leacock, Stephen. The Iron Man & The Tin Woman, With Other Such Futurities; A Book of Little Sketches of To-day and To-Morrow. New York: Dodd, Mead, 1929.

These are not stories but brief comic sketches, a few no more than a paragraph long, which satirize many of the popular topics from the robots of the title piece to the visit of a Marshian from Marsh, Chester County, Pennsylvania. Delightful in itself, it also acts as a measure of the popular response of the period to science and the future. Yet one suspects that Leacock is responding more to newspaper and magazine articles than to fiction

498. Legge, Ronald. The Hawk; A Story of Aerial War. New York: McBride, 1909.

M. Breul has a secret explosive rejected by England; he thus brings "Breuligen" to the U.S. The idea of the Channel tunnel between France and England is also in the background as England defeats a coalition of European powers.

499. Leggett, M[ortimer] D[ormer]. A Dream of a Modest Prophet. Philadelphia: Leppincott, 1890.

This is not a novel; there is no storyline. The first-person narrator does not know how he got to Mars, but he makes some observations about Martian society: the absence of cities; the temperance of the people; the universality of daily baths; the more equitable division of property. Evolution is the same, although Mars is at least 3,000 years in advance of Earth. Yet all of this is merely background in an essay which defends orthodox Christianity. He inveighs against the idea of a "first cause" as God, because such a belief is "mere soulless, intellectual awe...." On Mars they believe that eventually man will do all the wonderful things that Christ did.

500. Leonhart, Rudolph. The Treasure of Montezuma. Canton, Oh.: Cassidy, 1888.

After a preliminary remark that there is a universal dissatisfaction with social affairs at present, the narrator describes a twenty-five year experiment in which the treasures of Montezuma were used to build a utopian valley, Friedenstahl. It is, of course, socialist; land is held in common.

501. LeQueux, William [Tufnell]. The Great War in England in 1897. London: Tower, 1894.

Serialized in Answers (1893): the Russians and French attack Britain. Because Britain has lost control of the seas, India, Australia, and the colonies cannot immediately help. The French land in Sussex. Leith and Newhaven are bombarded and Edinburgh attacked. Birmingham falls, and the French attack London. Victory comes only after the Germans, faithful allies of the British, take Paris on 16 November 1897. Karl von Beilstein, a spy for Germany, is shot by a firing squad.

502. LeQueux, William [Tufnell]. The Great White Queen; A Tale of Treasure and Treason. London: White, 1896.

The first-person narrator, Richard Scarsmere, becomes the friend of Omar Sanom at Grammar School in Eastbourne. When Omar's mother summons him home to Africa to the Land Beyond the Clouds--also called Om--somewhere near the Niger, Richard accompanies him. Thus begins a journey that leads to a series of fights with natives and the Arab, Samony, who hate the Queen. Once in The City in the Clouds, Omar becomes involved in a revolt that deposes his tyrannical mother, the Queen Naya. He must then fight Samony again, and Richard rescues lovely Liola, daughter of the chief minister, from Samony's harem. The former queen, now insane, commits suicide. Richard returns to England as Omar and Liola rule the kingdom.

503. LeQueux, William [Tufnell]. The Invasion of 1910, With a Full Account of the Siege of London. London: Nash, 1906.

One of the most famous of the future war novels, originally serialized in the Daily Mail (March 1906); I. F. Clarke gives a good account of its impact in Voices Prophesying War. The Germans land at Weybourne, Norfolk, and Hull, and march through Essex. Their attack begins on 3 September. They lay siege to London, and by 21 September there are rebellions in such areas as Shoreditch and Islington. Although the British are driven from London, they rally west of Staines, counterattack, and destroy the Germans occupying London. The German occupation was a harsh one.

504. LeQueux, William [Tufnell]. Zoraida; A Romance of the Harem and the Great Sahara. London: Tower, 1895.

The first-person narrator ventures into the Sahara, where he finds the beautiful Zoraida, a queen among the Arabs, and brings her back to London as his bride. This reminds one more of The Shiek than a lost race novel.

505. Leroux, Gaston. The Bride of the Sun. New York: McBride, 1915.

Francis Montgomery--Dick--returns to modern Peru; he has long been fascinated by the legends of Pizarro and the Incas. At Callao he meets and becomes affianced to an old friend, Maria-Teresa de la Torre, daughter of a wealthy aristocrat. It is the time of an Indian festival. An old story says that every ten years the Indians send a Golden Sun bracelet to a young Spanish woman whom they intend to sacrifice to the ancient Gods. Maria-Teresa receives one; she is then kidnapped. The remainder of the novel becomes an account of her rescue sketched against the background of a threatened Indian revolt.

506. Lewis, Leon. <u>Andrée</u> at <u>the</u> <u>North</u> <u>Pole</u>, <u>With</u> <u>the</u> <u>Details</u> <u>of</u> <u>His</u> <u>Fate</u>. New York: Dillingham, 1899.

The narrative gives the dertails of Andrée's departure from Spitzbergen on 11 July 1897. It then becomes a vehicle for the concept that man first appeared on Earth in the region of the present Arctic. Andrée and his companions discover a hidden kingdom close to the Pole inhabited by "Polar Aryans" or "Polarians." The country is compared to Switzerland. In the political turmoil after the death of the King, Andrée and his friends flee aboard the balloon. three days later its wreckage lies on an ice field, no trace of survivors. There is also a love story involving a Polarian prince and Alice Haddon, rescued by Andrée from a shipwrecked vessel.

507. Lewis, [Harry] Sinclair (as Tom Graham). <u>Hike</u> <u>and</u> <u>the</u> <u>Aeroplane</u>. New York: Stokes, 1912.

Written for a juvenile audience, focusing upon Hike Griffin and Poodle Darby, the narrative concentrates upon the invention of a special tetrahedral aeroplane by Martin Priest. Since Hike is the son of a major in the Signal Corps, he can help Priest get his plane accepted over that of a rival, Lieutenant Jack Adeler. For the most part the storyline involves Mexican bandits and revolutionaries. This has significance primarily because of its date and because Lewis follows the conventions of popular fiction.

508. Lewis, [Harry] Sinclair. <u>It</u> <u>Can't</u> <u>Happen</u> <u>Here</u>; <u>A</u> <u>Novel</u>. Garden City, Doubleday, 1935.

Doremus Jessup, the Vermont newspaper editor, remains the protagonist of Lewis' dramatization of how dictatorship came to the U.S. Using quotes from <u>Zero</u> <u>Hour</u>, the book written by Senator Berzelius Windrip, to introduce many of the chapters, Lewis shows how the agony of the times, the Depression, swept this man into office in 1936 and how he outlawed Congress and the Supreme Court within the first days of his election. The story is complete with Minute Men, concentration camps, a war with Mexico, and the attempted rebellion by Walt Trowbridge--who had lost the election. Windrip's replacement by Lee Sarason--who had told him to write the book, had managed his campaign, and had been his Secretary of State--climaxes the take-over by 1939. Jessup is active in an underground movement, but the dictatorship remains in power as the novel ends. Con-

sidering the date of publication, Lewis' insight remains
extremely credible.

509. Lindsay, David. A Voyage to Arcturus. London: Methuen,
1920.

The best-known and most controversial of Lindsay's novels
centers upon the journey/transmigration of Maskull, symbolic of natural man, to the planet Tormance in the Arc-
turian system. He goes on a quest to learn the nature of
ultimate reality. Maskull dies on Tormance, but by doing
so, he releases his soul, Nightspore, to continue the
quest. Although Nightspore learns that there is a divine
plan, he also finds that there is a titanic battle between
truth (whose champion is Surtur) and deception (Crystal-
man). He learns that both the individual and reality
itself are constantly changing. Nightspore is to return to
Earth to continue the quest. Perhaps the most significant
point is that he discovers that on Earth Surtur gains
expression as pain. There is also the concept that one
must somehow lose/transcend the self before one can know
reality.

510. Linton, Dr. C[harles] E[llsworth]. The Earthometer and
Other Stories. Salem, Or.: Statesman, 1920[?].

In "The Ocean Cave at Heceta Head" the first-person narrator does little more than discover a woman who has spent
twenty years in a cave. She guides him out and leaves him.
"Rescue of the Cave Woman at Heceta Head" seems to get
sidetracked. A German Professor, T. Moshier, appears with
an "earthometer," a machine which he says will bring an end
to warfare. It uses a radium mixture and explodes, killing
the Indian who is helping them. In "Three Weeks Inside the
Earth" the Professor builds a larger machine which burrows
through the Earth. He makes a number of geological discoveries, including that the Earth is hollow. He also
discovers that two of the crew members are young women.
The last story, "The Hermit of Chimaso Island" takes a
first-person narrator to the moon in a flying boat; he
discovers that the four-legged creatures are human. One
suspects that these stories were intended as satires of the
field.

511. L'Isle, Adam. [See Jean Villers de L'Isle-Adam].

512. Llewellyn, Alun. The Strange Invaders. London: Bell,
1934.

Sometime in the future a new Ice Age has engulfed the
Earth; moreover, wars--referred to as the Destruction--have
devastated civilization so that man has fallen into a new
barbarism. Adun Bayatan lives on one of the rivers in
Russia. The rulers are called the Fathers; the symbol of

their rule is the Hammer and Sickle.   In the church are
three icons: Marx, Lenin, and Stalin.   A triangle develops
among Adun, the girl Erya, and Karasoin, leader of the
Swords.   The annual trading caravan does not return;
instead a horde of saurians besiege the town.   Karasoin
takes all power in the crisis.   Much of the narrative is
given to the struggle with the saurians, who are finally
overcome by the cold, although one is certain other hordes
will come again.   There is also a struggle for power which
ends only after Adun has killed Karasoin, thus rescuing
Eyra from him.   A third element is the appearance of the
Tartars (with the Rus, they make up the people); they are
forced outside of the town, and many of them fall victim to
the saurians.   Nothing is finally decided.   This narrative
must stand as one of the high points in British sf of the
1930s; its projection into a Russian scene of the future
makes it one of the most original novels of the half-
century leading up to it.

513. Lloyd, John Uri.   <u>Etidorhpa</u>; <u>or</u>, <u>The</u> <u>End</u> <u>of</u> <u>Earth</u>.
Cincinnati, Oh.: John Uri Lloyd, 1895.

Lloyd suggests that he has edited a manuscript which should
have been published by Llewellyn Drury.   Thirty years
earlier Drury had encountered a mysterious, aged man, who
told him the story.   Its narrator--called only "I-am-the-
man"--once belonged to a secret society of alchemists but
betrayed the group; as punishment he was granted lengthened
life and was sent on a journey to exotic caverns beneath
the surface.   He was to gain untold knowledge which he
would disperse.   The novel becomes a series of episodes
illustrating the inadequacy of modern science and the need
for a deeper spiritual truth.   It warns "beware the science
of man"; only in the 1914 edition does Lloyd achieve an
explicit statement of his basic theme: "A study of true
science is a study of God."   The novel is most notable for
the vehemence of its attack on biology.

514. London, Jack. <u>Before</u> <u>Adam</u>. New York: Macmillan, 1906.

Waterloo accused London of plagarism, saying this was taken
from <u>The</u> <u>Story</u> <u>of</u> <u>Ab</u>.   The plots were very similar; London
attempted to show the major discoveries leading to the
advancement of man taking place in a single generation.
London's chief innovation was the use of a first-person
narrator who dreamed of his life as a caveman because of
racial memory.

515. London, Jack. <u>The</u> <u>Iron</u> <u>Heel</u>. New York: Macmillan, 1908.

Presented as a manuscript published seven centuries after
it was written and footnoted as by an historian, the first-
person narrative (the Everhard Manuscript) is the account
by Avis Everhard of the career of her husband, Ernest

Everhard, who was one of the first leaders against the Oligarchy of Trusts which had seized Fascist-like powers in the early twentieth century. Everhard gave the Oligarchy the name, The Iron Heel. Of all the novels which dwelt upon the conflict between capitalism and labor, this must be regarded as the finest, at least by an American author, largely because of the strength of its narrative frame. After laying the necessary background, the narrative covers the period after the socialist victory in the elections of 1912, when they were not allowed to take their seats (a General Strike resulted) to the destruction of the Chicago Commune in the autumn of 1917. Chicago was made an example. The manuscript breaks off abruptly, as though Avis Everhard had been warned that mercenaries were on their way to arrest her and Ernest in New York, although the initial note of the first chapter refers to Everhard's arrest and execution in 1932.

516. London, Jack. The Red One. New York: Macmillan, 1918.

The title story is the most unique and memorable narrative of the period dealing with the encounter between man and extraterrestrial aliens.   It is also the most effective blending of literary naturalism and fantasy.   The American naturalist, Bassett, is lured into the jungles of Guadal-canal by a sound that he hears.   London portrays his degeneration from the effects of malaria as he lies a prisoner of the headhunter, Ngurn.   Knowing that the natives worship something called "The Red One" or "The Star Born," he agrees to allow Ngurn to kill him and shrink his head if he may see the god. He has previously seen it, for he has used the wizened, apelike woman, Balatta--so different from the princesses of the lost race motif--to help him gain sight of The Red One.   He realizes immedi-ately that a spaceship crashed in the jungles ages ago. Around it lie the bones of the countless natives who have been sacrificed to it.   He wonders about the nature of the creatures who built and flew it, but the ultimate question he can arrive at asks, "Was life, strife? Was the rule of all the universe the pitiless rule of natural selection?" In view of the importance of the theme of alien encounter, "The Red One" achieves an excellent irony.

517. London, Jack.   The Scarlet Plague.   New York: Macmillan, 1915.

In 2013 a new plague devastates the world, reducing the survivors to an inescapable level of barbarism.   At that time, Granser, then Professor James Howard Smith of the University of California, was twenty-seven; now on the coast of California, he tells the story of the onslaught of the plague to his grandchildren.   The United States had become a Fascist-type state dominated by the Trusts.   In 2012 Morgan the Fifth had been appointed president by the

Board of Industrial Magnates. Granser was a member of the
oligarchy who owned all of the land and all of the
machines; he refers to the workers as "food-getters,"
slaves. He remembers the beautiful Vesta Van Warden, whose
husband ruled the U.S.; after the plague she became the
woman of Bill the Chauffeur, a brutal man, who founded the
Chauffeur tribe. Granser married into the Santa Rosa
tribe; he refers to other tribes--the Sacrementos, the Palo
Altos, the Utahs. In a cave on Telegraph Hill he has
hidden books, hoping they will sometime be discovered; but
the remark of one of the boys makes him realize that
gunpowder will be discovered and used. Pessimistically, he
sees the cycle repeating itself. Together with the story,
"The Red One," and The Iron Heel, this seems the best of
London's fiction because he developed a narrative frame
sufficiently strong to give his material an objectivity, a
distancing, it frequently did not have.

518. London, Jack. The Star Rover. New York: Macmillan, 1915.

The only one of London's novels to be concerned with
transmigration of the soul: sentenced to life imprisonment
in San Quentin and tortured because the authorities believe
him to be a revolutionary who has hidden dynamite, Professor Darrell Sanding learns how to release his soul from
his imprisoned body. He seeks other periods of history: he
is a swordsman in sixteenth century France; he is a nine-
year-old boy in the American West trying to escape Mormons
and Indians; he is a seaman shipwrecked on the coast of
Korea. He can also wander freely in time and space.
Finally he dies.

519. Lorimer, George Horace. The False Gods. New York: D.
Appleton, 1906.

Focusing upon Ezra Simpkins, reporter for the Boston
Banner, Lorimer satirizes both yellow journalism and a
combination of Madame Blavatsky and Egyptology. Simpkins
comes to New York to work for Mrs. Athelstone, who announces that she is a reincarnation of Madame Blavatsky.
Simpkins gives his imagination free range, and Mrs. Athelstone announces that she is really the reincarnation of
Queen Nefruari, dead some 3,000 years. He sends an article
suggesting that she has killed her husband only to have the
AP report that Dr. Alfred W.R. Athelstone has arranged to
excavate newly discovered tombs in the area of Karnak. The
story ends as Simpkins goes off to city hall to investigate
a woman's theory that souls are red, white, or blue; "he
was back again serving false gods."

520. Lynde, Francis. <u>Scientific Sprague</u>. New York: Scribner, 1912.

Against a western background, the engineer-detective, Sprague, solves a number of mysteries and crimes which threaten a small western railroad. He relies upon his physical courage and Holmesian intuition to overcome such problems as the deliberate collision of trains, the blowing up of ralroad tunnels, and the flooding of the right-of-way.

521. Lytton, Lord Edward Bulwer. <u>The Coming Race</u>. Edinburgh: Blackwood, 1871.

In an unspecified country during a trip through a mine, the unnamed American protagonist gains access to a vast subterranean world inhabited by the Vril-ya, who have dwelt there since the Noachian deluge. They have an advanced technology, including robots and detachable wings so that they can fly; everything is powered by "vril," which Lytton suggests is a kind of "atmospheric magnetism." Unlike so many of his British contemporaries, Lytton does not object to machines. However, he is more interested in politics, social organization, evolution, world peace, and the occult. In view of the date one of the most important features of this utopian civilization is that the women are physically superior to the men, instigate courtship, and are the equals of men in all other ways. Zee, the seven-foot woman who falls in love with the narrator--called Tish among the Vril-ya--carries him to the mine after he has been sentenced to death and received no reprieve. This last results from a triangle involving Zee's sister, whom the narrator imagines he loves until Zee has left him behind. In the area of sexuality lies the bulk of Lytton's satire. Significantly, no other British novel was referred to more often by subsequent novelists.

522. Macaulay, Rose. <u>Orphan Island</u>. New York: Boni & Liveright, 1925.

In 1855 while escorting fifty orphans from London to San Francisco, Miss Charlotte Smith, Anne-Marie--the French nursemaid--and the drunken ship's surgeon, O'Malley, are castaway on an island when their ship sinks. In two open boats the captain and crew abandon them. In 1923 Mr. Thinkwell, lecturer in sociology at Cambridge, receives a letter from his aunts in Sydney, Australia, telling him that his grandfather, William Thinkwell, abandoned Miss Smith and her party. The note gives the precise location of the island. Thinkwell, his daughter Rosamond, and two sons organize a rescue party. They discover a very Victorian society in which the ruling class is the Smiths--descendants of Miss Smith and Dr. O'Malley. She is still alive and thinks of herself as Queen Victoria. The novel ends after her death at ninety-eight when the parliament changes the name of the island from Smith to Orphan. Thinkwell and his children have also been marooned on the island because their ship, Typee, never called to pick them up. The result is a delightfully clever satire of British class structure and manners. It must be regarded as one of the finest hybrids of the lost race motif during the period.

523. MacClure, Victor [Thom MacWalter].   The Ark of the Covenant; A Romance of the Air and of Science.   New York: Harper, 1924.

Published in London as Ultimatum; A Romance of the Air by Harrap (1924): the first-person narrator, Jimmy Boon, reports a number of bank robberies supervised by an airship which gases the area. Also gifts of radium bromide turn up. Dan Lamont is aboard a British ship from which gold is stolen; his companions include Lord Almeric and his niece, Kirsten Torrance--whom Dan loves--daughter of the physicist, David Torrance, who disappeared some twenty years earlier. Dan and Lord Almeric, aboard the airship Merlin encounter a mysterious airship, Ark of the Covenant, which has issued an ultimatum demanding that war end. They follow it to South America, to "The Plateau of the Red Star," where they find that the Master has formed a League to bring about the end of war. The narrative shifts to Shelto Seton, who supplies background information. Some three years earlier near the Amazon he found a man terribly burned by radioactivity. That was the Master. Among his other discoveries is the gas Aithon and the D-1 ray. The narrative shifts back to Jimmy as the Master and his ship approach Washington, D.C. in an attempt to communicate with the president. The Master is identified as David Torrance by the president, who becomes custodian of the powers because the Master, long in agony because of his burns, dies. Dan and Kirsten are united.

524. MacDonald, Raymond (pseud. of Edward McDonald and Raymond Leger). The Mad Scientist; A Tale of the Future. New York: Cochrane, 1908.

Against the background of an attack upon Wall Street (the name Morgerbilt is introduced), several scientists get into the action. Professor Kaye declares that the secret of invisibility is his. But Maxim Folk, knowledgable of radium and electricity, threatens to ignite the Atlantic Ocean. In St. Louis a convention of the United Laborers of America denounces the government and marches on Washington. "This modern Satan," Folk, helps them; he electrocutes some 15,000 troops near Washington and kills the president, Harold Markham, by means of an electrical device. Professor Kaye, with the aid of Detective Egan, helps capture Folk, who is brought to trial. He escapes, steals the battleship Behemoth, levitates it, and is seen at Callao, Peru, and a year later near New Guinea and Australia. Folk has an electric gyroscope which is destructive; he threatens New York and does sink the ship Hudson, but a lunar eclipse occurs. The gravitational force of the Earth, moon, and sun overcome Folk's powers so that the Behemoth crashes and burns, thus freeing the world from the "murderous amusements of the mad scientist."

525. Machen, Arthur [Llewellyn Jones]. The Terror; A Fantasy. London: Duckworth, 1917.

During the war a number of unexplained deaths terrorize rural England; rumor has it that somewhere there is a subterranean area filled with German soldiers. The novel ends after the death of the Thomas Griffith family; a manuscript suggests that because of the hatred and brutality of the war, the animals have allied themselves against man.

526. MacIsaac, Fred[erick John]. The Hothouse World. New York: Avalon, 1965.

Copyright 1931 by Popular Publications and issued in Fantastic Novels (1950): first-person narrator, George Putnam, is tricked by Professor Judkins so that he lies in suspended animation for a century until 2051. He awakens in the glass-domed Putnam Community on Lake Champlain. He learns that this is apparently the only society surviving the Great Catastrophe, which occurred when a comet struck Earth in 1987 polluting the atmosphere and causing a new Ice Age. He finds the group ready for revolt because of the attitude of the aristocracy, led by President Ames. A horde of barbarians attacks the dome and is beaten off; Putnam learns that they are from Carolina, and finding an airplane, he and Helen Ames, who has told him that she loves him and will choose him in the next marriage lottery, fly to the Gulf Coast. From the Carolinas south the country is like New England of 1951 rather than being covered by ice. When he returns to the Community, a revolution has taken place; he and Helen flee aboard the airplane. An appended note says that he rescued a thousand people and re-established civilization in the Carolinas.

527. MacIsaac, Fred[erick John]. The Mental Marvel. Chicago: A. C. McClurg, 1930.

When Roger Thule was a child, his father financially exploited his son's brilliance, but he did allow him to take lessons as a boxer. This provides the point of departure for a story that focuses both upon Roger's successful career as a boxer and the solution of his father's murder. His father had been cheated out of much of the money Roger earned. Roger pursues the killer into the South American jungle. Equally important is the story of his infatuation with Eloise Lane, a brilliant young woman who likes boxers. The predictable happy ending occurs.

528. MacIsaac, Fred[erick John]. The Vanishing Professor. New York: Waterson, 1927.

Despite an initial attack on the finances of the academic world, this becomes essentially a lighthearted love story. Professor Frank Leonard invents a means of making things invisible; because of his poor pay, he robs several banks, but his invention is stolen by the villainous John Craven. After sundry incidents, including a chorus girl who becomes invisible during her act, Detective Foster Gaines and Leonard split $50,000 gained because the War Department pays such a sum to have a means of making an airplane or submarine invisible. Leonard marries Lucy Ransome, daughter of a colleague whom he has loved since she first came back from Vassar to join her father.

529. Mackay, Donald. The Dynamite Ship. New York: Manhattan, 1888.

Irish revolutionaries bombard London, destroying the Houses of Parliament, to gain Irish liberty. By means of a flashback the novel explains how Heyward and Mellerkoff have invented a new and terrible gun; led by the Irishman, Lubin, the Irish League arms the yacht Atlantic. An ultimatum is delivered demanding that Ireland be freed within twenty-four hours. The Queen at first ignores it. Ireland is freed as Lubin dies. As a kind of aside the Standard Oil monopoly is attacked, and the remark is made that one barrel of crude petroleum will do the work of a ton of the best coal.

530. Malet, Lucas (pseud. of Mary St. Leger Harrison). The Gateless Barrier. New York: Dodd, Mead, 1900.

As Mr. Rivers is dying, his nephew Lawrence comes to him. After various remarks about the current state of belief, the nephew sees a girl's ghost. His uncle permits him to investigate, but he must not reveal what he finds to anyone but his uncle. Lawrence discovers letters dated from 1802-1805; the ghost is Agnes, referred to as "the scarlet woman," whom some believe his ancestor, Mr. Dudley, murdered. He loved her so deeply that briefly she returned to life.

531. Manley, R.M. The Queen of Ecuador. New York: Hagemann, 1894.

Much reference is made to Atahualpa, the last Inca, as well as to the Quiti Indians, who had a higher civilization than the Incas. Alexander Millard, physician, acts as guardian to the mysterious girl, Ellen. Some thirty years ago Bertram and Edwards explored South America and encountered "The Rainbow Kingdom," where the Indians have kept free from the Spanish. Its ruler, Ata, is the last of the Inca queens. Bertram apparently is her husband, although she dies. Some question remains as to whether or not Ellen is their daughter; much of the plot concerns the accusation that Ellen has killed the woman she is nursing. Manley changes the focus of the narrative so often in terms of time and place that the result remains confusing.

532. Mann, Horace. The World Destroyer. Washington: Lucas-Lincoln, 1903.

The first-person narrator, Edward Milton, is upset with the condition of the world. He tries to rearrange the politics as well as find a woman who can be his world empress. Although married to Alice, he desires Miriam Worthington. In the end the reader learns that he is mad.

533. Manson, Marsden. The Yellow Peril in Action; A Possible Chapter in History. San Francisco: Britton & Ray, 1907.

Supposedly written in 1912, the narrative calls to the attention of Congress and the public the possibility of war in the Pacific. In 1909 and 1910 China resumed boycotting American trade; the Japanese ambassador revealed a treaty with China dating back to 1906. In a great battle near Hawaii, "astounding use" is made of torpedo boats. Asiatic mastery of the Pacific has "paralyzing effects" upon the production of the U.S. Abruptly at the end a law of Congress forbids all immigration for ten years and denies the franchise to anyone not born on American soil. This is a twenty-eight page essay instead of a novel.

534. Marriott, Crittenden. The Isle of Dead Ships; A Tale of the Sargasso Sea. Philadelphia: Lippincott, 1909.

Frank Howard, formerly a naval officer, is arrested and being returned to the U.S. from San Juan. He married a beautiful Porto Rican girl who followed him to New York City; supposedly he strangled her. Aboard the same ship is Dorothy Fairfax, who is engaged to marry Lieutenant Loving, an officer acquainted with Howard and his wife. Frank declares to Dorothy that he is innocent. They are shipwrecked and drift into the Sargasso Sea, where they come under the tyranny of Captain Forbes, who has lashed a number of ships together in order to create a village. Forbes insists that she marry because of the shortage of women. She refuses, and Howard acts as her champion against Forbes. He wins. Forbes forces them to marry; then she has to shoot Forbes' great snake which he had attack Howard. They find a small submarine, and using five

tons of gold as ballast, they try to escape. An accumulation of seaweed keeps them from surfacing until the
missionary, Willoughby, volunteers to go outside and cut
the seaweed. He succeeds, and they are rescued by a ship,
one of whose officers is Lieutenant Loving. Willoughby
thinks that Loving is Howard, for he married him to Dolores
Montoro, who followed him to New York. Loving confesses
and kills himself. Howard is head of the Seashark Wrecking
Company, which will take salvage from the Sargasso.

535. Marshall, Edison. <u>Dian of the Lost Land</u>. New York:
Kinsey, 1935.

Dr. Adam Weismann, a specialist in a rare Oriental disease,
is shanghaied to keep an old sailor, Hull, alive in order
to lead an expedition to a lost tribe described as blond
Eskimos in Antarctica. Hull is the sole survivor of the
Gilbert expedition of 1939, some twenty years earlier.
From the beginning Adam is contrasted with the middle-
European, Karl Belgrade, an ethnologist and anthropologist.
They discover a tribe of Cro-Magnon people in a hidden
valley; the high priestess is the comely Dian, daughter of
Hull by a native woman. The debate between Adam and
Belgrade concerns the fate of the tribe if civilization
learns of them and traders, among others, exploit them. In
a final battle with a horde of Neanderthal men, Belgrade
and Weismann work together to defeat the Neanderthals.
Weismann remains behind as Dian's husband, while Belgrade
promises not to reveal the tribe's existence.

536. Marshall, Edison. <u>Ogden's Strange Story</u>. New York:
Kinsey, 1934.

Ogden Rutherford, who believes himself a superman because
of his intelligence and training, flies north to join a
party of friends. He does so only because his fiancée,
Ruth Prentiss, is a member of the party. When his plane
crashes, he suffers an injury which makes him revert to a
prehistoric man, Og, the Dawn Man. He has various adventures in the Yukon Rockies, but when he encounters the
Nahhane Indians, he kills Red Hawk and steals the girl,
She-Who-Laughs. They come to love one another. When a
search party pursues them, she commits suicide, while he is
taken to a hospital in Seattle. An operation restores him
to his identity and he marries Ruth Prentiss. But he is
haunted by the memory of She-Who-Laughes and has a sense
that some great adventure awaits him in the Hereafter.

537. Marshall, Sidney J[ohn]. <u>The King of Kor; or, She's
Promise Kept</u>. Washington: Marshall, 1903.

This novel attempts to complete Haggard's <u>She</u>. Taking
possession of Michael, the servant of Holly and Leo, Ayesha
guides them back to the Valley of Kor. Leo dies, assured

that he will be united with Ayesha.   Holly is also permitted a "soul mate," Iganit.

538. Mastin, John.   The Stolen Planet.   London: Griffin, 1906.

The first-person narrator, Jervis Meredith, whose "re-
creations" are engineering and chemistry, becomes the
friend of Fraser Burnley, whose specialty is electricity.
Together they control gravity and develop the "aerostat,"
Regina, which they use for a cruise exploring the universe.
They visit the planet "Silens," near Aquarius, which had a
culture and artistry equal to the finest of the ancient
Greeks, although life has apparently been destroyed by
volcanic action.   They go to the giant planet, Inimicus
Ingens, where the ship is placed on a table in a house;
they escape only after using chlorine gas to force the
people to open a window.   They investigate a comet and a
nebula.   Venus proves to be the planet of love where the
lion and lamb cavort together.   They have been in communication with Saxern of the Times; to save the paper's
reputation, they bring a planetoid near the Earth but send
it into orbit as Jupiter's seventh moon.   Faced with
lawsuits because they have disrupted the tides and caused
ships to go aground, they receive a full pardon after a
world-wide petition asks England and the King to pardon
them.

539. Mastin, John.   Through the Sun in an Airship.   London:
Griffin, 1909.

Centuries in the future, Dennis Oakland, last heir of
Jervis Meredith, owns the Regina, but the secret of its
operation has been lost.   He is joined by two friends, Ross
Ainley and Gilbert Eastern, and they solve the problem so
that they may fly to the planet Bona, which has come into
the Earth's orbit after a journey from a star system beyond
Neptune.   Many changes have occurred on Earth; among them,
electricity has changed the climate so that the northern
polar area is the "Garden of the Earth," and women have
obtained full equal rights, including participation in
Earth's government.   On Bona they learn that all planets
but Earth are in communication telepathically.   On Mars
they are arrested so that their ship may be used by Martians to leave that planet when it grows too dry, but they
escape.   They land on the opposite side of the moon and
journey to Jupiter.   For a time they are lost.   They pass
through high concentrations of solar energy and visit
several additional exotic planets before heading back to
Earth.   Mastin includes much discussion of scientific
material, seemingly, but one finds an almost casual dis-
regard for the actualities of spaceflight.   And, of course,
all planets are somehow like Earth, if only different in
size.

540. Mayo, W[illiam] S[tarbuck]. Kaloolah; or, Journeyings to the Djébel Kumri; An Autobiography of Jonathan Romer. New York: Putnam, 1849.

The first-person narrator travels from the western plains of America and the Congo, where he describes the slave trade, to northern Africa amid the Bedouins. Among his traveling companions in Africa are Kaloolah and Enphadde, princess and prince of the country of Framazugda in the northern interior of Africa. Its great city is Killoam, which is the equal of any European city, especially in its sewage system and air conditioning. The emphasis is upon personal health and municipal baths. It is culturally but not technologically advanced. Romer speculates as to their origin, deciding that they come from the East, although they are not Chinese or Egyptian; nor are they Cartha- ginian. He suggests that they come from somewhere such as Yeman. He marries Kaloolah, the princess. He sends his manuscript to be published; he does, however, hope someday to open commerce with the world.

541. McCardell, Roy. L. The Diamond from the Sky. New York: Dillingham, 1916.

This is one of those novels of the period with a deceptive title. In 1651 when Indians are about to execute Sir Arthur Stanley, who attempted to kidnap an Indian princess, a meteor falls from the sky containing a great diamond. The body of the novel is good Victorian family melodrama complete with murder and a lost heir.

542. McCord, P[eter] B. Wolf; The Memoirs of a Cave-Dweller. New York: Dodge, 1908.

Dedicated to Theodore Dreiser: the present editor inherited a manuscript which his grandparents had obtained in 1833 from an old Jesuit who had been in Indo-China as well as among the Indians of America. It stresses the tie between Amerinds and Asiatics. The manuscript is the first-person narration of the caveman Wolf. He and his brother Storm steal a woman from a stranger who kills Storm. Wolf kills a mammoth and carves images of a man and woman from its teeth. He plants grain; otherwise this is simply a re- counting of conventional adventures.

543. McDougall, Walter H[ugh]. The Hidden City; or The Strange Adventure of Eric Gilbert. New York: Cassell, 1891.

Several years earlier the balloonist, Eric Gilbert, crashed between the Wasatch and Elk Mountains, finding there the city of Atzlan. After the conventional incidents, he weds Lela and becomes governor of the city. The first impres- sion that this is a mixture of Vikings and Central American Indians is upset by the tales which the aged Iklapel, an

old blind high priest, tells.   The legends of the people
associate Atzlan with Atlantis destroyed by a comet, but
also suggest that everyone perished except for a white man
and a red woman from whom all humanity came.   What makes
the novel a unique handling of the motif arises from H. R.
Pierce and a wagon train of pioneers coming to the city
after a carrier pigeon has given Pierce Eric's location.
Pierce becomes the city's financial adviser and will
convert its gold into money while bringing modern equipment
and cattle into the valley to modernize Atzlan.

544. McIntyre, Margaret A.   The Cave Boy of the Age of Stone.
New York: D. Appleton, 1907.

Thorn and Pineknot are the cave children;   Strongarm and
Burr, their parents.   Their dog is Wow-wow.   McIntyre
shifts back and forth from thousands of years ago to the
present as she tries to instruct her readers about the life
of the cave people.   She treats them as though they were
Indians or other primitive peoples of the present or recent
past.   For example, she asserts that when Columbus discovered America, the Indians were in the Stone Age.   Such
obvious didacticism weakens the narrative.

545. McKesson, Charles L.   Under Pike's Peak; or, Mahalma,
Child of the Fire Father. New York: Neely, 1898.

The first-person narrator, Thomas Larnard, falls down a
shaft of an old volcano into an inner world.   He finds
there Oliver Esteller, who had disappeared in the same area
some two years ago.   He sees and falls in love with the
young woman, Mahalma.   She is descended from a people who
consciously left the surface when mankind had developed
into a brutish creature whom love could not control.   Hers
are a humane and civilized people, but their existence must
be kept secret.   Beyond this the narrative is little more
than an account of the triangle of the narrator, Mahalma,
and Esteller.   Eventually Mahalma dies, and the two men
return to Colorado Springs.

546. McLandburgh, Florence.   The Automaton Ear and Other
Stories. Chicago: Jansen, A.C. McClurg, 1876.

In the title story a professor tries to develop an instrument which will capture all sounds, even those from the
past.   He perfects it but chooses to keep it a secret.   A
deaf and dumb woman obtains it; he chokes her and gets it
back.   The ending suggests that he may have been mad
throughout the narrative.

547. McMasters, William H[enry].   Revolt; An American Novel.
Boston: Nickerson, 1919.

The novel attacks big money's control of American politics.
At the Harvard commencement in 1925 John Paine Morton gets
an honorary degree, while his son Roger gets an A.B. From
the beginning Roger is in love with Marta Falmouth, daughter of a Harvard professor whom the older Morton accuses of
being a socialist. By 1940 Falmouth points out to Roger
that his father, the head of Universal Trust Company, has
named the candidates for both parties in the past three
elections and will do so again. With no motivation other
than Falmouth's remark that his father "is a self-chosen
dictator," after asking what he should do to set things
right, Roger helps to organize a new political party, the
Revolutionist, and runs a classmate, Dan Holman, for
president. Two of the party planks assure government
ownership of all public utilities and a regular weekly
income for everyone sixty or over. There is, of course, a
women's branch to the party headed by Marta; it advocates
the franchise for all women. The Revolutionist Party wins,
and after Roger and Marta are married, there is a reconciliation with the elder Morton, who enjoys a hard fight
and wins appointment as Secretary of the Treasury.

548. McNeil, Everett.   The Lost Nation.   New York: Dutton,
1918.

This is one of a series intended for a juvenile audience.
Richard Orson and Harry Ashton join the scientist, Thane
Kendal, as he searches for a lost city of Toltecs in
Mexico. They find a city in a valley in the mountains.
Kendal falls in love with princess Exitl. When apemen
besiege and take the city, the professor, the boys, and
Exitl escape aboard a balloon conveniently left by a former
explorer who died. They are carried out to the Pacific but
are rescued by a ship. Kendal and Exitl marry.

549. McNeile, H[erman] C[yril].   Guardians of the Treasure.
Garden City, N.Y.: Doubleday, 1931.

Jim Maitland, British scientist, and Judy Draycott search
for her twin brother who disappeared several years earlier
into South America. Although there is reference to apemen
and a deserted ship, like the Marie Celeste, this is more a
straight adventure story in that they discover a treasure
left on Lone Tree Island about 1600 by Don Silva Rodriguez.
The villain is Emil Dresler, "blackmailer, white slave
trafficker, arch-scoundrel." Published by Crime Club, this
novel exemplifies how late writers were dressing up their
mysteries with the furniture of the lost race motif.

550. Meredith, Ellis. The Master-Knot of Human Fate. Boston:
Little, Brown, 1901.

An unexplained catastrophe maroons a man and woman, Adam
and Robin, in a cabin in the Rockies. Although they do not
at first love one another, they do by the end of the narrative, realizing that in their love they have found God and
that he has seen fit to begin things again with them.
Apparently all of the continent except the Rockies has
sunk. The only sign of human life is a derelict ship.

551. Merrill, Albert Adams. The Great Awakening; The Story of
the Twenty-Second Century. Boston: George Book, 1899.

As a result of an operation the first-person narrator
occupies the body of "a certain Richard Pangloss" at the
beginning of the twenty-second century. In part the novel
is an attack on the gold standard; after a revolution
in 2021 wealth was distributed equally and the population
was stabilized. Electricity provides the energy for
everything, including trains. Russia has fallen, while
famine and pestilence have annihilated the Chinese. The
Anglo-Saxon races have spread throughout the world.

552. Merritt, A[braham]. Burn, Witch, Burn. New York: Liveright, 1933.

Dr. Lowell, a psychiatrist, and Ricori, a gangster, join
forces against a witch, Madame Mandelip, who can capture
souls and then use them to animate mannikins which she uses
to carry out varous crimes. Although science and power are
unable to overcome her, Lowell's former nurse, now transformed into a doll, kills her.

553. Merritt, A[braham]. Creep, Shadow. Garden City, N.Y.:
Doubleday, Doran, 1934.

A sequel to Burn, Witch, Burn: the storyline traces a
number of murders to Dr. Keradel, a warlock who makes human
sacrifices to an ancient monstrous god, and his daughter
Dahut, a reincarnation of an ancient princess who captures
souls and makes them do her evil for her. Again Lowell and
Ricori are helpless before witchcraft. But Dahut kills her
father because she loves Lowell. Her captured souls rise
and kill her.

554. Merritt, A[braham]. Dwellers in the Mirage. New York:
Liveright, 1932.

Originally published in Argosy (1932): Merritt blends
together Nordic, Asiatic, and American Indian mythologies
as background for the linguist-anthropologist, Leif Langdon. Three years earlier in the Gobi he encountered
descendants of the ancient Uighurs, who hailed him as the

hero-warrior Dwayanu and let him participate in rituals calling up the monstrous god, Khalk-ru (the Kraken). Now in Alaska he and his companion, the Cherokee, Jim, are summoned by drums to the Shadowed Lands, a valley lying beneath a heavy fog. They encounter a race of pygmies whom Jim identifies as the Little People of Cherokee legend. They live in continuous guerilla warfare with Uighurs who fled Asia when the Gobi became a desert. For a time the two stay with the Little People; Leif loves the girl Evalie. But the spirit of Dwayanu possesses Leif so that he joins the Uighurs and becomes the consort of their queen, Lur. Warfare ensues. Only when Jim is killed does Leif gain freedom from Dwayanu. In the novel he and Evalie, who had originally come from the outside, leave the valley. In the manuscript Evalie was also killed; some later reprints have used this variation.

555. Merritt, A[braham]. The Face in the Abyss. New York: Liveright, 1931.

The novel combines two works published in Argosy All-Story and Argosy (1923, 1930): in the Ecuadorian Andes Nicholas Graydon and his companions discover the girl, Suarra, and learn of Yu-Atlanchi. Graydon alone survives the first encounter; he returns to search for Suarra, whom he loves. He becomes involved in the struggle between Nimir, the evil being whose stone face was in the abyss, and The Snake Mother, who fled from the Antarctic long before the Andes arose. Nimir was one of the creations of the Snake Mother's people. The climax comes after a titanic battle between Nimir and the Snake Mother. He is destroyed, and Graydon and Suarra (a handmaid of the Snake Mother) are united.

556. Merritt, A[braham]. The Metal Monster. New York: Avon, 1946.

Originally published in Argosy (1920): Dr. Walter Goodwin and his party venture into central Asia, where they encounter both the descendants of ancient Persians and an inorganic, matallic being who can change its shape as it wishes. The creature--referred to as the Metal Horde because it is composed of millions of cell-like units--wishes to conquer the world. A girl, Nordala, expelled by the Persians, uses the metal being to destroy them, but is herself destroyed when the units of the metal monster struggle among themselves so that it, too, dies.

557. Merritt, A[braham]. The Moon Pool. New York: Putnam, 1919.

The novel combines two works orginally published in All-Story (1918, 1919): the first-person narrator, Dr. Walter Goodwin, discovers Dr. David Throckmorton pursued by what

Goodwin calls a "Thing." Throckmorton explains that his wife Edith and his associates were taken by the Dweller in the Moon Pool on Nan-Tauach in the Carolines. He is seized/absorbed by a radiant pillar. Goodwin, Larry O'Keefe, and Olaf Huldrickson penetrate the chamber of the Moon Pool and enter the sub-oceanic country, Muria. Among its wonders are the Silent Ones, three survivors of an ancient reptilian race whose task is to kill the Dweller (also called The Shining One). Larry becomes involved in a triangle with Yolar, the lovely evil queen, and Lakla, the fair heroine. Because the ruling class of Muria intends to invade the surface and conquer the world, there is a civil war. In the final battle Olaf is killed. Goodwin has seen Throckmorton and Edith and now buries them. The Silent Ones destroy the Dweller; Goodwin kills the evil Russian scientist, Marakinoff, whose schemes were evil but never quite explicit. Goodwin finds himself alone on the surface, the gate to Muria (the moon door) vanished. Somewhere below Larry and Lakla remain united. Despite its extravagance, The Moon Pool had perhaps greater influence on subsequent science fiction than any work except those of Burroughs.

558. Merritt, A[braham]. Seven Footprints to Satan. New York: Boni & Liveright, 1928.

James Kirkham, an American explorer and adventurer, is kidnapped by a master criminal, seemingly an Asiatic who calls himself Satan, in order to have Kirkham steal the ancient necklace of the Egyptian princess Senusert from a museum in New York. He does, with the aid of Eve Demarest. Eventually Satan is destroyed in an explosion and fire, while Eve and Kirkham fall in love.

559. Merritt, A[braham]. The Ship of Ishtar. New York: Putnam, 1926.

John Kenton, an enthusiast rather than a trained archaeologist, receives a block of stone from an excavation in the Near East. When the stone splits, he discovers within it a miniature ship. Falling unconscious, he finds that he is aboard the ship, taking part in a cosmic struggle between good and evil: between the priests who worship Nergal, dark god of Babylon, and the followers of Ishtar. He falls in love with Sharane, her priestess. In the final battle the ship is sunk; Sharane is killed. Kenton's consciousness passes back and forth between the worlds. His body is found by his servants, but the implication is that Ishtar has joined the lovers together in eternity.

560. Meyer, John J[oseph].   The Deer-Smellers of Haunted
Mountain; The Almost Unbelievable Experiences of a Cerebroic
Hunter in the Hills of This World and the Lowlands of the
Universe with a Gypsy-Eyed Spirit Hunter, Humorously Tattle--
Taled. New York: Cerebroscope, 1921.

   The earliest treatment of an essentially occult theme: on a
   hunting trip to Haunted Mountain, Richard Reyem is captured
   by Germans who dwell deep inside the mountain.   After his
   psyche has gone on a number of cosmic journeys, Reyem
   defeats them.   The mysticism remains thoroughly murky, but
   essentially Cerebroism is a belief in God and has only one
   law: "Anything that brain can imagine is possible."   Tagged
   on is the love story of Ted Flynn, detective, and the
   golden-haired heroine of Haunted Mountain.   A further
   sub-title declares the book to be "a Bewitching, Inspiring
   Satire" so that one cannot be sure what Meyer is serious
   about.

561. Meyer, John J[oseph].   13 Seconds That Rocked the World;
or, The Mentator; A Romance of a Mankind Director in an Age of
Certified Reason. New York: Henkel, 1935.

   Six scientists, including Dr. Roneale and Professor Olney,
   gather to discuss the future of mankind.   Their basic point
   is that until Science can discover what thought is, it
   cannot deal with spiritual problems or prove the existence
   of God; therefore, scientists must proceed upon the idea
   that man is alone.   Given this premise they want the world
   governed by science and scientists.   To this end, they form
   United Science of the World, whose outstanding achievement
   is the development of an electric brain, first called Arty
   Dumbel, and then The Mentator.   They set up the Bahamas as
   the site of United World Science and make Grand Bahama
   Island Mentator Park.   The brain will gather the thoughts
   of all human beings into one unity.   The Mentator will take
   care of all human problems, including crime.   It is the
   supreme Mind and Power on Earth.   Tied to all of this
   mystic gibberish is a thin storyline; Joan Olney is kidnapped by Big Boy, head of the Western underworld, and
   taken to the Grand Canyon.   She is rescued by Mentator and
   united with her beloved Dr. Roneale.

562. Meyer, John J[oseph].   Try Another World; A Saga Coursing
Its Way Through the Six Adventures of Joe Shaun Which Thrilled
the Village of Carydale.   New York: Business Bourse, 1942.

   An additional subtitle proclaims, "Greater Dreams Hath No
   Man."   Dozing in the Catskills, Joe Shaun is whisked away
   on a cosmic voyage which culminates when he has revealed to
   him the world of the Mentator.   Through him it will prevent
   a reign of terror on Earth.   In a prefatory note, Meyer is
   called "a Jules Verne of the world of ideas."

563. Meyer, John J[oseph]. <u>20,000 Trails Under the Universe with the Cerebroscope; A Tale of Wonderful Adventures</u>. New York: "Privately Printed," 1917.

This is the first appearance of Richard Reyem; apparently the mystical mishmash was caused by the death of a child, here called Little John. The Cerebroscope permits communication with the dead. Reyem forms the Church of Universal Truth, and the Cerebroscope transforms the Earth into "the reign of the brotherhood of man."

564. Michaelson, Miriam. <u>The Awakening of Zojas</u>. New York: Doubleday, Page, 1910.

Dr. Rossi, a scientist who wishes to extend human lifespan, performs an experiment on Zojas, a brigand awaiting execution. It succeeds, but not before a revolution destroys the laboratory. Zojas plans to make himself king; Dr. Rossi refuses to be Prime Minister.

565. Mighels, Philip Verrill. <u>The Crystal Sceptre; A Story of Adventure</u>. New York: Fenno, 1901.

Sole survivor of a balloon crash on an island somewhere in the East Indies, the first-person narrator find himself in a struggle between two tribes of Missing Links. With the aid of gunpowder he helps the "Red Links" defeat the "Black Links" and becomes their king. He discovers gold, but more importantly he rescues a white girl whom he calls only "the goddess" because the Black Links worship her. Although his greed for gold almost causes their capture by the Black Links, they escape in a small boat and are picked up after two days by a steamer. Only in the characterization of one of the links as a faithful clown ("Fatty") who helps save him and the girl and in portraying a crippled child who dies as being more intelligent ("Little Man") does Mighels show any originality.

566. Miller, Leo E[dward]. <u>The Hidden People; The Story of a Search for Incan Treasure</u>. New York: Scribner, 1920.

Young Stanley Livingston and Ted Boyle search for Incan treasure in the Andes of Peru. They find the city of Patallaca in the Hidden Valley; it is ruled by Huayna Capac, the Inca, who befriends them. He makes them princes, but his jealous son, Quizquiz, has them arrested for treason and conspiracy. Condemned to exile beyond a great wall that divides the valley, they escape with the aid of Timichi, who had been banished to the area; he shows them a cavern of gold. They escape by an underground river and take with them a treasure in gold.

567. Miller, Leo E[dward].   In the Tiger's Lair.   New York:
Scribner, 1921.

Stanley and Ted return to the Hidden Valley, but Miller
intrudes a chapter in which they return to the U.S. and
join the air force because America is in World War I; he
then dismisses their war experience.   The device permits
them to fly to the Hidden Valley (though they had been
there on foot in the first chapter and had to return to
Cuzco for dynamite).   They find Quizquiz to be the Inca; he
calls himself the Tiger.   And of course he remembers them
and gives them trouble.   Eventually with the aid of Suncco
and an eclipse, they overcome the villainy of Quizquiz and
his priest, Villac Ulu.   The natives want to kill the two
scoundrels and make Stanley king.   They repair a wall to
keep out sabre tooth tigers, and they establish a new
government.   They take as much gold as a hundred men can
carry with them as they leave, but they promise Suncco not
to reveal the existence of the Hidden Valley.

568. Milne, Robert Duncan.   Into the Sun & Other Stories.
Edited by Sam Moskowitz.   West Kingston, R.I.: Donald Grant,
1980.

Between 1879 and 1899 Milne published some sixty stories,
primarily in The Argonaut in San Francisco.   The eleven
stories in this volume deal with a variety of popular
themes.   They range from "Into the Sun" (1882), in which
the protagonist, a balloonist, watches the destruction of
San Francisco because of the heat of a comet that has
fallen into the sun, and "A Family Skeleton" (1885), in
which a two-headed man commits suicide, to "The World's
Last Cataclysm" (1889), in which a comet causes a tidal
wave, and "A Question of Reciprocity" (1891), in which a
mad scientist threatens to destroy San Francisco with a
bomb if he is not paid twenty million dollars.

569. [Minor, John W.(pseud.)].   "Bietigham."   New York: Funk &
Wagnalls, 1886.

Presented as a series of three lectures, this narrative,
without creating individualized characters or dramatizing
action, reviews the causes and effects of the "momentous"
war of 1890-1891.   Briefly it touches upon the victory in
the 1888 election of a new American political party, the
Nationals.   In the summer of 1889 the visit of a young
German, a naturalized American citizen, to his birthplace
in Germany and his arrest for evading service in the German
army precipitated a crisis.   Britain, France, Italy, Spain,
and the U.S. fought Germany, Austria, and Russia.   Attention is given the defeat of a German Imperial Fleet
attacking New Orleans, but the victory of the Allied armies
at Bietigham, complete with a cavalry charge, crushes the
enemy.   In May the Treaty of Carlsruhe was signed.   By 1893

a general social revolution had begun on the Continent so that the conquered nations immediately went republican and by 1910 the United States of Europe had come into being. Russia did not join. The consequences of the end of imperialism and militarism advanced the standard of living everywhere. All of South and Central America are united in a similar republic. From the new nations the United States learns to use the direct popular vote rather than the old electoral college. The only danger is the possibility of a war sometime with China. Immigration from Europe has ceased. This is a richly textured narrative which merits study as an exercise in imaginary history.

570. Mitchell, Edward Page. The Crystal Man. Edited by Sam Moskowitz. Garden City, N.Y.: Doubleday, 1973.

In this collection of hitherto uncollected stories, Mos-kowitz calls Mitchell, an editor of the New York Sun, a major figure in nineteenth century science fiction, sug-gesting that even such a writer as Wells was indebted to him. The thirty stories written between 1874 and 1886 deal with a variety of popular themes. In "The Crystal Man" the protagonist achieves invisibility by bleaching the pigment of the skin. A watchmaker, "The Ablest Man in the World" (1879), develops a machine that can reason; he places it inside the skull of an idiot who is transformed into one of the world's leaders. Many of the tales, like "The Facts of the Ratcliff Case," deal with multiple personality; in this instance a young woman seems able to influence (drug) those to whom she gives her attention. The protagonist of "The Balloon Tree" (1883) is rescued by a tree and carried more than a hundred miles to his ship. He refers to it as "a plant-animal" and asserts that friends have seen it. Mitchell proves himself a competent, highly imaginative writer.

571. Mitchell, J[ohn] A[mes]. Drowsy. New York: Stokes, 1917.

The storyline concerns the love of Cyrus Alton and Ruth Heyward, beginning when they are children. A scientific genius, he develops an ultimate energy as well as an anti-gravity device which permit him to fly to the moon. He finds the ruins of a once great civilization there and returns with a fortune in diamonds. Setting out on a trip to Mars because he thinks that Ruth does not love him, he does reach Mars, but her psychic call--her declaration of love--draws him back. In returning he has an accident and ends up in a hospital where she nurses him. They announce a wedding date.

572. Mitchell, J[ohn] A[mes]. The Last American; A Fragment from the Journal of KHAN-LI, Prince of Dimph-Yoo-Chur and Admiral in the Persian Navy. New York: Stokes, 1889.

In 2951 a Persian expedition discovers the legendary continent of the "Mehrikans," landing in the harbor of ruined Nhu Yok. Later in Washington they encounter an old man, a girl, and a young man; both men are killed in the fight that occurs after a Persian, Ja-khaz, kisses the girl. In the period 1945-1960 severe climatic changes (since the diary entries for May refer to a wintry storm, one infers something caused a reversal of seasons) completed the catastrophe which had begun with other events. After the U.S. obtained a large share of the world's trade, a European coalition attacked and defeated her. In 1927 a massacre of Protestants was followed by the tyranny and chaos of the "Murfey" regime. All of this contributes to Mitchell's attack upon American materialism.

573. Mitchell, J[ames] Leslie. Three Go Back. Indianapolis, In.: Bobbs-Merrill, 1932.

During a flight from England to America the airship Magellan's Cloud witnesses a submarine earthquake. The August climate grows suddenly colder; wireless messages cease; the moon is full five days ahead of time. When the airship burns, Clair Stranlay--journalist and novelist--and Keith Sinclair manage to swim ashore. They are joined by Sir John Mullaghan. Somehow they have been cast 25,000 years back in time to the continent of Atlantis, where they fall in with a tribe of Cro-Magnards. Clair is attracted to a hunter, Aerte, and Sir John dies. The Cro-Magnards head toward Europe until they encounter a Neanderthal horde. In the final battle everyone is killed, but Clair and Keith revive to find themselves in 1932 in the Azores, in the same pass where the final battle took place. They realize that Keith is Aerte and plan to marry.

574. Mitchell, J[ames] Leslie. Gay Hunter. London: Heinemann, 1934.

The lovely Gay Hunter is projected into the future to a time when Britain has returned to barbarism. She finds Major Ledyard Houghton and Lady Jane Easterling there, but she is separated from them. She meets the hunter, Rem, and travels with him to his tribe, where she finds Houghton and Easterling captured and judged insane. Gay and Rem are married and go on a honeymoon; when they return, they find that Houghton and Easterling and some of the nomadic hunters have tried to establish a new civilization in what was once London. They fail, and Gay recovers consciousness back in the twentieth century. This is interesting only because of its variation on the theme of the reversion of modern civilization to barbarism.

575. Moffett, Cleveland [Langston]. The Conquest of America; A Romance of Disaster and Victory: U.S.A., 1921 A.D.; Based on Extracts from the Diary of James E. Langdon, War Correspondent of the "London Times." New York: Doran, 1916.

> Originally serialized in McClure's Magazine (1915): in 1921 Germany occupies the United States. Despite heroic resistance, the United States does not regain freedom until scientists and industrialists combine their efforts. First a German army is annihilated when Americans ignite thousands of gallons of gasoline (provided by Standard Oil) buried beneath the battlefield; the second victory occurs when a fleet of airplanes dumps tons of liquid chlorine on another German army; finally, Thomas Edison develops a radio-controlled torpedo enabling "an insignificant airforce" to destroy the German navy. While Cleveland defends the concept of Manifest Destiny and advocates reforms which would lead to socialism, he also suggests that "war may be a biological necessity in the development of the human race. . . ."

576. Moffett, Cleveland [Langston]. Possessed. New York: McCann, 1920.

> Supposedly the fulfillment of a medium's prophecy on the eve of the first war, this novel concentrates upon the psychological treatment of Mrs. Penelope Wells (widowed and decorated for valor under fire as a nurse) by Dr. William Owen, a psychiatrist who also developed toxic liquid containing a strain of deadly bacteria for possible use in warfare. His assistant, Captain Herrick, now is the lover of Mrs. Wells. The question remains whether or not Moffett was exorcising a demon who possessed Penelope or whether he simply used her to lash out at feminine sensuality. The "Epilogue" is subtitled "A Woman's Litany" and asks for the Lord's deliverance from "all defilements of love"; supposedly it was written by Penelope Wells.

577. Montague, C.E. Right Off the Map. Garden City, N.Y.: Doubleday, Page, 1927.

> This must be included in the future war motif, for it is a satire of the "unreasoning insanity and wasted effort of war." The struggle is between the republics of Porto and Ria over some desert land where gold was supposedly discovered. The attack is partly upon British colonialism in that the republic of Ria is a new country arising from the old state of Goya, which was heavily populated by British; but more of the satire is aimed at the neurotic, excitement-seeking Rose Burnage and her husband Cyril, who edits the newspaper, the Voice.

578. Montgomery, Frances Trego. On a Lark to the Planets; A Sequel to "The Wonderful Electric Elephant". Akron, Oh.: Saalfield, 1904.

Harold and Ione continue their adventures when the robot elephant flies to various planets. The incidents simply echo other books.

579. Montgomery, Frances Trego. The Wonderful Electric Elephant. Akron, Oh.: Saalfield, 1903.

In the Grand Canyon Harold Frederick comes upon a wonderful robot elephant. A dying old man inside the elephant says that anyone who buries him may have the robot to travel the world. Frederick does. His companion is a beautiful blonde--Ione de Valley--rescued from Indians. They go to the West coast and marry; then the elephant sprouts wings so that they can go to Japan, China, and Siam.

580. Moresby, Louis (pseud. of L. Adams Beck). The Glory of Egypt. New York: Doran, 1926.

Also published in England by Thomas Nelson (1926): the first-person narrator, Christopher "Kit" Ross, refers to various expeditions into Chinese Turkestan and Tibet which have found artifacts or heard reports of an ancient city. He and his friend Soames learn of "Touch-the-Sky Mountain where is the Splendour of Egypt"; it is also referred to as the "place of the One Woman" and of "the Things that Run." They are guided deep into Tibet, where they find an ancient Egyptian city dating from at least 1,200 B.C. The woman is its princess and has decided that Ross should be her husband. He must save her from the seemingly alien creatures who attempt to sacrifice her; as they escape, Soames, who has been growing more moody, attempts to kill Ross. The princess pushes him over the edge of a cliff, but she also falls to her death. Although this permits Ross to return to his English girl, Joan Boston, the princess haunts him and he thinks of organizing another expedition to the city, as though not convinced that she is dead.

581. Morris, Gouverneur. It and Other Stories. New York: Scribner, 1912.

Of these the most significant story is "Back There in the Grass," in which a foot-high, man-serpent creature is discovered. The suggestion is made that it is the end product of another line of evolution.

582. Morris, Gouverneur. The Pagan's Progress. New York: Barnes, 1904.

A pseudo-historical romance of the caveman, this novel focuses upon the growing spiritual awareness of primitive

man. The climax comes when the protagonist "sees" his dead
mate in a forest and realizes that man has eternal life
instead of "dissolution...decay...dust...nothing."

583. Morris, Gouverneur. The Voice in the Rice. New York:
Dodd, Mead, 1910.

The first-person narrator, Richard Bourne, is swept off the
deck of a boat as it passes the Santee River. He lands on
a swampy coast and finds a Southern society living much as
it would have before the Civil War. Lord Nairn makes the
laws, but significantly slaves can acquire and hold property. Against this background most of the narrative is
concerned with Bourne's love for Mary Moore, whose voice
he falls in love with. Although Nairn, a widower, wants
her, Bourne wins her. At the end the people scatter, but
Bourne gives his address as Georgetown, South Carolina.
Teitler lists this as a lost race novel, but Reginald does
not include it.

584. Morris, William. News from Norwhere; or, An Epoch of
Rest. London: Roberts, 1890.

Originally published in Commonweal (1890): Morris intended
this as a direct response to Bellamy. In the twenty-first
century Kensington is completely wooded; squalor, poverty,
all signs of urban industrialization have vanished. The
scene calls up Morris' much-loved fourteenth century. At
the heart of his nostalgia for the past are the concepts of
harmony with nature and a sense of beauty as well as
equality in the lives of all men and women. Morris uses a
dream-vision as a narrative frame; his dreamer finds no
competition, no politics, nor family strife. He learns
that after a massacre in Trafalgar Square, there came a
revolution, during which all machines were destroyed.
Morris' earlier The Dream of John Ball (1886-1887) had
pictured the Peasants' Revolt of 1381. His central idea is
that the fellowship of humanity will endure and that
consequently all persons will share equally.

585. Morrow, William C[hambers]. The Ape, The Idiot, and Other
People. Philadelphia: Lippincott, 1897.

The most significant of these stories is a variation on the
Frankenstein theme, "The Monster Maker," in which a young
man comes to a surgeon asking to be killed. He is subjected to an experiment, transformed into a beast which has
a "small metallic ball surmounting its massive neck." The
surgeon kills it as it tries to escape; everything is
burned. Much is said of the neurological makeup of man,
particularly of his motor abilities, in the terms of the
period.

586. Morrow, W[illiam] C[hambers]. <u>Lentala of the South Seas;
The Romantic Tale of a Lost Colony</u>. New York: Frederick A.
Stokes, 1908.

The first-person narrator, Mr. Tudor, and a shipload of
colonists are wrecked on an unknown South Seas island.
They are kept separate from the natives, but Tudor suspects
that white men have been marooned on the island and sacrificed to various gods. Two storylines develop. First,
Vancouver and Rawley attempt to foment revolt and seize the
island.   More important is the love between Tudor and
Lentala.   To be near him she disguises herself both as a
common maiden and a boy. Although a native, Gato, attempts
to seize control, Lentala ends as the queen of the island.
Tudor remains as her consort. She is of mixed blood, her
father having been an Englishman.   The novel is most
provocative because of its discussion of race.   It is
enigmatic in that neither the islanders nor the island is
ever identified.   Chapter headings are presented in the
manner of eighteenth century fiction so that one cannot be
certain of its time, though it seems the late nineteenth
century.   This must be regarded as one of the most noteworthy novels of the period, though it does not adhere
strictly to the conventions of the lost race motif.

587. Morton, A. S. <u>Beyond the Palaeocryptic Sea; or, The
Legend of Halfjord</u>. Chicago: Donnelly, 1895.

The narrator has been sent to Greenland in 1885 by a "scientific society" to study the area.   After two years at
Upernarvik, he goes northward and in 1888 discovers a
manuscript.   Dated "Nikiva, 1858," it is by Pierre Vach-
erson, who took part in the search for Franklin.   After
referring to the Symmesian theory, he comes upon people of
Scandinavian descent from a settlement in the ninth century.   Chief among the differences in custom is the complete lack of monogamous marriage.   His manuscript gives
the history of the colony of Halfjord, including its defeat
by Harold the Fair-Haired, who wanted to unite Norway under
one flag.

588. Mott, Laurence. <u>The White Darkness and Other Stories of
the Great Northwest</u>. New York: Outing, 1907.

The most significant story is "The Black Thing of Hatchet
Lake."   Jack Arnold drowns in the lake.   Batiste Clement
must take a message to someone; this requires him to pass
the lake.   He thinks he sees Jack.   In the morning he is
found frozen to death, his expression showing that he has
gone mad/been frightened to death.   The narrative recalls
some of Bierce's work.

589. Muller, Julius W[ashington]. The Invasion of America; A
Fact Story Based on the Inexorable Mathematics of War.   New
York: Dutton, 1916.

  Although called a novel this is an essay which recounts the
  complete conquest of America by a coalition of European
  powers.   There is no real storyline.   It anticipates
  Bywater. Muller also wrote The ABC of Preparedness.

590. Mundo, Otto (pseud.). The Recovered Continent; A Tale of
the Chinese Invasion. Columbus, Oh.: Harper-Osgood, 1898.

  In a clumsy framing structure, Mr. Esden falls onto an
  electric wire in 1874 and thus undergoes suspended animation. He is revived in 1926. The first part of the
  narrative celebrates a U.S. that dominates North America.
  Because of a deliberately changed climate, Greenland is now
  a habitable country, containing great resources.   An
  operation on a simple-minded individual successfully
  creates a genius, Toto Topheavy. After political bickering
  he leaves the West. Momentarily Esden thinks he has been
  asleep and is not certain whether he is in 1874 or 1926.
  The second part of the narrative deals with a war resulting
  from revolution in China and then throughout Asia. Britain
  and Russia are the main enemies. A terrible battle near
  Constantinople makes China victorious.   Toto, who has
  somehow aligned himself with the East, is declared to be
  the anti-Christ. An attempt is made to assassinate him,
  but he survives to go to Greenland, where he helps structure a universal federation of all of the nations of the
  world. He wants to use all the explosives in the world to
  cut a canal through Panama. At the end Esden wonders
  whether or not he can exist in both the nineteenth and
  twentieth centuries. This is a strange mixture of mysticism and racism which does not properly jell.

591. Mundy, Talbot (pseud. of William Lancaster Gribbon). Tros
of Samothrace. New York & London: Appleton-Century, 1934.

  A pseudo-historical novel (949 pages) dealing with the
  adventures of Tros, Prince of Samothrace, as he tries to
  defend Britain against Caesar in 55 B.C. By summer of 54
  B.C. Tros takes leave of Caesar, though they are not
  friends, declaring that he will sail around the world.
  Many of Mundy's novels dealing with India contain some of
  the furniture of the lost race motif, but none really
  qualifies. Granting personal preferences, one does feel
  that Tros best exemplifies his writing potential: atmosphere, action adventure.

592. Nelson, Arthur A. Wings of Danger; A Novel. New York:
McBride, 1915.

> Extremely Anglophile, speaking of "the Rhodes dream," the
> narrative focuses upon Sir Alan Severn, a hunter and free
> agent who is a friend of Rhodes. He saves Norma Rayles-
> croft from a cobra, but her father dismisses him, pre-
> ferring Lord Chalmes as a suitor. Eric Ivarsson knows of a
> manuscript in the British Museum, a Norse saga of "Ull the
> Old," whose Vikings ravaged the coast of Ethiopia. Driven
> inland, they settled near Skull Mountain. Ivarsson has the
> map of Ibrahim to guide him. Their companion, Ingulf, is
> an amnesiac found in the interior. Raoul de Rougement
> appears as their rival; he has Arab slavers and represents
> Belgium. As Severn's party treks for Skull Mountain, they
> fight the Matabeles, rescuing Norma and Lord Chalmes. They
> find a walled city on a volcano in a desert area; it is
> lighted by natural gas. Ingulf calls it Valkyria. In the
> court of King Fágu they meet the girl, Phaima, one of the
> few of pure Norse blood because of the centuries of mis-
> cegenation. Fágu has eyes for Norma, but Prince Hâkon
> starts a revolt, aided by Roguemort. Ingulf kills the
> king; as Hâkon dies, he reveals that Ingulf is the true
> heir. Fangari, an Ethiopian priest, ignites the gas well,
> and volcanic action destroys Valkyria. Ingulf stays with
> Phaima, but since Chalmes is also dead, Severn and Norma
> are united. Rhodes tells Severn that he has served England
> well; during Rhodes' trial, Severn is knighted.

593. [Newcomb, Cyrus]. The Book of Algoonah, Being a Concise
Account of the History of the Early People of the Continent of
America Known as the Mound Builders. St. Louis: Little &
Becker, 1884.

> Algoonah is the king of an Assyrian-Egyptian people forced
> to move from their country and wander through Asia. They
> finally colonize America and become the Mound Builders.

594. Newcomb, Simon. His Wisdom, the Defender; A Story. New
York: Harper, 1900.

> Presented as future history, the novel traces the rise to
> power of an American scientist, Archibald Campbell, Pro-
> fessor of Molecular Physics at Harvard. He forms a secret
> society, "The Angellic Order of Seraphim," among the young
> college men of the country. Subpoenaed by Congress, he
> reveals that he has discovered ultimate powers ("etherine"
> and "ferm") which would disrupt the world socially, finan-
> cially, and economically. Since his powers would bring
> about a crisis more severe than the Industrial Revolution
> because this crisis would occur so suddenly, he insists
> that he have personal authority to control the revolution.
> Reaction is not openly antagonistic until he proposes a
> consitituion for a federated world state with himself as

head.   Only after his weapons and the "seraphim" have
defeated the German army, the British navy, and a combination of French and Austrian forces, thus producing chaos
in Europe, do the nations of the world meet his demands.
He brings about a Golden Age of Man through a single
government and the abolition of war.   He does suggest that
"dependent peoples" may become members of the federation
when they are judged ready to govern themselves.

595. Nichols, Robert (pseud. of Malise Bowyer).   Fantastica,
Being the Smile of the Sphinx and Other Tales of Imagination.
London: Chatto & Windus, 1923.

"Golgotha & Co." bitterly projects a picture of Europe
after a second world war.   The first-person narrator
attacks science in particular.   The story culminates with
the Second Coming of Christ.   A lengthy "Epilogue" opens
with a denunciation of Wells's concept of an earthly paradise; in the story Ahasuerus represents Christianity as "an
other-world" religion; nothing in Christianity speaks of
this world as becoming a better place.

596. Niemann, [Wilhelm Otto] August.   The Coming Conquest of
England.   Trans. from the German by J.H. Freese.   New York:
Putnam, 1904.

Also published in London by Routledge (1904): Niemann
asserts that for centuries most wars have involved Britain.
After Japan's victory over China, he wonders whether or not
France, Germany, and Russia should hold off or join hands
against England, who had interest in China.   Much of the
fighting at first involves a Russian and Afghan incursion
into India.   German and French fleets force the landing of
an army in Scotland near Leith and Edinburgh.   Russia gets
to the Indian Ocean; Egypt goes to France; Germany sets up
an arrangement with the Boer republics.   The Kaiser will
lead triumphant armies into London.   Land must not be an
object for speculation, and there must be no socialism in
the new colonies.   A thin storyline recounts the love of
various women for sundry officers and diplomats.

597. Niswonger, Charles Elliott.   The Isle of Feminine.   Little
Rock, Ar.: Brown, 1893.

The first-person narrator and his companion go out in a
small boat; they drift for three days, and the companion
cuts his own throat.   The narrator awakens on an island
where Diana has ruled for 3,552 years.   He loves her, and
she makes him a prince of the island, naming him Angelo.
She declares that immortality occurs only in the absence of
passionate love.   She loves him passionately, throws
herself in his arms, dies, and withers.   The populace rises
against him, but he escapes from the island with Vesta,
whom he loves, as the island sinks.

598. North, Franklin H. The Awakening of Noahville. New York:
New York Publishing, 1898.

Described as "a lost city, in a lost kingdom beyond the
seas," Noahville portrays a strictly agricultural, medieval
society which is visited by two Yankees. It does not survive the impact of the nineteenth century. The nobility
strikes for higher wages and shorter hours. This is a
parody of the style and content of many of the utopian
novels of the period. A new moneyed class appears, and a
technological project--the building of a tunnel--floods the
country.

599. Norton, Roy. The Caves of Treasure. London: Hodder &
Stoughton, 1925.

After an interval of years, the first-person narrator,
Henri, tells how he, James Dalyrmple Wardron, and Dr. Paolo
Morgano--the last an authority on ancient civilizations of
Central America--discovered in 1912 a hidden city of Mayas
in a valley in Guatemala. Their guide is Ixtual. Henri
and Wardy leave the erratic genius, Morgano, behind when
they leave the city; he has become a blood brother in the
priesthood. They return to find Morgano the high priest.
Ixtual heads the so-called "Modern" faction which hopes to
use the city as a rallying place for the Mayan people
before seizing control of the Guatemalan government. Their
host is Dr. Manco. Wardy falls in love with his foster-
daughter, Marizda (of French and English parentage), whose
widowed mother Manco married in Paris. When Morgano
decrees that Henri, Wardy, and Wardy's servant, Beni
Hassan, must die, Morgano collapses. In the ensuing
turmoil, they all escape, though Morgano has to leave
behind his manuscript. Wardy and Marizda are married,
while Henri and Morgano return to Paris, where Morgano
discovers that he has brought back three immense diamonds.

600. Norton, Roy. The Flame; A Story of What Might Have Been.
London: Mills & Boon, 1916.

The mysterious figure of Naast destroys the German fleet
and the Krupp works at Essen. He has developed a powerful,
brilliant light ray. He uses it on the German army along a
two-hundred mile front; of the survivors, 500,000 are blind
and must be cared for. Germany surrenders. Naast is
revealed as Richard Wentworth and for twenty years before
his death acts as a benevolent dictator of a peaceful
world.

601. Norton, Roy. The Toll of the Sea. New York: D. Appleton,
1909.

Copyright by Street & Smith as The Land of the Lost (1909)
and published under that title in London by Stodder &

Houghton (1925): Dr. Pablo Martinez warns the world of impending earthquakes. Scoffed at, he disappears. Savage quakes devastate the Pacific so badly that it must be recharted; the coast of North and South America is changed. The cowboy, Bill Pape, discovers a golden fishhook in the abandoned city of Ayacucha in the Andes. He joins his friend Captain Jim Tipton aboard the Seattle as the ship looks for a lost American cruiser and other missing vessels. The Seattle is drawn magnetically into the narrow harbor of a new land. They learn it is Azonia, peopled by an Aryan race which colonized South America and the Mediterranean. Its ruler, Manco, explains much of the history of his people, the Quichas. They survived in a valley in the Andes; for a century they prepared for the cataclysm, although despite their knowledge of electricity and radioactivity, apparently they did not cause the quakes. Only Choto-Aucco and two assistants had been in the outside world. They seized Martinez because they were afraid that if his warnings were heeded, the modern imperialistic nations would claim any new land that rose. They had aircraft which brought them and their materials to the new land. Choto leads a rebellion to defy all the nations of the world; he is defeated but escapes. Pape fights him; both are killed. But Tipton finds his true love in Ayara, the daughter of Manco, whom he has loved from first meeting.

602. Norton, Roy. The Vanishing Fleets. New York: D. Appleton, 1908.

When a Japanese fleet and convoy attacks the Hawaiian Islands, it disappears. Angry notes are sent to Washington by European powers denouncing such annihilation of an enemy as inhuman. Soon the British North Sea fleet demonstrates off the coast of the U.S. and disappears. During a heavy fog in London and Berlin both the King and Kaiser are kidnapped, while one of the British dreadnaughts appears unharmed in the Thames. Only then does a flashback reveal that an American scientist and his daughter have developed several new weapons for America. The first is a new metal. When subjected to a current of electricity, that metal overcomes gravity. The scientist thus develops a "radioplane." In the battle with the Japanese, each plane seizes a ship and carries it to a lake near Seattle. The British fleet accepts such a journey when the power is demonstrated to them. The President asks the King and the Kaiser to meet with him to end war and establish an alliance which will lead the world onward to a utopian state. A prisoner in the wilderness of the Northwest, the Kaiser speaks of the profound effect the experience has had upon him. The alliance is achieved.

603. Noyes, Pierrepont B[urt].   The Pallid Giant; A Tale of Yesterday and Tomorrow. New York: Revell, 1927.

In the prehistoric grottoes in France, the first-person narrator, Walter, and his friend, Rudge, find the Grotto Glorieuse, in which they discover an ancient manuscript. They are aided by an old peasant, Leon, and the girl, Mraaya, who at one point goes into a psychic trance. With the aid of friends, they obtain a translation. Entitled "The Death-Ray," it is the narrative of Rao, son of Remil; he is the last of his people and is ready to die in a world made into a desert by man. For the manuscript tells of the destruction of a civilization millions of years ago. The few survivors bred with the "Brutes," but kept the half-caste girls, the "Gla-ni," separate to serve as priestesses and chiefs. The line comes down through the Cro-Magnon, and by implication Mraaya is one of them. At the end, Markham, a British agent whom the Germans trust, suggests that "they" have the ray and that doom once more awaits mankind.

604. "O" (pseud.).   The Yellow War.   New York: McClure, Phillips, 1905.

Neither fantasy nor science fiction as sometimes described, this narrative sketches various events in the Russo-Japanese war. Most are dated and were published in Blackwood's. It is included here only to emphasize the impact of the Japanese victory and military prowess on the Western imagination.

605. Ober, Frederick Albion.   The Silver City; A Story of Adventure in Mexico. Boston: Lothrop, 1893.

A book of 95 pages printed in double columns, the story must have appeared originally in some periodical. It is highly imitative of Jules Verne. Nineteen-year-old John North finds a lost city and caves filled with idols and treasure; the Indians return him to the coast when he predicts an eclipse. Ober also wrote The Last of the Arawaks; A Story of Adventure on the Island of San Domingo (1901), a highly jingoistic juvenile adventure which does not have a lost race element.

606. Odle, E.V. The Clockwork Man. Garden City, N.Y.: Double-day, Page, 1923.

Published in London by Heinemann (1923): during a cricket match a man-robot who has a clock built into him to regulate his experience appears in an English village. He comes from a future time when man has voluntarily surrendered his free will and permitted the rulers who had survived the last war to make him into--essentially--a sensitive automaton. He suggests that only when man began to respect his machinery did true history begin; he keeps referring to a multiform world, which he regards as a world set free. In this there is irony, for he speaks of the limit to human adaptibility; one also senses that he and others hope that God takes man seriously. Stableford regards this as the outstanding work of British science fiction during the 1920s.

607. O'Leary, Con. This Delicate Creature. New York: Elliott Holt, 1929.

Published in London by Constable (1928): Boda, a Mayfair society woman unfaithful to her husband, seduces Crowfeld, the anthropologist, in order to obtain a drug, Nirvabogoea, used by Central American Indians. She finds that she becomes all those persons and animals she has injured; she changes sex and species. Her experiences thus range from a parlormaid and chorus girl to a mouse and an Alsatian bitch. For a time "Boda was in the trenches." She also sees herself as her husband sees her. The result is a reconciliation between them.

608. Olerich, Henry. A Cityless and Countryless World; An Outline of Practical Co-operative Individualism. Holstein, Ia.: Gilmore & Olerich, 1893.

A Martian, visiting an American family, describes the co-operative system which makes up all of Mars. A thousand people (a family) live in each housing unit; those are built about a half mile apart so that 120 of them border a rectangle twenty-four by six miles. All farming is done by electrical power. Most importantly, women are not finan- cially dependent on men; women may also regulate their sexual affairs to suit themselves. Three chapters are devoted to sexual relationships and a denunciation of marriage.

609. O'Neill, Joseph. Land Under England. London: Victor Gollancz, 1935.

Anthony Julian, the first-person narrator, falls through a door in the Roman Wall and thus enters a strange subter- ranean world. There has been a family legend that various ancestors have visited such a land, only a few returning. His father disappeared, and Julian searched for him. But this narrative is unique in the degree to which it concen- trates upon Anthony, especially during his early period underground. He encounters Romans around a Central Sea. On a political level, he finds only automatons who have surrendered their individuality to the state. On a per- sonal level the narrative can be read as Freudian in that Anthony's father rejects him so that Anthony flees to the surface to his mother. He is found in a mine--reputedly a Roman mine going far beneath the surface--and is united

with his mother.   One must question the successfulness of
the symbolism, particularly on the personal level.

610.   Orcutt, Emma Louise.   The Divine Seal.   Boston: Clark,
1909.

In the far future, the first-person narrator, Uzzane Slav,
a master of English and German as they were spoken from the
eighteenth to the twenty-second century, goes on an Arctic
expedition to find the wonderful city of Zallallah.   Recent
excavations on the Isle of Atlantis (part of the lost
continent apparently) provided a written record covering a
million years; this prompted the expedition.   The potential
falls by the wayside of a love-story steeped with mysticism.   The narrator loves the girl Talma--identified with
the earliest Aryan race--and saves her from forced marriage
to a villain by finding Zallallah.   They are governed by
"the Power of Eternal Good."

611.   Osborne, [Samuel] Duffield.   The Secret of the Crater.
New York: Putnam, 1900.

In a prefatory note a first-person narrator, presumably
Osborne, laments that soon the world will have been completely explored.   Referring to Verne and Haggard, he
reports that in the Navy Department he found a letter
written by a man still alive which hints at a romance
comparable to those of the two authors.   The man, Deshon, a
doctor, explains that he long searched for the island where
the incident occurred.   He dies, and Osborne reconstructs
the story as he imagines it happened.   In 1839 the American
ship Falcon discovered a lost race of Carthaginians near
Easter Island.   The Princess Zelkah, daughter of the ruler,
confesses that she loves Second Lieutenant Vance.   When he
learns that she is to be sacrificed to a volcano god
worshipped by the Polynesian priests who have forced their
old religion on the Carthaginians, he begs his captain to
rescue the girl.   The captain lets him go ashore, but the
Falcon then sails away, abandoning him (the letter presumed
him dead).   Vance saves Zelkah and destroys the evil
priesthood in a battle; he remains with her, supposedly
becoming the ruler of the island.

612.   Osbourne, Lloyd.   The Adventurer.   New York: D. Appleton,
1907.

In Venezuela the protagonist joins an expedition searching
for the treasure of a ruined pre-Columbian city, Cassa-
quiari.   After facing mutiny, a reluctant heroine, and the
attacks of Indians, he successfully reaches the city and
returns to the main expedition with the treasure.   His awe
at the city--"a forgotten Rome"--is noteworthy.   The most
fantastic element of the narrative is the means of trans-

portation: a "land-ship"--an aluminum shell outfitted with
sails.

613. O'Sheel, Shaemas. It Never Could Happen; or, The Second
American Revolution. New York: House, 1932.

This political fantasy uses the dispersal of the Veterans'
"Bonus Army" in July 1932 as its point of departure. The
skeletal narrative is presented as a future history
published in 1982, The Veterans' Revolution of 1932, whose
first-person narrator is General Elmer Hicks, formerly
commander-in-chief of the U.S. forces. Calling for the
renascence of American principles and the ousting of a
corrupt Congress and government, the benevolent millionaire, Brian Barry asks Hicks to be c-in-c of the Army of
Washington, his name for the Bonus Army. He skillfully
brings about another collapse of the Stock Market. When a
communist army marches on Washington, he and Hicks tell the
government to use regular troops against the Reds, while
the army of veterans protects Washington. A combination of
"bankers and rich men" attempts a Fascist coup when the
"High Committee of National Safety" declares the suspension
of the Constitution. The Reds are defeated, the Fascists
tricked and captured, and both the Congress and president
put out of office because the regular troops support Barry
and Hicks. The only real fighting occurs when the criminal
"Army of Liberation" from Chicago fights after it has
pillaged Pittsburgh on its way to Washington. Barry rules
as a dictator for fity years, until "his wise measures"
cure democracy of its "vices" and Americans learn once
again to rule themselves. What his measures are never
becomes explicit.

614. Paine, Albert Bigelow. The Great White Way. New York:
Taylor, 1901.

In the Antarctic an expedition finds an Oriental-looking
race which Paine several times compares to the Incas.
They live in a pastoral valley described as "The Land of
Heart's Desire" and are governed by a beautiful princess
who, like the Inca, came from the sun to govern them.
Ferratoni, a scientist-mystic, is much affected by them;
renowned for his work with electricity, he is also a
psychic. He can communicate with the natives telepathically; when the princess selects him to be her husband, he
remains behind, foresaking the materialism of the outer
world. Paine emphasizes that they live close to nature and
distrust modern mechanical conveniences.

615. Paine, Albert Bigelow. The Mystery of Evelin Delorme; A
Hypnotic Story. Boston: Arena, 1894.

This is one of the earliest American imitations of Dr.
Jekyll and Mr. Hyde. Although Paine introduces no scien-

tific explanation within the body of the story, in an introduction he allows Dr. Herbert L. Flint, "the well-known hypnotist," to describe the case. Susceptible to hypnotic suggestion, Evelin asks the doctor to call up a second personality so that for a few hours, at least, she can be a "heartless, haughty, gay woman of the world." The transformations are repeated; a year later the doctor encounters her in the second personality, now dominant. In short, an experiment has gotten out of control. As Evelin March, she is a shrew; as Eva Delorme, she is gentle and kind. Both personalities love the same man. Off-stage, jealous and thinking that she is killing a rival, Evelin March/Eva Delorme commits suicide.

616. Pallen, Condé B[énoist]. Crucible Island; A Romance, An Adventure, and an Experiment. New York: Manhattanville, 1919.

Pallen denounces socialism. By secret agreement the governments of Europe for the past fifty years have allowed exiles to practice socialism in the Spielgarten on the island of Schlectland. The state is supreme; individualism is erased. Carl Ruden, a young revolutionary, is sent there. He falls in love with Mina Clausen. To widen the perspective, the story of her father, John Clausen, who has been on the island for many years, is included. Finally, after the discovery of gold, the young lovers and their companions leave the island for America.

617. Palmer, John H[enry]. The Invasion of New York. New York: Neely, 1897.

On 4 July 1898 the USS Maine is at Honolulu; reference is made to a treaty to annex Hawaii. The Japanese in Hawaii attack U.S. marines. The United States declares war on Japan and Spain. Torpedo boats are used, and magnets are placed in the New York harbor and cause invading ships to sink. The U.S. scores a decisive victory.

618. Parabellum (pseud. of Ferdinand Heinrich Grautoff). Banzai! New York: Baker & Taylor, 1908.

Also published in Toronto by Musson (1908): the fighting begins in the Philippines when the Monadnoch is blown up; the passenger ship Tacoma is seized and taken to Yokohama. In order to cover as wide a screen as possible, the action is episodic. Japanese immigrants in the U.S. rise in rebellion, as do the Chinese (Grautoff makes little distinction between them; they constitute the "yellow peril"). The Pacific fleet is destroyed, and the Japanese armies penetrate eastern Oregon. Australia and South Africa are threatened. "Old England" is cast as a villain in that she has given financial support to the Japanese. The Germans aid America by recognizing the Monroe Doctrine. A victory near Ft. Bridger brings an end to the invasion. A detailed, highly racist, anti-English account of the war.

619. Parrish, Randall. <u>Prisoners</u> <u>of</u> <u>Chance</u>; <u>The</u> <u>Story</u> <u>of</u> <u>What</u> <u>Befell</u> <u>Geoffrey</u> <u>Benteen</u>, <u>Borderman</u>, <u>Through</u> <u>His</u> <u>Love</u> <u>for</u> <u>a</u> <u>Lady</u> <u>of</u> <u>France</u>. Chicago: A. C. McClurg, 1908.

An historical romance of the American frontier which may be associated with the lost-race motif in that the suggestion is made that the Natchez Indians are descendants of the Mound Builders.

620. Parry, David M[aclean]. <u>The</u> <u>Scarlet</u> <u>Empire</u>. Indianapolis, In.: Bobbs-Merrill, 1906.

Off the eastern coast of the United States, the first-person narrator finds the sunken Atlantis, protected from the sea by a great glass dome. Although the storyline centers on the love of the narrator for the maiden Astraea, the novel is significant for the violence of its attack upon socialism. The Social Democracy of Atlantis is a decadent state dominated by a bureaucracy in which a quarter of the population serves as inspectors--or spies. They must see that each citizen smiles once an hour to show he is happy. A law prescribes how many words a day each individual may speak. The state never permits a handsome man to marry a lovely woman; it equalizes beauty by decreeing that the handsome marry the ugly so that in each generation everyone will be more equal. Every night the people are encouraged to smoke the so-called "Lethe weed," a narcotic which induces a feeling of exhilaration. The protagonist is informed that the energy running Atlantis' technology comes from radium, and he is reminded that Atlantis was the Edenic homeland of mankind where science and invention first developed. He and Astraea escape from Atlantis after he fires a torpedo which destroys the glass dome. They are picked up and return to America.

621. Peck, Bradford. <u>The</u> <u>World</u> <u>a</u> <u>Department</u> <u>Store</u>; <u>A</u> <u>Story</u> <u>of</u> <u>Life</u> <u>Under</u> <u>a</u> <u>Cooperative</u> <u>System</u>. Lewiston, Me.: Peck, 1900.

Percy Brantford falls asleep 31 December 1899 and awakens on 7 April 1925 to find that the cooperative city of Maine had been built during the quarter century. Money is the root of all evil: the nineteenth century with its gambling "hells," drinking places, and houses of prostitution proved that. Society must learn the true meaning of Christian brotherly love. Peck enlivens his portrait with three marriages, Harry and Alice, George and Mabel, and Percy Brantford and Helen Brown, whose honeymoon takes them as far as Chicago before returning via Niagara Falls and Montreal.

622. Perkins, Lucy Fitch.   The Cave Twins.   Boston: Houghton Mifflin, 1916.

One of her twins series, the volume has importance only in that it shows how popular the prehistoric scene was by World War I. The children are Firetop and Limberleg, and they spend much time with Granny. Little is original except, perhaps, the sentiment. At first woman hunted "all by herself," but gradually she surrendered the task to man. "Prehistoric Man and Prehistoric Woman did their part bravely and well...."

623. Pettersen, Rena Oldfield.   Venus.   Philadelphia: Dorrance, 1924.

Two Venusian women, De and Ve, arrive on Earth by space-ship; they are immediately absorbed into the Carter family group at Tide End. The visitors quickly become models of what women should be like instead of the "modern" genera-tion of Mary Carter and some of her friends. For example, they insist that Mary's friends "make too much of sex." They do allow Mary to see herself in previous incarnations, ranging from a cave woman and an Egyptian princess to a pioneer woman with a babe. Jim Carter proposes to De, and they honeymoon in space without benefit of marriage, for marriage is an earthly institution which Ve denounces. This is the major thematic point of the novel. Mary and Jack Dale fall in love, as do various pairs of their friends. Ve serves as a kind of Cupid, for she preaches love and peace.

624. Phelps, William Lyon.   A Dash at the Pole.   Boston: Ball, 1909.

The first-person narrator has always wanted to discover the North Pole. The narrative is a parody of the craze. For example, he encounters Eskimos who named their village Saliva because it is on a spit of land.

625. Pier, Garrett Chatfield.   Hanit the Enchantress.   New York: Dutton, 1921.

Professor Steven Ranney, who loves Susan Braintree, is the first-person narrator, as well as the head of the Yale expedition to Egypt. In recent excavations near the tomb of King Ahmenhotep, his party has discovered the bodies of Queen Hanit's murdered son, the beautiful slave girl Bhanar, and Princess Sesen; a friend writes to him telling him of the discovery of the mummy of Queen Hanit, the first wife of Ahmenhotep the Third, who was "put aside" for a beautiful Syrian, Queen Thi. Ranney has a fever and falls; he awakens some three thousand years earlier during the reign of Ahmenhotep the Third. What develops is a love story between him and Princess Sesen, attendant to the young queen Noferith, whom he identifies with Hanit. He awakens a second time in a hospital where Susan Braintree is his nurse. He identifies her with Sesen, though he is not sure whether he has dreamed or actually has been back in Egypt.

626. Pier, Garrett Chatfield. Hidden Valley. Boston: Stratford, 1925.

This is a pseudo-historical novel of Moses in Egypt.

627. Pope, Gustavus W. Journey to Mars. New York: Dillingham, 1894.

The first in a projected series entitled "Romances of the Planets": shipwrecked and caught in the ice in the Antarctic, Lieutenant Frederick Hamilton of the U.S. Navy encounters yellow, red, and blue men. At first he believes them to be from a Symmesian world, but when he saves their leader, Prince Altfoura, from a shark, he learns they are from Mars. He accompanies them to Mars, where he falls in love with the Princess Suhlamia, sister of the man he rescued. For a time he is the prisoner of a rival suitor, Prince Diavojahr, but he escapes and arrives in time to keep Suhlamia from signing a marriage contract which would guarantee his freedom. When a comet passes near Mars, a meteor storm threatens that world so that Hamilton and his friends lead an emigration to the south polar region of the Earth. Despite the continued threat, when they hear that Diavojahr has conquered their capital, they undertake a return to Mars. The narrative ends abruptly as Hamilton leaves his manuscripts near New Zealand. At one point Pope defends the scientific romance as a valid literary form. He also asserts that man would be the same "in Esse" on whatever planet he dwelt so that he becomes another advocate of parallel and progressive evolution. Yet he tells little of the Martian society. It is a monarchy. So advanced are Martian Therapeutics that diseases from insanity and consumption to cancer have been cured.

628. Pope, Gustavus W. Journey to Venus. Boston: Arena, 1895.

Lieutenant Hamilton and Princess Suhlamia journey to Venus, which is a younger world than either Earth or Mars so that it is still at a stage of prehistoric development. Pope uses this device to deal with some of the mysteries of Earth's prehistory. They find a sub-human apeman whom they identify as the missing link; they observe a giant "anthropopithekos" which they believe will develop into the true man of Venus; and they witness the sinking of a vast continent.

629. Pope, Marion Manville. <u>Up the Matterhorn in a Boat</u>. New
York: Century, 1897.

> The first-person narrator uses an aluminum balloon, the
> <u>Cloud Queen</u>, to fly above Mont Blanc. In danger of de-
> scending into a deep crevasse, the balloon is saved from
> accident by an Alpine blizzard. This is a parody of the
> various aerial and space voyages of the period.

630. Post, Melville Davisson. <u>The Revolt of the Birds</u>. New
York: D. Appleton, 1927.

> The first portion of the narrative tries to establish the
> mystery and horror of the Orient. In this it reminds one
> of Conrad, perhaps because Post uses a complex point of
> view. The first-person narrator repeats the stories told
> to him by two derelicts, the American Bennett and the
> English skipper, Chillingsworth. Their stories concerning
> Arthur Hudson, the heir of a number of coal mines in
> Pennsylvania, overlap. In order to straighten out fi-
> nancial matters, Hudson worked for five years in the coal
> fields. What sustained him was the memory of an English
> girl. But he never dreamed of her; instead he dreamed of a
> slim, dark-haired girl who always had a flock of birds
> about her. When he went to England and found the English
> girl being seduced (willingly) by Lord X, Hudson broke the
> noble's nose and fled to the Orient. There, abandoned by a
> Chinese skipper, he takes a sampan alone to an island
> crawling with insects. Amid this horror he finds a mis-
> sionary and his daughter--the girl he dreamed of. The
> island is infested because the missionary had poisoned the
> rice which the birds had fed on; the girl had tried to
> drive the birds away from the poison; finally the birds
> stopped coming to the island. Hudson rescues the two--
> their Chinese servant is devoured by the insects. The
> father dies, but birds come and form a sail for the sampan
> so that Hudson and the girl escape. But they disappear at
> sea; Bennett does not know what happened to them. While
> the narrator speaks in a mystical manner about Hudson's
> real and dream lives, the end of the story is science
> fiction in its concern for the insects. Only the birds
> protect man, wherever he is, from the terror of the
> swarming insects.

631. Powell, Frank. <u>The Wolf-Men; A Tale of Amazing Adventure
in the Under-World</u>. New York & London: Cassell, 1906.

> Professor James Mervyn, together with such friends as
> Seymour and Garth, tries to reach the North Pole aboard the
> submarine <u>Seal</u>. They encounter an ice barrier and then go
> through a tunnel in a dead volcano to reach a subterranean
> world. The narrative is episodic in order to contain as
> many adventures as possible. After they see bestial men
> pursuing a giant elk, they learn that other prehistoric

animals have survived, including great vampire bats. Because Seymour and Mervyn had explored a South Atlantic island, they are able to read a scroll that they find. It tells the story of Ayuti, a once mighty kingdom which sank beneath the sea. A remnant of its people fled through the tunnel of the volcano and for a time prospered, using the wolf-people as slaves. But an evil priest, Nordhu, led the wolf-people in revolt so that once again the Ayuti were almost exterminated. Eventually Mervyn and his friends escape to the surface. When their story is not believed by the press, Seymour presents Prince Chenobi and his mount, a mighty elk, as evidence; the audience is convinced.

632. Pratt Ambrose. The Living Mummy. New York: Stokes, 1910.

Despite the presence of the first-person narrator, Dr. Hugh Pinsent, this becomes a highly confused narrative involving spiritualism, the occult, black magic, and the implication, at least, of an elixir of life. Pinsent has been trans-lating a stele regarding Amen-hotep III [sic] when Sir Robert Ottley and his beautiful daughter May arrive, asking for Arabs to help them. Ottley has discovered the tomb of Ptahmes, the high priest of Amen-hotep IV, who became Akhnaten. The Arabs discover treasure in a sarcophagus. One of them is found dead in it; the mummy seems to have revived. Pinsent flees to England. Ottley becomes asso-ciated with the villainous Dr. Belleville, who attempts to kill Pinsent and marry May. The idea of the mummy's revival is dulled by the suggestion that a modern who somehow resembles him is responsible for most of the villainy. Amid confusion Pinsent and May marry.

633. Prentice, Harry. Captured by Apes; or, How Philip Garland Became King of Apeland. New York: Burt, 1892.

Originally published as The King of Apeland (1888): in 1871 Philip succeeds his father in the business of buying, selling, and training wild animals. He had been a natura-list specializing in monkeys. What follows reminds one of Jules Verne in the sense that it is episodic and varied--from mutiny and shipwreck to the story of an attempt to colonize an island. It is that island, containing a variety of apes, which provides Philip with his kingdom. He is rescued and brought back to New York, accompanied by two chimpanzees, Ben Bolt and Sweet Alice. A supposed treasure was never found.

634. Prime, Lord (pseud. of Walter Doty Reynolds). Mr. Jonnemacher's Machine; The Port to Which We Drifted. Phila-delphia: Knickerbocker, 1898.

The narrative is a study of the twentieth century, par-ticularly its last decade; it is written as though by historians of the twenty-first century. It celebrates

Philadelphia as the queen city of a U.S. that dominates the continent. The basic conflict occurs because of the development of a machine which can perform all the processes of textile manufacture without human laborers. When two-thirds of the workers are unemployed, bread riots and revolution begin. Machinery becomes the monster to be destroyed. Jonnemacher (a caricature of Wanamaker) is assassinated; yet the narrator says of him that he saw the problems and tried to put forces in motion which would correct the injustices, but crooked politicians prevented him from doing so. Significantly, his machine still exists, but its earnings go directly to a socialist government which provides compensation for all the citizens. The government regulates supply and demand at the distribution centers.

635. Pruning Knife (pseud. of Henry Francis Allen). A Strange Voyage; A Revision of the Key to Industrial Co-operative Government; An Interesting and Instructive Description of Life on the Planet Venus. St. Louis: Monitor, 1891.

Originally published in 1886: a beautiful maid offers to take the first-person narrator to the planet Venus. Transportation between the planets is possible because of currents which are also the source of heat and light. On Venus he sees a society containing most of the reforms emphasized in the period. Every building and dwelling is surrounded by a garden. The women share the responsibility of government. The narrator awakens from a dream.

636. Ramsey, Milton Worth. Six Thousand Years Hence. Minneapolis, Mn.: Roper, 1891.

After General Morton founds a city in the American West, he turns his attention to science. A sphere strikes the Earth near his home, tearing away the city. They observe Mercury, find the Sun is a great world (it has two surfaces, the outer one the source of heat and light). Princess Flontee, whose country they fight for, falls in love with Professor Hix. After they have sundry adventures, they return to Earth to find that 6,000 years have passed. It is 7902. The remainder of the narrative celebrates the technology of Earth, including a railroad that goes around the world. Electricity is the source of energy, and some of the buildings are a hundred stories tall. Minnepaul is a single city. In 2518 the Atlantic was bridged; both the Sahara and Gobi are fertile. At one point early in the novel, as they plunge toward the sun, they burn coal because it is cold in space. A globe of water long ago hit the Earth, causing the Noachian deluge. At the end, having attained longevity which the Earth knew before the Flood, General Morton dies at age 6065. His is a thoroughly Christian death as he bids farewell to friends; the occult knowledge he has gained makes him realize he will join his wife in blessed eternity.

637. Rathborne, St. George. A Goddess of Africa: A Story of the Golden Fleece. New York: F. Tennyson Neely, 1897.

Rathborne's portrayal of South Africa in 1896 is definitely pro-Rhodes and anti-Boer. He celebrates the Anglo-Saxon race and praises the British as colonists, although saying that they start "unprovoked" wars. The storyline imitates Verne, while the background is indebted to Haggard. Rex Hastings, a young fortune-seeking American; Professor Jules Verdant, a scientist searching for the "missing link"; Lord Bruno, an Englishman fighting the natives; and Jim Bledsoe, an American cowboy--these four join together to go through Matabele country to find a lost temple in the Zambodia area. Most of the action involves fights with and escapes from natives. They find an English-speaking girl whose father called her Maid Marian before he died. She has been worshipped as a goddess by the natives. The British South African Mounted Troop rescues the protagonists. One of the cowboys--Little Phil--proves to be a girl whom Lord Bruno abandoned. He marries her, and Rex and Maid Marian wed in England. Despite Bledsoe's death the others plan to return to search for hidden treasure.

638. Raymond, James F. The Lost Colony. Philadelphia: Peterson, 1891.

A series of narratives is concerned primarily with the Civil War, complete with Confederate spies, a court martial, acquittal, and descriptions of a number of the major battles and campaigns. Much of the storyline concentrates upon the Baxter family of Virginia and the military career of "Duke" Steele, who ends as a general and an ambassador for the Grant administration. Two elements of fantasy intrude into the melodramatic work. When the British nobleman, Sir Eldred Romayne, builds a ship and puts it at the disposal of the Confederates, two men will not swear allegiance to the Confederacy so that Herman, Captain Perkins, and his cook Caesar are put ashore on an island. Penetrating inland, they discover a utopian agrarian society. Subsequent manuscripts give the history of the colony, founded after the wreck of a ship which departed New England in 1672. The colonists are, of course, Pilgrims. Together with Joshua Sparks, Perkins and Herman attempt to leave the island by balloon. Only Joshua is found by the ship Northumberland. When a government expedition searches for the island, it finds the place where Herman, Perkins, and Caesar were, but it cannot find the "lost colony." Both in narrative technique and ending the novel remains a notable blending of realism (the Civil War) and the lost race motif.

639. Rees, Arthur J[ohn]. The Threshold of Fear. New York:
Dodd, Mead, 1926.

> Also published in England by Hutchinson (1925): in the
> framing narrative, the first-person narrator, Haldham,
> takes a job as chauffeur for Colonel Gravenall in Cornwall
> near Penzance. His chief duty is to drive Edward Ches-
> worth, the invalid nephew of the Colonel. He is attracted
> by Eleanor Chesworth, the Colonel's niece. He soon en-
> counters Dr. Penhryn, an alienist and student of Freud and
> Jung, who is treating Edward for an apparent nervous
> disorder. Edward is the sole survivor of the Herbert
> Musard expedition which had gone into a mysterious part of
> South America two years earlier. In a story-within-a-
> story, Edward gives a first-person account of the accident
> which killed all of his companions as well as his journey,
> alone, into the "Valley of Ghosts" to reach "The Hidden
> Place . . . the Island of Death." There he met the Indian,
> Munyeru, who apparently can bring people back to life, if
> "the Master of Life, the Compassionate," intercedes with
> Death. Edward believes that he was dead, lying at the
> bottom of a lake for four days and nights before being
> brought back to life. The framing narrative resumes;
> Edward is terrified because various signs, like a drumming,
> suggest that Death has come for him. Haldham is fired
> because he thinks that Colonel Gravenall is victimizing his
> nephew; he remains in the area with a detective friend,
> grey, to solve the mystery. Dr. Penhryn dies; his note-
> books indicate that he was using Edward to explore the
> unknown. The narrative ends ambiguously, emphasizing the
> power of the unconscious mind and the imagination. This is
> one of the most successful psychological studies of the
> period.

640. Reeve, Arthur B[enjamin]. Atavar, The Dream Dancer. New
York: Harper, 1924.

> Natalie Lisle provides Craig Kennedy with one of his most
> effective studies of dual personality. In everyday life
> she dances the role of Astarte at the American Opera. She
> dreams that she is the Stone Age woman, Gel, pursued by two
> paleolithic men and rescued by a third. In everyday life
> Roger Gerard and Guy Hawtrey pursue her, while a third man,
> Gordon Gaunt, has studied with Jung and Freud. When
> Hawtrey is killed, Kennedy must find his murderer.

641. Reeve, Arthur B[enjamin]. The Film Mystery. New York:
Harper, 1921.

> When Stella Mara, an idol of the screen, is found dead with
> a small puncture in her arm, Craig Kennedy must find her
> murderer.

642. Reeve, Arthur B[enjamin]. <u>Gold</u> <u>of</u> <u>the</u> <u>Gods</u>; <u>The</u> <u>Mystery</u> <u>of</u> <u>the</u> <u>Incas</u> <u>Solved</u> <u>by</u> <u>Craig</u> <u>Kennedy</u>--<u>Scientific</u> <u>Detective</u>. New York: Hearst's, 1915.

> The theft of an Incan dagger from the University Museum starts Kennedy into action, especially after the stolen dagger is used to kill Don Luis de Mendoza. The curse of the Inca ruler, Cacique Mansiche, upon anyone who searches for a lost treasure provides further background, but the action scarcely moves outside of Manhattan as Kennedy works with several of his gadgets as well as his knowledge of such drugs as <u>curare</u>. Professor Allan Norton, who recently returned from an expedition to Peru; a love affair between Chester Lockwood and Inez de Mendoza; Stuart Whitney, who hopes to gain mining concessions to search for the gold; and Senora de Moche, a member of an old Indian family--all provide Kennedy with suspects. The novel is most important for showing how thoroughly popular fiction was fascinated by the legends of Incan treasure.

643. Reeve, Arthur B[enjamin]. <u>Pandora</u>. New York: Harper, 1926.

> Potentially the most significant of the Craig Kennedy novels, the narrative concentrates upon the efforts of the country of Centrania to destroy the American economy and make the U.S. a vassal state. It introduces the chemical synthetol into the market, thereby undercutting the gasoline and oil, the automotive, the coal, and the transportation industries. Rumor has it that synthetol may be used to produce synthetic foods. As synthetex it can destroy the textile industry, while in another form, synthesite, it becomes a deadly gas capable of destroying all cell life. Centrania uses spies, purchases newspapers to act as propaganda agents, and infiltrates the American Liberal Party. On "Black Friday" a major panic occurs on Wall Street when two million shares are sold. Even Britain cannot aid the U.S. but must protect its own market. The novel is highly interesting for its attitude toward women and its condemnation of jazz as a destroyer of American morals. Against this background, the storyline centers upon the beautiful Pandora Paget, who marries wealthy Townsend Woodward (he dies of exhaustion and heart attack during the panic), and the young chemist Lee Wyndham, whose love for Pandora and America lead him back from the depths of the jazz culture to discover Protonic Force (atomic power), thereby saving the American economy, to say nothing of its morality. A beautiful Centranian agent and a young girl who sells birth control information both serve major roles. Centrania is specifically called a white nation and cannot be identified with Russia or Asia.

644. Reeve, Arthur B[enjamin]. The Silent Bullet; The Adventures of Craig Kennedy, Scientific Detective. New York: Dodd, Mead, 1912.

From 1910 until November 1915 the Craig Kennedy stories appeared monthly (except November 1912) in Cosmopolitan. For a decade he was one of the best known heroes of American popular fiction. The Silent Bullet was the first book collection of the stories. He exploited current developments in all fields of science--mechanical "gadgets," medical discoveries, physical and chemical data, and the field of psychology. He invented many of his devices in his own laboratories, for like his contemporaries, he sought the utlimate energy and had developed a super-metal, selenium. His confidant, Walter Jameson, a society writer for a New York paper, is the narrator. Kennedy's adventures cover every field from assassination and adultery to witchcraft and white slavery. Someone comes to him, or he goes to the scene of a crime. He interviews the principal suspects or finds a seemingly meaningless clue. He calls all of those involved together, and after the description of a theory or a new "gadget" forces a confession.

645. Reeve, Arthur B[enjamin]. The War Terror. New York: Hearst's, 1915.

Only the title story, in which Fortescue invents a new explosive, fortescite, and an electric magnetic rifle, ties directly to the war. Other inventions are mentioned, such as a new flare that will help night defenses against torpedo boat and airplane attacks. "The Artificial Kidney" deals with a "system" developed by the doctors at Johns Hopkins. The final story, "Psychanalysis" [sic] presents one of his fullest early uses of Freudian material.

646. Renard, Maurice. New Bodies for Old. New York: Macaulay, 1923.

The novel is dedicated to H. G. Wells. The first-person narrator, Nicolas Vermont, concentrates upon the experiments of his uncle and guardian, Dr. Frédéric Lerne, Professor of Clinical Medicine. Having started as exercises in grafting, those experiments have proceeded to changing a frog into a plant and trees into animals. Lerne early advances the argument that the automobile bears a "striking" resemblance to the body of a vertebrate. He is able to switch the brain of one creature into the body of another, but his aim is to switch personalities without changing bodies. At one point he transfers Nicolas's brain to the body of the black bull, Jupiter. Lerne's assistant Otto Klotz takes possession of Lerne's body, and when he himself dies in an automobile wreck, Klotz transfers his brain into the mechanism of the car. Nicolas keeps the car locked up until it decays; while he is certain that Klotz is dead, he is not certain what has become of his uncle's other assistants. An added dimension to the storyline occurs because Nicolas loves the flirtatious Emma Bour-dichet, who finally rejects him. Much is made of the essence of life being related to electricity and of any form, animate or inanimate, as a kind of mechanism. As Nicolas himself suggests, the result is both frightening and comic.

647. Rhodes, H. Henry. <u>Where</u> <u>Men</u> <u>Have</u> <u>Walked</u>; <u>A</u> <u>Story</u> <u>of</u> <u>the</u> <u>Lucayos</u>. Boston: Clark, 1909.

A foreword refers to the Lucayos, islands off the coast of Florida, and to Cavalaro Bay, with a "treacherous Wind Cave." The first-person narrator and his companion, MacFayden, are cast adrift in a small boat after their ship sinks. They wrestle; MacFayden is killed by a snake; the narrator falls exhausted on an island. After a discussion of hypnotism in terms of electricity and batteries, he revives in the company of an old man who tells him that he is "in the Year of the Earth the 101,000th" and that he will see the great city of Bunavere (the implication is that this represents some great civilization of the past). There follows a long discussion with the sage Lovidorosa in which sin is dismissed as "discord and ignorance," while electricity is equated with God and the soul. All in-dividuals are in perfect harmony. Once this dialogue ends, he meets the woman, Buna Vere, who initially rejects the idea of wife as a "word created solely for the ruin of maidens." One cannot be certain at what time period this initial encounter occurs; she declares that she has been searching for him for years. At last, after he suggests that this is the day of her resurrection (apparently after she falls at the Wind Cave), they sail away from the island for his home in the Blue Mountains. This again exemplifies those works which grow obscure because they attempt to state a pervasive mysticism in terms of science.

648. Rhodes, William H[enry]. <u>Caxton's</u> <u>Book</u>. San Francisco: Bancroft, 1876.

In a prefatory note sketching Rhodes' life, the editor of this posthumous volume, Daniel O'Connell, describes Rhodes as the equal of Jules Verne and acknowledges "scientific fiction" as a distinct genre. In "Phases in the Life of John Pollexfen" a photographer-chemist searches for the perfect lens and makes one after analyzing a "living" eye. The youthful protagonist of "The Telescopic Eye" can describe in detail such distant objects as the moon because of the structure of his eyes. Rhodes uses this device to satirize his contemporaries' concepts of lunar society. "The Aztec Princess" deals with the transmigration of an explorer to pre-Columbian times; the narrator discusses the works of Stephens and Norman at length. "The Earth's Hot

Center" involves an attempt to dig to the center of the Earth.   Perhaps his best known story, "The Case of Summerfield" introduces a mad scientist who threatens to destroy the oceans of the world if he is not paid a ransom.   It was reprinted separately (San Francisco: Paul Elder, 1918).

649.   Rice Elmer [Leopold].   A Voyage to Purilia.   New York: Cosmopolitan, 1930.

This novel uses a parody of imaginary voyages and societies --as well as a touch of other forms like the western--to effect a devastating satire of modern America, its topics ranging from sexuality, the jazz age, and poverty to racism and war.   Employing the Winsted Gravitator, the first-person narrator and his companion, Johnson, journey into space to reach Purilia.   Though it lacks modern science and industrialism, it is not an idyllic pastoral world.   For example, small rural homesteads are usually either owned or mortgaged by wealthy landlords who threaten eviction if the daughters do not marry them or otherwise give in to their desires.   The most venerated of its five castes is that of the Umbilicans, made up only of mothers who have suffered. Next highest are the Pudencians, young women between eighteen and twenty-two, whose chief characteristics are virginity and blondeness.   Soon after arriving, they meet Pansy Malone; eventually they must rescue both Pansy, whom the narrator finds attractive, and Mollie, whom Johnson likes, from the underworld of "the Chinks"--specifically, from Wu Long Ti, ruler of the subterranean city of the Chinks.   All native chieftains "are dominated by lust" and desire to "possess some beautiful Pudencian."   No summary can do justice to the novel, for Rice combines many of the conventions of popular literature and society to achieve his result.   Johnson is gunned down by Killer Evans on the eve of their return to Earth.   The marriages of Pansy and Mollie at the end allow the narrator a final opportunity to lash out at modern morality.   Purilia is, of course, "a white civilization."

650.   Roberts, Charles G[eorge] D[ouglas].   In the Morning of Time.   New York: Stokes, 1922.

Originally published as a series of short stories in Cosmopolitan (1914-1915) and first issued in book form in England by Hutchinson (1919): Roberts begins with a description of "The World without Man."   These inter-related stories present another portrayal of the caveman as he begins his ascent toward modern humanity.

651.   Robertson, Morgan [Andrew].   The Grain Ship.   New York: McClure & Metropolitan, 1914.

A selection of short stories: "From the Darkness and the Depths" presents an invisible sea monster which is photo-

graphed with ultra-violet light so that it can be killed.
"Extracts from Noah's Log" pretends to tell what really
happened aboard the ark.

652. Robertson, Morgan [Andrew]. Over the Border. New York:
McClure, 1914.

A selection of short stories: although revealed as a dream,
"The Last Battleship" has a dreadnaught destroyed by a
bombing plane; it also introduces a submarine. "Absolute
Zero" introduces a device like radar to warn against
icebergs.

653. Robertson, Morgan [Andrew]. The Wreck of the Titan; or,
Futility; Paranormal Experiences Connected with the Sinking of
the Titanic. New York: McClure & Metropolitan, 1914.

Of these stories the most purely science fiction is "Beyond
the Spectrum," in which inventors transform ultra-violet
rays into a weapon which helps the U.S. defeat Japan. "In
the Valley of the Shadow" deals with three persons who are
trapped aboard a submerged submarine and are endangered by
the resultant gases.

654. Robinson, Charles Henry. Longhead; The Story of the First
Fire. Boston: Page, 1913.

At first no laws, social organization, or love exist among
a people that has short, rounded heads. Longhead is a step
forward. He becomes the leader; Broken Tooth promises that
she will remain with him as his mate. The episodic novel
moves from the discovery of the use of fire to the first
attempts at art and religion.

655. Rock, James. Thro' Space. Boston: New England Druggist,
1909.

Rock acts as editor of a manuscript given him. The first-
person narrator and his companion fly to a utopian Venus on
a ship that resembles a submarine, making use of hellium
[sic]. They reach Venus in forty days; the side toward the
sun is desert. The Venusians, Um and Ux, remark about
earthly life, commenting that in the U.S. the unbounded
freedom itself leads to a kind of bondage. The moon,
incidentally, is inhabited by huge, ungainly creatures.

656. Rockwood, Roy (pseud.). The City Beyond the Clouds; or,
Captured by Red Dwarfs. New York: Cupples & Leon, 1926.

The orphans, Jack Darrow and Mark Simpson, remain with Amos
Henderson, who has developed a telescope with which to view
Mars. A new kind of plane, developed by Gustavus Hertz,
crashes nearby. After repairing it, they join Hertz in a

flight to a dark satellite of Earth and rescue his son and beautiful daughter.

657. Rockwood, Roy (pseud.). Five Thousand Miles Underground; or, The Mystery of the Centre of the Earth. New York: Cupples & Leon, 1908.

Professor Henderson now develops the Flying Mermaid, which can serve as a plane or a ship, in order to explore the vast hole that they previously discovered on an island in the Atlantic. Neither a whale, a cyclone, nor fourteen sailors who repay their rescue from a burning ship by mutinying can deter the adventurers. No mention is made of Symmesian theory. The inner world is characterized by giantism. Its inhabitants range from ten to fifteen feet in height, but they are soft--described as being like putty--perhaps as a result of atmospheric and gravitational forces. The adventurers are rescued by King Hankos, a student of science, who built a cylinder and gained the surface of the Earth by being forced upward on a great geyser. King Hankos smuggled himself aboard the Flying Mermaid before its descent because otherwise he could not return to his kingdom. Because the entrance through which they descended into the inner world is closed by an earthquake, they must use the geyser as a means of escape, making use of a cylinder life raft that Professor Henderson thoughtfully and secretly provided. At the end, Professor Henderson, "getting quite old," closes his workshop and settles down, while Mark and Jack resolve to gain an education before building more ships for further voyages.

658. Rockwood, Roy (pseud.). Lost on the Moon; or, In Quest of the Field of Diamonds. New York: Cupples & Leon, 1911.

Having attended the Universal Electrical and Chemical College, and having interrupted their studies to journey to Mars, Jack and Mark now join Professor Henderson and Professor Santell Roumann, whose development of the energy Etherium had allowed the flight to Mars, in a journey to the moon. A Martian newspaper has announced the existence of vast diamond fields on the moon. Roumann now develops a Cardite motor (using a Martian mineral), and George Axtell, brother of the maniac who tried to sabotage the Martian flight, tries to stop this flight. For a time he disguises himself as Mark, whom he has kidnapped. But Mark gains his freedom, and the journey to the moon takes place. Mark and Jack are temporarily lost from the ship Annihilator but are saved before the lunar night falls. They discover a petrified city and return to the Earth with a petrified man, as well as diamonds, most of which are put to industrial use.

659. Rockwood, Roy (pseud.). <u>Through the Air to the North</u>
<u>Pole</u>; <u>or</u>, <u>The Wonderful Cruise of the Electric Monarch</u>. New
York: Cupples & Leon, 1906.

The orphans, Mark Sampson and Jack Darrow, fall in with
Professor Amos Henderson, who has invented the airship, the
<u>Electric Monarch</u>. This is highly imitative of Jules Verne
in its episodic adventures involving sea lions, polar
bears, and the rescue of Andre Christiansen, who is being
held by Esquimaux. The humor is provided by Henderson's
black servant, Washington. They reach the pole.

660. Rogers, Lebbeus Harding. <u>The Kite Trust</u>; <u>A Romance of</u>
<u>Wealth</u>. New York: Kite Trust, 1900.

First in Hamilton and then in Springfield, Ohio, the boys--
Mickey Flynn, Fred Schmidt, Sam Forbes (the inventor), and
Ed Webster (the brains) develop a fine kite and begin to
sell it. They must produce fifty-three dozen by next week.
Rogers calls the book a "first lesson in political economy." Sarah Matilda Flynn, whom Ed Webster likes, has a
teacher who advises her to place $10.00 of $14.42 in a
"savings institution." God originally created everything;
man has only to put the various elements together into
things "we want."

661. Rousseau, Victor (pseud. of Victor Rousseau Emanuel).
<u>Draught of Eternity</u>. London: Long, 1924.

Originally published in <u>All-Story Weekly</u> (1918) by Victor
Rousseau; in book form issued under a second pseudonym,
H.M. Egbert. Experimenting with marihuana, Doctors Clifford and Candra Pal send themselves into a future incarnation to a primitive America (New York), where the de-
graded white race has been enslaved by an Oriental race
named Yuki. Clifford tries to lead a revolt, but is defeated by the prince who is Candra Pal. Clifford has
fallen in love with Princess Alma; by taking marihuana,
they escape together back into the present.

662. Rousseau, Victor (pseud. of Victor Rousseau Emanuel). <u>The</u>
<u>Messiah of the Cylinder</u>. New York: A.C. McClurg, 1917.

Also published in England by Hodder & Stoughton (1918): as
a result of a deliberate experiment, the protagonist,
Pennell, is kept in suspended animation for a century; he
revives in 1984 to find a world dominated by socialism and
science. He finds that his tomb is a chapel with a cru-
cifix. He learns how the world was made over; during a
period following revolution and the decay of democracy,
1945-1978, the works of Wells were rediscovered. Dr.
Sanson appeared about 1980 and was regarded as a kind of
anti-Christ, but he did become the ruler in a state based
on pure reason. Marx, Darwin, Mendel, and Nietzsche are

honored in the hall of fame. However, there has been the legend that Pennell will awaken and look upon the sleeping princess and thus bring about a new world. He finds that his girl friend, Esther, was also put into suspended animation by her father. Together they overthrow the Marxist state and establish a Christian community. One observation declares that science must be kept within its own domain and not be relied upon too much.

663. Rousseau, Victor (pseud. of Victor Rousseau Emanuel). My Lady of the Nile. London: Hodder & Stoughton, 1923.

Published in book form under the pseudonym, H. M. Egbert: told by a first-person narrator, this is a love story and adventure rather than fantasy or sf. Another novel, Eric of the Strong Heart (London: John Long, 1925) also published under the Egbert pseudonym is a very orthodox lost race story involving Norse in the Arctic in the city of Rangarok. The first-person narrator, Eric Silverstein, brings the Princess Editha back to America with him.

664. Rousseau, Victor (pseud. of Victor Rousseau Emanuel). The Sea Demons. London: Long, 1924.

Originally published in All-Story (1916) by Victor Rousseau; issued in book form under the pseudonym H.M. Egbert. Lieutenant Donald Paget, new commander of submarine D-55, encounters Captain Jonathan Masterman, whose scientific standing has been discredited by Ira MacBeard, because Masterman has asserted that mammalian life exists at the sea bottom and has said that he saw a sea monster off Aberdeen. Masterman dies, but in his laboratory Paget finds a specimen of the humanoid undersea life; MacBeard attacks him and steals Masterman's letter. The plot develops along three lines. First, Paget and his crew rescue Ida Kennedy from the sinking ship Boeotia and in the submarine descend to the ocean bottom to discover that the undersea creatures are real and are a threat to civilization. Secondly, MacBeard wishes to use the sea creatures to conquer the world, but he falls in love with Ida. Thirdly, the sea creatures are described as being like bees. When their new queen develops, the swarm (also called the herd) attacks England and other countries. The invasion results from the call of their queen who would mate with Paget; she does not and dies. Her death causes the swarm of drones to kill themselves in Skjold Fjord. MacBeard is destroyed by them. The world is saved because the queen lives for only three weeks. Paget (now an admiral) and Ida are united. The nations of Europe end the Great War because they realize the need for the unity of humanity if such threats as that from which Paget saved them may occur.

665. Roy, Lillian Elizabeth.   The Prince of Atlantis.   New
York: Educational Press, 1929.

> This is cast as an historical record written by Yolen,
> chief scribe of Atlantis. The main action traces a great
> exodus from Atlantis to the headwaters of the Nile after
> earthquakes. No explicit scientific cause is given for the
> sinking, although "evil vibrations" and the restlessness of
> mankind are referred to. The Atlanteans, however, recog-
> nize that the female is "the more vital and virile of the
> human species."

666. Royal, Matthew J.   The Isle of the Virgins.   Buffalo,
N.Y.: Wenborne-Sumner, 1899.

> John Fairfax is one of five men who survive a shipwreck and
> reach an island governed by women. Originally settled by
> Romans who got lost trying to sail around Africa, the
> island was visited two centuries after the discovery of
> America by French explorers who married into the people.
> There is some suggestion that those with French blood have
> remained an aristocracy. The ruler is Alzira, a beautiful
> but suspicious empress. All young women between fourteen
> and twenty-two are kept on Virgin Island. Twice a year
> there are games or marriage. Men have no voice in the
> matter of wedlock. Women hold all the important offices.
> Fairfax is named Ozito, meaning "The Beautiful." He is
> warned not to fall in love with either Ayzala or Numeni,
> the queen's daughters. Instead he falls for Sione, the
> lovely blonde commander-in-chief of the military forces.
> Numeni secretly invites him to her boudoir and flirts with
> him. She talks her way out of possible trouble when they
> are discovered. Queen Alzira chooses to marry him, but he
> refuses. By various machinations he, Sione and Numeni--
> both of whom love him--and twenty virgins secure passage to
> Valpariso and subsequently to England. A prefatory note
> intrudes the opinion that science will yet show that Earth
> is the center of the universe and that sun and planets
> revolve around it.

667. Ruck, Amy Roberta.   The Immortal Girl.   New York: Dodd,
Mead, 1925.

> Also published in England by Hodder & Stoughton (1925):
> Martha Marigold Owen is given her youth a second time. The
> formula works only with women. She first loves Bill Iffley
> (at the end of the nineteenth century) who is killed in a
> train accident. Later Colonel Stock refuses to marry when
> he learns how old she is. Once again the theme emphasizes
> the unhappy consequences of eternal youth.

668.   Russell, Addison Peale.   Sub-Coelum; A Sky-Built Human
World. Boston: Houghton Mifflin, 1893.

This presents an essentially pastoral utopia.   Education
stresses manners and character.   Youth and beauty--in
simple dress--are emphasized. The income tax takes care of
government expense.   Everyone is advised to practice
Christianity.   Godliness provides a mystery the people do
not understand.

669.   Russell W[illiam] Clark.   The Frozen Pirate.   London:
Sampson, Low, Marston, 1887 (2 vols.).

Mistakenly classified as science fiction, this narrative
concentrates upon the survival of Paul Rodney, a British
seaman, after his ship, The Laughing Mary, strikes a huge
iceberg and sinks.   After four days in an open boat, he is
cast upon the ice and discovers an old schooner.   The
narrative focuses upon his realistic, first-person, detailed account of what happened to him.   Fantasy enters
when he revives a Frenchman, Tassard, and learns that the
schooner is the Boca del Dragon, lost in 1753.   The present
year is 1801.   Tassard tells him of a treasure and they
find it by the end of volume one.   In the second volume
Tassard dies, Rodney is alone, the schooner frees itself,
and he is discovered by the Susan Tucker, whaler, of New
Bedford, Josiah Tucker commanding.   The remainder of the
story concerns the return of the Boca del Dragon and the
treasure to England.   A final chapter reports Paul Rodney's
death in 1823, suggests the amount of the treasure was
over-estimated, and verifies the existence of vast icebergs
in the Antarctic in the 1850s.

670.   Sabin, Edwin L[egrand].   The City of the Sun.   Philadelphia: Jacobs, 1924.

In the nineteenth century against the background of the
ancient city, Tonatuah-huac, the storyline centers on the
love of Robert McClung of Kentucky and Felicia Bobadella.
She is to be a virgin sacrifice to the great snake, but
together with the Mohican Indian, Eagle Heart, McClung
rescues her.   They go back out of the desert country as the
city and temple in the lake are destroyed.

671.   Saki (pseud. of Hector Henry Munro).   When William Came; A
Story of London Under the Hohenzollerns.   London: Lane, 1914.

Perhaps the finest example of the future war motif, the
narrative provides more than adequate warning by portraying
London society after England has been occupied by the
conquering Germans.   Cecily Yeovil provides the portrait of
the young woman who survives such an occupation by becoming
a part of the social scene.   Her husband, Murry Yeovil,
learned of the war while traveling in Siberia.   The em-

phasis is therefore upon character rather than melodramtic incident.   Herr Von Kwarl enunciates a major theme and prepares for the climax by stating that the Germans must capture the hearts and minds of the British youth.

672. Savage, Juanita.   The City of Desire.   New York: A.L. Burt, 1930.

Professor Desmond Warwick hopes to solve the disappearance of Professor Lancaster, who vanished some twenty years ago. He is the first to recognize the importance of the ruins found at Milta.   With him is his daughter, Nora Warwick, whom he has never quite forgiven for being a girl.   In the mountains after passing through a tunnel, she finds a great city and is regarded as a goddess.   On the throne is a white man, El Ray.   He loves her and presses his suit; she finally succumbs and realizes that she loves him.   He is identified as Ray Lancaster, son of Professor Lancaster and an American wife.   Denis O'Mara, who has also pressed his suit, settles for the girl Ixia.   This is another of those romances where an individual from modern society falls in love with someone from a primitive culture.   That El Ray is identified as "a white man all through" simply recognizes the racism which existed during the period.

673. Savile, Frank.   Beyond the Great South Wall.   New York: New Amsterdam, 1901.

The first-person narrator, Captain Jack Dorinecourte, inherits two manuscripts which suggest the existence of a Mayan civilization in the Antarctic.   One comes from a sixteenth century ancestor, a sea captain; the other, from a Mayan Indian, who tells of an exodus before oncoming Spaniards and of the discovery in a land of ice of an incarnation of the god Cay.   Dorinecourte ventures south-ward; after taking time to rescue his beloved Gwen Delahay from the sinking ship of Lord Denvarre, he penetrates the Ross Ice Barrier--the Great South Wall.   In an ice-encased gorge, he finds the ruins of a Mayan temple.   He also finds the god Cay, a lone brontosaurus, which pursues various members of the expedition throughout the remainder of the book.   It traps Dorinecourte and Gwen in a cave; instead of fainting, she informs the Captain that she was never engaged to Lord Denvarre.   After a convenient earthquake kills the dinosaur, they are free to return to England to marry.

674. Schindler, Solomon.   Young West; A Sequel to Edward Bellamy's Celebrated Novel "Looking Backward".   Boston: Arena, 1894.

Julian West died in the second year of his marriage because his cells failed to reproduce themselves.   This is the story told by his son reflectively at the age of seventy.

Electricity and the school system are emphasized; during high school teen-aged boys and girls are separated; however, sex education is stressed, although "all coarseness" is removed, while the "sanctity and holiness" surrounding the "mystery" are dwelt upon. Young West goes through a successful presidential campaign. His father's letters are given by Edith Leete West. They reveal that West was not psychologically able to adapt to the new social organization. No person from the nineteenth century could have made the adaptation. This point of the problem of adaptation remains perhaps the most significant theme of the novel; it seems unique in that emphasis.

675. Sedberry, James Hamilton. Under the Sign of the Cross. Boston: Clark, 1908.

Billed as a prophetic historical novel and dated 2005, the narrative does portray a war between the Caucasian and Asiatic races, with the battlefield primarily in Turkey. More importantly, it portrays a love story which romanticizes the Old South (Virginia) and the English country gentry. William Hastings rescues Mary Barkesdale and Katherine Van Roy when their horses run away. On the James River he again rescues Mary and Ralf Davenport, but Katherine is kidnapped by Edward Falstaff, a villainous English sea captain who loves her. The narrative shifts to England concentrating upon General Rayman Clifton, commander of the Christian forces, and his daughter, Beatrix. She is betrothed to a kinsman, Sir Lambert Saville, because her father is indebted to his family. William saves Beatrix when her horse almost runs off a cliff into the Bosphorus. Her father rejects him, and he fights a duel with Lambert after Beatrix is elected queen of a ball. Then the fighting begins in earnest, and William becomes commander-in-chief of the American forces. Using "electric devices of death," the Western powers win. William and Beatrix are united after Lambert has tried to kidnap her. Earlier Davenport had rescued Katherine. The novel closes on a scene years later when Taric-El Kadar, a friend and servant of William's, tells Oriental stories to the children of William and Beatrix.

676. Seeley, Charles Sumner (pseud. of John William Munday). The Lost Canyon of the Toltecs; An Account of Strange Adventures in Central American. Chicago: A.C. McClurg, 1893.

The first-person narrator, David Nelson, reports how he, Professor Adolph Bernstein, and Kiran Cadwallader search for Sir Reginald Bunsen Taylor in the Isthmus of Panama. With them is Mary Taylor, dear to David Nelson. In the interior she and her maid, Amelia Caxton, disappear, kidnapped by Indians who dwell in a city surrounded by little fields and irrigation canals and containing a pyramid temple. Much is made of the natural background as

well as the idea that the Toltecs were a peaceful tribe
driven into Central America by the warlike Aztecs. After
appropriate adventures, Mary and her father are rescued.

677. Senarens, Luis Philip. The Frank Reade, Jr. series. New
York: Frank Tousey.

Under the pseudonym "Noname," Lu Senarens wrote almost two
hundred stories about the youthful American inventor, Frank
Reade, Jr., for Frank Tousey during the 1880s and 1890s.
He took the place of Harry Enton. The most recent selection of his work is the two-volume The Frank Reade
Library edited by E. F. Bleiler (Garland, 1979). This
group of thirty-five tales presents an adequate cross-
section of young Reade's exploits. Perhaps three observations are adequate here. First, beginning with a "new
steam horse," most of the stories focus upon inventions
which can be put to practical use in terms of transportation. Secondly, those inventions allow him to travel to
locations already made popular by other authors. Thirdly,
in reflection of the spirit of the period, the youthful
Reade became wealthy through his inventive efforts. In
short, rather than a major source of other juvenile works
and a direct influence upon subsequent science fiction, one
should emphasize that they adapted material already a fixed
part of popular fiction to a juvenile audience.

678. Service, Robert A. The Master of the Microbe; A Fantastic
Romance. New York: Barse & Hopkins, 1926.

The first-person narrator, Harley, loves his cousin,
Rosemary, but cannot marry her because of some dreadful
secret. Most of the narrative focuses upon his eccentric
Uncle Cyrus Quin, who is partially paralyzed and afraid of
microbes. He has discovered a microbe which might be
developed into a vaccine against the Polish Grippe--called
the Purple Pest because it turns people purple. Quin dies
under a vitriol bath and there is some suggestion that he
is mad. Particular emphasis is made at one point that all
diseases are caused by bacteria.

679. Serviss, Garrett P[utnam]. A Columbus of Space. New
York: D. Appleton, 1911.

Dedicated to the readers of Jules Verne's romances: the
scientific genius, Edmund Stonewall, develops inter-atomic
energy and uses it for a flight to Venus. The story is
told by a first-person narrator, one of three friends whom
Stonewall literally kidnaps for the journey. They land on
the night-side of Venus and find gorilla-like creatures who
worship the Earth and its moon. Traveling to the sunny
side of Venus, they become involved with Queen Ala and a
jealous noble, Ingra. Although Stonewall is attracted to
Ala, it is incorrect to regard this as a love story. for

most of the storyline is given to escapes from Ingra's
machinations.   He kills Juba, their companion from the
night-side, just before the entire population goes mad when
the sun--which they worship--shows itself through a break
in the clouds.   Apparently the solar radiation somehow
destroys their minds, including those of Ingra and Ala.
They return to the dark side to bury Juba and then to
Earth.   Three months later Stonewall disappears and the
narrator reveals that a year has passed since he vanished.
The narrator implies that Stonewall has undertaken some
other voyage.

680. Serviss, Garrett P[utnam].   Edison's Conquest of Mars.
Los Angeles: Carcosa House, 1947.

A sequel to Wells's The War of the Worlds, originally
serialized in the New York Evening Journal early in 1898:
although the Martians who survived Earth's bacteria returned to their home planet, flashes there portend another
invasion.   Edison invents both a spaceship (it utilizes an
anti-gravity power) and a disintegrator (it uses vibrations) and leads an international armada in a war of
retribution.   After sighting a giant footprint on the moon
and learning that some of the asteroids are solid gold, the
fleet arrives on Mars.   The Martians are giant humanoids (a
contradiction to Wells).   Their culture is dominated by a
military class, and they are capable of brain culture,
developing especially the brains of those who are to be
soldiers.   Edison declares that this is a war between the
evolution of Earth and that of Mars.   He wins by flooding
the planet after opening the canals, but many Martians fall
victim to the disintegrator at the emperor's palace.
Edison exacts a promise that never again will they attack
Earth.   The expedition finds the girl Aina, a representative of the Aryan race which dwelt in the Valley of
Cashmere; her people were used as slaves to build the
pyramids when the Martians attacked the Earth 9,000 years
earlier.   She returns to Earth and marries Sydney Phillips.
Lord Kelvin is a member of the expedition.

681. Serviss, Garrett P[utnam].   The Moon Metal.   New York:
Harper, 1900.

Discovery of vast gold deposits near the South Pole make
gold as common as iron so that the world's finances are
reduced to chaos.   The mysterious Dr. Syx appears before a
council of bankers and offers to replace gold with a new
metal, artesium, which comes only from his mine in the
Grand Tetons of Wyoming.   In return he asks for military
protection for his mine as well as payment of one percent
on the circulated money, together with the privilege of
setting aside a set amount of artesium to be used in the
arts.   Though it gives him a monopoly, his plan is accepted.   Another scientist, Hall, begins an investigation

and learns that both the mine and the reducing works are fakes. He finds a strange machine which operates only when the moon is above the horizon; by experiment--using a new form of electrical energy--he learns that there is a flow of molecules between Syx's pretended mine and the moon. After Syx's monopoly has been broken, he disappears from the United States and teaches scientists around the world how to obtain artesium. Hundreds of rays devastate the moon and almost reduce the Earth to ruins because of the metallic dust. At last the governments restore order. At one point Syx shows lantern slides of a world catastrophe; by implication the slides reveal the death of civilization on the moon. In a final scene Syx disappears before Hall's eyes. Both Hall and the narrator agree that Syx resembled the man in the moon. Such an ending is out of tone with the rest of the novel.

682. Serviss, Garrett P[utnam]. The Second Deluge. New York: McBride, 1912.

First serialized in Cavalier Magazine (1911): when Cosmo Versal learns that the Earth will plunge through a watery nebula, he builds an ark to save a few chosen people (no lawyers) and animals. The public, including Professor Pludder, scoff at him. During the flood Versal uses the submarine Jules Verne to explore sunken Paris and the Sphinx; later he uses a diving bell to see submerged New York. A geological phenomenon causes the Rockies around the Pike's Peak area to rise above the water so that some three million people, including Pludder, are saved. The novel is presented as a future history; Versal has founded a new society based upon eugenics and scientific principles. One of the scientists he saved, Costaké Theriade, has developed atomic energy.

683. Severy, Melvin L[inwood]. The Darrow Enigma. London: Richards, 1904.

This transitional novel blends psychological material with detection, in this case the solution of the murder of Darrow in a crowded, semi-darkened room. Severy clutters the novel with much talk of the occult, actually devoting its middle section to a pursuit of a Hindu fakir in India. The young scientist-playing-detective proves that the inspector of police investigating the crime is the culprit; through an elaborate method of post-hypnotic suggestion he controlled the agent committing the crime by making him introduce a poisonous snake into the semi-darkened room.

684. Shanks, Edward. The People of the Ruins; A Story of the English Revolution and After. New York: Stokes, 1920.

Also published in England by Collins (1920): against the background of a threatened general strike and the outbreak

of civil conflict, Jeremy Tuft is buried alive in the
cellar of a house on Lime Court in Whitechapel. Accidental
exposure to a new ray puts him into suspended animation.
He awakens in 2074 to find Britain in a state of decadence
rather than complete barbarism. The survivors refer to
"The Troubles," which lasted some fifty years and destroyed
all of the nations of Europe as well as Britain: war,
disease, famine. Much of southern England has become
Catholic, and modern education disappeared during The
Troubles. Society has been fragmented. Jeremy is sought
after by the Speaker, the hereditary ruler of the London
area taking his title from the Speaker of the House of
Commons, because Tuft has some knowledge of artillery. His
knowledge and action defeat an army of northerners, but in
a second battle the forces of the President of Wales
triumph. London is razed, while the Speaker, Jeremy, and
Lady Eva--the Speaker's daughter whom Jeremy loves--must
flee. Several matters make this novel unique: first, the
old struggle for power continues because society has not
been obliterated; secondly, Thomas Wells, called the
Canadian, represents an area which supplies mercenary
troops to anyone (the U.S. no longer exists); thirdly, the
idea of inevitable progress through science and technology
is questioned from the outset. Its potential may be
lessened by the emphasis upon battles, but the final
pessimism is effective.

685.   Shaw, W[illiam] J[enkins].   Cresten, Queen of the Toltus;
or, Under the Auroras. New York: Excelsior, 1892.

Published as Under the Auroras (1888): Amos Jackson, the
first-person narrator and an investigator of natural phenomena, and his companion, John Harding, build a metallic
balloon and penetrate to an inner world. Jackson finds and
marries Cresten, queen of a people who speak Norwegian as
it was spoken a thousand years ago. For fifteen years they
live together; then she dies, and he buries her. There is
implication early in the narrative that the narrator is
deceased and is telling the story from the spirit world.

686.   Shearer, W. B. Pacifico. New York: Tait, 1926.

Aided by Captain St. Johns of the British navy, Commander
Truxton Rodgers, U.S.N., and Rena Garrett attempt to keep
military secrets from falling into the hands of such agents
as Captain Yamamoto, though he is the best of the Japanese
because he trained with the British navy. The American
industrialist, Currens, is introduced to emphasize the
desire of America to trade with China, but much emphasis is
given to Japanese domination of Chinese economics. The
arch-villain, however, remains Count Komura, son of a
German father and a Japanese mother, who has given his
allegiance to a militant Japan. Much is made of Japan's
having learned from Germany. The climax comes when a

Filipino Junta, led by Senor Reyes and reinforced by
Japanese soldiers of fortune as well as Japanese living as
civilians in the Philippines, fails in an attempted coup
d'etat.   Truxton and Rena are in love.   The League of
Nations is called a failure, as is Bolshevism.

687.   Sherman, Harold M[orrow].   Tahara Among African Tribes.
Chicago: Goldsmith, 1933.

Under Jess Sylthe's influence a band of Arab slavers attack
the Taharans and Gorols.   In face of the odds, Queen Vanga
of the Taharans and Chief Wabiri of the Gorols call upon
the medicine man, Cimbula, for aid.   He is captured, as is
Veena, the handmaiden of the queen who has always admired
Dick.   The remainder of the novel becomes a pursuit of the
savage Muta-Kangas, who also hold Professor Oakland and Ray
prisoners through the added treachery of Sylthe.   With the
aid of Mahatma Sikandar, an Indian who can foresee the
future and control the minds of both men and animals, Dick
and Dan defeat the Arab slavers and their native allies,
although they gain additional aid from the fierce Kungoras,
whom Sikandar has ruled.   The crown which Dick discovered
proves to be the ancient crown of Solomon, which Sikandar
much wants to see.   The Taharan, Raal, kills Cimbula and
rescues Veena, whom he loves.   Kurt and Kurul, two tribesmen who supported Dick from the first, accompany him and
his American friends as they fly Sikandar to India.

688.   Sherman, Harold M[orrow].   Tahara, Boy King of the Desert.
Chicago: Goldsmith, 1933.

Dick Oakland and his friends Dan and Ray Carter (Ray is a
lovely young girl) join their fathers, Professor Hector
Oakland and the wealthy Rex Carter, in an expedition to the
Sahara.   The fathers are most interested in watching a
solar eclipse from Pomegranate Oasis, although there is
rumor of a lost Stone Age tribe somewhere in the Sahara.
The treacherous Jess Slythe and Suli, the Arab, attack Dick
during an airplane flight.   He parachutes into the desert
where he becomes involved with a Stone Age tribe who
believe him to be the sun god, Tahara.   Cimbula, a one-eyed
medicine man, is Dick's chief antagonist in a struggle for
power.   As Tahara, Dick gives the tribe the bow and arrow
and leads them in a war against the darker Gorols, called
"Missing Links."   Slythe brings Dan and Ray to the Gorols
so that one of the main lines of action is the rescue of
his two young friends.   He causes the image of the Great
Gorol to be broken, and finds that it contains the ancient
crown which unites the tribes.   They proclaim him king as
Cimbula vanishes, and Dick refuses the offer of Rex Carter
to bring in guns and machinery to civilize the tribes.   He
wishes to guide their advancement without such modern aids.

689. Sherman, Harold M[orrow].   Tahara, Boy Mystic of India.
Chicago: Goldsmith, 1933.

   In India the Taharans, Kurt and Kurul, inadvertently
   desecrate the golden monkey temple in Benares. A priest
   curses the party, declaring that death will come to them
   within three weeks. Dick sets out to find the so-called
   Master, Bhagavan Vamadeva in the mountains of Kashmir.
   Although Kurt and Kurul die, Dick encounters Bhagavan
   Vamadeva and finds that he himself is adept at the mystic
   arts. He must rescue Dan and Ray from the Maharaja Zakar
   Singh, who is forcing Ray into an unwanted marriage. A
   final note from Bhagavan Vamadeva sends them to Yucatan.

690. Sherman, Harold M[orrow].   Tahara in the Land of Yucatan.
Chicago: Goldsmith, 1933.

   In Yucatan, Dick and his companions meet Jacques Romano,
   who for three years was a student of Bhagavan Vamadeva.
   With his aid they find a ruined Mayan city beyond Chichen
   Itza. He tells Dick and Ray that they spent one of their
   incarnations as lovers in that Mayan city, where Bhagavan
   Vamadeva was king. Romano had then caused their deaths by
   throwing them to snakes, but this time he rescues them from
   their treacherous guide, Antonio Martinez, leader of a
   "fiendish" gang of bandits, who has kidnapped Dick and Ray
   for 25,000 pesos ransom. Reference is made to the past
   glory of Atlantis, which had aerial-submarines, among other
   technological wonders. Throughout the last three novels of
   the series whenever the occult is discussed, the human mind
   is compared to a radio which is capable of receiving
   thoughts telepathically. The novel ends after Dick has
   finally confessed his love for Ray.

691. Shiel, M[atthew] P[hipps].   The Lord of the Sea. London:
Richards, 1901.

   A massacre of Jews in Prague spreads throughout Europe and
   leads to an exodus of Jews to England, where they immedi-
   ately gain control of much land and the national finances.
   The result must be regarded as the most viciously anti-
   Semitic novel of the period. Early the reader learns that
   Richard Hogarth, raised as an Englishman, is actually a
   Jew, but he seems not to have heard his foster father tell
   him this. For some two hundred pages the storyline concentrates upon the villainous Baruch Frankl, who tricks
   Hogarth so that he is imprisoned for murder, and who traps
   Margaret Hogarth into an asylum when she will not surrender
   to his desires. Richard loves Frankl's daughter, Rebekah,
   though she will not seriously consider him. When Hogarth
   realizes in prison that "land tenure" is the cause of all
   social evil, he escapes. Fortunately a great asteroid has
   burned up in the Earth's atmosphere, and he gains untold
   wealth from the diamonds in a fragment of it. With this

wealth he literally buys Europe and proclaims himself the
Lord of the Sea, building immense floating fortresses which
control the sea-lanes. With the aid of the priest O"Hara
(there is also an element of anti-Catholicism in the
novel), Hogarth's aims are defeated. But in the new state
of Israel, which European legislation has created, Hogarth
rules in his true name, Spinoza, for sixty years. Israel
is a kind of utopian state and Hogarth/Spinoza is regarded
as something of a messiah. Frankl is satisfactorily killed
by one of his henchmen. But the entire first half of the
book is unnecessary.

692. Shiel, M[atthew] P[hipps].   The Purple Cloud.   London:
Chatto & Windus, 1901.

A purple gas from a volcano in the Pacific wipes out civilization while Adam Jeffson, the first-person narrator,
ventures to the North Pole. He kills one member of the
expedition, but the gas finishes the others. When he
returns alone to England, he loots a deserted London. He
breaks the narrative off for some seventeen years. He has
wandered the world and developed the habit of burning such
cities as Calcutta, Peking, and San Francisco. In Istanbul
he discovers a young woman of Circassian blood, but he
refuses to accept the idea that he must be the Adam to her
Eve. He speaks at length of the struggle within him of
"the White" and "the Black," the latter of which he is
certain governs his soul. He is sure, for examplle, that
God loves the young woman and hates him. Although he wants
to kill her at one point and deliberately separates himself
from her (he is in England; she, in France), he finally
accepts her as his wife and envisions them as parents of a
new race. As usual there are religious overtones throughout Jeffson's tormented suffering. This remains perhaps
the finest of Shiel's novels, primarily because he uses
traditional science fiction materials--the catastrophe
motif and the theme of the last man--to explore the ab-
normal psychological state of his protagonist.

693. Shiel, M[atthew] P[hipps].   The Yellow Danger; or, What
Might Happen if the Division of the Chinese Empire Should
Estrange All European Countries. New York: Fenno, 1899.

Also published in England by Grant Richards (1898): in this
volume Shiel introduces the concept of the "yellow peril,"
which was to become part of Western mythology as late as
World War II, at least. Its protagonist, John Hardy, hates
the Asiatic races. When Dr. Yen How is rejected by Ada
Seward, a "nanny" in Fulham, his evil mind seeks revenge,
especially since a British soldier lays hands on him. Yen
How plays the European powers against one another because
of their greed for Chinese territories. The British fleet
wins a victory over ships from Germany, Russia, and France.
Hardy goes overland to Asia and becomes involved in fight-

ing in China. After escaping from Yen How, he returns to Britain in time to take part in another major victory over European navies. But Yen How has released an army of over a hundred million Asiatics who sweep through Europe. Time is taken out while Hardy rescues Ada Seward from Yen How, and then a final battle against the Asiatic horde degenerates into "a debauch of hell." The remnants of the Asiatic army are released along the coast of Europe and are infected with a plague. Europe becomes a "charnel-house" swept by "putrid cholera." Hardy does not live to enjoy this final decimation, for he is killed by a French duelist whom he has angered earlier. As in The Lord of the Sea, Shiel reveals himself as a thoroughgoing racist who is almost sadistically pleased with the concept of genocide.

694. Sibson, Francis H. The Stolen Continent. London: Melrose, 1934.

A sequel to The Survivors, this narrative gains its uniqueness in that it concerns itself primarily with the efforts of corrupt politicians, like Senator Wannstead, and organized crime to take over control both of the U.S. and the new Atlantean continent. The so-called United States League of Defence is the front organization for the criminal element, but it is opposed even in America by the United States Fighting Services. Because the League of Defence tries to colonize the new continent and because its leaders kidnap Joan Archdale, she and Fennlake are once again on the new land. The American Ralston sacrifices himself in a successful attempt to destroy the criminal airplanes. After that success the Squadron of Peace makes a final appearance, carrying the two flags of "Anglo-Saxondom"--America and Britain.

695. Sibson, Francis H. The Survivors. Garden City, N.J.: Doubleday, Doran, 1932.

Also published in England by Heinemann (1932): volcanic action and subterranean earthquakes raise an island continent in the area of the Sargasso Sea. Aboard The General Longstreet, the Southern girl, Joan Archdale, survives the initial wreck, but she is trapped below deck. On board the British cruiser, Maple Leaf, Lt. Commander Fennlake is the chief protagonist. The narrative alternates between the two ships as it details both the loneliness and suffering of Joan and Fennlake and their efforts to survive. Fennlake goes to her rescue after receiving radio signals from the Longstreet. Although the Maple Leaf has been damaged and grounded, it is refloated. As Joan and Fennlake depart the new continent aboard the Maple Leaf, they finally hear radio reports that Great Britain has not been destroyed. They have falllen in love; indeed, she asks if he would have cared had they been the last man and woman alive. Anticipating The Stolen Continent, one passage, at least, refers to crime and political corruption in the U.S. but speaks of the "real solid Nordic stuff" underneath.

696. Sibson, Francis H. Unthinkable. New York: Smith & Haas, 1933.

Also published in England by Methuen (1933): most of the narrative concerns the wreck of the South African Antarctic Expedition and their survival on the ice as they wait for a relief ship. When none comes, they find a ship which has been adrift for at least a year and sail the derelict vessel back to South Africa. John Dane is the protagonist. On their journey to Antarctica they had heard radio reports of a Franco-Italian dispute. As they near the southwest coast of Africa, they become increasingly aware that civilization has destroyed itself in a terrible war invovling gas and both incendiary and explosive bombs. There is no explicit statement (other than the early radio report) as to what nation(s) actually started the war. Something in the destructive forces has affected the higher brain cells of the few survivors, but the crew resolves to build civilization again--"and build better."

697. Simpson, Helen [De Guerry]. The Woman on the Beast, Viewed from Three Angles. London: Heinemann, 1933.

The narrative pictures "The Indies" (1579), "France" (1789), and Australia (1999). Its chief concern is with the existence of evil. Emma Jordan Sopwith is a religious leader and produces the Sopwith Bible in 1987. Her organization is the New Gospel Workers. One must regard this as another of the strange mystical documents which had such popularity during the period. Perhaps its most significant detail is that she wants a society in which there are no books nor newspapers.

698. Simpson, William. The Man from Mars, His Morals, Politics, and Religion. San Francisco: Beattle, 1900.

This is the third edition of a book originally published by Bacon under the pseudonym Thomas Blot (1891). Its lengthy preface extols Christianity but denounces the churches, especially the "supernatural horrors" which they so long taught. The preface ends with the author speculating as to how many worlds are inhabited. At that point the man from Mars enters and becomes the first-person narrator. He elaborates a Martian culture far in advance of that of the Earth, and he assures the author that science will eventually strengthen belief in future existence. The book's chief claim to notice lies in an extended chapter condemning attitudes toward women. The Martian praises women's affinity for knowledge and virtue. The author leaves open the question of whether or not the dialogue was a dream or an actual visitation, but one of his final points is that there will definitely be a Second Coming.

699. Slee, Richard and Cornelia Atwood Pratt. Dr. Berkeley's Discovery. New York: Putnam, 1899.

Dr. Berkeley prefers research to medical practice; he is particularly interested in "cerebral localization" and develops a means by which to photograph the content of specific memory cells. In Paris he had met Aline Lefevre and later married her; now, exhausted by his research, he awaits her return from a visit to France. He becomes involved in the investigation of the murder of a Madame Massoneau in a hotel in New York; to his horror he discovers that the dead woman is his wife Aline. When the suspect is arrested, Berkeley is called to give evidence. His photographs prove the accused guilty but, more importantly, they prove that Aline did not deceive him. The murderer, an aristocrat, had intended to seduce her but failed. All of this is too much for Berkeley; he flees to his old tutor and dies without revealing his secret. Interestingly there is very little dialogue or representational detail.

700. Small, Austin J. The Avenging Ray. Garden City, N.Y.: Doubleday, Doran, 1930.

Also published in England by Hodder & Stoughton under the pseudonym, "Seamark" (1930): while a guest at Deepvale Manor, Geoffrey (Gerry) Windermaine discovers a yard-wide scorched streak across the Devon fields and meets the girl, Rosaine, who lives at Rose Cottage with Carlo Damian, called the "mad scientist." Rosaine warns him to leave the area, but he feels that Damian is about to do something more. He is correct in that a pond, called the Black Deep, vanishes; only a hole remains. Ranting against the armaments makers and militarists, Damian proclaims that he is the chosen instrument of God to wreak vengeance upon the sinful world. He has developed a "Degravitisor," which disrupts the cohesion of molecules. On the eve of the day he intends to destroy the world, Damian goes into the Pendine Caves, where his great electric machine is storing energy; Rosaine leads Windermaine into the caves. She reveals that she is Damian's daughter. With the aid of Scotland Yard and others, Windermaine shuts down the so-called "accumulators," which may explode at any moment. Damian dies of a heart attack as he is handcuffed, while Windermaine and Rosaine plan to go away. Valerie, the daughter of Windermaine's host, Sir Robert Harrigan, whom her father wanted to marry Windermaine, understands and returns his ring.

701. Small, Austin J. The Death Maker. New York: Doran, 1926.

A madman, Jann Vorst, develops deadly poisons by combining
bacteria from various diseases. He intends to inject these
into the world's food supply in order to destroy the population of the world. Kellard Maine, who was framed by
Vorst some fifteen years earlier and served time in prison
for Vorst's murder, becomes involved when several individuals die of poisoning. Coralie Warden, a singer who is
the "Nightingale of Ten Capitals," introduces Vorst to
Maine as her father. Maine goes to the "germ farm" created
by Vorst, kills him, breaks the vials of germs, and traps
Vorst's gang so that they are poisoned before the germs
dissipate.

702. Smile, R. Elton (pseud. of Elton R. Smilie). The Man-
titlans; or, A Record of Recent Scientific Explorations in the
Andean La Plata. Cambridge, Ma.: Riverside Press, 1877.

In a series of narratives the novel reports the findings of
the Teutonic corps of the R.H.B. Society of Berlin, led by
M. Hollydorf, as they explore the headwaters of the Para-
guay and its tributaries. The reports are sent as letters
to Berlin, and replies from such officials as the Kaiser
are included in the book. They early encounter Correliana
Adinope, whose people dwell in the walled city of Heracles
by the Falls and are descended from noble Roman families
whose ship was driven across the Atlantic to South America,
where they settled in the Betongo valleys. The original
city was destroyed when the natives, treated like slaves,
revolted and massacred many of the rulers. The new city
has remained constantly under siege. The greater discovery
comes, however, when with the aid of the tympano-micro-
scope, the explorers find the petals and pistils of a
flower peopled by diminutive human beings, the Manatitlans.
Correliana introduces Manito, the Praetor of Maniculae,
principal city of Manatitla. From that point the narrative
becomes a description of Manatitlan society, especially its
system of education. Their society is 11,000 years old,
dating from the imaginary date of Mauna Che's advent as
their deity. It becomes a means of satirizing European society. The narrative concludes with the statement signed
by all of the European explorers that the account given is
true.

703. [Smilie, Elton R.]. Investigations and Experience of M.
Shawtinbach, at Saar Soong, Sumatra; A Ret or Sequel to "The
Manatitlans." San Francisco: Winterburn, 1897.

Originally published anonymously: this is a defense of the
Bible against Darwinism. It is a heavy-handed satire in
that the major portion of the narrative begins with the
story of the "First Foundling of Orang and Darwing Ex-
traction."

704.   Smith, Garret.   Between Worlds.   New York: Stellar, 1930.

On Venus in an essentially static society, the first-person
narrator, Scribner, joins Hunter, who wishes to sail
through the unknown Circle of Darkness to discover new
lands.   The action develops along three lines.   First,
Hunter discovers that the Queen of Darkness is the daughter
of a kinsman who disappeared some time ago.   She loves him.
His ship is the first to sail around the world, thereby
changing the concept of the universe.   Secondly, the so-
called Lady of the South, who also loves Hunter, leads a
suffragette movement which demands that women not work but
be permitted to care for their homes and children, as well
as being supported by their husbands, whom they will marry
for love.   To remove the disruption caused by these two
women, Hunter takes them with him when he flies a ship to
Earth.   They arrive at the time of World War I.   The narrative telegraphs that they will be the source of the legend
of the Angels of Mons.   The Queen of the Night is captured
by a German U-boat commander, while the Lady of the South
becomes involved with another U-boat commander who is taken
to Siberia.   The narrator suggests that both women are
responsible for the emergence of the "Bolsheviki" and are
fomenting plots.   To save the Earth, Hunter releases a
Venusian plague, causing the Spanish influenza epidemic of
1918.   The book is strongly anti-German.   The narrator and
Hunter both fall in love with the Fanwood sisters--British
--and thus remain on Earth.

705.   Smith, Homer W.   Kamongo; or, The Lungfish and the Padre.
New York: Viking, 1932.

This has historical significance because it provides a late
dialogue on the nature of evolution and the universe.   A
skeletal narrative frame permits Joel, a physiologist, to
meet a Padre as they travel through the Suez Canal and Red
Sea.   Several years earlier Joel had been to Africa to
search for the lungfish and take them home alive; they are
important to him because they are the living animal closest
to the extinct link between fish and land animals.   From
this point of departure Joel, especially, advances the idea
that evolution is not progressive but is simply a matter of
change.   Although the Padre stresses faith and the unknown,
Joel concludes that there is no goal (purpose) to evolution
except that life continue living.   In a sense, perhaps,
that view concludes the running debate which had so colored
sf and fantasy with various shades of mysticism during the
period.

706.   Smith, Mrs. J. Gregory [Ann Eliza Smith].   Alta; The Story
of the Lost Island.   New York: Harper, 1886.

This is another account of the sinking of Atlantis.   Its
principal city is Atlan.   The author refers to it as "this

Eden of the West" located where the Sea of Sargasso is. Among its final rulers are two princesses: Astera, "impulsive, ardent, passionate"; and Alta, "dignified, spiritual, tranquil." Although earthquakes destroy the island, its descendants escape to Central America, Central Asia, Northern Europe, and the Pacific Isles. Through Princess Alta come the Phoenicians and Greeks, while through Astera come the Aztecs and Toltecs.

707. Smith, Mrs. J. Gregory [Ann Eliza Smith]. Seola. Boston: Lee & Shepard, 1878.

Accidentally the narrator finds the oldest tomb in the world in the mountains of northern Syria. In it he discovers a manuscript, "The Journal of Seola, wife of the patriarch, Japhet." The narrative thus pretends to be a history of the period of the Noachian deluge. Retitled Angels and Women, it was reissued in 1924.

708. Smith, Titus K[eiper]. Altruria. New York: Altruria, 1895.

The narrative is presented as the letter of John Optimus written from Altruria, Iowa, on 4 July 1893. He dislikes the fact that during the present era everything is measured by its economic value. He stresses that all honest, industrious persons are dependent upon one another. The town of Altruria has 3000 inhabitants, and they are served by a "central kitchen or hotel," although they all work in the country. In its last chapters he compares New York unfavorably to the small town. He also calls for both universal free trade and uniform money in a "world-wide republic of all civilized states."

709. Smyth, Clifford. The Gilded Man; A Romance of the Andes. New York: Boni & Liveright, 1918.

In a "Foreword" Richard Le Gallienne praises this novel as one of the best of its kind, comparing it to Haggard's King Solomon's Mines. After establishing David Meudon and Una Leighton as lovers, the narrative focuses upon psychology and the nature of thought, making mention of an "Electric Psychometer." Harold Leighton gives David a word association test which leads him to Bogota and Lake Guatavita, the sacred lake of the Chibchas. He joins Raoul Arthur in a search for El Dorado. In a great cavern lighted by a radium sun David finds a remnant of the Chibcha tribe. For a time David has amnesia and does not remember Una. In a moment of peril Una sends a psychical message to him. When he recovers and must return to America and Una, Sajipona, the Indian princess who loves him, throws herself into the radium sun. The Indians make use of radium baths to strengthen moral character because of the affinity of certain radium colors for certain moral attributes.

710. Snell, Edmund. <u>Kontrol</u>. Philadelphia: Lippincott, 1928.

Also published in England by Benn (1928): in a sense this
should be compared to Wells's <u>The Island of Dr. Moreau</u>. The
mad scientist, Dr. Guriev, starts to transplant magnificent
brains into magnificent bodies. He produces some 378 of
these creatures, and Count Marchette provides him with an
island where his creatures--described as being dead--begin
to build a technological center. Marchette is certain that
the next war will be one of chemistry and electricity.   A
volcano finally destroys the island.   The protagonist is
Denis Wildash, who was wounded in the Great War and patched
up.   Sonia Ingerstrom, who loves him, says after the destruction of Marchette's island and Dr. Guriev that the
creatures are searching for Wildash to destroy him in order
to keep their secret.

711. Snell, Edmund.   The <u>Sound-Machine</u>.   London: Skeffington,
1932.

Professor Gerardo invents a machine which emits vibrations
that cause structures to collapse.   Peter Enright, attracted to Gerardo's niece, Agnes, pursues the mad scientist until he is destroyed in his palace on the Riviera.

712. Snell, Edmund.   The <u>Yu-Chi Stone</u>.   New York: Macaulay,
1926.

Also published in England by Unwin (1925): Glynn Haverstock, manager of the Maitam rubber plantation, finds a
Dutchman, Stahl, who has escaped from Kang Yin, a mysterious Oriental having a private kingdom in the interior
of Borneo. Stahl bears the burns of the Yu-Chi stone.
Then Lois Stroud comes to the plantation, searching for her
weakling brother, Gilbert, whom she believes to be enslaved
by Kang Yin. The millionaire yachtsman, Rex Hermanos, has
aided her thus far, and so the three of them venture into
the interior.   Captured by Kang Yin and Korungau, the
priest of the Yu-Chi stone, Lois is to be sacrificed to the
goddess of the stone, but Haverstock rescues her. A final
attack brings about the downfall of Kang Yin and his
soldiers.   Hermanos and Kang Yin are both killed, while
Gilbert has died.   An added attraction is provided by the
lovely jungle girl, Tiana, who loves Haverstock and helps
him rouse the Chinese against Kang Yin.

713. Snell, Edmund.   The <u>"Z" Ray</u>.   Philadelphia: Lippincott,
1932.

Also published in England by Skeffington (1932): in this
variation the mad scientist develops a death ray. The most
notable point is the description of radiation as "X ray
dermitology" which no one knows how to stop.

714. Snell, Roy J[udson]. The Seagoing Tank. Chicago: Reilly
& Lee, 1924.

Intended for a juvenile audience, the narrative centers on
Curlie Carson and Joe Marion. Because they are wireless
operators, they are valuable in the testing of a submersible, seagoing tank which is hailed as one of the indis-
pensible weapons of the future. No nation is safe. In
addition, they are instrumental in finding the papers which
prove that a number of Oriental yachtsmen are really spies
trying to steal U.S. secrets.

715. Speller, Robert and Jane. Adam's First Wife. New York:
Macaulay, 1929.

A slight and playful narrative told in the first-person by
Lilith, who was born in 5018 B.C. and writes this partial
memoir in the twentieth century. Raised as a ward of King
Urech of Akkad--a colony of Atlantis, as were the Medi-
terran countries and the land of the Mayas--she must spend
one night with the King before being given in marriage to
the male he has chosen for her. Thus she becomes the first
wife of Admu, a blonde barbarian, who becomes obsessed with
the idea that he will be remembered as the first man. All
who came before him will be forgotten. Her marriage to
Admu is dissolved and she weds another. Although only men
during her time were permitted to enjoy longevity, she
gained her apparent immortality by eating the sacred
mushrooms.

716. Springer, Norman. The Dark River. New York: Watt, 1928.

The setting is the Straits and New Guinea. The narrative
shifts back and forth between two principal charaacters.
Eric Waithe is a former soldier whose racial memory was
activated by a shell explosion in France after he and some
comrades found a cave once inhabited by Cro-Magnon men.
This atavistic element controls him a good part of the time
and leads him to fall in love with a golden woman, a
"hybrid of the Straits," Mata. The second character, Dan
Murdock, is marooned in New Guinea during his exploration
and for a time is a prisoner. What ties the two together
is their search for the Raiaroka--or Sky People--a legendary lost race deep in the interior. An added compli-
cation occurs because Doc McToole is convinced that Neanderthal man is not extinct. In this he is correct, for
Neanderthal exists as the Sukakara in the interior of New
Guinea. The Sky People, now thoroughly integrated by
centuries of intermarriage, may have come from as far west
as Egypt. They have a young white woman as a goddess who
must be rescued. An amusing touch, perhaps, is that the
Neanderthal, like everyone else, suffer from an epidemic of
mumps. This intricate plot and narrative technique are

satisfactorily worked out.   Eric's atavar is surpressed when he hears reveille.

717. Stacpoole, H. deVere. The City in the Sea. New York: Doran, 1925.

The foreword refers to several recent discoveries of ancient submerged cities. The storyline concerns the finding of the city of Hyalos in the Aegean. Although the villain makes much of stealing artifacts in an effort to cover his own attempted theft, Jacob Behrens asserts that he will hold the city and its treasures in trust for Greece and the world.   It is also the love story of Bobbie Lestrange and and Martia Hare.

718. Stapledon, [William] Olaf. Last and First Men; A Story of the Near and Far Future. London: Methuen, 1930.

The first of Stapledon's books, this novel has been praised by such writers as Arthur C. Clarke and has influenced many subsequent authors.   More essay than dramatic novel, the narrative projects two billion years into the future, forecasting the cycles of catastrophe and progress that result from man's actions.   The near future deals with a series of wars which ruin contemporary civilization and finally a Martian invasion which destroys both worlds. Fifth man (the fifth species of man) migrates to Venus. From his world on Neptune, Eighteenth man reflects upon history which was dominated by a Darwinian struggle for survival; his astronomers have learned that an unusual nova will annihilate man.   Stapledon remarks that mankind's existence has always been precarious.   The last species wishes to know the past thoroughly and hopes somehow to develop an artificial human seed and project it among the stars.   The narrative ends with a eulogy of man as potentially godlike, but when set against the idea that in all probability he will vanish as a continuing species, the tone must be regarded as melancholic at the best.   The narrative ends with two remarks: "It is very good to have been man. . . .   For we shall make after all a fair conclusion to this brief music that is man."

719. Stapledon, [William] Olaf. Last Men in London. London: Methuen, 1932.

One of the last men returns to the twentieth century through an Arctic settlement called the Portal to the Past. Calling himself a "parasite," the traveler becomes a part of the boy Paul and comments upon the twentieth century, beginning with the era of World War I and giving most attention to the war.   Through Paul he tries to awaken the Race Mind; Paul asserts that man must master himself and make a better world.   One senses that this narrative is much more personal, more autobiographical, than Last and

First Men because one of Paul's acquaintances is the author of that book (Stapledon does not name himself). As in the case of the former book, Stapledon tries to assemble an epilogue sent to him from Neptune by the last man.

720. Stapledon, [William] Olaf. Odd John; A Story Between Jest and Earnest. New York: Dutton, 1936.

Also published in England by Methuen (1936): the first-person narrator writes the biography of John Wainwright, whom he had known since infancy. Significantly, in the first chapter the author refers specifically to J. D. Beresford's "account of the unhappy Victor Stott." A mutant so advanced is John that he represents a new species of man far in advance of homo sapiens intellectually. After John declares that man has learned little from the experience of World War I, he seeks others like him and establishes a colony on an island in the Pacific. (At this point his contact with his biographer is merely through letters.) When a fleet representing nations from Britain and the U.S. to the Soviet Union reaches the island, a Japanese officer attempts to arrest one of the colonists. The mutant drops dead. They are thus left unharmed until the military receives instructions from its governments. The biographer--called Fido--departs amid their avowals that they love him. He reports that when a large invasion force landed on the island, the colonists first repelled them by inducing fright telepathically; then instead of surrendering, they destroyed themselves and their works by causing the island to sink. The narrator dates the event as 15 December 1933. He also calls the mutants "super-normals." Although the narrative voices Stapledon's biases, it remains perhaps the finest early novel in which mankind is unable to accept and live with advanced muta-tions (supermen).

721. Stapledon, [William] Olaf. Sirius; A Fantasy of Love and Discord. London: Secker & Warburg, 1944.

Although written later than the period under consideration, this novel deserves attention because it is one of Stap-ledon's finest works. The first-person narrator finds Plexy Trelone, whom he loves, with her dog, a Border Collie, Sirius. The dog is the subject of experiments which artificially enhance his intelligence; he becomes at least the equal to human beings. He also proves to be one of the most effective critics of modern men. Society enrages him, and he finally dies, but he loves Plexy, who returns his love. This may well be Stapledon's finest novel.

722.   Stapledon, [William] Olaf.   <u>Star</u> <u>Maker</u>.   London: Methuen, 1937.

On the eve of "a catastrophe worse than that of 1914," the first-person narrator, a contemporary Englishman, projects his consciousness throughout time and space. He encounters other planets and sentient beings, but the high point comes when he perceives the Star Maker at work. It is this being--symbolic of the perfection of the life force--who creates universe after universe, each better than its predecessor. Stapledon defines him as "the eternal and perfect spirit which comprises all things and all times" and spends his time in creation and contemplation. Returning to Earth, the narrator sees the basic struggle as one between the human will which wants change and perfection and that element of humanity which is afraid of change. Stapledon is as much a mystic as any who tried to defend orthodox Christianity during the period; he must represent the awed, wishful voice of humanity in a secular, uncaring universe. Therein lies his strength and his tragedy.

723.   Stark, Harriet.   <u>The Bacillus of Beauty; A Romance of Today</u>.   New York: Stokes, 1900.

Helen Winship, a midwestern country girl who is a brilliant chemistry student, goes to New York, where Professor Darmstetter, "a great biologist," gives her a bacillus which makes her the most beautiful woman in the world. She becomes the first-person narrator as the novel becomes a study of her increasing pride, selfishness, and greed. She insists, for example, that her father mortgage his farm in order to provide her with money. John Burke, who was once her teacher, loves her and wishes to marry her, but she rejects him. Dated as though they are diary entries, most of the chapters take place between Christmas and June. The last section is made up of the notes of Burke. She dies; the final chapter is dated a year later. While the chief concern is with feminine beauty and pride, the novel also becomes a satire of the standards and actions of high society.

724.   Stevens, Rowan.   <u>The Battle for the Pacific</u>.   New York: Harper, 1908.

The lead story by Stevens centers upon the "remarkable chemist," Adams, whose inventions help defeat the Japanese after they seize Honolulu and Pearl Harbor. Other contributors, like Yates Stirling, Jr. and William J. Henderson, describe other battles, most of them involving advanced weapons. One story, at least, deals with an episode in a conflict between Venezuela and Great Britain. The entire book is extremely jingoistic.

725. Stevenson, Robert Louis. The Strange Case of Dr. Jekyll
and Mr. Hyde. London: Longmans, Green, 1886.

This novel remains the classic presentation during the
nineteenth century, at least, of the phenomenon of dual
personality. From his youth Dr. Jekyll becomes aware of a
streak of wickedness within him. He develops a potion
which makes that wickedness dominant and thereby transforms
him physically into Hyde. The lawyer Utterson presents the
mystery, but only a manuscript, the statement of Henry
Jekyll, gives a full explanation of the relationship
between him and his alter ego. Throughout the period all
subsequent treatments of dual personality are to some
degree indebted to Stevenson.

726. Stilgebaurer, Edward. The Ship of Death; A Novel of the
War. Trans. from the German by M. T. H. Sadler. New York:
Brentano's, 1918.

Also published in England by Cassell (1918): the narrative
divides itself into two parts. The first concerns the
sinking of the ship, Gigantic, and is obviously patterned
after the Lusitania. Much of the focus is upon the lovely
young Lady Mabel Roade, though the figure of de Chate-
lanard, a leader of the Christian Scientists in Philadelphia, is also emphasized. Some regard him as a saint
and believe that nothing will occur so long as he is on the
ship. He goes aboard a small boat to Brest, and the
Gigantic is sunk as it heads for Liverpool. The captain of
the submarine reads Lady Roade's diary after she has been
killed and becomes enmeshed in the ropes of the submarine.
The second part of the narrative concerns thirteen reincarnations that the U-boat captain undergoes as punishment
for his deed.

727. Stockton, Frank. The Great Stone of Sardis; A Novel. New
York: Harper, 1898.

The narrative focuses upon the adventures arising from two
inventions of the idealized scientist, Roland Clewe. The
first of these, to which most detailed attention is given,
is the successful voyage of the submarine Dipsey to the
North Pole despite the efforts of Ivan Rovinski to sabotage
it. Clewe also develops an Artesian ray capable of seeing
through the strata of the Earth. His ray penetrates
fourteen miles and then shows a shining area which implies
that the Earth is hollow. Clewe cannot accept this, nor
the idea that the core is molten. He builds an automatic
shell, eighteen feet in length and four in diameter, that
cuts a shaft through the Earth. Clewe discovers that the
core is a gigantic diamond and brings back a piece which he
calls "the Great Stone of Sardis," named after his extensive laboratories and industrial works. The love interest
is between Clewe and Mrs. Margaret Raleigh, his partner and

the majority owner of the works. They marry and are rich
enough to have anything they care to possess. Rovinski,
meanwhile, died when he attempted to go down the shaft the
shell had cut.

728. Stockton, Frank. The Great War Syndicate. New York:
Collier, 1889.

Originally serialized in Collier's Weekly: when warfare
between Britain and America begins, a group of twenty-three
men, "all great capitalists," assumes full control of the
war effort.   They insist that the armed forces, still
controlled by the government, must engage only in defensive
action.   The Syndicate then develops three weapons: a
heavily-armored vessel; a submarine-like "crab" which
seizes a ship's propeller in a crab-like claw, thereby
rendering the ship immobile; and the "Instantaneous Motor,"
detonated by electricity instead of gunpowder. They demon-
strate their power against a small Canadian fort and
against an English coastal fort. The "Motor Bomb," as it
is called, has an effect, in appearance at least, like the
A-bomb.   Peace is soon concluded, and an Anglo-American
Alliance is signed which outlaws all future war and promises to lead civilization to new heights. In many ways
the novel reads almost like an essay.

729. Stoddard, Thomas A. The Quest. New York: Cochrane, 1909.

Mary Williams sends away a mother whose child is suffering
from diphtheria, although her husband, Dr. James Williams,
has an antidote.   Apparently this must be regarded as a
major sin demanding retribution; Williams disappears and is
accused of murdering Enos Holmes. As Adams he sails to the
Orinoco River, where with the aid of an Irishman, Pat--"my
man Friday"--he encounters a number of Indian tribes,
including one blue-eyed tribe which speaks Gaelic.   His
major accomplishment is the Christianizing of one of the
more brutal tribes.   His wife finds him; he is ill and
delirious for forty days, and when he regains consciousness, she reads him the confession of Holmes' killer. He
does not know where he is or what he has done and wonders
whether he has been living for five years in a "sub-con-
scious state." He and his wife return to America, but Pat
remains with the Indians.   This is another of those books
whose chief interest is with religion and the nature of the
human mind/soul.

730. Stone, Idella Purnell. The Forbidden City. New York:
Macmillan, 1932.

Jimmie Miller and his friend Ned go into the interior of
Mexico, beyond Guadalajara, and find both a primitive--
though not lost--tribe, the Huichol, and a gold mine.

731. Stone, Idella Purnell. <u>Lost</u> <u>Princess</u> <u>of</u> <u>Yucatan</u>. New
York: Holt, 1931.

Two girls, the American Anne and the Mayan Lupe--are
classmates at an American school in Yucatan. The ranch
where they live is mortgaged to a Senor Bala, but the girls
find Mayan artifacts and give them to the young scientist,
James Butler, who sells them to Harvard and thus saves the
ranch. Lupe has the Book of Nal, and invaluable contribution to the history of the Mayan people, and Anne discovers a golden disc which proves to be a Mayan Rosetta
Stone.

732. Stoneham, C[harles] T[hurley]. <u>The</u> <u>Lion's</u> <u>Way</u>; <u>A</u> <u>Tale</u> <u>of</u>
<u>Men</u> <u>and</u> <u>Lions</u>. London: Hutchinson, 1931.

The lioness, Kali, keeps a child, Kaspa, as her cub. He
grows to be leader of the pack and becomes the lion-god of
the Bomogo tribe. When white authorities learn of him,
James Horton, Canadian newspaperman, offers a reward for
his capture, Jan Cloete traps him, and Martin Sefton
befriends him but takes him to Canada, where he is recognized as the heir of the deceased millionaire, Denison
Starke. His parents were killed in Africa. At a circus he
kills a tiger and wants to purchase two lions. Orphaned
Madeline Moore, paid companion of his great-aunt, declares
her love for him. He incurs the enmity of his cousin
Lucian and of Harold Reeves, while Sefton tells him that
he is not a fit mate for Madeline. He returns to Africa.
Lucian and Reeves plan to kill him to obtain his money,
hiring Cloete to shoot him. Kaspa avoids the killers, but
he is wounded. Madeline declares her love for him again,
and he abandons the lions for her, although the implication
is that he will build a home in Africa. Effete, money-
loving civilization is denounced throughout the book;
Madeline is charmed by the primitive strength of Kaspa and
hates the emptiness of her role as an impoverished companion.

733. [Stout, Rex]. <u>The</u> <u>President</u> <u>Vanishes</u>. New York: Farrar &
Rinehart, 1934.

Published anonymously: Europe is again at war, and in order
to avoid delivering a message to Congress which will result
in a declaration of war, President Stanley disappears. The
storyline follows the attempts of Lincoln Lee, head of the
Gray Shirts, to come to power. But Stout attacks munitions
makers (those industrialists who truly govern the nation),
labor unrest, and communism. Lee kidnaps the president,
but after suitable searching, the president is rescued.
The novel ends with a long passage asserting that the U.S.
must not become involved in another war.

734. Stringer, Arthur (pseud. of John Arbuthnot). The Woman
Who Couldn't Die. Indianapolis, In.: Bobbs-Merrill, 1929.

In a prefatory sequence, Sigurd Blödaxe kidnaps Thera,
daughter of the Jarl of Hordoland and betrothed of Haakon.
Blödaxe sails toward Greenland to escape pursuit. Re-
calling adventures which occurred some twenty-seven years
earlier in Canada, the first-person narrator, David Law of
Glasgow, explains how he obtained an old manuscript having
a map, showed them to Carlo Pareso--a scientist--and
learned that Blödaxe and Thera had fled into the Northwest
Passage, had been captured by Indians, and through the
treachery of the Indian chief, Oolah, Thera had been
entombed in a cake of ice. Law, Pareso and Knutsson head
into the Yukon. There they first find a blonde Indian
girl, Ota, whom Knutsson tries to kidnap. Then they find a
blonde tribe, whom Pareso identifies as being at least
partly Norse. The Indians tell them of a blonde goddess
asleep in a temple in the mountains. Pareso revives her,
but Law must teach her to speak English. She declares that
she is in love with him, but she is also attracted to
Knutsson. Pareso also desires her. With Ota, they attempt
to flee the valley. Pareso is killed, Knutsson and Thera
seem to perish fighting the Indians in the mountains, and
only Ola and Law flee successfully to the south, ending up
in Vancouver.

735. Sullivan, [Edward] Alan. In the Beginning. London: Hurst
& Blackett, 1927.

A letter from Withers, who has been found dead near Quidico
in South America, leads John Caxton, Burden, and other companions to the interior of that continent because Withers
reported that he had seen the body of a recently dead
Megatherium. In the Andes they find an area which has not
known climatic change since the Pleistocene; there they
find a tribe of cavemen. Burden reverts to a primitive
creature, becoming one of the tribe and loving the cave-
woman, Mam-lo. Caxton's daughter, Jean, is used to make
comparisons to the primitive beauty since Jean, too, is
attractive. The end comes when fire devastates the valley,
killing Burden and Mam-lo as well as the animals there.
Caxton, Jean, and the others escape, but the film they have
used is accidentally destroyed so that no one will believe
their reports. A final letter from Burden--delivered by
young Harrop--explains his atavism and acknowledges that he
wishes to remain in the valley.

736. Sutphen, [William Gilbert] van Tassel. The Doomsman. New
York: Harper, 1906.

By 2015 American civilization has been reduced to a primitive level. Some ninety years earlier the "Terror"--a
plague--had ravaged all the nations of the world. In

America the government decreed that all cities must be burned. Three classes of people have survived: a hybrid of the Indian and Negro races dwelling in the forest; whites living in fort-like communities surrounded by stockades; and descendants of criminals released at the time of the plague. The last have gathered in the ruined city of Doom (obviously New York). Against this background Sutphen builds a melodramatic story which has more of the flavor of the past than the future. Constans, a young Stockader, gains the enmity of Quinton Edge, a Cavalier from Doom with whom Constans' sister Issa wants to elope. After his community, Greenwood Keep, is destroyed in a raid by Doomsmen, Constans first goes to his uncle in the town of Croye and then ventures into Doom itself. He is captured but escapes with the aid of the young woman, Esmay, and a young man who simply vanishes from the plot. Three years later Constans returns to Doom, where Edge holds Esmay a prisoner, a kind of pawn in a struggle for power. As Doom burns, Constans and Esmay escape; they return to a rebuilt Greenwood Keep and marry. Issa and Edge have died together in the ruined city.

737. Swayne, Martin (pseud. of H. Maurice D. Nicoll). The Blue Germ. New York: Doran, 1918.

The first-person narrator, Richard Harden, joins his friend, Professor Sarakoff, a Russian scientist who has developed a strain of germs which prevents death. They release it into the reservoir at Manchester; the ensuing epidemic of immortality--called the "Blue Disease" because of the coloration it causes--sweeps through England. The major theme of the novel emphasizes that immortality is not desirable. It leads to warfare between the young and the old, it prevents people injured in a terrible railroad accident from dying, it reveals both the selfishness of a beautiful singer who does not want anyone else to have immortality as well as the tragedy of a young woman who cannot marry so long as her invalid father lives. In short, death is desirable, for immortality brings with it "the end of disease and the end of desire." The populace falls asleep, and when it awakens, the infection is gone.

738. Sweven, Godfrey (pseud. of John Macmillan Brown). Riallaro, The Archipelago of Exiles. New York: Putnam, 1901.

In a prefatory note the author explains how he and his companions rescue a man from the ocean near New Zealand. When he recovers, he seems to remember the period from a generation ago. He then describes a number of unknown societies which he has visited. His narrative is most important because he idealizes the country of Aleofane, with its devotion to truth, and he denounces Tirralaria, a communist society. Not only has that society had difficulty with labor, but its morals have so decayed that the institution of marriage has been destroyed.

739. Taine, John (pseud. of Eric Temple Bell).   Before the Dawn. Baltimore, Md.: Williams & Wilkins, 1934.

Because Sellar, the archaeologist, wishes to date some Mayan artifacts, Langtry, the inventor, develops what is called an "electronic analyzer," a device which transforms into visual images the light rays which have touched an object.   Together with Bronson, the president of the American Television Corporation, they view images from prehistory; the first time they are trapped within the image for a hour--the duration of time they instructed the technicians to keep the machine going.   After that they refine and control the images.   The narrative celebrates prehistory, focusing upon the figure of Belshazzar, a Tyrannosaurus rex, beginning with his birth and ending with his death.   Belshazzar is highly anthropomorphized, and Taine slips into an editorial "we" as he presents the narrative, but the tale remains one of the most vivid accounts of the age of the dinosaurs.

740. Taine, John (pseud. of Eric Temple Bell).   The Gold Tooth. New York: Dutton, 1927.

Because Jim Blye has collected fossilized dinosaur eggs in Manchuria and Cho-sen, he is named to head a new expedition which ventures into the unknown northern mountains of Korea.   There he discovers an ancient race which has metallurgical knowledge surpassing anything the modern world knows.   For a time he is attracted by a young woman whom he calls Eve and describes as "almost Caucasian, at least Aryan."   The villain is the Samurai, Okada, who penetrates the region and wants to give the secret metal (of which he makes a tooth) to the emperor of Japan.   For a time the American girl, Geraldine Shortridge (who is most critical of women's colleges and for whose parents Okada has worked in Boston) is infatuated with the Samurai. Volcanic action destroys the ancient race and their secret, but Blye has obtained a catalyst from the area which changes mercury into gold.   It promises to "revolutionize" the gold standard, and its use proves a commercial success. By the end Okada has died, Geraldine and the American Secretary of State have become engaged, and Blye has forsaken all rewards from either Japan or the U.S. in order to return to fossil hunting.   There is a strong anti-Japanese feeling through the narrative.

741. Taine, John (pseud. of Eric Temple Bell).   The Greatest Adventure. New York: Dutton, 1929.

Despite a love of biology--particularly the puzzle of the source of life and the creation of living organisms by

artificial means--Dr. Eric Lane turned to geology. He made
a fortune as a mining engineer through his discoveries of
coal. From the Antarctic Captain Anderson brings him the
preserved body of a monstrosity--a kind of winged rep-
tile--one of many specimens brought to the surface by a
subterranean eruption which also produced a flow of oil.
Anderson and his first mate, Ole Hansen, have pictures of
smooth rocks covered with pictographs. With the young
archaeologist, John Drake, and his daughter Edith (a
pilot), Lane hires Anderson to return to the Antarctic.
They find a beach covered with the corpses of monsters, and
Ole and Edith fly into a great circular valley having
15,000-foot cliffs. At the foot of those cliffs they find
living monsters as well as caverns so large that they can
fly their plane in them. After deciphering the pictographs, they deduce that an intelligent race discovered the
secret of life--created life. Imagining the monstrosities
which could result from the discovery that they could not
control, they attempted to encase the entire area in
cement, a job that took generations and cost them their own
annihilation. The arrival of Lane's party causes spores to
begin to grow; they must make an effort to destroy the
spores before they can spread.

742.   Taine, John (pseud. of Eric Temple Bell). Green Fire; The
Story of the Terrible Days in the Summer of 1990, Now Told for
the First Time. New York: Dutton, 1928.

Independent Laboratories (James Ferguson and family) and
Consolidated Power (Jevic) compete fiercely to develop
atomic energy. Ferguson would use it to aid humanity;
Jevic, to gain personal profit. When Jevic succeeds, his
efforts begin to destroy matter. Distant nebulae take on a
green glow and then are obliterated. With the aid of
MacRobert, Ferguson is able to stop the destruction of the
universe at the Andromeda galaxy. Jevic is another of
Taine's mad villains.

743.   Taine, John (pseud. of Eric Temple Bell). The Iron Star.
New York: Dutton, 1930.

Presented as a mystery, the narrative focuses upon Swain,
who for twenty years was a medical missionary in Africa.
Dr. Colton asks him if he was ever addicted to drugs. At
times Swain is animal-like; his wife who is shot resembles
an ape. He joins Colton, the father-and-son Blake team
(Big Tom and Little Tom) on an expedition into the Congo-
Uganda area. They are joined by youthful Lila Meredith.
Swain leads them to a giant meteorite that fell millions of
years ago. They also discover a giant, intelligent gray
ape (called Captain) who is an implacable enemy of Swain.
Ever more animal-like, Swain drowns as he leads them to a
series of caves near the meteorite. In one cave they find
an ancient drawing. The meteorite contains a new element,

asterium. One of its side effects acts as a drug on man
and transforms human beings into beasts. It has done so
since it fell to Earth. Swain went to Africa to study apes
in order to disprove Darwinian theory. He launched a
vendetta, with the aid of natives, to annihilate apes, thus
destroying the physical evidence of a theory which he
regards as blasphemous. The ape, Captain, was the geologist McKay, who got Swain, his daughter Edith, and
Swain's wife addicted to the drug effect. He himself
degenerated from a human to an ape. At least once the
effect of the meteor-drug is referred to as the fork in
evolution. Its users became beasts; others, men. Colton
and the Blakes destroy the meteorite, while the Captain
dies saving them. The idea of an ancient race again
occurs, and one infers that Taine meant to dramatize the
conflict between science and religion.

744. Taine, John (pseud. of Eric Temple Bell). The Purple
Sapphire. New York: Dutton, 1924.

Taine's first novel, the narrative concentrates upon the
efforts of John Ford, Rosita Rowe, and Captain Montague
Joicey to find Evelyn, daughter of General Weederburn, who
was kidnapped twelve years earlier and taken into Tibet.
The three find that she serves as a kind of goddess (a wise
woman) to descendants of an ancient race which in its
greatness controlled what seems to be a kind of atomic
power and was able to transmute metals. Much of the narrative is spent either in getting to the scene deep in Tibet
or explaining the former greatness of the ancient race. An
earthquake, volcanic action, and a blue flame which is
perhaps radioactive destroy the entire area where the race
dwells. Ford and Joicey and the two women escape back to
India and bring with them a treasure in sapphires.

745. Taine, John (pseud. of Eric Temple Bell). Quayle's
Invention. New York: Dutton, 1927.

David Quayle discovers a way to extract gold from sea
water. When he asks the banker, Cutts, whose daughter
Sheila he loves, to finance the development of his invention, Cutts calls him and his "hellish device" a threat to
civilization. He lures Quayle to the western coast of
Australia and abandons him there in the desert. He has
Quayle's blueprints and data. A flashback reveals that for
some three years--since the Lucerne Gold Conference--Cutts
has begun to fail mentally and morally. He tries to save
Russia from Bolshevism by persuading the money powers to
finance Russian agriculture for a year with gold needed to
save the French franc. Ruinous weather foils his effort.
Another venture fails when the German chemical works,
B.F.T., explode with enough force to leave a crater having
a radius of fifty miles. He has taken the brilliant but
unscrupulous young chemist, Barton, into his confidence.

When Barton begins to blackmail him, Cutts goes insane and eventually dies. Barton intends to gain profit from the secret. Meanwhile Quayle has survived and with the aid of bushmen has mined a rich gold vein. He does this under the name of King; he seeks revenge against Cutts. Reunited with Sheila, he confronts Barton and survives an attempt to kill him and Sheila. When Barton dies and he regains his blueprints, he tells Sheila that they can control and change the world. She persuades him that he should forget the secret; they go off together. One feels that once again Taine has unnecessarily complicated the plot, perhaps in order to voice political and social opinions.

746.   Tarde, [Jean] Gabriel de.   Underground Man.   Trans. from the French by Cloudesley Brereton.   London: Duckworth, 1905.

H. G. Wells wrote a laudatory preface, emphasizing the "satisfaction" which the supposed future historian shows toward the changes which have taken place in society. Although the narrative opens with a description of an Asiatic-American-European confederacy--a utopian state-- which one hundred and fifty years of war had established, by the late twenty-fifth century the death of the sun brings about a catastrophe resulting in drought, famine, and new glacial ages. A new leader, Militades, suggests that man survive by burrowing deep into the Earth. In doing so, man alone endures, for he takes with him neither animal nor plant. Chemistry and psychology prove to be the sciences which shape the new humanity, whose number is necessarily limited to fifty million. Love dominates mankind's thought and society. With a minimum of utilitarian work and a maximum of aesthetic expression, a society powered by marvelous machines allows man to reach undreamed of heights.

747.   Taylor, C. Bryson.   In the Dwellings of the Wilderness. New York: Henry Holt, 1904.

Archaeologists open the bewitched tomb of an Egyptian princess. She returns to life, luring them into the wilderness, where one goes mad and another blind.

748.   Taylor, William Alexander.   Intermere.   Columbus, Oh.: XX Century, 1901.

When the ship Mistletoe sinks near the fortieth parallel south, the first-person narrator, Giles Henry Anderton, survives, awakening in the country of Intermere. Xamas, the First Citizen, is his initial host. Anderton describes the country as existing around an inland sea some four hundred by two hundred miles in size so that its twelve hundred mile shoreline is "studded" with farms, towns, villages, and both private homes and public buildings. Once he equates it with Atlantis, and once he is told that

he is "within the mundande sphere," but the geography
remains deliberately vague. Nor is the society presented
representationally in any detail. By "evolutionary processes" its people have unlocked most of the secrets of the
universe and are far in advance of the outside world. The
closest that Anderton comes to learning the secret of
Intermere occurs when another host, Remo, speaks of control
of a direct current of electricity. All people are equal
and individual; this is no socialist state. Its three
modes of transportation are the Medocar (land), Aerocar,
and Merocar (boat). At the end while unconscious, Anderton
is returned to the known world and picked up by a ship and
taken to Singapore. Incidental mention is made of the
Boxer Rebellion, though not by name (Albert Marshall, a
sergeant of Marines, his foster brother is killed during
that engagement). Again, specific warning is made that the
Chinese and associated peoples are dangerous.

749. Thomas, Chauncey. The Crystal Button; or, Adventures of
Paul Prognosis in the Forty-Ninth Century. Boston: Houghton
Mifflin, 1891.

An accident impairs Paul Prognosis mentally for some ten
years; on Christmas Eve 1872 he bids good night to his wife
and awakens in the year 4872 in the city of Tone. Professor Prosper acts as his host and describes the utopian
society. Electricity and compressed air provide the forms
of power, while the metal is aluminum. The predominant
structure of the period is the pyramid. There is a World
Council of Nations, and all of the conventional reforms
have been effected. In the twentieth century appeared the
prophet John Coster, who advocated a society and morality
based upon truth. Prognosis learns that technocracy
operating at the municipal level is the most efficient form
of government. The passage of the comet Veda (which caused
the Noachian deluge and also appeared the year before
Coster) provides the framework for the description of the
society. Prognosis wakens on Christmas Day to find that
his new electrical engine has been put to work and that his
idea of the city of Tone, with its pyramids, has been
implemented. The narrative uses the idea of brain damage
as a supplement to the usual dream framework. Prognosis
has regained his mental alertness. A prefatory note
suggests the novel is intended to complement Bellamy's
Looking Backward.

750. Tooker, Richard. The Dawn Boy. Philadephia: Penn Publishing, 1932.

Intended for a juvenile audience, the narrative follows the
adventures of No-Ma-Ka-Ta. Called the limping bear because
of a crippled foot, he overcomes that handicap to unite his
Cro-Magnon people. Much of the tale concerns his invention
of the bow and arrow and the catapault so that he can

conquer the great mammoths. Traveling westward alone, he discovers not only the graveyard of the mammoths but a pleasant tropical land inhabited by blacks. He returns to his people and leads them from a drought-stricken land across a desert and mountains to the "promised land" which he had found. Before they can settle, the Cro-Magnons must fight the blacks (called Grimaldi men) in a seven-day battle. From the migration and the battle, they learn to live as a tribe. In a cave they paint many creatures, but they live in a village. At the end No-Ma marries Ya-Ya, one of the few women to survive the harrowing migration, and takes her to his tree house. This tale is unique in emphasizing warfare with the blacks and in stressing that Cro-Magnon men were the ancestors of modern humanity.

751. Tooker, Richard. <u>The Day of the Brown Horde</u>. New York: Payson & Clarke, 1929.

In the valley which forms the present northern end of the Gulf of California, the tyrannical Ag-Tar, ruler of a tribe of prehistoric cave people, decrees that the infant Kaa, the Unnamed, must die because he is supposedly a weakling. Ag-Tar kills Ka-Mat, Kaa's father, while his mother, O-Wat, flees with the infant into the mountains. Youthful Kaa learns to swim, and he and his mother worship the bison. Kaa wears the bison horns. Ag-Tar kills O-Wat, and Kaa is alone. Eventually he literally pursues the maiden, Chee, not knowing she is the daughter of Ag-Tar's youngest wife. He mates with her. Ag-Tar has established a religion worshipping the plesiosaurs. Kaa kills three of the plesiosaurs with ten spears, while Chee perhaps inadvertently kills Ag-Tar. Kaa becomes chief. But then volcanic action and earthquakes precipitate a cataclysm which causes the sea to fill the valley. Kaa is saved by a bull bison, but Chee dies. The final scene, however, shows Kaa as the patriarch of a tribe that has prospered. The implication suggests that these are ancestors of the American Indian.

752. Tooker, Richard. <u>Inland Deep</u>. Philadelphia: Penn Publishing, 1936.

Robert Langtree, the first-person narrator, joins Roger Anson in an expedition to Commanche Cave in western Colorado. Willa Anson accompanies them. They find a footprint as well as a skeleton that can be no more than 500 years old in the cave; then they hear a warbling and a laughing. Using dynamite to chase the creature away, they open an inner cavern which contains "an inland sea." There they sight a sauranodon, but much of the narrative centers on their contact with the so-called frog men, described as "a mongrel species of anthropoids." At one point they must rescue Willa from the frog men who accidentally cause a flow of lava into the body of water. The three of them escape along a subterranean river and end up in one of the gorges of the Grand Canyon. One of the aims of the story is to prove that prehistoric man did live in America.

753. Tracy, Louis. The Final War; A Story of the Great Betrayal. New York: Putnam, 1896.

In one of the most extravagant novels to portray a future war, Germany and France attack Great Britain in May 1898. Russia stands aside when promised India. The British fleet wins an initial victory off Worthing. Then when the British blockade the Straits of Gibraltar and destroy the Suez Canal, the enemy fleets are helpless in the Mediterranean. Britain lands armies at Le Havre and Stralsund near the Kiel Canal; they are victorious. Initially the U.S. claims Canada (to Canadian indignation), but Rockefeller declares that U.S. business interests lie with Britain. When Russia (in exchange for the Near East and Turkey) declares war and sends a fleet into the Irish Sea, the American admiral, Mahan, defeats the Russians off Cardiff even before the U.S. declares war. Meanwhile the Indian army invades Asiatic Russia. A "brave champion of Russian freedom," Pochowski, leads a rebellion against the Tsar. U.S. and British armies take Paris after a glorious campaign, while the Indian army wins at Kharkof even as the rebels blow up the Tsar's family in the chapel of St. George in the Kremlin. The Kaiser comes to realize that he should be allied with his Anglo-Saxon colleagues and emerges a sympathetic portrait. Cavalry and artillery dominate the military day; machine guns are mentioned once in passing. Romantic interest, culminating in a double wedding, are provided by Captain Edward Harington and Lady Irene Vyne and Ethel Harington and Frank Rodney. Both men behave bravely and rise in command. The Anglo-Saxon Alliance ensures the future peace of the world.

754. Train, Arthur [Chesney] and Robert Williams Wood. The Man Who Rocked the Earth. Garden City, N.Y.: Doubleday, Page, 1915.

Originally serialized in The Saturday Evening Post in the autumn of 1914: by 1 July 1916 the stalemated European war has involved all nations but the United States of North and South America. An unknown scientist, calling himself PAX, demands that hostilities cease; if they do not, he will slow the rotation of the Earth. His ultimatum ignored, he causes a series of quakes which slow the Earth by five minutes. A second series of quakes brings about the International Assembly of Scientists. PAX then cuts through the Atlas Mountains, diverting the waters of the Mediterranean into the Sahara. But his ship, called the Flying Ring, is seen; his weapon is the Lavendar Ray. When a German general ignores the proposed armistice by bombarding Paris with the Relay Gun (a cannon able to fire a series of shells a hundred kilometres), PAX destroys his headquarters at the village of Champaubert. The remainder

of the novel becomes a race between a German Expeditionary
Force and the American scientist, Bennie Hooker, to reach
PAX in Labrador. The German force is annihilated; Hooker
finds the Flying Ring, but PAX, who has gone mad and
threatened to shift the Earth's axis so that Europe will be
the new Arctic, kills himself during a further experiment.
The nations of Europe have combined into the United States
of Europe, destroyed their armaments, and established a
capital at The Hague, with an International Police Force to
enforce its authority. The ending announces that Hooker
has developed a Space-Navigating Car, with which he plans
to explore the Solar System. PAX had, of course, conquered
atomic power.

755. Train, Arthur [Chesney] and Robert W[illiams] Wood. The
Moon Maker. Hamburg, N.Y.: Krueger, 1958.

Not in either edition of Bleiler; copyright by Kenneth J.
Kreuger (1958): no information about the history of the
slight story (84 pp.) is given. This narrative continues
the adventures of Bennie Hooker after he returns the Flying
Ring to Washington. When the asteroid Medusa threatens to
collide with the Earth, Bennie and his companions, among
them Miss Rhoda Gibbs, a fellow scientist, fly the Ring and
bombard the asteroid. They return to Earth; the remnant of
Medusa becomes a second moon; and Bennie and Rhoda are
married.

756. Turner, George Kibbe. Red Friday. Boston: Little, Brown,
1919.

The first-person narrator is an American Christian Socialist, and much of the narrative becomes a kind of
dialogue between him and Plangonev, a Russian Marxist.
Plangonev tries to bring about a revolution, partly through
controlling Charlotte Black and thus her father, a wealthy
banker, who dies. He refers to women as the "most attractive form of property." Despite the difficulties that
America has gotten herself into because of the differences
between capital and labor, the narrator finally declares
himself an individualist and denies Marxian law, which has
been equated with scientific law and Evolution.

757. Twain, Mark (pseud. of Samuel Langhorne Clemens). A
Connecticut Yankee in King Arthur's Court. New York: Webster,
1889.

In Warwick Castle Twain obtains the first-person manuscript
of Hank Morgan, master mechanic and superintendent of the
Colt Arms factory in Hartford. Knocked unconscious, Morgan
awakens in Arthur's Camelot, where he becomes the "Boss."
Despite this "transmigration of souls," some critics have
called this the first time travel story. The complexity of

themes as chivalric Britain and the technological nineteenth century confront one another, leading to the massacre at the Battle of the Sand Belt, need not be elab-
orated here.   Morgan himself dies, mumbling of dreams.
Whatever else, this novel becomes a bitter attack upon the
materialism of the nineteenth century.

758. [Tweed, Thomas Frederic]. Gabriel Over the White House; A
Novel of the Presidency. New York: Farrar & Strauss, 1933.

Hartley Beekman, secretary to President Judson C. Hammond,
is the first-person narrator. After an auto wreck Hammond
is much changed in personality and political view.   He
sides with the unemployed against his conservative cabinet
and a corrupt Congress.   Dismissing his Cabinet and ad-
journing Congress, he rules as a benevolent dictator,
controlling public opinion through the use of government-
controlled television.   When the government manufactures
all liquor, gangsters start terrorist activities.   Hammond
federalizes all police forces into the Federal Mobile
Police (they use motocycles).   After anti-gun laws, he
establishes a concentration camp on Ellis Island, where
nine out of ten criminals using guns are executed.   War is
essentially brought to an end after the Americans bomb the
Japanese fleet, proving that air power makes fleets anti-
quated, and after new detection devices make submarines
ineffective.   His final action is to establish a Council of
Nations.   Then the last criminal ("Wolf" Miller) tries to
assassinate him.   Hammond falls, striking his head.   He
becomes the man he was three years earlier, and when he
learns what he has done, he plans to repudiate his actions
on national TV just prior to an election which he has
called for, an election in which the opposition is strong
because of the new-found prosperity.   His Cabinet decides
to take action against him, but he dies of a heart attack.
His niece, Pendie Malloy, suggests that during the three
years when he was apparently near insanity because of a
brain injury in the original auto wreck, he may have been a
divine agency to save the U.S. in a time of peril.

759. Van Zile, Edward [Sims].   A Magnetic Man, and Other
Stories. New York: Lowell, 1890.

"A Magnetic Man" concerns itself with the career of Marcus
Rodney, inventor and electrician, who feels that other
people do not like him--find him unattractive--because of
the flow of electric currents.   He refers a number of times
to the work of Ampère.   He learns to control electrical
currents, but although he wishes to marry Margaret Durand,
who initially refuses him, he will not use science to make
her fall in love with him.   She must love him naturally,
and at the end she asks that he renew his proposal of
marriage because now she will agree.   "Chemical Clair-
voyance" concerns Maurice Danton, who can see into the

future. The idea that the future leaves impressions on
objects that can be photographed is toyed with. The
remainder of the stories are not concerned with fantasy or
science, only with love.

760. Vaux, Patrick. The Shock of Battle. New York: Putnam,
1906.

Except for locating much of the early action in the Caribbean off the island of St. Thomas, this is essentially a
conventional account of the British defeat of Germany. The
great sea battle, comparable to the Nile or Trafalgar, is
fought near Wilhelmshaven and is won basically by the
British torpedo fleet.

761. Verne, Jules. An Antarctic Mystery. Trans. from the
French by Mrs. Cashel Hoey. Philadelphia: Lippincott, 1899.

Surely the weakest of Verne's efforts, the narrative
concerns the journey of Mr. Joerling, a man of science,
from the Kerguelen Islands to the South Pole. This is
intended as a sequel or completion of Poe's Arthur Gordon
Pym, but it becomes a detailed account of the actual
voyage, shipwreck, and mutiny. Joerling sails aboard the
Halbrane, commanded by Len Guy, brother of William Guy,
master of the Jane of Poe's tale. One of the sailors
(Hunt) proves to be Dirk Peters. The sailor Patterson
cannibalized after the wreck of the Grampus was in reality
Ned Holt, brother of the sailing master of the Halbrane.
They find Pym's frozen body at the foot of a giant magnetic
lodestone seemingly shaped like the sphinx; indeed, this
phenomenon gives the French edition its title, Le Sphinx
des Glaces. Len Guy finds his brother, and the survivors
are picked up in the Pacific by the Tasman and returned to
safety. Significantly, no mention is made of Symmes'
theory in Verne's narrative. All of Poe's tone of mystery,
as well as the natives of the Island of Tsalal, are excised
from the narrative. (Pym's dog Tiger appears on the island
and is mad so that he drives most of the natives from it;
the island itself is made barren by an earthquake.)

762. Verne, Jules. Around the World in Eighty Days. London:
Sampson, Low, 1874.

Serialized in Le Temps and then published in Paris by
Hetzel (1873); published as A Tour of the World in Eighty
Days in Boston by Osgood (1873): this was the most popular
of Verne's novels. The journey of Phileas Fogg and his
servant, Passepartout--traveling eastward in order to gain
a day--draws heavily on several journals as well as the
promotional literature of Thomas Cook's agency, which was
planning an around-the-world journey for tourists. The
incidents in India, where Fogg encounters Aouda, widow of
the rajah of Bundlekund, and in the Western United States

are largely inaccurate and follow materials conventional to other fiction. Perhaps the best example of this indebtedness occurs in the long aside devoted to the Mormons, a topic used by both FitzJames O'Brien and Mark Twain.

763. Verne, Jules. The Begum's Fortune. London: Sampson, Low, 1879.

Originally published in Paris by Hetzel (1879): undoubtedly inspired by Verne's hatred of Germany as a result of the Franco-Prussian War, this narrative remains one of Verne's most provocative stories. Dr. Sarrasin, a scientist devoted to the study of hygiene, inherits a fortune from an Indian rajah; Professor Schultz, a scientist who wishes to conquer the world for Germany, contests the will. They split twenty million pounds. In the wilderness of Oregon, Sarrasin builds Frankville, a utopian city. Some thirty miles away Schultz founds Stahlstadt, a symbol of authoritarianism and militarism. Through the use of heavy artillery, a gun weighing three hundred tons, Schultz seeks to destroy Frankville. One kind of shell will release carbonic acid gas which will freeze anything within a radius of some thirty yards. Schultz is killed in an accident so that Frankville survives, while Stahlstadt breaks up. The image of Stahlstadt anticipates later totalitarian fortress-cities.

764. Verne, Jules. Five Weeks in a Balloon; or, Journeys and Discoveries in Africa. New York: D. Appleton, 1869.

Originally published in Paris by Hetzel (1863): the first of Verne's voyages extraordinaires, this tale established the conventions which he employed throughout his fiction. Dr. Ferguson is accompanied by his servant and young Dick Kennedy as he flies the Victoria across Africa. Captures and escapes dominate the storyline; most notable is the abundance of factual material about the geography of Africa. Verne's only innovation is a device to heat the hydrogen in order to navigate the balloon. Perhaps the most interesting detail of the book involves Ferguson's speculation that when the continent of Europe is exhausted, its people will make Africa their future home.

765. Verne, Jules. From the Earth to the Moon, Passage Direct in 97 Hours and 20 Minutes. Newark, N.J.: Newark, 1869.

Originally published in Paris by Hetzel (1869): members of the Baltimore Gun Club--formed during the Civil War and devoted primarily to ballistics--grow restless during peacetime. When their president, Impey Barbicane, suggests that they launch a projectile to the moon, they undertake the project enthusiastically, led by J. T. Maston. America contributes $4,000,000; the nations of Europe, as well as Mexico, more than $1,400,000; Great Britain, not a penny.

Verne loads the narrative with information about the formation of the moon, various aspects of artillery, and data about such matters as escape velocity (12,000 yards per second). They build an observatory in the Rockies to observe the shot. They select Stone Hill, near Tampa, Florida, in which to dig a shaft nine-hundred feet deep and lined with iron; named the Columbiad, it will serve as the cannon. For a moment Barbicane and Captain Nicholl (a rival scientist) threaten to duel one another because of differing views. Together with the Frenchman, Michel Ardan, they make up the crew of the cylinder. The explosion on December 1 so disturbs the natural order of things that a cloud cover prevents sighting the projectile until December 11. Although some satire is undoubtedly intended, Verne hails the Yankees as the world's finest mechanics and engineers.

766. Verne, Jules. _A Journey to the Centre of the Earth_. London: Griffith & Farran, 1871.

Originally published in Paris by Hetzel (1864): Verne makes the novel a virtual textbook of geology and biology as he begins the story with one of the established conventions. Discovering the sixteenth century manuscript of the Icelandic alchemist, Arne Saknussemm, Professor Hardwigg and his nephew, Harry descend into the Earth through the volcano Sneffels. One can debate whether or not Verne knew Symmes' theory. The professor and his nephew discover an underground sea, glimpse a giant man-like being herding mammoths, and see a plesiosaurus. It is the first novel to give attention to the theory of evolution. (In the French edition the protagonist's name is Lidenbrock and his nephew, Axel.)

767. Verne, Jules. _The Mysterious Island_. London: Sampson, Low, 1875.

Originally published in Paris by Hetzel (1874-1875): five Union prisoners--including Cyrus Harding (engineer) and Gideon Spillet (newspaperman) as well a sailor, Harding's black servant, and a boy--escape from Richmond by means of a balloon. Storms and winds drive them into the Pacific, where they crash land near an island. This is Verne's Robinsonade, for through Harding, the men utilize the resources of the island to create many nineteenth century inventions; in this sense the novel is a tribute to nineteenth century progress. But a number of unexplained happenings--all of which help them--lead to the discovery of Captain Nemo aboard the _Nautilus_ in a cavern. As he dies, he tells his story, thus clearing up all of the mysteries involving his life. Educated extensively in Europe, he was Prince Dakkar of Bundlekund. He became involved in the Sepoy Mutiny of 1857, and after defeat, with a price on his head and his family destroyed, he retreated to this island, where he designed and built the Nautilus. When he dies, the Americans place him aboard the submarine and sink it. He leaves them a treasure of diamonds and pearls, and they are rescued just before a volcano destroys Lincoln Island.

768. Verne, Jules. Round the Moon; A Sequel to From the Earth to the Moon. London: Sampson, Low, 1873.

Originally published in Paris by Hetzel (1870): Barbicane, Nicholls, and Ardan are knocked unconscious during the launch. Their cylinder misses a small second moon of Earth (an invention of Verne's), which causes their craft to be slightly deflected. Instead of striking the moon, it circles it. So close is the vehicle to the lunar surface that the bulk of the moon prevents them from seeing any details of the dark side of the moon. Momentarily they do see what they infer is a volcano, and a meteor burns close to their ship. Heading back to Earth and glowing with heat, the cylinder lands in the Pacific close to the Mexican coast. J. T. Maston is among those who join the crew of the Susquehanna as it searches the sea floor for the wreck. After searching in vain for more than two days, the ship heads for San Francisco and finds the cylinder afloat, flying the American flag. The voyagers and the Gun Club are received as heroes.

769. Verne, Jules. Twenty Thousand Leagues Under the Sea. London: Sampson, Low, 1872.

Originally published in Paris by Hetzel (1870): by the time Verne wrote this novel, more than twenty successful submarines had been tested. His only real innovation is to have the Nautilus powered entirely by electricity. When ships around the world are mysteriously attacked, Professor Arronax, his assistant Conseil, and the Canadian whaler-- Ned Land--undertake investigation. They attack the supposed sea monster only to find that it is Captain Nemo's submarine. For seven months they cruise amid the wonders of the unknown undersea world. Verne draws upon all the conventional plot devices of the period; he allows them to view the ruins of Atlantis, fight a giant octopus, and find open water at the South Pole. At the end Arronax, Conseil, and Ned Land escape from the Nautilus as it is sucked down in the maëlstrom. The mysterious Captain Nemo, who hates the imperial navies and lives off the treasures which he finds at the bottom of the sea, remains Verne's most memorable character.

770. Verrill, A[lpheus] Hyatt. The Boy Adventurers in the Land of El Dorado. New York: Putnam, 1923.

Harry and Fred accompany Dr. Woodward to Georgetown, British Guiana, and go up the Essequibo River. Once again

Woodward seeks the ancient tribe which worships the idol,
Billikins. Most of the narrative is simply a jungle
adventure, but at the end they first find a cavern filled
with skulls of an ancient race as well as some gold; then
they discover ruins of a city near which stands a golden
statue of Billikins. Around it they find some skulls of
white men. Entering the ruins, they find themselves
confronting two naked black savages who resemble the
creature the boys have seen in the forest. After 258
pages, the narrative breaks off abruptly as they face the
savages. There is much talk of Sir Walter Raleigh, El
Dorado (as a man who has been coated (gilded) with gold),
and Manoa as the city of a race which may antedate the
prehistoric American civilizations. But nothing is developed from these suggestions. The novel opens with
references to their having been to Panama, where they found
a lost city peopled by savage Kuna Indians. This title is
not listed in Reginald or Bleiler.

771. Verrill, A[lpheus] Hyatt. The Boy Adventurers in the Land
of the Monkey Men. New York: Putnam, 1923.

With their uncle, Dr. Woodward, Harry and Fred venture into
British Guiana in South America. They have a small black
idol which leads them to quest for "that radium stuff," but
the narrative takes them through sundry adventures, mostly
captures and escapes, among various Indians. At one point
they wire a chief's throne so that he receives a shock.
The superlative is used to describe everything, including
the strange valley they encounter in which the grass and
foliage are scarlet, though no explanation is given. One
tribe is described as giant monkey men.

772. Verrill, A[lpheus] Hyatt. The Boy Adventurers in the
Unknown Land. New York: Putnam, 1924.

Once again Harry Woodward, his cousin Fred, and Dr. Woodward go into the jungles of British Guiana near the border
of Brazil. They still have the idol--Billikins--while
searching for radioactive material, but all they find is
the ruins of a prehistoric city. This title is not listed
in Bleiler or Reginald.

773. Verrill, A[lpheus] Hyatt. The Golden City; A Tale of
Adventure in Unknown Guiana. New York: Duffield, 1916.

This is Verrill's most effective treatment of the lost race
motif. Exploring in the back country of the Essequibo
River near Mount Roraima, the teen-aged protagonist, Frank,
and an official of the government of Guiana find the lost
city of Manoa (El Dorado) in an isolated valley on the
shores of a circular lake. Since its ruins extend out into
the lake, they conclude that it was destroyed by a meteor.
They are kidnapped and taken far into the jungle by the

guardians of the city in order to keep the city untouched. They also solve the mystery of the so-called "Dido," a legendary creature. Black-skinned and red-maned, with feet and hands that terminate in talon-like claws, the Dido is judged to be the original inhabitant of the continent, perhaps the western hemisphere, exterminated by the Indians. This provides one of the few instances suggesting a separate line of evolution which has vanished.

774. Verrill, A[lpheus] Hyatt. The Radio Detectives under the Sea. New York: D. Appleton, 1922.

Another juvenile series, this features Tom Pauling and Frank Putney, who work with Tom's father. They have a diving suit which needs no hose or lifeline, for which oxygen is produced by chemicals. At one point Mr. Pauling asserts that radio and the theory of electrons upset "all our old-fashioned" ideas. The storyline features the arch-criminal "Smernoff" as well as a submarine, a fight with a giant octopus, and capture by African "devil dancers." This title is not listed in Bleiler or Reginald, but deserves notice because it represents another juvenile series in which there is much talk about science.

775. Villiers de L'Isle-Adam, Jean. The Eve of the Future Eden. Trans. from the French by Marilyn Gaddis Rose. Lawrence, Ks.: Coronado, 1981.

Apparently composed between 1880-1886, this narrative builds primarily upon a dialogue at Menlo Park between Thomas Alva Edison, the "electrician," and his friend and benefactor, Lord Celian Ewald. Ewald would like to be in love with Alicia Clary, a stylish and witty young woman who wants a career in the theatre, but he is put off by some of her mannerisms. Through the use of photosculpture, Edison adapts one of his inventions, an android, Hadaly, so that she is a duplicate of Alicia. She is so perfect that Ewald does not perceive that she is the imitation. Against a background that includes an element of the occult to which Edison himself responds--there is his assistant Sowana, who seems a creature of the afterlife--the narrative is perhaps most important for the detail given to an explanation of the creation of Hadaly/Alicia. Edison reads of a shipwreck in which Hadaly/Alicia is destroyed by fire and receives a letter from Ewald suggesting suicide. Alicia, incidentally, was programmed for only sixty hours.

776. Vinton, Arthur Dudley. Looking Further Backward, Being a Series of Lectures Delivered to the Freshman Class at Shawmut College by Professor Won Lung Li (Successor to Prof. Julian West). Albany, N.Y.: Albany, 1890.

Won Lung Li is both a mandarin and the historian in charge of the northeastern division of the Chinese Province of

North America. Although he regards Bellamy's Looking
Backward as "one of the wonders of the age," he addresses
himself to "the American Barbarians." He notes that on 6
January 2012 a riot broke out in Marseilles after the
government ordered the curtailment of the manufacture of
toys; France had become dependent on China and annually
paid a tribute. On 29 September 2020 China declared war on
the U.S. One of the points that Won Lung Li makes is that
under Nationalism no attention was paid to American defenses. He cites Julian West's diary, but most of his
attention is given to the manner in which the Chinese navy
defeats the Americans. Boston is cut off, and West's son
is a victim of influenza. Washington falls without a shot,
Philadelphia surrenders, and New York is reduced to ruins
because she resists. The conquerors declare the Nationa-
list credit cards to be worthless, for "wealth without
production to support it is an element of weakness." The
Chinese begin to move American citizens and replace them
with Chinese; otherwise they could not successfully implant
the Chinese culture and system of government on a population of two hundred million. Moreover, in the new set up,
women no longer compete with men but become the "hand-
maidens of male humanity."

777. Vivian, E[velyn] Charles.   Fields of Sleep.   London:
Hutchinson, 1923.

Six years earliier after the suicide of his father, Clement
Delarey journeyed to Sapelung in Batavia to work with his
cousin Pierre. He has since disappeared, but he is an heir
to six million francs left him by an uncle, Armand Delarey.
Victor Marshall agrees to search for Clement. Also to save
Stephanie Delarey from her foster mother, he marries the
girl and by contract assures himself of half a million
francs. He travels to Sapelung and then into the interior,
where he becomes the friend of Erasmus Whauple. At Mah-Eng
he finds Tari-Hi and his daughter, Aia, who loves Marshall;
they are descendants of Babylonian sailors who came here to
mine gold. In a valley close by Clement is one of several
thousand men and women who have become addicted to a drug
which permeates the atmosphere of the valley. One of its
effects is that the power of speech is lost. No vivid
picture of the culture is presented. Eventually as a
result of a rock fall the valley is flooded, and all of the
people in it, including Clement, are drowned. Marshall
must also fight off various attempts by the villainous
Pierre to prevent his finding Clement. After the valley is
flooded, he and Whauple return to England, with but little
gold. Marshall wants Stephanie to be his wife, although he
has been haunted by the beauty of Aia.

778. Vivian, E[velyn] Charles. A King There Was--. London: Hodder & Stoughton, 1926.

In a "Prelude" Felipe Gutierrez, the Torero, explains that he will write down two stories which have been told in the oral tradition and come down to the present from a race that is older than any of the great tribes--Incas, Caras, or Quitus. What follows is a pseudo-historical novel of prehistoric South America. It focuses upon the warrior, Leonti of Tarasin, and King Ronal, although part of it is supposedly told by Cloa, a priest. It ends with the destruction of the kingdom when it is overrun by hairy men; a great earthquake and volcano also occur. One infers that the destruction of the city of Entiros refers to an ancient city drowned in the waters of Lake Titicaca. A love story between Ronal and the Lady Alua is also included. Apparently this is the destruction of the western empire of Atlantis. But the narrative does not realize its potential because Vivian is more poetic than representational.

779. Vivian, E[velyn] Charles. People of the Darkness. London: Hutchinson, 1924.

After Stephanie dies in childbirth, Victor Marshall and Erasmus Whauple return to Mah-Eng to find Tari-Hi and Aia, who disappeared when the valley was flooded. They enter a series of great caverns and find there a sightless people. When they are guided to Pas-Eng, where they find Tari-Hi and Aia, Tari-Hi explains to them that the last king of a western continent [Atlantis] tore the eyes from the ancestors of these people and forced them into the caverns to mine for gold. Never since have the people known light. The vast lake breaks through the walls of the mine and floods the caverns. Tari-Hi remains to die in the area, but Aia returns to civilization with Marshall. Once again one feels that the potential of the narrative has not been realized. After Marshall and Whauple emerge from the caverns into Pas-Eng, the chief concern of the narrative is with the love of Marshall and Aia.

780. Vorse, Albert White. Laughter of the Sphinx. New York: Drexel Biddle, 1900.

The volume is made up of a number of stories/sketches published in newpapers and magazines during the 1890s. Concerned with the two expeditions led by Johann T. Bundergup to explore Greenland, the narrative provides a parody of polar exploration, both real and fictional. The North Pole is called "The Sphinx of the North." The patron who finances Bundergup is a retired brewer who would like to have geographical places named for him. Most of the scientific men come from a German background, although the principal hunter comes from an old New York family. Both expeditions fail; the last story ends with a group of dead Eskimos.

781. Walker, J[ohn] Bernard. *America Fallen! The Sequel to the European War*. New York: Dodd, Mead, 1915.

More essay than novel, the narrative warns against unpreparedness. Germany defeats and occupies the U.S.

782. Wallace, King. *The Next War*. Washington, D.C.: Martyn, 1892.

This novel is unique during the period in that it focuses upon a secret society made up of all persons in America having any Negro blood who plot against the white race. Taking positions in the white households of the country, they intend to poison all of their employers' families on a given date. The only inclusion of scientific material occurs when they attempt to procure from the scientist-protagonist the formula for a poison he has developed to exterminate English sparrows. Under torture augmented by the pleadings of his sweetheart, he gives them a dilute form of the poison. When the plot fails, the blacks, like lemmings, disappear into Southern swamps and are seen no more.

783. Walsh, J[ames] M[organ]. *Vandals of the Void*. London: Hamilton, 1931.

One of the first novels of interplanetary warfare, this is the story of the first-person narrator, Jack Sanders, Captain of the Inter-Planetary Guard. He flies for Mars aboard the liner *Cosmos*, but finds a drifting ship which is cold and whose crew is asleep. He receives warning that the ships of the three planets--Earth, Mars, and Venus--are being subjected to attack. Homo Kell is the villain, a spy for the forces of Mercury, who are attempting to take control of the system. Although the *Cosmos* is forced down on Venus, the Mercurians are annihilated by a combined fleet. Against this space-opera background, more attention is actually given the love story of Sanders and the Martian woman, Jansaa Dirka. They are married ("mated") before the principal battle begins. Interesting as an example of the few space operas which saw book publication during the period: all of the paraphernalia, from mysterious ray guns to atomic energy, is present.

784. Ward, Herbert D[ickinson]. *A Republic Without a President, and Other Stories*. New York: Tait, 1891.

In the title story the president and his wife are kidnapped and held for ransom by Colonel Oddminton, who owns a small island off South Carolina. He is the dupe of anarchists, and the story is a warning that America must not be defenseless. The colonel develops an electric yacht. In "The Lost City" a cataclysm destroys the city of Russell, the "greatest producer of electro-motor power" in the U.S., when uncontrollable electric power erupts. The city is compared to a battery which has been abused. The story is reported for newspapers by Ms. Insula Magnet. In "A Terrible Evening" Dr. Alaric Randolph experiments upon Harland Slack, an alcoholic, and cures him by "hypnotic therapeutics." Slack believes that he has killed a young woman who does not exist. In the final story, "Colonel Odminton" [sic] the villain of the title story returns the ransom to the president. He dies a man without a country in the Everglades. His son is a "middy" aboard a torpedo boat during a war between the U.S. and Patagonia, a war brought on by jingoism.

785. Warner, William Henry. The Bridge of Time. New York: Scott & Seltzer, 1919.

In ancient Thebes Prince Rames, a pupil of the high priest of Amen-Ra, drinks a potion which allows him to enter another time period in order to study it for a year. But he must not surrender to any woman. In Venice in February 1914 he becomes acquainted with Iris Waverly of New York, who resembles his beloved Teta. Although Iris loves him, he returns to Thebes only to find that invaders have destroyed the power of Egypt. He declares that he will somehow return to Iris/Teta. He becomes Captain Richard Lackland of the French Foreign Legion. Wounded, he is nursed during World War I by Iris. Their love conquers time. It is noteworthy really only because of the reverse incarnation/time travel.

786. Warren, B[enjamin] C[lark]. Arsareth; A Tale of the Luray Caverns. New York: Lovell, 1893.

A study of the occult and Theosophy serves as a framework for a journey by one of the lost tribes, thus explaining the origin of the American Indians. John Elton finds a treasure in a copper box in the caverns and seals their entrance. The storyline also concerns his love for Alice Davis, daughter of a student of the occult. The narrative ends with their marriage. The manuscript reporting the journey is that of the first-person narrator, "Obal, of the tribe of Ephraim, of the children of the Captivity"; he gives Virginia the name Asareth.

787. Waterloo, Stanley. Armageddon; A Tale of Love, War, and Invention. Chicago: Rand, McNally, 1898.

A European coalition attacks the United States after its engineers complete a Nicaraguan Canal. Victory comes only when an American scientist develops a dirigible-type bomber. Then an Anglo-American Alliance is signed and the victors proclaim that the Anglo-Saxon race is destined to govern the world. Centuries may pass before the inferior peoples of the world are capable of conducting their own affairs. An American scientist asserts that the controlling powers must have "such power of destruction" that no nation will challenge them. He promises that American science will continue to seek such a weapon. Aluminum and electricity are again enshrined.

788. Waterloo, Stanley. The Seekers. Chicago: Stone, 1900.

The narrative serves as a vehement attack on both patent medicines and faith healers, including Christian Science. The protagonist, Yule, declares that the miracles of the New Testament have lost their power over the modern mind. He also suggests that the only evil is not to know truth. In the storyline Yule marries Kate Vaughn, and they find her sister, Narcissa, who has run off to the faith farm of the corrupt Dr. Zadski. Notable only because Waterloo wrote it.

789. Waterloo, Stanley. A Son of the Ages; The Reincarnations and Adventures of Scar, the Link; A Story of Man from the Beginning. Garden City, N.Y.: Doubleday, Page, 1914.

By combining the ideas of reincarnation and racial memory, Waterloo traces his protagonist from Scar, the Link, through the Phoenicians, the Germanic tribes, and finally the Vikings. In this way he can show the developments taking place outside of a single lifespan. One of his later episodes, entitled "The Deluge," portrays by implication at least, the sinking of Atlantis. The story made its first appearance in Argosy (May 1914).

790. Waterloo, Stanley. The Story of Ab; A Tale of the Cave Man. Chicago: Way and Williams, 1897.

Because this novel does not give attention to religion, as did Bierbower, it establishes the basic form for the treatment of the development of the cavemen. He fights Oak for possession of the woman, Lightfoot, marries her, and begets a number of children. But he accomplishes all of the deeds--conquering fire, hunting the mammoth, inventing the bow and arrow, learning to swim--which start man on his upward evolution. Significantly, Waterloo insists that there is no missing link; ". . . experiment, adaptation, discovery . . ." explain the progress between the Paleolithic and Neolithic ages.

791. Waterloo, Stanley. The Wolf's Long Howl. Chicago: Stone, 1899.

Some of these love stories have an element of science. In "Love and a Triangle" Nell Morrison, whose interest in astronomy was "Vassar-born," and Julius Corbett, a civil engineer, become involved with the astronomer Marston in an attempt to communicate with Mars. Geometric figures laid out on the Argentine pampas bring about the figure of a right triangle on Mars. The problem of exact communication remains. In "Professor Morgan's Moon" the young astronomer Morgan wins the hand of Lee, daughter of a rival astron- omer, Professor Macadam, when he proves that mathematics can lie by suggesting that the moon caused an eclipse at a time before such scientists as Macadam believe the moon existed. In "Love and a Latch Key" Ned Simpson's invention of an electric key wins him the hand of Jason B. Grampus' daughter. In "Christmas 200,000 B.C." the cave girl Red Lips helps Yellow Hair kill a rival suitor as well as her father before they take possession of her parents' cave.

792. Webster, F[rederick] A[nnesley] M[itchell]. The Curse of the Lion. London: United, 1922.

Bruce Logan tells these stories of Africa to Hugh Trent and Jack Spenser. In the title story Tom Harden is cursed by a native lion priest after he has killed a lion. Frightened, he dreams of lions and wastes away; he is found dead--as though struck by a lion's paw--in front of the lion house at the zoological gardens. In "The Power of the Spirit" Henry Warren buys the girl Azizun on the slave market and after caring for her, leaves her; when the Arab Ibrahim bin Hassan kidnaps her, she seizes a talisman Henry gave her and calls upon him to aid her. He comes and kills the Arab. An eminent anthropologist hopes to disprove Darwin, but in "The Ape People" Logan tells of a safari from Nairobi which found an Englishman, an Oxford graduate, who had reverted to the level of an ape. After his wife and child were killed, he kept to himself, avoiding men and joining a group of white apes. He was captured when hunting alone.

793. Webster, Henry Kitchell. The Sky-Man. New York: Burt, 1910.

At least four years earlier Captain Fielding discovered a fog-enshrouded valley heated by a giant geyser some 300-500 miles north of Cape Barrow. The area is rich with gold. His journal contains detailed scientific observations as well as personal reflections. His daughter, Jeanne, has been given a bottle containing a message from him; it has drifted at least four years, but she obtains a yacht and goes to look for her father. The crew, led by the giant Roscoe, who reminds one of the beast-men of London and the early naturalists, tries to steal the ship. Jeanne is marooned. She has met Philip Cayeley, who resigned from the army in the Philippines after being accused of mo- lesting a man "of Spanish blood" and raping his daughter. The real culprit was one of his closest friends so that he

could not reveal the truth. As a result he abandoned
mankind for the Arctic, and in this region he has dwelt
alone while developing a wing-like device which enables him
to fly/glide as effectively as the birds. Much of the
storyline takes place during a winter when Roscoe, Jeanne,
and Philip are abandoned on the ice. Roscoe tries to
ravage Jeanne; Philip knifes him, but Roscoe attempts to
use the wings to escape; he falls to his death. Philip and
Jeanne are rescued by an enthusiast of "aerial navigation"
who declares that Philip's device could not possibly have
worked.

794. Webster, J. Provand. The Oracle of Baal; A Narrative of
Some Curious Events in the Life of Horatio Carmichael, M.A.
Philadelphia: Lippincott, 1896.

Also published in London by Hutchinson (1896): a conventional treatment of the lost race motif, in which Carmichael finds a lost city of Carthaginians in Africa.
Witchcraft is also woven into the storyline.

795. Wells, H[erbert] G[eorge]. The First Men in the Moon.
London: Newnes, 1901.

Using negative gravity, Bedford and Cavor journey to the
moon, where they find that the Selenites have evolved a
highly complex, insectlike social order based upon intellectual specialization. The Grand Lunar is simply a giant
brain. Separated, Cavor is recaptured, while Bedford flees
to the Earth. His adventure and his recounting of it (he
serializes the story using "Wells" as his pseudonym)
comprise what may be regarded as a conventional account of
a lunar visit, but it is interrupted when Cavor begins to
send radio signals giving his description and analysis of
Selenite society. Bedford is controlled by his desires and
individualism (he thinks of returning to the moon to obtain
more gold), whereas Cavor represents the inquiring scientific mind. Significantly, Cavor both recognizes the
horror inherent in the Selenite organization of society and
yet is destroyed by the very intellect that recognizes that
horror. Quite possibly Bedford and Cavor dramatize opposite forces within Wells himself.

796. Wells, H[erbert] G[eorge]. The Food of the Gods, and How
It Came to Earth. London: Macmillan, 1904.

Bensington, a chemist, and Redwood, a physiologist, discover a nutrient which causes giantism. In the initial
stages, emphasizing such creatures as wasps, rats, and
ants, for example, the narrative reads like a horror story.
It takes on symbolic importance when the food is given to
children who grow to be more than thirty feet tall.
Conflict between society and the giants begins, especially
when the Princess of Weser Dreiburg and Redwood's son fall

in love. A treaty proposes that the giants go into exile,
that no more food be produced, and that the giants have no
children. At the end the giants are preparing for battle
in order to survive. Ignoring the importance of the
giants' desire to help the poor, one can read the narrative
as symbolic of the conflict between the concept of change
and the desire to maintain the status quo. One can also
infer that the giants may be the next advancement in the
development of man.

797. Wells, H[erbert] G[eorge]. The Invisible Man; A Grotesque
Romance. London: Pearson, 1897.

In "The Epilogue" Wells remarks that with the death of
Griffin comes the end of "the strange and evil experiment
of the invisible man." Late in the narrative, Dr. Kemp, a
fellow scientist who is at least initially sympathetic,
calls Griffin "mad . . . inhuman . . . pure selfishness."
Griffin has made his discovery, but he chooses to use it to
gain personal power. From the first he instigates a reign
of terror and crime so that although he tells his story to
Dr. Kemp, one does not sympathize with him as one does with
both Dr. Frankenstein and his nameless monster. This novel
must remain Wells's statement that in the hands of an evil
genius, even the most miraculous developments of science
can be misused and lead only to destruction and death. It
is this feeling--together with his small regard for humanity's social conscience/intelligence--which gives all of
Wells's work an element of ambiguity, uncertainty.

798. Wells, H[erbert] G[eorge]. The Island of Dr. Moreau.
London: Heinemann, 1896.

Edward Pendrick, the first-person narrator, is cast away on
Nobel's Island in the Pacific after the wreck of the Lady
Vain and thus not only witnesses Moreau's experiments but
listens to the rationale behind them. Pessimism broods
throughout the novel. The human attempt to codify behavior
("The Law") is absurd, for Moreau's creatures revert to
bestiality. After Moreau's death the concept of natural
man is satirized. When Pendrick returns to civilization,
he becomes aware of the face of the beast in every human.
The result unnerves him and, one infers, Wells himself.
Moreover unlike Dr. Frankenstein, for example, Dr. Moreau
feels no sense of guilt or remorse, nor does he have any
compassion for his creatures. Both he and his world are
therefore much more brutal than the earlier world of Mary
Shelley.

799. Wells, H[erbert] G[eorge]. A Modern Utopia. London:
Chapman & Hall, 1905.

In an introductory chapter Wells instructs his readers to
imagine that a man, simply called the Voice, is recounting

"the adventures of his soul among Utopian inquiries"; a second person, the Botanist, is also present but will never speak; one can know his reactions to the ideas through the Voice's asides. Descending from Lucendro Pass, the two men somehow enter a world like Earth beyond Sirius. The Voice insists that the possibilities of Utopia be considered within the limits of human "possibility" and within the "inhumanity [and] insubordination of nature." He also insists that it be a world-wide state because it cannot be localized or made static, as previous utopian societies have been, and that its citizens must speak a single language. He stresses the versatility of the worker in Utopia, and argues that possible failure can be cut short by "wise marriage laws" (and therefore the size of population) and by recognizing that a "scientific mechanical civilization will always replace labor by improved machinery." Most importantly, he calls upon a voluntary, intellectual group of persons -- he calls them Samurai -- who will take responsibility as administrators. These are the people of good will that he will seek throughout the remainder of his career. Perhaps his major emphasis, however, is on the need to realize that the concept of Utopia will always change; indeed, each generation will have its own concept of a utopian society.

800. Wells, H[erbert] G[eorge]. The Time Machine; An Invention. London: Heinemann, 1895.

One of the Time Traveler's dinner guests provides a first-person framework for the Traveler's own account of his journey into the future. The split of the human race into the Eloi and Morlocks has been interpreted so frequently as Wells's verdict on the Marxian class struggle that the other concerns of the period which are implicit in that dichotomy have not received adequate attention. Certainly the idea that nineteenth century man cannot control his own destiny has not been adequately explored. To move away from a strictly politico-economic interpretation of the novel, one has only to recall that the Traveler journeys to the end of the world -- the image of the dying sun and the crab-like creature on the beach providing an unforgettable glimpse of the death of the Earth. Nor should one forget that although the Traveler stresses the need for "intellectual versatility," the narrator of the frame stresses that if mankind is to vanish and the world to die, then "it remains for us to live as though it were not so."

801. Wells, H[erbert] G[eorge]. The War in the Air, and Particularly How Mr. Bert Smallways Fared While It Lasted. London: Bell, 1908.

Serialized in Pall Mall Magazine (1908): the novel expresses Wells's concern about the apparently growing inability of mankind to deal socially and morally with new technological developments. In this case Germany, England, the Orient, and the U.S. all develop some form of aircraft. This leads to an ever-spreading warfare, beginning when a German dirigible fleet attacks New York City and is itself attacked by Oriental airplanes.   One of Wells's keenest insights is that aircraft can destroy cities, but they cannot occupy them. Thus only destruction can result. The Purple Death follows so that civilization is destroyed. Bert Smallways, adrift in Alfred Butteridge's balloon, ends up in a German army camp so that he conveniently accompanies the dirigible fleet as it destroys the American navy and thus renders all battleships obsolete. He ends up on Goat's Island above Niagara Falls, as does Prince Carl Albert, who launched the German attack. He last remarks essentially that war should not have happened. The discovery that the narrative has been written by a future historian does not lessen the feeling of pessimism.

802. Wells, H[erbert] G[eorge].   The War of the Worlds. London: Heinemann, 1898.

Serialized in Cosmopolitan (1898): much of the impact of the novel occurs because the nameless first-person narrator recounts the destruction of familiar places -- Horsell Common, Weybridge, Shepperton (though that makes necessary the intrusive shift to his brother's account of what occurred in London itself).   The description of the Martians as octopuses adds to the horror and provides one of the earliest occasions when the aliens are not humanoid, a skillful means of underscoring his theme. The annihilation of the Martians by bacteria also measures his intellect and artistry, especially after the reactions of the Artilleryman and Curate.   But one must not overlook that this is perhaps the most pessimistic of Wells's early novels. Although the narrator tries to emphasize the "gifts to human science" which the invasion brought, it also destroyed forever man's naive certainty of his unique place in the universe and the security of his life, present and future, on Earth.   Whatever hope the narrator holds out, the invasion marks a point in Wells's increasing pessimism and desperation which turned him toward the insistence upon the need for a utopian society.

803. Wells, H[erbert] G[eorge].   When the Sleeper Wakes. London: Harper, 1899.

When the Sleeper, Graham, wakes, he finds that he owns half the Earth; a Council rules in his name and is itself perhaps a satire of capitalism. In this novel one sees the beginning of the split which will evolve into the Eloi and Morlocks, for the Council has regimented the workers into the Labour Company.   However, in the face of all Marxist evaluation of this novel, one should not forget that Graham aids Ostrag, the leader of the rebellion against the

Council, until he learns that Ostrag, certainly an authoritarian figure, plans to betray the workers whom he supposedly leads. Thus Graham dies while bringing down the transports filled with African troops whom Ostrag is bringing to crush the rebellion.

804. Westall, William. The Phantom City; A Volcanic Romance. New York: Harper, 1886.

After preliminary adventures, including the sinking of the ship Guadalquivir, the first-person narrator uses a balloon to fly to Phantomland in Yucatan, where he finds an American aboriginal race lighter in color than the Indians, although he suggests they are related to the Toltecs. He successfully removes a tumor from the wife of Ixtil, saves Ixtil from falling into the crater of a volcano, and finds the king's two daughters, Zoe and Suma, attractive. After overcoming a plot of scheming priests, he and Suma are to be married. She agrees to return to civilization with him, and they will keep the existence of the valley a secret.

805. Westall, William. A Queer Race; The Story of a Strange People. London: Cassell, 1887.

The narrative divides itself into two parts, both told by the first-person narrator, Sidney Erle, who loses his place as an underwriter for the Oriental and Occidental Marine Insurance Company after its bank collapses. He goes to sea with Captain Peyton aboard the Diana, which takes the derelict Lady Jane, a fever ship, as prize. Rats bring a plague of yellow fever to the Diana. Only Erle and an old boatswain, Tom Bolsover, survive. Their ship drifts through fog and comes to an unknown island south of the equator. Tom has the journal of Robert Hare, chaplain of the Hecate, which captured the Spanish treasure ship, Santa Anna, in 1744. The people inhabiting the island are descendants of those who survived the wrecks of the Hecate and Santa Anna. They are a queer race in that intermarriage with Caribs and a black race, the Cariberoes, has left them piebald. Queen Mab, a "decided brunette," rules Fair Island from its capital, Fairhaven. After sundry adventures, including being cast adrift aboard the Diana near the island, a tidal wave, and a final battle with invading Cariberoes, Queen Mab declares that she loves Erle. They are married, return to London briefly with a fortune in pearls--leaving the treasure of the Santa Anna intact on the island--and return to Fair Island. Erle suggests that Westall will be the editor of his manuscript and hopes that one day he may reveal the location of the island so that his readers can visit the kingdom.

806. Weston, George.   His First Million Women.   New York:
Farrar & Rinehart, 1934.

    Martin Cavanaugh invents a zoometer which measures sexual
    potency; he suggests that life and electricity may be
    interchangeable terms. When Comet Z appears near Earth, it
    causes great electrical disturbances and renders all men
    except David Glendenning sterile. The novel then becomes a
    satire of the new Adam theme. By touching men, David can
    transmit a "Secondary Influence" which renders them tem-
    porarily virile; an arrangement is made for an "Inter-
    national Drawing," although the president and other auth-
    orities want David to have as many sons as possible so that
    his descendants will be immune to Comet Z and America can
    be politically dominant.   There are riots; there are
    special parties where one hundred men and young women are
    temporarily married so as to take advantage of that "Sec-
    ondary Influence."   Although the president decrees that
    David may marry every twenty-four hours and have each
    marriage annulled after that period, Glendenning begins to
    be attracted by Sylvia Vanderpool. A Dr. Barnes theorizes
    that Comet Z appears every 10,000 years; the biblical Adam
    was one of the men immune to it. Just as David discovers
    that he can use his power to bring about such social
    reforms as disarmament and an end to poverty, Comet Z
    disintegrates. All men are again sexually potent, and the
    world forgets David Glendenning.

807. Wetmore, Claude H[azeltine].   Sweepers of the Sea; The
Story of a Strange Navy.   Indianapolis, In.: Bowen-Merrill,
1900.

    A political movement originates to transform Peru into
    Incaland.   After developing a navy, Incaland goes to war
    against Great Britain and defeats Britain and Chile in a
    battle in Valpariso harbor.   The U.S. helps Peru/Incaland
    short of going to war. After a victory over Spain, Inca-
    land signs a treaty with the U.S.   One of her leaders,
    Pedro Garcia y Garcia, forsees the Western hemisphere
    ruling the world peacefully because of its military and
    economic power.   The U.S. rules northward to the Arctic,
    while the United States of Incaland rules southward to the
    Antarctic.

808. Wharton, Edith.   Tales of Men and Ghosts.   New York:
Scribner, 1910.

    Wharton gives a biographical sketch of the scientist, Galen
    Dredge, in "The Debt."   A protégé of Professor Lanfear,
    whose Utility and Variation has been judged the basic,
    final statement of Darwinian theory, Dredge attacks the
    theory after Lanfear is dead and Dredge has been given his
    chair at Columbia.   He reminds his critics of Lanfear's
    assertion that an hypothesis lasts only until new evidence

introduces something different. In "The Bolted Door" the protagonist kills his uncle; when he tries to confess, he is judged insane and placed in an asylum. The protagonist of "The Eyes" tries to explain the eyes which haunt him in terms of hallucination. The implication exists that the hallucination results from guilt involving homosexuality.

809. White, Stewart Edward. The Sign of Six. Indianapolis, In.: Bobbs-Merrill, 1912.

A mad scientist sends notes and wireless messages to the capitalist McCarthy, who "quite simply" owns New York, demanding he surrender himself for judgment and punishment. To prove his power, the madman blacks out the Atlas building, cuts off sound around the building, and finally causes the failure of light throughout the city. Percy Darrow, Schermerhorn's assistant, realizes that the scientist has developed a method for cutting off all vibrations. He finds the culprit and burns the document containing his formulae, for while it is the greatest achievement of modern science, it would give man power that belongs only to the gods.

810. White, Stewart Edward and Samuel Hopkins Adams. The Mystery. New York: McClure and Phillips, 1907.

One of the most effective novels of the period, the narrative divides into three parts. First, in the South Pacific the U.S.S. Wolverine discovers the derelict Laughing Lass, the ship of the scientist, Karl Augustus Schermerhorn, who has disappeared. Twice prize crews disappear; after the ships are separated the second night, the navy crew observes volcanic and electrical disturbances to the southwest. In the morning they find only one of the yacht's lifeboats; in it exhausted, lies a well-known journalist, Ralph Slade. He relates the second part of the novel telling how he smuggled himself aboard Schermerhorn's ship in order to get a story. He deals not with Schermerhorn's experiments themselves, but with the effects of the voyage on the motley crew. When the volcano where the experiments take place explodes, the crew kills Schermerhorn and steals the ship. The ship begins to burn, and the crew is lost. When Slade suggests that Percy Darrow, Schermerhorn's assistant, may be alive on the island, the Wolverine returns and finds him. He gives the account of Schermerhorn's attempt to find the ultimate energy, celestium. Schermerhorn could cure or kill mankind because of the power he would have; instead he is killed by ignorant men who think he is an alchemist with a chest of gold.

811. Wickham, Harvey. <u>Jungle Terror</u>. Garden City, New York: Doubleday, Page, 1920.

In South America after the First World War, the American, Ross Purdy, and his companion, Tommy, agree to investigate stories of a dragon which destroys villages in the jungle. They discover a mad German scientist, Hans Krieg, who has developed an advanced airplane as well as a form of atomic power (novalite); he actually stole the secret from an American in New York just before the Armistice. He sees himself as a new Kaiser. The narrative becomes a tale of Purdy's pursuit of Krieg and Krieg's eventual death. Purdy is further motivated by the love of Marie Kocian, an agent of Serbia, though she appears French. Maria was married to Krieg in name only as she attempted to foil his plot as well as prevent the persecution of her Serbian people by Bulgaria and a nameless state. At the end after Krieg's death, she and Purdy are together; Tommy goes back into the jungle to destroy Krieg's lab as well as any papers that may be there.

812. Wicks, Mark. <u>To Mars Via the Moon</u>; <u>An Astronomical Story</u>. London: Seeley, 1911.

Dedicated to Percival Lowell: Wicks' narrative reads like a textbook, citing not only information about Mars and space travel but entering into lengthy discussion of the controversy regarding the canals and the intelligent habitation of the planet, until his voyagers reach the planet. The first-person narrator, the sixty-three-year-old Wilfrid Poynters, encounters his deceased son, Mark, now reincarnated as Merna on Mars. Little is given regarding the society of Mars, for Poynter is given to much astronomical observation. He does learn that Martians are adept at telepathy and that Merna has been trying to reach him in order to have him fly to Mars. The theme once again is the concept of parallel and progressive evolution; Poynter emphasizes this with his remark about "Onward" and "Upward." He decides to remain on Mars and sends the manuscript back with those who return. A final "Addendum" by John Yiewsley Claxton includes Professor Lowell's account of photographs taken of Mars in 1909 which prove that the canals are "<u>certainties</u>" and that intelligent life must exist on the planet. He also observed water vapor in the atmosphere. In a way this undercuts the narrative, although Claxton wonders if he were to return to Mars, would he again meet the attractive girl, Siloni.

813. Willard, T[heodore] A[rthur]. <u>Bride of the Rain God</u>; <u>Princess of Chichen Itza, the Sacred City of the Mayas</u>. Cleveland, Oh.: Burrows, 1931 [?].

Using himself as a character, Willard pictures five people sitting around the Sacred Well in Chichen Itza on 20

February 1930. He reads a manuscript which he hopes
eventually to edit and publish; it is a pseudo-historical
novel. King Canek of Chichen Itza defeats the warriors of
the city of Mayapan, whose army takes Princess Lolniche
prisoner. Although she is intended as a sacrifice to
ensure peace, she and the heir to Mayapan fall in love.
Their marriage brings peace to the two cities.

814. Willard, T[heodore] A[rthur]. The Wizard of Zacna, A Lost
City of the Mayas. Boston: Stratford, 1929.

The narrative frame is the story of the young American,
Thomas Cranton, who is attracted to Delores and Lolita, the
daughters of his wealthy Spanish friend, Pedro Cocom. In
the jungle Cranton rescues Ahman, an old man, who becomes
the first-person narrator of an adventure which took place
in his youth. Captured, he is taken to the Mayan city then
known as Luumilkay, where he is attracted to the two
daughters of the king, Ixkan (blue eyed and blonde) and
Ixlol (brunette). He is used by Ixhan as she attempts to
bring her lover, Ekchan, to power and later to assassinate
her father, the king. Ixlol, who really loves him, saves
his life at the cost of her own during the struggle for
power. As Ahman dies, Cranton is uncertain how much of his
story to believe.

815. Williams, Francis Howard. Atman; The Documents in a
Strange Case. New York: Cassell, 1891.

Williams pretends to be the editor of a variety of papers,
including letters from the year 1887 and several journals,
as well as an extract from the Times. One of the journals
is that of Professor Perdicaris, a student of psychic
philosophy. All of them are concerned with the French
woman, Felise, who supposedly has no soul and thus is "the
highest development of the animal woman." Perdicaris tries
to combine the body of Felice with the "pure spirit" of
Margaret Haviland. He fails; he commits suicide as Margaret dies. An epilogue suggests that the artist, George
Wolff, saves Sister Mary Agatha from a fire; she is really
Felise and confesses her love for him. This is a strange
treatment of the occult which tries to gain objectivity by
reliance upon a number of documents to increase the cred-
ibility of the action.

816. Williams, Harper. The Thing in the Woods. New York:
McBride, 1924.

The first-person narrator, Dr. Haverill, takes up practice
in a small Pennsylvania town. For the most part the narrative is presented as a mystery: Aaron Manning is sought on
the charge of manslaughter involving his brother Jake.
Only after Haverill struggles with a misshapen creature in
the forest and after it is killed with a silver bullet does

the reader learn that "Jakey," who had been an acrobat and a "false" wild man in a circus, killed Aaron and was a werewolf.

817. Williams, Neil Wynn.   The Electric Theft; A Story. Boston: Small, Maynard, 1906.

Also published in London by Greening (1906): the early portion of the narrative introduces Reginald Burton, a young electrical engineer, and allows him to save Blanche Ferguson after an anarchist, Stavinski, tries to rob a train in France, causing an accident. This is a prelude to the major action. The anarchist, Boleroff, discovers a "natural electrolytic 'bath'" in a great cavern beneath St. Paul's Cathedral. It exists because of a natural "earth current"; Boleroff makes it into a great magnet which disrupts all forms of electrical power and service in London. This appears to bring about the financial ruin of Ferguson, who controls electric power financially in London; when the catastrophe strikes, the stock market falls and his shares are worthless. Boleroff insists that Ferguson give him Blanche, though the anarchist has no intention of marrying her. Ferguson refuses. Burton converts the dome of St. Paul's into a giant megaphone, magnifying all of the sounds in London; eventually he uses it to preach against the anarchists. Boleroff is killed in an attempt to stop Burton, the electric current stops flowing for some unknown reason in the lake in the cavern beneath St. Paul's, Burton and Blanche are married, and the megaphone preaches "on the great and exceeding value of Love." Williams very carefully explains his supposed science, even referring to chapters where he has previously introduced some idea.

818. Wilson, William Huntington. Rafnaland; The Strange Story of John Heath Howard. New York: Harper, 1900.

A thoroughly conventional story of a lost tribe of Vikings in the Arctic.

819. Windsor, William. Loma, A Citizen of Venus. St. Paul, Mn.: Windsor & Lewis, 1897.

Edward Bell, physician and scientist, watches an unknown young man rescue a woman drowning in Lake Michigan. The man identifies himself as Loma, a citizen of Venus, and tells Bell that the young woman whom he saved is Myrtle Burham, who tried to commit suicide because she is pregnant. The narrative becomes an attack on orthodox Christianity--Presbyterianism is named specifically--but at the same time it is a defense of certain traditional values and events. Venus first communicated with Earth when it established Adam and Eve--two exceptional persons--in the Garden of Eden. Orthodox religion is also attacked because it is based upon a theology having its origins in the decrees of "a lone masculine God" and forgetting completely the "motherhood of God." Myrtle gives birth to a son in a chapter entitled "Nativity"; after further instruction from Loma, she and Dr. Bell are married. Eventually, after others from Venus have briefly joined him, Loma ascends to Venus. Windsor announces that his intention is to help free women from "Sex Slavery"; he also ends the book with a chapter on phrenology after the story itself is finished. In many ways this is one of the most ardent attempts to reconcile traditional religious belief with the new century, although it is equally radical in its language and treatment of women.

820. Winger, F.S.   The Wizard of the Island; or, The Vindication of Prof. Waldinger.   Chicago: Winger, 1917.

The entire narrative is presented as though it were a lecture to the American Society of Scientific Research. The first-person narrator was one of the crew of the airship, America, which took part in a race across the Pacific, making use of three International Floats devised to maintain a constant latitude and longitude in order to make the trans-Pacific flight possible. Their plane was diverted to a mysterious island by Professor Waldemar, who takes them into his laboratory--referred to as "The Fairy Land of Science"--in order to show them his Vibrometer. Using the steam from the volcano on the island as his source of power, Waldemar can with his Vibrometer generate or annul any existing force. By his control of vibration he can mix the sense perceptions (that is, he can make one hear a color or see an odor). He then gives the crew a lecture on the "Dominant Ether." He has achieved all of this because some ten years ago, Professor Turner, present as a member of the crew, and others scoffed at his theory. He then isolated himself and his daughter Bessie on the island. He and Turner are killed accidentally. Bessie flies his spaceship back to San Diego and then, with everyone safe, she sets the controls of the Electron, as it is called, so that it flies alone into space. Waldemar's secrets die with him. Bessie marries George Kepner, another member of the crew.

821. Winsor, G[eorge] MacLeod.   Station X.   London: Jenkins, 1919.

A preliminary note asserts that such Imperial Telephone Stations as X are necessary to the military (naval) security of Britain. Alan Macrae is posted to Station X near Australia. After his companions, Lt. Wilson and a Chinese, kill one another, he sinks into a coma. Upon recovering, he finds that he has communicated the news while unconscious. When the ship Sagitta arrives, its crew finds Macrae again in a coma, but Dr. Anderson, a specialist in

brain and nervous disorders, finds a diary with a tran-
script of Macrae's conversations with a citizen of Venus
(called a Venerian in the text). He tells Macrae that long
ago when the moon was a dying world the Lunarians seized
control of the Martians. The Martians, transported to the
moon, died. The Lunarians/Martians are aggressive beings
with tremendous mental power. Macrae leaves the Station,
but returns with Professor Rudge, the inventor of the
system of "telephony." The remainder of the narrative
becomes the attempt of a Martian to seize control of
Macrae. He does. After a trip to London, Rudge returns
with a fleet, but the Martian has seized the ship Sea Lion.
Rudge manages to steal important parts ("coherers") of the
communication system so that more Martians cannot be
brought to Earth. Although three Martians, including
Macrae, have submarines, they are defeated by bombing
planes. May Traherne, initially Macrae's girl to whom he
wrote letters, is to become Lady Rudge. Important as an
early alien invasion, the narrative's weakness lies in its
reliance upon psychic possession and warfare in terms of
traditional naval weapons.

822. Winsor, G[eorge] MacLeod. Vanishing Men. New York:
Morrow, 1927.

The first-person narrator, Sir Henry Fordyce, tells of the
"Mysterious Disappearance Cases" which have baffled Scotland Yard. Everyone knows that Arthur Seymour is the
criminal and that he used a place called Chennel as his
base. He disappears, and Chennel burns. Only then does
Fordyce find the diary which recounts Seymour's career.
Fordyce summarizes it, saying that it "made horrible
reading." Seymour is capable of destroying matter and
discovers a new "matter," which he calls levium. This has
the power of anti-gravity so that he can kill his victims,
put a belt of levium around them, and allow them to ascend
into space. He also developed a means for flying, a
gyropter, which made use of levium. Seymour is, of course,
a mad scientist, although he gave the radium which was a
by-product of his other experiments to hospitals. Incidental to the narrative is Fordyce's love of Miss Arnold,
which ends in marriage.

823. Wodehouse, [Sir] P[elham] G[renville]. The Swop! or, How
Clarence Saved England; A Tale of the Great Invasion. London:
Rivers, 1909.

This is a most delightful parody of the future war motif.
In a prefatory note written from "The Bomb-Proof Shelter,
London W.," Wodehouse apologizes for the "lurid colours" of
the realism with which he has depicted the invasion.
Muttering "England, my England," Clarence Chugwater, a boy
scout, is the only member of his family who gives attention
to the invasion of Essex by a German army. Eight other

invaders have descended upon England: Russia at Yarmouth; the Mad Mullah at Portsmouth; the Swiss navy at Lyme Regis; the Chinese at the Welsh watering place, Lllgxtplll; Monaco at Auchtermuchty on the Firth of Clyde; "boisterous" Young Turks at Scarborough; while Brighton and Margate have been seized by Moroccan brigands and warriors from the isle of Bollygolla, respectively.   Moreover, the army has been previously abolished so that the defense of the land is entrusted to Territorials, The Legion of Frontiersmen, and the Boy Scouts.   At the height of the "Silly Season" letters pour into editors, but the response to the threat is made ridiculous.   The Boy Scouts make their camp in Aldwych.   The invaders suffer from colds and coughs.   No summary can do justice to Wodehouse's wit.   Significantly, this appears to be the one book of his which has not seen innumerable reprintings.

824. Wonder, William (pseud. of Thomas Kirwan).   Reciprocity (Social and Economic) in the Thirtieth Century; The Coming Cooperative Age: A Forecast of the World's Future.   New York: Cochrane, 1909.

Departing from Boston in the summer of 1907, the first-person narrator arrives near White Water Junction, Vermont, in 2907.   He finds there a utopian community made up basically of small farms, although the reader learns that New York City now has a population of thirty million. Electricity is the source of all energy, although society is not highly technological.   The emphasis is upon the basic goodness of human nature.   There is, for example, little illegitimacy because the young are taught to curb their passions.   Government is run much like the traditional New England town meetings.   The narrator wakes from his dream.

825. Wood, Walter.   The Enemy in Our Midst; The Story of a Raid on England.   London: Long, 1906.

The novel opens with an attack upon the presence of aliens in England; a procession of the unemployed march on Hyde Park, their posters demanding, "England for the English!" Captain Mahler, a spy, organizes the German citizens in England to fight in London, while German fleets strike at such places as Southampton and Dover.   The arrival of the Atlantic fleet brings a naval victory, but the invaders have wide success across the country.   John Steel and Lt. Richard Grenville become the protagonists as England eventually triumphs.   The chief emphasis is upon the importance of the navy.

826. Worts, George F[rank]. The Phantom President. New York:
Cape & Ballou, 1932.

    Although Theodore K. Blair is "the cleverest practical
economist in America" and runs its greatest corporation
successfully even in the Depression, the "Big Four," who
run American politics, decide that he does not have the
charisma to be elected president, though his ability is
much needed. They come up with the idea of substituting a
look-alike, the villainous Peter Varney, for Blair on all
public occasions. He wins in a landslide but insists that
he wants to be the president all of the time. Blair tries
to assume power and keep Varney a prisoner. Complications
occur when the communist, Zarinov, indicates that he knows
there are two presidents and insists the U.S.S.R. be fully
recognized and be given full endorsement. Varney escapes.
No one knows for sure which man is the real Blair. When
Varney is assassinated, Blair leaves Washington so that one
of the kingmakers, Senator Pitcairn, must become the new
president. Blair decides that one man should not be able
to impose his wishes upon an entire population and that
power is "a great mistake."

827. Wright, Allen Kendrick. To the Poles by Airship; or,
Around the World Endways. Los Angeles: Baumgardt, 1909.

    This is an essay instead of a work of fiction. In six days
the air ship New Era circles the globe from New Orleans.
The author stresses three advantages of the trip: the speed
of 325 mph; the observation of the effects of climatic
changes on nature and society; and with the aid of adjust-
able-telescopic-lens-windows, the ability to see entire
continents. On the fifth day near the South Pole, they
observe a large land tract containing the ruins of an
ancient capital; although the name Atlantis is included,
the author wonders if the ruins were peopled by the lost
tribes of Israel. He also praises the South American
continent highly. The essay becomes a tirade against the
Jews and against Japan for fomenting trouble in the Philippines and Hindustan, as well as inciting China to inaugurate commercial war with the U.S. In the Near East the
author observes a great battle between Western forces,
including Russia and the U.S., and the legions of China,
Turkey, Japan, and India. A Western victory brings lasting
peace. It ends with a general denunciation of war; now
that peace has been established, the governments can spend
their money on schools of invention. Young people need "a
vision of largeness"--passing allusion being made to "a
summer outing trip to Mars"--and the realization that next
to God, man is the "largest and most wonderful being ever
created." This deserves notice because it reinforces so
many ideas of the period.

828. Wright, S[ydney] Fowler. Dawn. New York: Cosmopolitan,
1929.

A sequel to Deluge: although the narrative begins by
focusing upon such a character as Muriel Temple, it soon
returns to Martin, Helen, and Claire. Its emphasis is
primarily upon Martin's attempts to create a peaceful
society, although his work is threatened by groups of
essentially brutish men, particularly Captain Cooper, who
would conquer Martin and impose their old-world power
values. Cooper is killed by a man, Burman, who reluctantly
cooperates with Martin. Claire, again the character who is
most active, kills Joe Harker. Martin realizes at the end
that he is the ruler of the group, but he also realizes
"the futility of all endeavor." Upon his meditation comes
an "indifferent dawn." Certainly this narrative becomes an
important statement of the sense of pessimism and futility
which marked British fantasy especially after World War I.
That emphasis is particularly noteworthy since Martin (and
Claire) have established a new beginning.

829. Wright, S[ydney] Fowler. Deluge; A Romance. New York:
Cosmopolitan, 1928.

A great convulsive earthquake destroys much of Europe,
India, and America. The narrative focuses at first upon
Martin Webster and his wife Helen. They are separated, and
Martin meets Claire Arlington; they fall in love. Many
passages in the narrative deal with the solitary figure of
Martin, especially, or Claire as they search through the
remnant of England for survivors. They join the group led
by Tom Aldworth, and they are opposed by Joe Harker and a
giant, Bellamy. Claire kills Bellamy, and when they find
that Helen is alive with Aldworth's group, Claire first
rescues Helen when Joe kidnaps her; then, most importantly,
because women have the right to choose their mates, she
chooses Martin although he already has a wife. The emphasis is upon the "fresh" and "free" beginning of a new
society. The relationship of Martin, Helen, and Claire
receives greatest attention, although at the end it appears
that Martin will become the leader of the group. The emphasis upon Claire implies that the position of women in
society needs serious reconsideration. She remains the key
figure in all of the action.

830. Wright, S[ydney] Fowler. Dream; or, A Simian Maid.
London: Harrap, 1931.

Rita Leinster goes to the magician who has put her in
trances so that she has lived in Babylon and Atlantis. Now
she wishes to be a prehistoric woman. He puts her in a
trance for fourteen days. Several hours later Stephen
Cranleigh pays to have him and the girl Elsie share the
same dream. Although there is the implication that this is

a triangle, those two awake as Stele and Elysa, sister and
brother. They find Rita wounded; she is a tree woman, a
kind of ape. Elysa has killed Amul, who wanted her as his
fourth wife; so they must flee. With another tribe Elysa
is mated to Thelmo, while Stele and Rita are attracted to
one another. In their wanderings both couples die. When
Rita awakens in the modern world, Cranleigh proposes to
her. She accepts somewhat reluctantly, as though the
victim of ennui (which, by implication, may have made her
undergo the trances as an escape).

831. Wright, S[ydney] Fowler. The Island of Captain Sparrow.
London: Gollancz, 1928.

Adrift in a small boat after a wreck, Charlton Foyle comes
to an unknown Pacific island. A century earlier it had
been the haven of Andrew Sparrow, a pirate; he was caught
and hanged, but members of his crew lived on the island and
bred with a race of satyrs so that they have become degen-
erate. At the time they came to the island, there was also
a small number of an ancient civilized race, but diseases
of the white men killed most of them off within a six-week
period. Now only the priest of Gir survives, with his wife
and daughter, living in an ancient temple. Foyle meets a
French girl previously shipwrecked on the island, Marcelle
Latour. They fall in love, and the narrative becomes an
account of their survival. The pirates kill the priest,
and the pirates themselves are drowned as they try to
escape the island in Foyle's boat. He and Marcelle remain
on the island in a kind of Adam and Eve climax.

832. Wright, S[ydney] Fowler. The War of 1938. New York:
Putnam, 1936.

Published as Prelude in Prague; A Story of the War of 1938
in London by Newnes (1935): Germany demands that all communists and all persons suspected of plotting against
Germany be expelled from Czechoslovakia and turned over to
German authorities for suitable punishment. The storyline
involves the death of Herr Johann Schmidt, a German agent
who leaves his papers which are found, and the discovery by
Secret Service Agent 973 of a subterranean German aero-
drome. When the Czechs do not meet the ultimatum, Prague
is bombed. Reference is also made to a freezing gas
created by Leunawerke. That part of Prague not destroyed
by the bombing is obliterated when Herr Neidlemann sets off
a system of mines beneath the city. At least once there is
reference to a "Nazi plot." The narrative has its greatest
value for the concept (even before the Spanish Civil War)
of the effect of mass bombing. Some of its incidental
observations, such as that regarding the annexation of
Austria, also are intriguing.

833. Wright, S[ydney] Fowler.   <u>The World Below</u>.   London:
Collins, 1929.

> The narrative is made up of two parts: "The Amphibians" and
> "The World Below." Its premise is that young Danby is sent
> 500,000 years into the future both to explore that world
> for a year and to find out what happened to Harry Brett and
> Townsend, who did not return from earlier journeys in the
> Professor's Time Machine. (At least one direct reference
> is made to Wells.) He finds the world dominated by two
> races, the Amphibians and the Dwellers, the latter of whom
> are giant humanoids. There is a third race, the Killers,
> described at least once as three-foot-high beings of a
> bright warm pink color. One of the Amphibians, who com-
> municate by telepathy, remains Danby's companion throughout
> most of the narrative. The resultant narrative is a kind
> of surreal nightmare. It reminds one somewhat of Lindsay
> or Hodgson. The symbolism does not coalesce, though one
> infers it has to do with the limitations of humanity. The
> reference to a war with an insectlike type of being and the
> Dwellers' near extinction suggest a dark pessimism. He
> finds that Townsend is dead and Brett driven mad. He
> himself is experimented upon though the Amphibians cause
> his release. Danby is called back to the present after his
> year is over. He promises to write his book, and he may
> again explore the future if his wife Clara will accompany
> him.

834. Wylie, Philip [Gordon].   <u>Gladiator</u>.   New York: Knopf,
1930.

> In Indian Creek, Colorado, Abednego Danner, a professor of
> biology, discovers a chemical that increases physical
> strength phenomenally. After experiments with a tadpole
> and a kitten, he gives his pregnant wife, Matilda, an
> opiate and then injects the chemical into her blood stream.
> Their son Hugo is a superman from his birth. The episodic
> narrative traces his experiences through boyhood, Webster
> University, World War I, and afterward. A number of
> episodes, such as his boxing with the professional Ole and
> his stint as a sideshow strongman, are particularly amus-
> ing, as is the account of his relationships with various
> young women. But the thematic tension is obvious from the
> outset: he is isolated because his feats of strength cause
> society to fear him. This is reinforced by his inability
> to find any lasting emotional relationship. When his
> father dies, the old professor gives Hugo the notebooks
> containing his secrets; when Hugo joins an expedition to
> the Mayan city of Uctotol, the scientist, Dan Hardin,
> echoes his father's belief: Hugo must begin a new race of
> supermen. As Hugo meditates upon his destiny, calling upon
> God, he is struck dead by lightning.

835. Wylie, Philip [Gordon].   The Murderer Invisible.   New
York: Farrar & Rinehart, 1931.

The chemist, William Carpenter, seeks a means of attaining
invisibility, partly because his own size (six feet, six
inches) has made him think of himself as a freak. He falls
in love with Daryl Carpenter, supposedly his orphaned
niece, though actually she was adopted. Bromwell Baxter
becomes his assistant. The novel is not nearly so successful or entertaining as The Gladiator for several
reasons. First, one has no sympathy for Carpenter; he is
simply another mad scientist who issues the ultimatum that
he is to rule the world. To show his power, for example,
he destroys Grand Central Station. Secondly, Daryl and
Baxter fall in love, and they aid the authorities in trying
to capture him. One of the better sequences occurs when
Carpenter appears only as a skeleton because he has taken
too small a dose of his potion. Daryl finally provides the
means by which he is shot and killed.

836. Young, Laurence Ditto.   The Climbing Doom.   New York:
Dillingham, 1909.

Waric Vagan joins Dr. Steinfield Kinder on an expedition
into South America to discover a lost city. After facing
such hazards as Andean rock ants (fire ants), they discover
a towered, white city ruled by Queen Zarra, who is "little
more than a girl." She speaks Spanish and declares that
she is descended from Pizarro. Despite the opposition of
such natives as Gonja, she marries Vagan, whom she has
loved from first sight. They have a daughter, Zarrine.
When Vagan leaves, taking the daughter with him, Zarra
kills herself. The second part of the novel occurs after a
time lapse. Various villains attempt to steal the emeralds
Vagan and Zarrine have, but the thrust of the narrative
ends with the marriage of Sylvester Cosmo Del and Zarrine.

837. Yoursell, Agnes Bond.   A Manless World.   New York: Dillingham, 1890.

Arthur Fielding visits his Uncle Matthew at Catskill Landing. He is engaged to Estelle Whitmore. His uncle suggests that there is a new disease in the sense that man has
lost his procreative powers. He suggests that this happened at least once to prehistoric man, but that after a
time man reappeared. No explanation is given. Meanwhile
an epidemic spreads throughout the world; science can give
no explanation. An organization called the American
Alliance forms to control landed interests. The novel
becomes a tirade against the Jews after a Dr. Henry Gold-
stein gives a young woman a potion that is supposed to
restore her procreative powers but instead kills her. The
world exterminates the Jews, beginning in America. But the
power of the American Alliance dissolves and the world is

controlled by anarchists, who are followed by a plague. The implication grows that the entire narrative has been nothing but the fantasy of Uncle Matthew. Arthur declares that his uncle must have had an unfortunate experience in love early in life. Yet the ending is ambiguous for while Arthur and Estelle meet on the evening of their betrothal, the narrative suggests that he is still in the house of his uncle. One can only infer that the theme builds on the idea that love overcomes fear.

838. Zamiatin, Evgenii [Ivanovitch]. We. New York: Dutton, 1924.

This is one of the major early dystopian novels, a satirical portrait of the United State of the far future. The State is an enclosed city peopled by survivors of a great war who have chosen to separate themselves from the irrational, natural world outside. The authorities carefully regulate all emotions and activities so that there is no chance of individualism. The storyline concerns the protagonist, D-503, who is building a spaceship, Integral, whose purpose will be to carry the State's enlightenment to other worlds. For a moment when he falls in love, he becomes somewhat human, but a revolt fails, and he remains an automaton. To ensure this, the authorities subject him to brain surgery. An attack upon the U.S.S.R., the novel has never been published in Russia. Despite other warnings, the dystopian vision of We marks the beginning of what has become one of the dominant moods of twentieth century science fiction.

AUTHOR INDEX

M

Macaulay, Rose 522
MacClure, Victor 523
MacDonald, Raymond 524
MacHarg, William 040
Machen, Arthur 525
MacIsaac, Fred 526-528
Mackay, Donald 529
Malet, Lucas 530
Manley, R.M. 531
Mann, Horace 532
Manson, Marsden 533
Marriott, Crittenden 534
Marshall, Edison 535, 536
Marshall, Sidney 537
Mastin, John 538, 539
Mayo, W.S. 540
McCardell, Roy L. 541
McCord, P.B. 542
McDougall, Walter 543
McIntyre, Margaret 544
McKesson, Charles L. 545
McLandburgh, Florence 546
McMasters, Henry 547
McNeil, Everett 548
McNeile, H.C. 549
Meredith, Ellis 550
Merrill, Albert A. 551
Merritt, A. 552-559
Meyer, John J. 560-563
Michaelson, Miriam 564
Mighels, Philip Verrill 565
Miller, Leo Edward 566, 567
Milne, Robert Duncan 568
Minor, John W. 569
Mitchell, Edward Page 570
Mitchell, J.A. 571, 572
Mitchell, J. Leslie 573, 574
Moffett, Cleveland 575, 576
Montague, C.E. 577
Montgomery, Frances T. 578, 579
Moresby, Louis 580
Morris, Gouverneur 581-583
Morris, William 584
Morrow, William C. 585, 586
Morton, A.S. 587
Mott, Laurence 588
Muller, Julius 589
Mundo, Otto 590
Mundy, Talbot 591

N

Nelson, Arthur A. 592
Newcomb, Cyrus 593
Newcomb, Simon 594
Nichols, Robert 595
Niemann, August 596
Niswonger, Charles E. 597
North, Franklin H. 598
Norton, Roy 599-602
Noyes, Pierrepont 603

O

"O" 604
Ober, Frederick 605
Odle, E.V. 606
O'Leary, Con 607
Olerich, Henry 608
O'Neill, Joseph 609
Orcutt, Emma L. 610
Osborne, Duffield 611
Osbourne, Lloyd 612
O'Sheel, Shaemas 613

P

Paine, Albert B. 614, 615
Pallen, Condé 616
Palmer, John H. 617
Parabellum 618
Parrish, Randall 619
Parry, David 620
Peck, Bradford 621
Perkins, Lucy 622
Pettersen, Rena 623
Phelps, William L. 624
Pier, Garrett C. 625, 626
Pope, Gustavus W. 627, 628
Pope, Marion M. 629
Post, M.D. 630
Powell, Frank 631
Pratt, Ambrose 632
Pratt, Cornelia A. 699
Prentice, Harry 633
Prime, Lord 634
Pruning Knife 635

Q

Quien Sabe 362

Walsh, J.M. 783
Ward, Herbert 784
Warner, William H. 785
Warren, B.C. 786
Waterloo, Stanley 787-791
Webster, F.A.M. 792
Webster, Henry K. 793
Webster, J. Provand 794
Wells, H.G. 795-803
Westall, William 804, 805
Weston, George 806
Wetmore, Claude 807
Wharton, Edith 808
White, Stewart Edward 809,
  810
Wickham, Harvey 811
Wicks, Mark 812
Willard, T.A. 813, 814
Williams, Francis H. 815
Williams, Harper 816
Williams, Neil 817
Wilson, William H. 818
Windsor, William 819
Winger, F.S. 820
Winsor, G. Macleod 821, 822
Wodehouse, P.G. 823
Wonder, William 824
Wood, Robert W. 754
Wood, Walter 825
Worts, George F. 826
Wright, Allen K. 827
Wright, S. Fowler 828-833
Wylie, Philip 040, 041, 834,
  835

Y

Young, Laurence 836
Yoursell, Agnes 837

Z

Zamiatin, Evgenii 838

SHORT-TITLE INDEX

"Bess" 240
Between the Dark and the
  Daylight 431
Between Worlds 704
Beyond the Great South Wall
  673
Beyond the Paleocryptic Sea
  587
Beyond the Selvas 316
"Bietigham" 569
Black Spirits and White 204
Bladed Barrier, The 013
Blake of the 'Rattlesnake'
  443
Blindman's World, The 056
Blue Germ, The 737
Boats of the 'Glen Carig' 423
Book of Algoonah, The 593
Bowl of Baal, The 061
Boy Adventurers in the Land of
  El Dorado, The 770
Boy Adventurers in the Land of
  Monkey Men, The 771
Boy Adventurers in the Unknown
  Land, The 722
Brave New World 437
"Breath of the Jungle" 270
Bride of the Rain God 813
Bride of the Sun, The 505
Bridge of Time, The 785
Brigands of the Moon 224
British Barbarians, The 010
Burn, Witch, Burn 532
By Airship to Ophir 023

C

Caesar's Column 253
California Three Hundred Years
  Ago 171
Call of the Savage 469
Camberwell Miracle, The 066
Can Such Things Be? 073
Captain Jinks; Hero 216
Captain Kiddle 300
Captain of the "Mary Rose,"
  The 166
Captive Goddess 101
Captured by Apes 633
Cast Away at the Pole 190
Cave Boy of the Age of Stone,
  The 544
Cave Girl, The 106
Cave Twins, The 622

Caves of Treasure, The 599
Caxton's Book 648
Centuries Apart 088
Certainty of a Future Life on
  Mars, The 350
Chalk Face 308
Chattering Gods 207
Children of the Morning 334
Christ of the Red Planet, The
  466
City Beyond the Clouds, The
  656
City in the Sea, The 717
City of Desire, The 672
City of Endless Night 405
City of the Sun, The 670
Cityless and Countryless
  World, A 608
Climbing Doom, The 836
Clockwork Man, The 606
Collapse of Homo Sapiens, The
  347
Columbus of Space, A 679
Coming Conquest of England,
  The 596
Coming of the Amazons, The
  453
Coming Race, The 521
Coming Storm, The 435
Coming Waterloo, The 132
Connecticut Yankee in King
  Arthur's Court, A 757
Conquest of America, The 575
Conquest of the Moon, The 494
Crack of Doom, The 209
Creep, Shadow 533
Cresten, Queen of the Toltecs
  685
Crucible Island 616
Crystal Button, The 749
Crystal City, The 495
Crystal Man, The 570
Crystal Sceptre, The 565
Cupid Napoleon 482
Curse of the Lion, The 792

D

Dark River, The 716
Darkness and Dawn 283
Darrow Enigma, The 683
Dash at the Pole, A 624
Daughter of the Dawn, The 422
Daughter of the Sun, The 362

Reciprocity . . . 824
Reckoning, The 185
Recovered Continent, The 590
Recreations of a Psychologist
  391
Red Friday 756
Red Gods, The 246
Red Napoleon, The 337
Red One, The 516
Red-Headed Goddess, The 181
Republic Without a President,
  A 784
Return of Frank Stockton 237
Return of Tarzan, The 116
Revi-Lona 198
Revolt 547
Revolt of Man, The 071
Revolt of the Birds, The 630
Revolution 067
Riallaro 738
Rice Mills of Port Mystery,
  The 416
Riddle of the Sands, The 160
Right off the Map 577
Romance in Radium, A 400
Romance Island 322
Rondah 250
Round the Moon 768
Round Trip to the Year 2000, A
  193
Royal Enchantress, A 247
Ru the Conqueror 363

S

Sacred Giraffe, The 238
Scarabaeus 492
Scarlet Empire, The 620
Scarlet Plague, The 517
Scientific Romances (Hinton)
  421
Scientific Sprague 520
Sea Demons, The 664
Sea Girl, The 227
Seagoing Tank, The 714
Second Deluge, The 682
Secret of the Crater, The 611
Secret of the Earth, The 050
Seeds of Enchantment, The 309
Seekers, The 788
Seola 707
Seven Footprints to Satan 558
Seven Sleepers, The 054
Shadow World, The 329

She 383
She and Allan 384
Ship of Death, The 726
Ship of Ishtar, The 559
Shock of Battle, The 760
Sign at Six, The 809
Silent Bullet, The 644
Silver City, The 605
Sirius 721
6,000 Tons of Gold 140
Six Thousand Years Hence 636
Sky-Man, The 793
Skystone, The 420
Slayer of Souls, The 146
Smoky God, The 281
Social War of the Year 1900,
  The 487
Solarion 294
Solaris Farm 274
Sometime 415
Son of Tarzan, The 117
Son of the Ages, A 789
Sons of the Mammoth 084
Sound-Machine, The 711
Spotted Panther, The 271
Spreading Stain, The 298
Star Maker 722
Star Rover, The 518
Starkenden Quest, The 177
Station X 821
Steam Man of the Prairies, The
  286
Steel Grubs, The 280
Stolen Continent, The 694
Stolen Planet, The 538
Stone Giant, The 230
Storm of London, The 248
Story of Ab, The 790
Strange Case of Dr. Jekyll and
  Mr. Hyde 725
Strange Case of William Hyde,
  The 138
Strange Discovery, A 232
Strange Invaders, The 512
Strange Manuscript Found in a
  Copper Cylinder, A 239
Strange Voyage, A 635
Struggle for Empire, The 174
Sub-Coelum 668
Submarine Tour, A 036
Suitor from the Stars, A 203
Survivors, The 695
Sweepers of the Sea 807
Swop!, The 823

T

About the Compiler

THOMAS D. CLARESON, Chairman of the Department of English at the College of Wooster (Ohio), has edited *Extrapolation: A Journal of Science Fiction and Fantasy* since 1959. One of the founders of the Modern Language Association (MLA) Seminar on Science Fiction in 1958, he was also the first president of the Science Fiction Research Association (SFRA) from 1970 to 1976. He is the author of *SF: The Other Side of Realism*, *A Spectrum of Worlds*, *SF Criticism: An Annotated Checklist*, *Robert Silverberg*, and *Robert Silverberg: A Primary and Secondary Bibliography*. He is the editor of *Science Fiction Periodicals, 1926-1978* (Greenwood Press, 1975, 1978), a collection of twenty magazines and one critical journal on microfilm. He has brought together a group of almost one hundred important novels to be microformed by Greenwood Press in conjunction with *Science Fiction in America, 1870s-1930s*; in addition, he is completing *Some Kind of Paradise,* a historical appraisal emphasizing American contributors to the field in the nineteenth and early twentieth centuries, for Greenwood Press.